INTO THE

# LAW OF NEGRO SLAVERY

IN THE

## UNITED STATES OF AMERICA.

TO WHICH IS PREFIXED,

An Historical Sketch of Slavery.

BY

## THOMAS R. R. COBB,

OF GEORGIA.

ISBN: 978-1-63923-816-3

Printed: March 2023

Published and Distributed By:
Lushena Books
607 Country Club Drive, Unit E
Bensenville, IL 60106
www.lushenabks.com

ISBN: 978-1-63923-816-3

# PREFACE.

I ENTER upon an untrodden field. Stroud's "Sketch of the Law of Slavery" is and was intended only as an Abolition pamphlet; Wheeler's "Law of Slavery" professes to be only a compend of abridged decisions on prominent questions. An elementary treatise, purporting to define the Law of Slavery as it exists in the United States, has not been brought to my notice.

As a pioneer I doubt not I have, like others, frequently deviated from the true course. Reflection has induced me to change many positions which I had committed to paper. Subsequent reflection, and the exposition of other minds, may induce me to change some now committed to the public.

This work has been prepared at leisure hours, in the midst of a laborious practice. These have varied in length from a few moments to a few days. The natural result—disconnection and incoherency —may be detected by experienced eyes.

Residing in an interior village, I have felt the want of access to extended libraries. I have taken advantage of occasional sojourns in the cities of

Washington, Philadelphia, and New York, to examine references previously noted, and such books as
related to my subject.    I have added also a number
of works to my own library, which I could not otherwise examine.    Never having visited the extensive
University Library at Cambridge, I took the liberty
to apply to the lamented Greenleaf, before his death,
to examine and copy for me from several authors
that I could not find elsewhere.    With a courtesy
and kindness, equalled only by his ability and accuracy as a lawyer and a scholar, he cheerfully complied with my request.    The MSS. sent me are in
his own handwriting, and I prize them as relics of
a great and good man.

From the causes before stated, I have been forced
to rely on the accuracy of others for some of the
references made.    In almost every case I have noticed, at the time, the person on whose authority I
cite.

My book has no political, no sectional purpose.
I doubt not I am biassed by my birth and education in a slaveholding State.    As far as possible, I
have diligently sought for Truth, and have written
nothing which I did not recognize as bearing her
image.    So believing, I neither court nor fear criticism; remembering that "*veritas seapius agitata,
magis splendescit lucem.*"

ATHENS, GEORGIA, August, 1858.

# CONTENTS.

## HISTORICAL SKETCH OF SLAVERY.

### INTRODUCTION.

### CHAPTER I.

### CHAPTER II.

### CHAPTER III.

# CHAPTER VI.

# CHAPTER VII.

## CHAPTER VIII.

CHAPTER IX.

## CHAPTER XII.

## CHAPTER XIII.

## CHAPTER XIV.

## CHAPTER XV.

## CHAPTER XVI.

## CHAPTER XVII.

## CHAPTER XVIII.

# LAW OF NEGRO SLAVERY.

# CHAPTER XVIII.

# CHAPTER XIX.

# CHAPTER XX.

# CHAPTER XXI.

# CHAPTER XXII.

# TABLE OF CASES.

**

AN

# HISTORICAL SKETCH OF SLAVERY,

FROM THE

EARLIEST PERIODS TO THE PRESENT DAY.

.

# HISTORICAL SKETCH OF SLAVERY.

## INTRODUCTION.

PHILOSOPHY is the handmaid, and frequently the most successful expounder of the law. History is the groundwork and only sure basis of philosophy. To understand aright, therefore, the Law of Slavery, we must not be ignorant of its history.

A detailed and minute inquiry into the history of slavery would force us to trace the history of every nation of the earth; for the most enlightened have, at some period within their existence, adopted it as a system; and no organized government has been so barbarous as not to introduce it amongst its customs. It has been more universal than marriage, and more permanent than liberty.[1] All that we can propose for ourselves here, is a limited and brief glance at its existence and condition during the several ages of the world.

Its beginning dates back at least to the deluge. One of the inmates of the ark became a "servant of servants;" and in the opinion of many the curse of Ham

---

[1] See Bancroft's United States, vol. i, ch. v. "Liberty and Tyranny have kept pace with each other. The helots at Sparta, the slaves at Rome, the villains of the feudal system, bear testimony to this melancholy truth." Brown's Civil Law, i, 97.

is now being executed upon his descendants, in the enslavement of the negro race. From the familiarity with
which Noah spoke of the servile condition of his young-
est son, it seems probable that the condition of servitude
must have existed prior to the flood.

In every organized community there must be a laboring class, to execute the plans devised by wiser heads:
to till the ground, and to perform the menial offices
necessarily connected with social life. This class have
generally been slaves, and, in the opinion of Puffendorf,
their bondage naturally arose, in the infancy of society,
from their occupation. The poorer and less intelligent
applied to the more opulent and intelligent for employment. The return was food and raiment, at a time
when there was no currency. With the removal of the
employer—mankind at that age having no permanent
abode—the employee moved also, and with him his
family. His children, as they grew to youth and man-
hood, naturally aided the parent in his labors, and received the same reward; and thus, either by express
contract or custom, the one, with his descendants, became attached to and a part of the household of the
other. Certain it is, that Abraham had his man-servants
and maid-servants, born in his house and bought with
his money; and that Sarah, his wife, was a hard mistress to Hagar, her handmaid, who became a fugitive
from her hand, and returned only by the direction of the
angel of the Lord. The slave-trade too, was of early
origin, as we find Joseph sold to Midianitish merchants,
and resold by them in Egypt. The transfer of slaves
from parent to child, was of still earlier origin, as we
find Rebecca, on her marriage to Isaac, carrying her
damsels home with her; a custom followed by Laban,
on the marriage of Leah and Rachel to Jacob. The
slavery in these patriarchal days, was undoubtedly mild;
and the relations between the master and slave, of the

most familiar character. Job protested before God, that he despised not the complaint of his man-servant or his maid-servant, when they contended against him; and gave, as his reason, that both master and slave were fashioned by the same hand.[1] The servant frequently had control of all his master's goods;[2] and in default of children, became his nominated heir.[3]

[1] Job 31 : 13, 15.          [2] Gen. 24 : 10.
[3] Gen. 15 : 3 ; Prov. 17 : 2. Our Saviour alludes to this in the parable of the wicked servants who slew the son—the only heir—that the inheritance might be theirs.

# CHAPTER I.

THERE were, among the Jews, two distinct classes of slaves, distinguished by great difference of treatment and *status*, as well as by the duration of their bondage. The one class consisted of their Hebrew brethren; the other of strangers and heathen. The bondage of the first expired on the seventh year; unless the servant " shall plainly say, 'I love my master, my wife, and my children. I will not go out free.' Then his master shall bring him unto the judges; he shall also bring him unto the door or doorpost; and his master shall bore his ear through with an awl, and he shall serve him forever."[1] Thus the Hebrew servant became one of the other class, whose bondage was perpetual.[2] On the seventh year, the Hebrew servant, when he went free, took with him his wife, if she came with him. But if his master had given him a wife, she and her children

---

[1] Exodus 21 : 5, 6 ; Deut. 15 : 16.

[2] I am aware that abolitionists, including learned prelates in the British House of Lords, have explained the word " forever" to mean only until the year of Jubilee. I am not a sufficient Hebrew scholar to enter into this controversy or to pretend to decide the question. I would remark that the same argument is resorted to, by those contending for universal salvation, to meet and refute the orthodox doctrine of eternal punishment. The curious on this point are referred to Fletcher's Studies on Slavery; Priest's Bible Defence of Slavery, 136 ; Gill's Commentary ; Lev. 25 : 44; Michaelis's Comm. on Mosaic Law, vol. ii, art. 127.  This learned author supposes that even the Hebrew servant in some cases served till the year of Jubilee.

belonged to the master, and remained with him, while the man-servant went out by himself.[1] He was not sent forth penniless, but was furnished " liberally out of the flock, and out of the floor, and out of the wine-press."[2] This limitation upon the servitude of Hebrews did not, at least under the first law, apply to Hebrew women that had been purchased as concubines for the master or his son. If she ceased to please him, " then shall he let her be redeemed." If not, food, raiment, and marriage duty were not to be diminished; on failure of either, she was enfranchised.[3]

The Hebrew servants consisted of those that, from poverty, either sold themselves or their children, or were sold for debt or crime.[4] If the Hebrew sold himself to a stranger, he was subject to be redeemed, either at his own instance or that of his near relatives, by paying the wages of a hired servant up to the year of Jubilee.[5] If his master was a Hebrew, the right of redemption does not seem to have applied.

A marked difference was made in the law as to the *status* of a Hebrew servant and one bought from the heathen. He was not to serve as a bond-servant, but as a hired servant and a sojourner.[6] He was not to be treated with rigor, but as a brother " waxen poor."[7] He lost, in his bondage, only his liberty, none of his civil rights. He was still a citizen, and might acquire property of his own.[8] Tiba, one of Saul's servants, possessed twenty slaves of his own.[9] In case of war, the

---

[1] Exodus 21 : 3, 4.    [2] Deut. 15 : 14.    [3] Exod. 21 : 7–11.
[4] Lev. 25 : 39; 2 Kings 3 : 16–28, 4 : 1; Ex. 22 : 2; 2 Chron. 12 : 8; Neh. 5 : 4, 5; Is. 50 : 1; Matt. 18 : 25; Michaelis's Comm. vol. ii, 160, et seq.
[5] Lev. 25 : 42, 47–51; 1 Kings 9 : 22; Neh. 5 : 5.
[6] Lev. 25 : 39, 40.    [7] Lev. 25 : 39, 43.
[8] Lev. 10 : 49; Priest's Bible Defence of Slavery, 139.
[9] 2 Sam. 9 : 10.

slaves "born in the house" were frequently armed and went forth to battle with their master.[1] The condition of the other class, the bond-servants, bought from the stranger and the heathen, or the captives taken in war, was very different.[2] They were pure slaves, considered as "a possession," and "an inheritance for their children after them," to inherit them for a possession. They were "bondmen forever."[3] These were very numerous, and rigorous treatment of them was tacitly allowed. That many of them were Africans and of negro extraction, seems to admit of but little doubt. Josephus says, "King Solomon had many ships that lay upon the Sea of Tarsus. These he commanded to carry out all sorts of merchandise, to the remotest nations, by the sale of which silver and gold were brought to the king, and a great quantity of ivory, apes, and Ethiopians."[4] These were doubtless sometimes taken captives in the wars of Israel,[5] and frequently obtained in exchange of goods, as there was undoubtedly a slave-trade at that time, in which the Jews sometimes engaged.[6] This practice and trade are negatively proved by the prohibition to sell the Hebrew women that were

[1] Lev. 25 : 49.

[2] Gen. 17 : 13; Exodus 12 : 44–45; Deuter. 20 : 14, 21 : 10, 11; 1 Kings 9 : 20–22; Michaelis's Comm. vol. ii, art. 123.

[3] Lev. 25 : 44, 45, 46.

[4] Antiquities of the Jews, Book VIII, ch. 7, p. 293. In another edition translated "negroes." See 2 Chron. 9 : 21; 1 Kings 10 : 21. I am aware of the strictures of Gliddon and others upon the common acceptation of the term "Ethiopians." I am inclined to believe that the term was applied to all *black* races, the Hindoo as well as the negro. See remarks of Abbé Grégoire on this subject, in his work *De la Littérature des Nègres*, ch. i.

[5] See 2 Chron. 14 : 9; 1 Kings 9 : 20, 22; Isaiah 20 : 3, 4; 1 Chron. 9 : 2; Josephus, Antiquities of the Jews, Book III, ch. ii, p. 85. The Abbé Grégoire cites and approves a statement of J. Ch. Jahn, in his Archæologia Biblica, that the Hebrews had negro eunuchs. Littérature des Nègres, p. 7.

[6] Joel 3 : 8; Ezek. 27 : 13.

slaves, "unto a strange nation."[1] Among the Egyptians, with whom the Jews carried on a brisk commerce, we shall see there were numbers of negro slaves. Their existence among the latter nation, therefore, is a matter of no great surprise.[2]

The negro among the Jews, as everywhere he is found, was of a proscribed race. He was even forbidden to approach the altar to offer the bread of his God.[3]

The treatment of this class of slaves, among the Hebrews, was extremely rigorous. Corporal chastisement was customary, and sometimes resulted in death. In such event, if the death was immediate, the master was punished; but if the slave lingered "a day or two," he was not punished: "For," said the law, "he is his money."[4] If the slave was maimed by loss of an eye, or a tooth, the penalty was his enfranchisement.[5] The slave sometimes escaped,[6] in which event, the master had the right of recaption. This right seems to have extended to the territory of the neighboring nations, as was exemplified in the case of Shimei pursuing his fugitives into the territory, and even the house of the King of Gath.[7] With the characteristic exclusiveness of the Jews, they denied this right to other nations, whose slaves sought refuge among them.[8]

The *status* of this class of servants was very different from that of the Hebrew servant. He was entitled to no civil rights; could make no complaint against his master, and could not be heard as a witness. He could not redeem himself, because he could acquire nothing.

---

[1] Exodus 21 : 8.

[2] The curious are referred to a very ingenious argument by Rev. J. Priest, in his Bible Defence of Slavery, to prove that all the Canaanites were black, and that "heathen" refers entirely to the black race.

[3] The flat-nosed must refer to the negro. Lev. 21 : 18.

[4] Exodus 21 : 20, 22; see Michaelis's Comm. vol. iv, art. 277.

[5] Exod. 21 : 26, 27.　　　　[6] 1 Sam. 25 : 10.

[7] 1 Kings 2 : 39, 40.　　　　[8] Deut. 23 : 15, 16.

Nor was it allowed, among the Jews, for a stranger to possess the land. Hence, the argument that the bondage of these was determined by the year of Jubilee, fails, for they had no "possession" to which they could return. Their descendants also were slaves, following the condition of the mother. Thus Solomon says, "I got me servants and maidens, and had servants born in my house."[1]

The value of slaves doubtless varied with their qualities and other circumstances. In the event of a slave being killed by a vicious ox, the price was fixed by the law, without regard to the circumstances, at 30 shekels.[2] In the case of releasing a person from a vow, a more discriminating scale of value was affixed, which we may safely take as the customary value of the times. A child under a month was valued at nothing. From 1 month to 5 years, males were valued at 5 shekels, females at 3. From 5 years to 20, males were valued at 20 shekels, females at 10. From 20 to 60 years, males at 50 shekels, females at 30. Upwards of 60 years, males at 15 shekels, females at 10.[3]

There were public slaves as well as private, among the Jews. These were attached to the sanctuary, and performed the menial labors for the priests and Levites.[4] Thus the Gibeonites, for their deceit, were condemned to be "hewers of wood and drawers of water."[5] Their posterity were called *nethinims* (meaning *presented as gifts*), and are mentioned on several occasions.[6] Samuel was a public servant, attached to the sanctuary, being so devoted from his mother's womb.[7]

Manumission was allowed among the Jews. The

---

[1] Eccles. 2 : 7. See also Gen. 17 : 13, 23 ; 15 : 3 ; 14 : 14 ; Ex. 23 : 12 ; Psalm 86 : 16.    [2] Ex. 21 : 32.

[3] Lev. 27 : 1–8 ; Michaelis's Comm. vol. ii, art. 124 ; see also Hosea 3 : 2.

[4] Lev. 31 : 40, 47 ; Michaelis's Comm. vol. ii, art. 126.

[5] Josh. 9 : 27.    [6] 1 Chron. 9 : 2 ; Ezra 8 : 17, 20.

[7] 1 Sam. 1 : 11.

effect of it, however, was not to confer any political privileges upon the freed man. His very name signified "uncleanness."[1]

At the Jewish feasts, the Mosaic law required the slaves to be invited, and, for a time, to enjoy them equally with their masters. The Sabbath was also, expressly, a day of rest for them.[2]

Slavery continued among the Jews so long as they were an independent nation. Even in their captivity they did not lose them; for we find, upon their return under Nehemiah, *one-sixth* of the people that came up from their captivity were "men-servants and maid-servants," exclusive of the children of Solomon's servants.[3] In the days of the Saviour, they still retained them.[4] Nor did he hesitate to avow the rightful superiority of the master, and to illustrate his precepts by this relation.[5] The kindly feeling existing towards the slave, is exemplified in the centurion whose sick slave was " dear unto him."[6]

When Nebuchadnezzar and his hosts came and "pitched against Jerusalem," the Jews, alarmed at their situation, made a covenant with Zedekiah, their king, to manumit all their Hebrew servants. After the immediate danger was removed, however, they reduced them again to servitude. It seems that the provision of the law, requiring them to be released on the seventh year, after six years of bondage, had been disregarded, and it was for this, among other sins, that Jeremiah prophesied that captivity which soon overtook them.[7]

---

[1] Michaelis's Comm. vol. ii, art. 126.

[2] Deut. 12 : 17, 18; 16 : 11. Michaelis conceives that the provision prohibiting the muzzling of the ox while threshing the corn, Deut. 25 : 4, was extended to the slaves eating of the provisions they prepared for their masters. Vol. ii, art. 130.     [3] Neh. 7 : 57, 66.

[4] Mark 14 : 66.

[5] John 13 : 16; 8 : 35, 36; Luke 17 : 7, 8, 9; 22 : 27.

[6] Luke 7 : 2.     [7] 2 Kings 25 : 1; Jer. 34 : 8-20.

# CHAPTER II.

## SLAVERY IN EGYPT.

NEXT to the Jews, the Egyptians have the earliest authentic history; and as Ancient Egypt was not only the cradle of the arts and sciences, but has been justly said to be " the first that found out the rules of government, and *the art of making life easy and a people happy*,"[1] our attention seems to be properly called next to the history of her system of slavery.

The bondage of the Israelites shows that the Egyptians were not only slaveholders at an early day, but hard taskmasters.[2] That they had slaves, not only agrestic, but domestic, attached to the person of the master, is abundantly shown by the inscriptions upon the numerous monuments of their ancient grandeur.[3] It is, moreover, well agreed from these monuments, that many of these domestic slaves were of pure negro blood.[4] In one of them, a large number of negroes are represented as prisoners of war.[5] Herodotus confirms this conclusion,

---

[1] Rees's Cyclopædia, Article " Egypt."

[2] Slaves constituted a part of the present the King of Egypt gave to Abraham. Gen. 12 : 16.

[3] Egypt and its Monuments. By Dr. Hawks. 2d ed. p. 144.

[4] The curious on this point are referred to Nott and Gliddon's Types of Mankind, p. 248, et seq. These monuments show negro slaves in Egypt at least 1600 years before Christ, p. 255, 262, 268, 307. That they were the same happy negroes of this day is proven by their being represented in a dance 1300 years before Christ, p. 263. The negro mummy, described on page 267, puts their existence beyond cavil.

[5] Wallon, Histoire de l'Esclavage, tom. i, p. 24, 27, n. Sir G. Wilkinson

and informs us that Ethiopia furnished Egypt with gold, ivory, and slaves.[1] Slave-markets undoubtedly there were, as the history of Joseph exemplifies; and it is said, that a city founded by fugitive slaves was one of the principal slave-markets.[2]

Upon one of the monuments at Thebes, an Egyptian scribe is represented as registering negroes as slaves, both men, women, and children.[3] Upon another, the victorious Egyptian king is represented as putting to flight a troop of negroes.[4] In still another, they are re-presented as indulging in their favorite amusement of this day,—the dance.[5] These representations are so per-fect, that the most unpractised eye would recognize them at a glance. A negro skull was exhumed in the Island of Malta, among the ruins of Hadjerkem.[6]

Purchase and conquests seem to be the principal sources of Egyptian slavery.[7] A law abolishing slavery for debt, and referred to by Diodorus, shows that prior to that time this was another prolific source. He also notices the substitution, by one of the emperors, of slavery, for the penalty of death.[8] Such commutation made the recipients public slaves, of which there was a vast number. These were engaged upon the public

says, "It is evident that both white and black slaves were employed as servants." Egypt and its Monuments, p. 169. A picture of this inscrip-tion may be found in Types of Mankind, p. 250. See also Pulszky's contribution to Indigenous Races of Man, for other and farther proofs on this point, pp. 150, 189.

[1] Herod. 3 : 97.

[2] Plin. Hist. Nat. vi, 34, cited by Wallon, tom. i, p. 25, n. See re-marks of Sir Gardner Wilkinson, quoted by Dr. Hawks, Egypt and its Monuments, p. 168.

[3] See representation of this in Types of Mankind, 252.

[4] Types of Mankind, 269.      [5] Ibid. 263.

[6] Wilkes's Exp. Exp. vol. ix, 186.

[7] Wallon, tom. i, p. 23 ; Odyssey, Bk. XIV, 260 ; Egypt and its Monu-ments, by Dr. Hawks, p. 164, 168.

[8] Diod. i, 75, 79.

works, and it was the boast of the Pharaohs, that the hand of no Egyptian labored in their erection.[1]

Though the negroes in Egypt were generally slaves, "prejudice of color" does not seem to have been so great as at this day, as we find in one of their inscriptions, the representation of the negro queen of one of the emperors receiving equal homage with himself.[2]

Among the Egyptians we first find an account of eunuchs, exhibiting a feature of ancient slavery, perhaps the most cruel and barbarous.[3] Moses sought, by every means, to deter the Jews from such a custom, yet we find eunuchs among the king's household,[4] and the prophet offering such consolation.[5]

The treatment of slaves by the Egyptians was very rigorous. Homicide was punished in every one except the master, but as to him there seems to have been no penalty. In the whole kingdom there was but one temple (that of the Egyptian Hercules, near Canope) in which fugitives might take refuge from cruel treatment.[6] "From the monuments," says Taylor, "we find that the mistress of a mansion was very rigid in enforcing her authority over her female domestics. We see these unfortunate beings trembling and cringing before their superiors, beaten with rods by the overseers, and sometimes threatened with a formidable whip, wielded by the lady of the mansion herself." Other scenes upon these monuments indicate kinder treatment. "In a tomb at Thebes," says Dr. Hawks, "is a representation, copied by Wilkinson, of a lady enjoying the bath, who is waited on by four female servants, where nothing

---

[1] Wallon, Hist. de l'Esclavage, tom. i, p. 28 ; Egypt and its Monuments, p. 168.

[2] Wallon, tom. i, p. 29, n. ; Types of Mankind, 262.

[3] Gen. 37 : 36. The word here translated " officer" means literally "eunuch." See Egypt and its Monuments, p. 169.

[4] 2 Kings 9 : 32.                     [5] Is. 56 : 3.

[6] Wallon, Hist. de l'Esclavage, &c., tom. i, p. 30.

appears to indicate any other feeling than that of mutual kindness, and on the part of the attendants respectful affection."[1] Other representations, upon the monuments, show the cruelty of the taskmasters, and the use of the bastinado.[2]

Whenever, from the excess of the supply over the demand, labor becomes so cheap that the free laborer can make for his wages only his food and clothing, there ceases to be value in property in slaves; on the contrary, the ownership is a burden, because the old, the infirm, and the infant, require care, clothing, and food, without remunerating labor. The feudal system in Middle Europe and Britain laid the foundation for the emancipation of the serfs, at this stage of society. In Egypt and the East, a more refined system of bondage was adopted in lieu of that of personal slavery, which continued the degradation of the slaves, while it relieved the masters from the obligations of ownership. This system was that of castes, by which the proprietorship of the lands and the holding of the offices of government were restricted to those and their descendants who were the former masters, while the laboring classes and their descendants were arranged in subordinate castes, ranking in dignity according to the supposed honorableness of their occupations; and that this might be a perpetual condition, the children were prohibited, under severe penalties, from attempting, under any circumstances, to improve their condition by obtaining a position in a higher caste.[3] The transition from a state of slavery to that of an inferior caste was gradual and

---

[1] Egypt and its Monuments, p. 144, 2d ed.

[2] Egypt and its Monuments, p. 219, 220. A remarkable picture in the Tomb of Rosché, at Thebes, gives so accurate a representation of the Jews engaged in the making of bricks, overlooked by their Egyptian taskmasters, as to cause doubts to be expressed of its authenticity. Ibid. p. 222.

[3] Prichard's Analysis of Egyptian Mythology, Book IV, ch. iii, sec. 1.

easy; and the fact that the laborers were chiefly
foreigners and captives and their descendants, the preservation of the distinctive castes became an easy matter, the line being drawn by nature herself in the different races.[1]

The number of these castes in Egypt (about which
there is disagreements in different authors), may be reduced to five. 1st. The sacerdotal order, or priesthood.
2d. The military. 3d. The herdsmen. 4th. The agricultural and commercial class. 5th. The artificers or
laboring artisans,[2] ranking in dignity as they are named.
To the two former classes belonged, by inheritance, the
lands and the enjoyment of all the honorable offices of
the government. The three lower classes differed only
in their occupations, and might, indeed, be properly
ranked together, as Strabo has done in his classification.[3]
These were the original slaves of Egypt, and by the
change have reaped no benefit. The privileged orders
keep them in complete subjection; laboring without
hope of advancement, "and for wages," says Volney,
"barely sufficient to sustain life."[4] "The rice and corn
they gather are carried to their masters, and nothing is
reserved for them but dourra or Indian millet, of which
they make a coarse and tasteless bread, without leaven."[5]

This system of castes gives, necessarily, a permanent
and remarkably uniform character to a nation; and
hence Egypt, to-day, would be, in her internal polity, the
same as Egypt in the time of Herodotus and Diodorus,
had not change of government and Mussulman rule crip-
pled more completely her energy, and stagnated her industry. Recent travellers testify, that the cultivators of
the present day retain of the fruit of their industry

[1] Wallon, de l'Esclavage, &c., tom. i, p. 22.
[2] Prichard, as above, p. 377, and authorities cited by him.
[3] Strabo, Lib. XVII.
[4] Prichard, 378; Wallon, de l'Esclavage, &c., tom. i, p. 22.
[5] Rees's Cyclopædia, Art. "Egypt."

barely enough to support existence. Their cattle and agricultural implements even, belong to the landlord.[1] Over them the landlord exercises unlimited control, with power to punish for offences, and to settle all disputes, without liberty of appeal.[2]

While the system of castes seems thus to have removed from the Caucasian races the *status* of personal slavery to the negro, it brought no relief, for the slave-market of the present day, in Cairo, offers still to the purchaser the children of Ethiopia, from whom are supplied the personal domestics of Egypt.[3]

There is one other class of slaves, at the present day, bought and sold in Egypt. These are the pure white Circassians, from whom the harems are supplied; and many of whose youths are purchased and educated, sometimes, for the highest offices in the state.[4]

[1] Olin's Travels in the East, vol. i, p. 40.

[2] Ibid. p. 43.

[3] Ibid. p. 61; Stephens's Egypt, &c., vol. i, p. 39; Types of Mankind, 251. Mr. Gliddon states the price of a negress to be about fifty dollars; Wilkes's Expl. Exped. vol. ix, p. 185.

[4] Olin's Travels in the East, vol. i, p. 34.

# CHAPTER III.

WE turn naturally from Egypt to India, for the remarkable similarity in their law of castes seems hardly
to be a coincidence, but indicates, in some way, a common origin. According to Menu, all men were created,
respectively, from the mouth, arm, thigh, and foot of
Deity; and separate duties were allotted to each, according to their origin. The first class (from the mouth),
had wisdom to rule and to sacrifice. The second (from
the arm), had strength to fight and protect the others.
The third (from the belly and thighs), were allotted to
provide nourishment for the whole, by agriculture and
traffic. The fourth (from the feet), were naturally *servile*, formed to labor and to serve.[1] There were subdi-
visions of some of these classes, corresponding, with
striking similarity, to the Egyptian castes. The first
class among the Hindoos (originally Brahmans,[2] now
Bramins), and the military, or second class, as among
the Egyptians, monopolized all the priesthood, the government, and the learning. The agriculturists were
mere tenants, having no interest in the land. And the
fourth, or servile class, were declared by Menu, to be

---

[1] Richard's Analysis, &c., note to Book IV, ch. iii, p. 397 ; Rees's Cyclopædia, Article " Caste ;" Institutes of Menu ; Wallon, tom. i, p. 31.

[2] Some have supposed Brachman to be a contraction of Abrachman,
and thus seek to trace this leading caste of the Hindoos to a descent from
Abraham and his wife, Kiturali. Rees's Cyclopædia, Article Brachman.

naturally slaves.¹ To serve a Brahman, was declared their most laudable action.²

The same provision existed and exists in India as in Egypt, in reference to the immutable *status* of the different castes, and similar penalties inflicted for any effort to seek to migrate from the one to another.³ The effect of which is, that India, to-day, is comparatively the same as India three centuries before Christ, when Megasthenes accompanied Alexander in his conquest, and left a record of his impressions.⁴

Though the servile class, or *Soudras*, were declared by Menu to be naturally slaves, yet we find, in modern times, many of them that, either from the clemency of their masters or the unprofitableness of their labor, are emancipated from the control of any particular master. And while those that belong to the military and agricultural castes seem originally to have been free, yet we find, in later times, from voluntary sale or other causes, many of them have become slaves to their superior castes; there being only one restriction, according to Hindoo law, and that is, that no one shall become a slave to a master of his own or an inferior caste.⁵ In the event of a marriage between persons of different castes, the offspring followed the condition of the inferior parent.⁶

By the Hindoo law, slaves might become such, by voluntary sale, by sale or gift of children, by sale for

¹ Institutes of Menu, ch. viii, v. 414; Adam, on Slavery in India, p. 13; Wallon, tom. i, p. 32.

² Wallon, tom. i, 32, n. 5. It will be perceived that, by this means, slavery became a part of the religion of the Hindoos. Ibid. 35.

³ Rees's Cyclopædia, Article "Caste;" Wallon, tom. i, p. 34, 35.

⁴ Arrian, Strabo, and Diodorus derived all their information from Megasthenes. See Prichard's Analysis of Egyptian Mythology, note to Book IV, ch. iii, p. 397.

⁵ Adam on Slavery in India, pp. 12, 13, and authorities cited by him; Wallon, de l'Esclavage, &c., tom. i, p. 32.

⁶ Wallon, tom. i, p. 34.

debt, by captivity, by birth, by marriage to a slave, or by
sale as punishment for crime.[1]   Children follow the condition of their mother; and all slaves are inherited as a
part of the estate of a deceased master.   The agrestic
slaves (such as are attached to the soil), are subject to
the laws of ancestral real property; while the domestics,
attached to the person, pass under the laws regulating
personal property.[2]

The Hindoo law gave the master unlimited powers
over his slaves.   "It makes no provision for the protection of the slave from the cruelty and ill-treatment of an
unfeeling master, nor defines the master's power over
the person of his slave.   It allows to the slave no right
of property even in his own acquisitions, except by the
indulgence of his master."[3]

The modes of enfranchisement, by this law, were
various.   Among others, the preservation of the master's
life; or the bearing to him a son, by a female slave,
operated as a manumission.[4]

When India passed under Mussulman rule, the Mohammedan law of slavery became engrafted upon that
of India, and, until the possession by Britain, was the
paramount law.

The Mohammedan law recognized but two legitimate
sources of slavery, viz.: captive infidels, and their descendants; these are subject to all the laws of contract,
sale, and inheritance, as other property.   They cannot
marry without the consent of their masters; they cannot testify as witnesses; they cannot be parties to a suit;
they are ineligible to all offices of profit and trust; nor
can they contract, or acquire, or inherit property.

---

[1] Adam, on Slavery in India, 14, citing Colebrooke's Digest of Hindoo
Law, vol. ii, pp. 340, 346, 368; Menu's Institutes of Hindoo Law, ch.
viii, v. 415; Wallon, de l'Esclavage, &c., tom. i, p. 30.

[2] Ibid.

[3] Colebrooke, quoted by Adam, p. 17; Wallon, de l'Esclavage, &c., tom.
i, 33.          [4] Adam, on Slavery in India, 17, 19.

The master's control over the slave is very great; and his murder subjects the master to no punishment. If another person kills him, his master may commute the punishment for a pecuniary compensation.

This description of slaves cannot be emancipated. There are other or qualified slaves who, under certain circumstances, such as bearing children to the master, become free.[1]

When India, through the agency of the East India Company, passed under British rule, it became a matter of grave concern, how far the laws of Britain should be substituted for the native regulations. After various provisions, looking wisely to the adoption of laws "suitable to the genius of the people," it was finally established, in 1793, that, "In suits regarding succession, inheritance, marriage, and caste, and all religious usages and institutions, the Mohammedan law, with reference to Mohammedans, and the Hindoo law, with regard to Hindoos, are to be considered the general rules by which the Judges are to form their decisions." Under this provision, it was held that the Hindoo and Mohammedan laws of slavery were established, as to those coming under their respective influence; and these laws were enforced by the British East India Court, from the date of this regulation (1793) until the nominal abolition of slavery by the East India Company.[2]

Slavery in British India, however, was not confined entirely to those so declared by the Hindoo and Mohammedan law. There were slaves, made so originally and directly under the law of the British Government.

[1] This summary of the Mohammedan law is extracted from Macnaghten's Principles and Precedents of Mohammedan Law, as cited by Adam, on Slavery in India, pp. 20, et seq., 41, 63, et seq.; see also Buchanan's Travels in Mysore, &c., vol. ii, 495.

[2] See Adam, on Slavery in India, 24–27; Harrington's Analysis of the Laws and Regulations, vol. i, p. 1, et seq.; Macnaghten's Hindoo Law, vol. i, p. 113.

Thus, in 1772, certain bands of robbers, termed Decoits, infesting the public roads, upon conviction, were to be executed publicly ; *" and the family of the criminal shall become the slaves of the state, and be disposed of for the general benefit and convenience of the people, according to the discretion of the government."*[1] Thus, by the Hindoo law, men were enslaved for their own crimes ; by the British law, for the crimes of their parents. This law was repealed in 1793.

The servile class in India are very nearly the color of the African negro. There are, however, distinguishing characteristics, showing them to be of different races. The negro proper, however, has found his way to India, and is there, as he is everywhere, in a state of slavery. The East India Company early discovered his adaptation to the labor of this hot climate, and worked their most extensive plantations of the nutmeg and clove by African labor.[2] And even at the time that British cruisers were hovering on the western coast of Africa, more effectually to prevent the African slave-trade, on the eastern coast a similar trade was being prosecuted, within their knowledge and to their own dominions, declared by an order of the Vice-President in Council, on 9th September, 1817, to be " of a nature and tendency scarcely less objectionable than the trade which has been carried on between the western coast of Africa and the West India Islands."[3] Prohibitory regulations were afterwards adopted, the effect of which, according to Mr. Chaplin's Report, was to " increase the price, without putting a stop to the traffic."[4] Mr. Adam, an

---

[1] Adam, on Slavery in India, 38 ; Colebrooke's Digest of the Regulations, Supplement, p. 7, 114; Harrington's Analysis, vol. i, p. 308.

[2] Adam, on Slavery in India, 40.

[3] Harrington's Analysis, vol. iii, p. 755 ; Adam, on Slavery in India, 78, 149.

[4] Report, pp. 150, 151 ; Adam, 149.

eyewitness, gives it as his opinion, that the trade had not entirely ceased in 1840.[1]

Slaves cannot be valuable where free labor demands only about four cents per day for wages; and, hence, we are not astonished to find the prices of slaves varying from eleven shillings to £2 5s.[2] The treatment of the slaves in British India was generally mild. "The slave is a favorite and confidential servant rather than an abject drudge. . . . The mildness and equanimity of the Indian's temper (or his apathy and slowness, if this better describe the general disposition of the people), contribute to insure good treatment to the slave."[3] The food and raiment allowed them were scanty, but fully equal to that of the free laborers of that class.[4] In India, as in all Eastern countries, many of the slaves are eunuchs.

The East India Company have lately abolished slavery within their dominions. This was necessarily merely nominal. The slaves remain with their old ma receiving as wages what they formerly received as food and raiment. Their actual servile condition remains unchanged. The number of them, in 1840, was estimated at about one million.[5]

---

[1] Slavery in India, 151.   [2] Adam, 107.
[3] Mr. Colebrooke's official paper of 1812.
[4] Buchanan's Travels in Mysore, &c., vol. ii, 370, 491.
[5] Adam, 129.

# CHAPTER IV.

## SLAVERY IN THE EAST.

AMONG the earliest records of the Assyrian Empire, we find the model of that system of slavery which distinguishes all oriental nations. Tradition ascribes to Queen Semiramis the introduction of the barbarous custom of making eunuchs of slaves. The Zendavesta, the most ancient of their records, and containing the pretended revelations of Zoroaster, recognizes four classes or castes: the priests, the warriors, the agriculturists, and the artisans. Infidels and negroes (*les fils des ténèbres*), taken captive in war, were reduced to slavery.[1]

The Medes and Persians, the successors to the religion of Zoroaster, exhibit oriental slavery in its full perfection. The number of domestic slaves attending the person and the various household duties was very great. The sources of slavery were chiefly captives taken in war, and children purchased either from their parents or from slave-dealers. The merchants of Phenicia and of Greece made them one of the articles of commerce. Hence the slaves were very numerous at Tyre and in the Phenician cities. The satrap of Babylon and of the Assyrian country, furnished annually to the Persians five hundred young eunuchs. And in the expedition against Ionia, the most beautiful children were reserved and condemned to this condition.[2] The fidelity of the eunuchs made them, according to Herodotus,

[1] Rees's Cyclopædia, Art. Zendavesta; Wallon, de l'Esclavage dans l'Antiquité, tom. i, 45, 47.

[2] Wallon, de l'Esclavage dans l'Antiquité, tom. i, 47. In speaking of the

highly prized among barbarous nations, and they consequently filled the highest offices in the households of
the nobles.[1]

The power of the master over the slave, among the
Persians, was almost unlimited. Herodotus says, it was
not allowed a Persian to punish one of his slaves cruelly
for a single fault, but if, after due consideration, his
faults were found to outnumber and outweigh his virtues,
the master might then follow the dictates of his anger.[2]
Sometimes the slaves revolted, as at Tyre, where they
massacred the freemen, and took possession of the city.[3]

Frequently the nobles armed their slaves, and led
them in battle. The Parthians are said to pursue the
same course.[4] At Babylon there was a custom, at a certain fête, for the masters to obey their slaves for five days.
One was selected to rule as king. At the expiration of
the fête he was killed.[5]

What has been said of Persia is true of all the surrounding countries. In fact, in the countries of the East,
slavery is universally an element of the social organization. A celebrated French writer upon this subject, in
summing up, says, "Comme on vient de le voir par ce
rapide aperçu pour l'orient, cet antique berceau du genre
humain et de la civilisation du monde, l'organisation
sociale se résume en deux mots qui sont, pour ainsi dire,
les deux termes d'un même rapport: despotisme, esclavage."[6] China, with her wonderful self-existing and
self-perpetuating civilization, forms no exception to this
remark. At least twelve hundred years before the
Christian era, captivity and other sources furnished
slaves to the Chinese. The most fruitful source, was

number of domestics, he enumerates "legions of cooks, musicians, dancers, valets de table, porters, and keepers of baths." Cyrus, we recollect,
among the Medes, acted as a wine-bearer. Xen. Cyrop.

[1] Herod. viii, 105.  [2] Herod. i, 137.  [3] Wallon, tom. i, p. 50.
[4] Xenophon, Cyrop. viii, 8, 20; Wallon, tom. i, 52, note.
[5] Wallon, tom. i, p. 51; Dion. Chrysost. Orat. iv, De Regno, p. 69.
[6] Wallon, tom. i, p. 52.

the sale of themselves and their children by the poor. The children of slaves were slaves by birth; and on the master's death, were the subjects of inheritance.

The treatment of slaves in China was milder than in the East generally. The law protected his life and his person. The branding of a slave with fire worked his enfranchisement. "Thus," says Wallon, "the mark of slavery became his title to liberty."[1]

When the Greeks and Romans successively overran the East, they introduced no change in the system of slavery. It was, if different, more lenient in practice than their own. When Arabia, under the infatuation of religious zeal, brought the surrounding nations, at one time, under her power, and to the knowledge of the faith, she found nothing in slavery that was not only consistent with, but expressly commanded, in that great miracle of the Prophet, the Koran.[2] Years and ages, hence, have made but little change in the law of Eastern slavery, though much of Eastern glory has departed.

Here, too, we find the negro still a slave.[3] The numbers, in ancient times, we cannot estimate. In later days, a brisk trade has been and even now is carried on with the eastern coast of Africa by Arab dealers, who supply Persia and Arabia with African slaves.[4]

Commodore Perry describes the Japanese slavery of the present day as of the most abject and wretched character. The poor frequently sell themselves as slaves, the price varying from two to ten dollars. The different ranks in society were distinguished by the metal of which the hair-pin was made, whether of gold, silver, or brass.[5]

---

[1] See Wallon, tom. i, p. 40. He refers to and cites freely M. Biot, Mémoires sur les Chinois.

[2] By its provisions, homicide of a freeman only was murder, and allowed the retribution by the avenger of blood. Chap. ii, 173.

[3] Texier's Arménie, Perse, et Mésopotamie, 1842, Pl. 113. Quoted in Types of Mankind, 254.

[4] Harrington's Analysis, vol. iii, p. 748; Adam, on Slavery in India, 78.    [5] United States Japan Exped. vol. i, pp. 219–226.

# CHAPTER V.

It has been considered a striking contradiction in the character of the Greeks, that while they professed to be worshippers of liberty, during their whole history they not only tolerated but encouraged slavery, and in such a form, that it became a proverb, that " at Sparta the freeman is the freest of all men, and the slave the greatest of slaves."[1] Whether this is really a contradiction we shall elsewhere consider, when we examine the political and social influences of slavery; and perhaps we may find that true philosophy confirms the conclusions of Aristotle and Plato, that this is an element essential in a true republic, for the preservation of perfect equality among citizens, and the growth and encouragement of the spirit of liberty.

Our inquiry now is as to the facts, and we find slavery among the Greeks from their earliest authentic history. True, it is stated, that among the Hellenes, in the earliest times, there was no slavery.[2] Yet, in the time of Homer, we find it in general use; not only of captives taken in war, but of slaves purchased for a price.[3] The familiar use of the institution in illustration, by the poets, dramatists, and writers of Greece, shows how completely it was interwoven into their entire system.[4]

---

[1] Plutarch's Lycurgus.      [2] Herod. vi, 137.

[3] Odyssey, xiv, 339 ; xv, 483 ; xxii, 421 ; Iliad, iii, 407 ; vi, 460 ; Eurip. Hecuba, 442, 479.

[4] The curious will find a large number of extracts and illustrations,

The legitimate use of these by the historian, is beauti-
fully defended by M. Wallon: " Car les muses sont
filles de la mémoire (Mnémosyne) et dans ces premiers
temps, fidèles à leur origine, elles puisent aux traditions
nationales le sujet de leurs chants."[1]

The Hellenes were not the earliest inhabitants of
Greece. The Ante-Hellenic period, however, is so
legendary, as to be almost fabulous. Even the name of
the people, Pelasgi, is said, and believed by many, to be
without a corresponding race, in fact, and those who
are said to be their descendants, occupied, in Ancient
Greece, an inferior position in society.[2] We may, therefore, well doubt the statement that there ever was a
period in which the Hellenes did not practise and recognize slavery. The barbarous aboriginal inhabitants
formed too convenient a material to be disregarded by
their superiors; and the right to and practice of enslaving the conquered, were recognized by all the surrounding countries. These, of all others, saw a wider
difference between themselves and barbarians, and were
the least likely to doubt the right or discourage the practice of enslaving barbarians. Certain it is, that from the
earliest period of their authentic history, we find conquest
a fruitful source of slavery among the Greeks.[3] An intelligent French writer concludes, after a full investigation, that the critic may rightfully determine that slavery
existed in Greece prior to that time at which we have
the evidence to demonstrate its presence.[4] So deeply im-

collected by the research and industry of Mr. Fletcher, in his Studies on
Slavery, p. 516, et seq.; See Eurip. Hecuba, 442; Troades, 186, 282;
Plautus, Casina. Captivi; Aristophanes, Plutus, et passim ; Sophocles,
Trachiniæ.                         [1] De l'Esclavage dans l'Antiquité, tom. i, 58.
   [2] Grote's History of Greece, vol. ii, 261, et seq., and authorities cited.
   [3] Xen. Cyr. vii, 5, § 73. Homer gives a graphic description of the
taking of a city and its consequences in the address of the old knight,
Phœnix. Iliad, ix, 585–600.
   [4] Wallon, de l'Esclavage dans l'Antiquité, tom. i, p. 56.

pressed was slavery upon the Grecian institutions in
the heroic age, that we find it transplanted among the
Gods, and Apollo serving as the slave of Admetus, as a
penalty for the murder of the Cyclops.[1]  And Hercules,
sold to Omphale a barbarian, completes a year in her service.  Enraged at this indignity, he seeks revenge upon
Eurytus, whom he looked to as the cause, and taking
an advantage of Iphitus, the son, while his eye is turned
in another direction, hurls him from a towering height.
Jupiter, incensed at this cowardly trick, condemned
Hercules again to slavery.[2]  In a fragment of Panyasis,
he says, " such (slavery) was the lot of Ceres, of the
illustrious blacksmith of Lemnos, of Neptune, of Apollo,
of the terrible Mars, bending under the fatal will of his
father."[3]

In the Grecian mythology, Mercury was the peculiar
God of the slave, who protected and partook of his
thefts.[4]

The sources of slavery among the Greeks were the
same as those we have noticed among other nations,
until the celebrated Seisachtheia (Σεισάχθεια) or Relief
Law of Solon, the insolvent debtor was the slave of his
creditor.  This act forbade the pledge of the person as
a security for the debt, released many debtors, who were
suffering the penalty of slavery, and even made provision for the repurchasing and bringing back in liberty,
many insolvent debtors, who had been sold and exported.
Solon farther forbade the sale by parents of their children as slaves, except in the case of an unchaste daughter.[5]  The policy of their laws from that time discou-

[1] Eurip. Alcestis, i, 2.
[2] Sophocles, Trachiniæ, 225–293 ; Æschylus, Agam. 1020.
[3] Quoted in Wallon, tom. i, 81.
[4] Aristoph. Plutus, 1140, et seq.   Quoted in Wallon, tom. i, p. 300.
[5] Grote's Hist. of Greece, vol. iii, p. 98 ; Plutarch's Life of Solon.  In
the other Grecian states, except Athens, the sale of children into slavery
continued.  Wallon, i, 158.

raged the enslavement of Greeks, and looked to the barbarians alone for a supply,[1] although, in some states, the debtor still remained the subject of sale.[2]

Expeditions were fitted, and wars undertaken frequently, merely for the purpose of procuring slaves.[3] Such expeditions filled up the leisure hours of the Greeks during the siege of Troy. The stealing of beautiful girls and boys for the purpose of enslaving them was a common practice with the maritime nations. The touching story of the swineherd Eumæus told Ulysses, illustrates this truth.[4] Piracy formed also a continual source of supply, which kept even pace with the demand.[5]

The children of female slaves followed the condition of their mother, even if the master was their acknowledged father. An excepted case was that of a master's living with a female slave as παλλακή, or concubine, in which event the children were free.[6] Ulysses was the offspring of such a connection, and he gratefully acknowledged that his father honored him equally with his legitimate sons.[7] Though free, their position, however, was precarious, and depended more upon the will and power of the father than any fixed rights. Hence, Tecmessa appealed to Ajax in behalf of her son, the issue of such concubinage, in the event of his dying during the son's tender years, lest she "should eat the

[1] See the speech of Callicratidas, Xen. Hellen. vi, 14.

[2] Isocr. Platocens, 19 ; Becker's Charicles, 272 ; Smith's Dict. of G. & R. Antiq. "Servus" (Greek). In the intestine wars among the different Greek nations, and even in the civil wars in the several states, the enslavement of the vanquished was enforced. See Wallon, i, 162, 163, and the authorities cited.

[3] Odyssey, xiv, 250 ; Sophocles, Trachiniæ, 253, et seq. Aristotle maintained the justice of such wars. Polit. iv, 7 ; xiii, 14.

[4] Odyssey, Bk. XV, 375, 500. Plautus, Captivi.

[5] Wallon, i, 166, et seq. ; Smith's Dict. "Servus" (Greek).

[6] Becker's Charicles, Excursus to Scene vii, p. 27 ; Wallon, i, 157.

[7] Odyssey, xiv, 200–210.

bread of slavery with her son."[1] This concubinage did not emancipate the mother. In the same appeal Tecmessa acknowledges her state of slavery.[2]

Another source of slavery among the Greeks was from the sale of strangers, residents in the city, Metics, who, upon failure to discharge their obligations to the state, or upon fraudulently, by marriage, introducing themselves into the family of a citizen, were condemned to slavery.[3]

Sometimes slavery was voluntarily submitted to as an expiation for an offence, especially homicide.[4]

There were two kinds of slavery among the Greeks, which may be denominated agrestic, attached to the land, or serfs, and domestic or personal servants. The former consisted chiefly of the conquered inhabitants of a country, who were first made the slaves of the community, and were retained in the possession of the conquered territory.[5] Among conquered nations, however, there was a difference in the degree of servitude, arising from the circumstances under which the conquest was effected, and the degree of force used therein. Of some, tribute only was required, and an acknowledged state of dependence, with a liability to answer the calls of the conquerors for men and munitions of war. Such were admitted to bear arms in the wars, and sometimes to hold offices, though their condition was still inferior to that of citizens. In Laconia, these were termed Perioiki, occupying a middle rank between the freemen and the Helots.[6]

In other cases, when the resistance was obstinate, or, after subjection, the vanquished were rebellious, a more

---

[1] Sophocles, Ajax, 485–518.  [2] Ibid.
[3] Wallon, i, 160.  [4] Wallon, i, 63.
[5] Wallon, tom. i, 56 ; Smith's Dict. " Servus" (Greek).
[6] Wallon, tom. i, 94, et seq.; Grote's Hist. of Greece, vol. ii, 364. The original meaning of the word περίοικοι is, " surrounding neighbor states," and is thus used by Thucydides, i, 17, by Isocrates, De Pace, p. 182.

rigorous servitude was enforced.  Such were the Helots
of Sparta, pure slaves, having no rights and allowed but
few privileges ; restricted from bearing arms, except as
attendants of their masters, or even from self-defence.
The tradition was, that they derived their name from
the inhabitants of Helos; who, refusing to accept the
same terms with the other Perioiki, were reduced to a
more severe bondage, and this gave an appellation to
this class of slaves.[1]  The Helots were the property of
the state, though their services were given to individuals.  The state reserved the right of emancipating
them, and sometimes exercised it.[2]  They constituted
the rustic population of Laconia ; sometimes working
the lands for a fixed rent, and sometimes under the immediate direction of a master.[3]  By reason, however, of
their being the slaves of the state, they were subject to
the control and order of every citizen.[4]  The rent that
he paid for the land was fixed by the state: a certain
portion of barley and a proportional of oil and wine.[5]
Being the slave of the state, the Helot was never sold,
especially out of the country; and feeling the pride of
Grecian birth and descent, frequently on the field of
battle won his freedom.  They were permitted to possess a small amount of property, how much is not certain.[6]  These circumstances gave them a marked superiority over the barbarian slave population of Athens
and Chios ; while, at the same time, they rendered them
more rebellious and unruly, requiring for their subjection a greater degree of rigor.  Instances of great
cruelty and inhumanity are recorded of the Spartans, in

[1] Smith's Dict. "Helotes."  A more satisfactory definition is from
the obsolete verb, ἕλω, to take or conquer. See Wallon, tom. i, 100–
101 ; Grote, vol. ii, 374.        [2] Smith, as above; Wallon, tom. i, 103.
[3] Smith, as above; Grote's History of Greece, vol. ii, 373.
[4] Wallon, tom. i, 103.
[5] Plutarch, Lyc.; Wallon, i, 103; Smith, as above.
[6] Grote's Hist. vol. ii, 375.

their treatment of the Helots. Some of them bear marks of exaggeration, which justify incredulity; such as the story of the disappearance of two thousand of them immediately after emancipation. The truth seems to be, that they sought to break the spirit of their unruly slaves by exhibitions of ostentatious scorn; and, at the same time, to inspirit their youth with a detestation of the degradation of slavery, and an unconquerable determination to preserve their own *status* as freemen. Such was the twofold motive for exhibiting them to their youth in a state of drunkenness. The result of such teaching would, naturally, lead to cruelty from the youth to the slaves; and the absence of a specific master to protect them (being slaves of the state), frequently, without doubt, subjected the unfortunate Helot to cruel oppressions.[1]

The other states of Greece had their agrestic slaves, as well as Athens and Sparta. The Penestæ of Thessaly resembled very much the Helots of Sparta, their condition being generally superior. They were slaves of particular masters, and not of the state. They are supposed to have been the descendants of the aboriginal inhabitants, and, like the Helots, were more ungovernable than the purchased slaves of Athens.[2]

So the Klarotæ, or Perioiki, of Crete, according to Aristotle, occupied a similar position with the Helots of Sparta. Some of them, however, were the property of particular masters, while others belonged to the state. The latter worked the public lands, and attended the public flocks—the principal source of their public revenue—attended at the public feasts, and performed similar duties on public occasions. Even those belonging to particular masters, were generally occupied with rural

[1] Grote's Hist. vol. ii, 375 ; Smith's Dict. " Helotes;" Wallon, i, 104.
[2] Smith's Dict. " Penestæ."

E

labors. The menial duties of domestics were performed by purchased slaves.[1]

At Corinth, also, we find the agrestic slaves.[2] So at Argos, Epidaurus, Sicyone, and at Delphos.[3]

In almost every Grecian state we find the public slaves. Those at Athens were termed "Demosii." They were educated to fill subordinate offices, such as heralds, clerks, &c. Sometimes they formed a part of the city guard, and preserved order in public assemblies. It is supposed that these possessed superior legal rights to the private domestic slave.[4]

In every portion of Ancient Greece we find the domestic slave. In Sparta they were selected from the Helots.[5] In most of Greece they were purchased slaves, generally barbarians, and bought in the slave-markets. These markets were regularly opened; the supply, from wars, commerce, piracies, and kidnapping, being ample. The largest and most remarkable were held at Chios and at Athens.[6] In these, the purchaser could supply himself with slaves from different countries and of different qualities, according to the service for which they were bought. Their very names indicated their different origin.[7] Those of the North were large, rough, and sometimes unruly. Those from Egypt were accustomed to burdens, and were very enduring. From Egypt principally came the supply of negroes. These were prized for their color, were kept near the persons, and were considered slaves of luxury.[8] The prices of slaves varied

---

[1] Grote's Hist. vol. ii, 364; Wallon, tom. i, 121–125.

[2] κυνόφυλον, literally race of dogs; Wallon, i, 127.

[3] Ibid. 130.      [4] Smith's Dict. verb, " Demosii."

[5] Grote's Hist. of Greece, vol. ii, 375.

[6] Becker's Charicles, 272. Both at Athens and at Rome the market took its name from the stone on which the sale was made.

[7] Wallon, i, 169, et seq.; Smith's Dict. " Servus."

[8] Wallon, i, 169; Theophe. Char. xxi; Becker's Charicles, Exc. 1, and Scene vii, 275. See Indigenous Races of Man, pp. 190, 191, for cuts of Etruscan vases, showing the perfect negro face and head.

very much, according to their qualities, and the object for which they were purchased. Artisans were sometimes very valuable. They never, however, reached those exorbitant rates which were afterwards paid for them at Rome. They were generally stripped naked when sold.[1]

As we have seen, the negro was a favorite among slaves. The opposite color, "white," does not seem to have enjoyed the same favoritism. According to Plutarch, in his Life of Agesilaus, when that king made an expedition into Persia, he ordered his commissaries, one day, to strip and sell the prisoners. Their clothes sold freely, "but," says the historian, "as to the prisoners themselves, their skins being soft and white, by reason of their having lived so much within doors, the spectators only laughed at them, thinking they would be of no service as slaves." Eunuchs were common among the slaves in Greece.[2]

In the later days of Greece, it denoted poverty to be seen without an attendant. The number of these varied according to rank and wealth, but never was so great as at Rome. In Greece, slaves were looked to as a source of income and revenue; but in Rome, merely as ministering to their pride and luxury. No individual in Greece ever swelled out the number of his slaves to the enormous limit common at Rome. But the most of the Grecian slaves were artisans, or skilled in some way to be profitable to the master.[3] Hence there were no learned slaves, as at Rome; nor slaves kept for mere pleasure, as actors, dancers, musicians. When attend-

[1] Smith's Dict. "Servus" (Greek); Xen. Mem. ii, 5, § 2; Becker's Charicles, as above. See Wallon, tom. i, 197, et seq.

[2] Herod. viii, 105.

[3] See Becker's Charicles, as above; Smith's Dict. "Servus;" Arist. De Repub. ii, 3, iii, 4; Aristoph. Eccl. 593; Xen. Mem. i, 7, 2; Plato, Leg. v, 742, vii, 806. When Phocion's wife had only one female slave to attend her, it was the subject of remark at the theatre. Plutarch's Phocion.

ing his master in the streets, the slave preceded, and did
not follow.   The reason for this custom was the frequent
escapes of fugitive slaves.[1]   More than 20,000, we are
told, escaped at one time during the occupation of De-
celea by the Lacedemonians.[2]   The master had the right
to pursue and recapture the fugitive, and the penalty
was, frequently, branding in the forehead, to prevent a
repetition of the offence.[3]   The delivery of fugitive
slaves was frequently a subject-matter for treaties between the different states.[4]   In the later days of the
republic, there were offices where insurance was taken
to respond, in the event of the flight of the slave.[5]

The number of female slaves about the house was not
proportionally great, many of their offices being performed by men.[6]   They were under the direction of a
stewardess, as the men were under a steward.   The
slaves on a farm were controlled entirely by an overseer;
the master and owner residing generally in the city.[7]

The number of slaves in Greece was very large.   Their
imperfect census, however, leaves the exact number and
proportion doubtful.   The better opinion is, that they
were three or four times the number of the free population.[8]

The condition of the Greek slave was much more
tolerable than that of the Roman.   He was much more
familiar with his master than the Roman.   Plutarch's

[1] Becker's Charicles, as above; Lucian, Amor. 10.

[2] Thucyd. vii, 27.

[3] Xen. Mem. ii, 10; Plat. Protag. p. 310; Smith's Dict.; Becker's
Charicles, 279; Athenæus, vi, 225; Aristoph. The Birds, 758; Wallon,
tom. i, 317.                    [4] Thucyd. iv, 118.

[5] Smith's Dict. "Servus" (Greek).   Antigenes, of Rhodes, was the
first to establish such an insurance.   Ibid.

[6] Becker's Charicles, 275.

[7] Xen. Econ. xii, 2; ix, 11; Aristot. De Repub. i, 7; Wallon, i, 310.

[8] Smith's Dict. "Servus" (Greek); Becker's Charicles, 273.   The subject is elaborately considered by Wallon, Histoire, &c., tom. i, 220, et
seq.

anecdote concerning " Garrulity," evidences the latter
thus : Piso invited Clodius to dine, a slave being the
bearer of the invitation; the dinner was delayed by the
non-arrival of Clodius. At last the host inquired of the
slave if he was sure he invited him. The reply was,
" Yes." " Why doesn't he come then ?" "Because
he declined the invitation." " Why did you not tell me
that before ?" " Because you never asked me about it,"
was the slave's reply.[1] Euripides represents the depriva-
tion of the liberty of speech as the greatest of ills, and
adds, that this is the condition of a slave.[2] While, however, the legal right was absent, the privilege was extended almost *ad libitum* to the Athenian slave at least.[3]
Plato objects to this practice as evil, and adds, " The
address to a slave ought to be entirely or nearly a command ; nor should persons ever in any respect jest with
them, whether males or females, acts which many persons do very foolishly towards their slaves, and by
making them conceited render it more difficult during
life for their slaves to be governed, and for themselves
to govern."[4]

The result of this kind treatment was a corresponding fidelity on the part of the slave. Thus, Plato bears
witness, that "many slaves, by conducting themselves
with respect to all virtue, better towards some persons
than brothers and sons, have preserved their masters
and their possessions, and the whole of their dwellings."

" Other masters," he says, " by frequent use of goads
and whips, cause the very souls of their servants to become slavish."[5]

[1] De Garrul. 18; Plaut. Stech. iii.    [2] The Phenician Virgins, 391, 3.
[3] Becker's Charicles, Exc. Sc. vii, 276 ; Dem. Phil. iii. The comedies
of Aristophanes abound with confirmations of this fact. See especially
The Frogs, 51, et passim, Pseudolus; see also Terence, Andr. vi, 676 ;
see also Plautus, Casina (Prologue), Epidicus.
[4] De Leg. Bk. VI, ch. xix, Burges's Trans.
[5] De Leg. Bk. VI, ch. xix.

Occasionally the slaves were allowed feasts and holidays, at which times they enjoyed unrestrained liberty. The master frequently furnished the feast luxuriously.[1] There were also certain public feasts, in which the slave participated freely with his master; such were the Anthesteria feasts of Bacchus; at the conclusion of which the herald proclaimed: "Depart, ye Carian slaves, the festivals are at an end."[2]  So, even at Sparta, during the feast of Hyacinthia, the slaves were admitted to the same table and sports with the masters.[3]  In Thessaly, during the feasts of Jupiter Pelorius, the masters exchanged places with them and served them. During the feasts of Saturn, in Greece as well as at Rome, unrestrained liberty was allowed to all.[4]

The affection of the master frequently followed the slave to the grave; and more than once they lay in a common sepulchre. The inscriptions on several monuments at Athens testify to the high esteem and sincere grief of the surviving master.[5] Euripides gives us a touching proof of this affection in the death-scene of Alcestis. " All the servants wept throughout the house, bewailing their mistress, but she stretched out her right hand to each, and there was none so mean whom she addressed not, and was answered in return."[6]

The life and person of the slave were protected by law at Athens, and an action lay by the master for injury done to his slave.[7] If the slave was cruelly treated by his master, he could take refuge in the Thescion, or

---

[1] Plautus, Stechus, Act III, Sc. I.

[2] Potter, Gr. Ant. vol. i, p. 422, et seq.; Wallon, tom. i, p. 299.

[3] Wallon, tom. i, 299, 300.          [4] Wallon, tom. i, 300.

[5] Bœckh. P. II, Inscrip. Atticæ, Cl. XI, Nos. 939, 1002, 1890, 1891, 1792, 2009, 2327, 2344; Wallon, tom. i, 301.

[6] Alcestis, 175, et seq.; see also Odyssey, xvii, 33; xv, 363, et seq.; xxiv, 226; Iphigenia in Aulis, passim, and the old nurse in Media.

[7] Xen. De Rep. Ath. i, 10; Æschin. in Timarch, 41; Demosth. in Mid. 529.

at some other altar, and then the master was forced to sell him.[1]  The reason is given by the poet : " The seat of the Gods is a common defence to all !"[2]  In some cases the master lost all right of property upon the slave's taking refuge.  Thus the temple of Hercules, at Canope, kept possession of all slaves seeking an asylum there.  So that of Hebe at Phlius, gave liberty to the fugitives, suspending their chains upon the boughs of the sacred trees.[3]  For the greater protection of the slave, who could not always reach the asylum, the mere presence with him of a consecrated relic, was an amulet and a charm against the master's cruelty : such were crowns of laurel from the temple of Apollo, and sometimes small bands or mere strings worn around the forehead.[4]

The homicide of a slave at Athens, by any one other than the master, was punishable in the same manner as that of a freeman.[5]  With the master, the punishment was exile and religious expiation.[6]  Plato, in his laws, proposes for the former, indemnity to the master for the loss of the slave, and religious purification.  In the case of the master, religious purification solely.[7]

Slaves were not considered as persons in the Greek law.  Marriage was not recognized between them, although a kind of contubernial relation existed.  This was entered into with the same solemnity, and sometimes with the same feasting, as a regular marriage.  Hence, in the prologue to Casina, the question is asked, " Are slaves to be marrying wives, or asking them for themselves, a thing that is done nowhere in the world?

[1] Becker's Char. Exc. Sc. vii, 277 ; see note 33, in Appendix to Wallon, tom. i, p. 482.
[2] Eurip. Heracl. 260 ; see also Androm. 260.
[3] Herod. ii, 113 ; Pausan. ii, xiii, 4.
[4] Wallon, tom. i, 313 ; Aristoph. Plut. 20.
[5] Dem. in Midias ; Eurip. Hec. 288.
[6] Wallon, tom. i, p. 315.          [7] Bk. IX, ch. viii.

But I affirm that this is done in Greece and at Carthage, and in our own country, in Apulia."[1]

The slave could not appear as a suitor in the courts, except in the single case of a suit for his liberty, when he appeared by a guardian.[2]  He was sometimes permitted to testify in the courts, but always under torture—a proceeding which shocks our sense of justice and humanity, but was approved and defended by the orators of that time.  Neither age nor sex was a protection against this cruelty, and if the master refused to permit it, he was himself subjected to punishment.[3]  Though deprived by law of any right of property, still the slave was allowed by usage his *peculium*.[4]

Wherever in Greece slaves were private property, they were the subject of sale.  They frequently constituted a part of the dowry of a daughter upon her marriage.[5]

The manual labor was almost entirely performed by slaves.  The working of the mines, of the oars of the vessels, of the fields, of the machinery, was chiefly performed by them.[6]  It is said, that, when from old age they became useless, they were abandoned in their misery; but I have not been satisfied, from the evidence, that this allegation is well founded.[7]

It is unquestionably true, that the laws governing slavery were more rigid than the practices of the community.  Wallon, speaking on this subject, says, " Mais la loi est moins puissante que les mœurs, et les mœurs grossières encore, n'étaient point communément cruelles."[8]  It is also true, that generally the slaves were

[1] Plautus, Casina ; Wallon, tom. i, 290.

[2] Wallon, tom. i, 324.

[3] Wallon, Ibid. ; Plato, De Leg. xi, 937 ; Plautus, Truculentus, Act. IV, Sc. iii : Dem. in Onet, i, 874.

[4] Wallon, tom. i, 293 ; Plautus, Aulul. III, Sc. v, 422.

[5] Clytemnestra's dowry ; in Iphigenia in Aulis ; Eurip.

[6] Becker's Charicles, 280.

[7] Wallon, tom. i, 332.

[8] Histoire de l'Esclavage, &c., tom. i, 81, 291, 334.

coarse and vulgar, incapable of noble feelings, their chief praise being their freedom from crime.[1]

For offences committed by the slave, corporal punishments alone were inflicted. If the offence was worthy of death, it could be inflicted only by process of law, and not by the friends, as the avengers of blood, nor by the master.[2]

Manumission of the slave was allowed in all the Grecian states. The effect of this manumission differed according to the manner and circumstances attending it. The manumitted slave, at Sparta, did not become a citizen thereby, nor was he even entitled to the privileges of a Perioikus without a special grant for this purpose, from a Perioikic township.[3] At Athens he came under a double tutelage. He occupied, in the state, the position of a metic, or alien resident. As to his former master, he became his client, and lived under his patronage. His condition was intermediate the slave and the citizen, tending rather to the former. In order to become a citizen, he must be *adopted* by the vote of an assembly of at least six thousand citizens.[4]

It is supposed, by some, that the slave could force the master to manumit him upon the payment of a certain price. The authorities cited in favor of this view, are not sufficient to warrant this conclusion, in the silence of so many other writers.[5]

[1] Becker's Charicles, Exc. Sc. vii, p. 279.

[2] Becker's Charicles, Exc. Sc. vii, p. 278, gives a full description of the various fetters and machines used. Wallon, i, 316, et seq.; Eurip. Hec. 287, 288.

[3] Grote's Hist. vol. ii, 379; Dion. Chrysos. Orat. xxxvi, p. 448, b.

[4] Wallon, i, 345, 350. There is some doubt whether even then he was entitled to the full privileges of citizenship; 351–2. The privilege seems to have been voted so freely and frequently as to have been a matter of complaint; 353. See also Smith's Dict. "Libertus."

[5] Plautus. The expression of Olympio, "Why do you frighten me about liberty? Even though you should oppose it, and your son as well, against your will and in spite of you both, for a single penny, I can become free." Act II, Sc. v.; Dion. Chrysos. xv, 240, 241.

In the earlier days of Rome, during the reign of her kings, and the beginning of the republic, slavery, though it existed, occupied an unimportant place in the political and domestic economy. The Romans, in this heroic age, were a rude, martial people, their greatest wealth being their land (hence *locuples*, a rich man), their source of revenue their flocks (*pascua*), and their very name for money (*pecunia*), having cattle for its root.[1] In their organization, however, were elements whose fruits must eventually be slavery. These elements were their spirit of conquest, the unlimited paternal power, and generally that devotion to and tendency towards the development of the principle of "power," which formed the basis of all her institutions, and the secret of her unparalleled success. In these, we find the fruitful sources of that slavery which, in the later days of the republic, and under the emperors, held in bondage so large a portion of the subjects of the Roman power. We will consider more minutely these sources.

And first of the paternal power. This was without parallel among civilized nations. "Nulli enim alii sunt

[1] Pliu. Nat. Hist. xviii, 3 ; South. Quart. Rev. vol. xiv, Oct. 1848, art. 4, p. 391, Slavery among the Romans. This article is supposed to be from the pen of Judge Campbell of the Supreme Court of the United States. From the known ability and accuracy of its author, I have not hesitated to use it freely in the preparation of this sketch.

homines qui talem in liberos habeant potestatem, qualem nos habemus."[1]  The potestas vitæ et necis, the power to expose the infant without liability to punishment, the power to sell into slavery, these were the legitimate elements of the paternal power.  It was not until the days of Constantine, that the exposure and abandonment of infants became penal; and a decree of Diocletian contains the first formal denial of the power of sale, though Troplong suggests, that the influence of Christianity had rendered the usage obsolete before that time.[2]  Children thus sold became absolute slaves, without the power of redemption, either in the parent or themselves.[3]  It was otherwise of children exposed.  The preserver held them subject to reclamation.  Many instances are given of such reclamations.[4]

Another internal source of slavery was the power of the debtor, either to sell himself directly into slavery, or to pledge his body (*nexus*) for the payment of his debt. In default of payment, he was, after a certain time of imprisonment, taken for three successive days before the prætor, and payment demanded.  He was then ordered to be sold, out of the city, and became what was called *addictus*.[5]  Though the debtor thus lost his liberty, he was not in precisely the same situation with an ordinary slave.  He could not be killed by his master, but might claim the protection of the law as a freeman; could inherit property, and retain his name.  " Ad servum nulla lex pertinet; addictus legem habet.  Propria liberi, quæ nemo habet, nisi liber, prænomen, nomen, cognomen, tribum, habet hæc addictus."[6]  And again, the slave when manumitted, became a " *libertinus*."  The *addictus*

---

[1] Gaius Inst. Com. i, 55.
[2] Influence du Chr. sur le droit civil, pt. ii, ch. ii.
[3] Wallon, Esclav. dans l'Antiq. tom. ii, p. 21.
[4] Plin. Epist. x ; Suet. De Illustr. Gram. 21 ; Wallon, as above.
[5] Wallon, ii, 23; Becker's " Gallus," 201.
[6] Quinctil. vii, 3, § 27 ; Arnold's Hist. of Rome, ch. xxvi, p. 224.

became a citizen (*ingenuus*). The slave, without the consent of his master, could not obtain his liberty. The
*addictus solvendo*, by redeeming his price, could demand
his release.[1]

The purchaser took with the debtor, all that belonged
to him, and hence his children, unless previously emancipated from the paternal power, went into slavery
together with their father. This power of the creditor
over the debtor, caused frequent disturbances, and was
much weakened by the Licinian laws.[2] Its final abro-
gation happened in this wise: A young man, Caius
Publilius, of extreme youth and beauty, surrendered his
person for his father's debt, to one Papirius, a cruel
usurer. He, excited with lust, approached the youth
with impure discourses; and then by threats, and finally
by stripes, endeavored to compel his assent. With the
marks of the scourge upon him, the young man rushed
into the street. A large concourse of people gathered
around him in the forum, and from thence in a body
went to the Senate-house. The consuls called the Senate,
and as each senator went in he was shown the lacerated
youth and told the tale of cruelty. The consequence
was, a law abolishing this penalty upon the insolvent
debtor.[3]

Another internal source of slavery was the penalty
for violating various laws. The person who withdrew
himself from the census, or who avoided military service, the open robber, and the free female who maintained sexual intercourse with a slave, severally forfeited
their freedom.[4] After the battle of Cannæ, the dictator,
pressed by the necessity, offered liberty to all such as

---

[1] Ibid. Wallon, ii, 24, 25.          [2] Arnold's Hist. ch. xxvi.
[3] Livy, Bk. VIII, § 28.
[4] So. Quart. Rev. xiv, 393; Wallon, ii, 31, 32; Gaius, iii, 189. The
latter was by senatus-consultum Claudianum. For its provisions, see
Smith's Dictionary. The master of the slave might relieve her of the
penalty by consenting to the cohabitation.

would enrol as soldiers. Six thousand availed themselves of this offer.[1]

The most fruitful sources of slavery were the continual wars of the Romans. The number of captives brought home into slavery appears sometimes incredible. It became common to release them sometimes upon the field for a ransom. A small tax was laid upon such contracts, and the revenue derived therefrom was very considerable. The captives were divided with the spoils upon the battle-field, and each soldier provided for the slaves allotted to him. Hence, it became common for the slave-dealers (mangones) to accompany the army for the purpose of purchasing the captives. The prices at such times became very trifling, sometimes as small as four drachmæ, about seventy-five cents, federal currency. Every nation of the then known world, as it bowed its head before the Roman Eagle, yielded at the same time its beauty and sinew to satiate the appetite and perform the labor for its victorious master. According to Josephus, 97,000 captives followed the destruction of Jerusalem. Africa, Asia, Greece, Germany, Gaul, and even Britain, brought their quota to swell the mighty mass. The valley of the Danube for a long time furnished the greater number, and gave the generic name of Scythian and afterwards slave (sclavi) to the whole class.[2]

While the Roman arms subdued the land, and destroyed the marine of all rival nations, yet Rome at no period of her history sought to become powerful upon the sea. This was then truly an unoccupied ocean, and numberless pirates soon took possession of the Mediterranean. The prisoners taken by these robbers of the sea, were made profitable booty in the Roman slave-

---

[1] Livy, xxiii, 14; Wallon, ii, 31, 2.

[2] Wallon, ii, 32–40; So. Quart. Rev. xiv, 394; Smith's Dict. of Gr. and Rom. Ant. "Servus," Roman; Plautus, "Captivi," Prologue; Henry's Hist. of Eng. ii, p. 225.

market; and hence, piracy is to be numbered among the fruitful sources of Roman slavery. It is said that the Cilician pirates imported and sold as many as 10,000 slaves in one day.[1] Men of the highest rank in Rome engaged in this honorable calling (*metier honorable*), and they constituted a powerful organization, threatening the security of the citizen himself.[2] Upon the land they built gaols, in which they secretly confined their victims, many of whom were kidnapped upon Roman territory.[3]

The tyranny of the Roman proconsuls in levying and collecting the tribute was another abundant feeder of the slave-market. Unable to respond to the heavy exactions, they borrowed money at exorbitant usury. The protection of the debtor in the city was not extended to the provinces, and hence, in a few years, numbers were sold into slavery. When Marius demanded a quota of troops from the King of Bithynia, his reply was, that his kingdom was depopulated by this process of exaction, extortion, and sale.[4]

The children of slaves always followed the condition of the mother; and hence the maxim of the law, "*servi nostri nascuntur aut fiunt.*" The breeding of slaves, until the latter days of Rome, was encouraged, it being cheaper to rear than to buy. For this reason a kind of marriage relation (*contubernium*) was recognized among them.[5]

Under the oppressions of the Empire of Rome, so great was the abhorrence of the citizens to holding the

---

[1] Strabo, xiv, 664–8; Smith's Dict. as above; Wallon, ii, 44, 45.

[2] Ibid. For an account of the power of the pirates and its final overthrow, see Plutarch's Life of Pompey.     [3] Wallon, ii, 47, 8.

[4] Diod. Fragm. xxxvi, iii, 1; So. Quart. Rev. vol. xiv, 394; Wallon, ii, 44.

[5] So. Quart. Rev. xiv, 400; Wallon, ii, 209; Plut. Cato, the Censor. Columella, in his work De re rust., recommends that a female slave, the mother of three children, should be relieved from hard work, and, for a greater number, should be granted her liberty; i, 8, 18.

civil offices of the government, that many voluntarily subjected themselves in preference to a state of slavery.[1]

Slaves constituted an important article of commerce, and also of revenue, in the tariff laid upon their importation and exportation, and also upon their sale. Carthage itself dealing largely in slaves, working the mines of the Peninsula exclusively with their labor, carried on a brisk trade in them. Delos and Chios also were slave-marts. But Rome was the centre of the trade, and the slave-market at Rome gives us the most perfect idea of its extent and variety. Slaves of peculiar beauty and rarity were kept separate and apart, and sold privately. The slaves generally were sold at auction, standing upon a stone, so that they might be closely scrutinized. Frequently they were stripped naked, to avoid the cheats the dealers were noted for practising. Sometimes the advice of medical men was obtained.[2] Newly imported slaves had their feet whitened with chalk.[3] Those from the East had their ears bored. All of them had a scroll (*titulus*) suspended around the neck, giving their ages, birthplace, qualities, health, &c., and the seller was held to warrant the truth of this statement. He was bound to discover all defects, especially as to health, thievishness, disposition to run away, or to commit suicide.[4]

If the seller was unwilling to warrant, instead of the *titulus*, he placed a cap (*pileus*) upon the head of the slave, and exposed him thus.[5] A crown upon the head indicated a captive taken in war.

The seller would cause the slave to run, leap, or perform some other act of agility. They possessed the art of causing their limbs to look round and their flesh

---

[1] Edwards's Eccl. Journ. § 18.

[2] Claudian in Eutrop. i, 35.          [3] Juv. i, 111 ; vii, 10.

[4] Cic. de Off., iii, 17 ; Aul. Gell. iv, 2 ; Smith's Dict. "Servus" (Roman) ; Wallon, ii, 53.          [5] Gell. vii, 4.

young, and to retard the appearances of age.[1]    They
vaunted loudly the praises of their good qualities.  Varro
and Seneca, Pliny and Quinctilian give warnings, to the
purchasers, of these arts, and rules of recommendation
for their protection.  Still the sellers succeeded in de-
frauding, and finally an edict declared, " that those who
sell slaves must acquaint the purchaser with the diseases
and vices of each, and declare whether he has been a
runaway or vagabond, or the contract of sale will be
avoided.  These declarations must be made publicly and
aloud before the sale.  If a slave is sold contrary to
these stipulations, or if he does not answer to the things
affirmed or promised when he was sold, the purchaser or
his assigns may rescind the sale.  Moreover, if the slave
has committed any capital offence, or has attempted
suicide, or has fought with wild beasts in the arena, it
must be made known at the sale, or it can be avoided."[2]

Slaves newly imported, were preferred for labor.  Those
who had served long were considered artful.[3]    The pert-
ness and impudence of those born in the master's house
were proverbial.[4]    The nativity of the slave gave some
indication of his qualities.  Thus, the Phrygian was
timid; the African vain; the Cretan mendacious; the
Sardinian unruly; the Corsican cruel and rebellious; the
Dalmatian ferocious; the Briton stupid; the Syrian
strong; the Ionian beautiful; the Alexandrian accomplished and luxurious.[5]

Dealing in slaves was, nevertheless, considered a degrading occupation.  They were denied even the name

---

[1] Wallon, ii, 56.  Hence, *mangozinare*, from *mangones*.

[2] Wallon, ii, 57, 8.  A vast number of questions arose under this edict
as to what was a defect.  For some of them see Wallon, as above.  For
the manner in which the auctioneer communicated the vices, but at the
same time covered them up with praises, see Horace, Epist. ii, 2.

[3] Terence, Heaut. v, 16.          [4] Hor. Sat. ii, 6, 66.

[5] Wallon, ii, 64, 65; So. Quart. Rev. xiv, 394; Juvenal, v. 73; Cic. ad
Att. Lib. iv, 16.

of merchants (*mercatores*), but were called *mangoncs*. They amassed large fortunes, yet they had not the cón- fidence of the community. Plautus makes his chorus speak of their faithlessness and dishonesty.¹ It seems there was, and ever has been, something in the prosecu- tion of this traffic, which either repels the good man, or else deadens his sensibility, and soon destroys his virtue.

To attest the early day at which the negro was com- mouly used as a slave at Rome, the following description of a negress, written in the second century, serves well:

"Interdum clamat cybalen; erat unica custos.
Afra genus, tota patriam testante figura,
Torta comam, labroque tumens et fusca colorem,
Pectore lata, jacens mammis, compressior alvo,
Cruribus exilis, spatiosa prodiga planta,
Continuis rimis calcanea scissa rigebant."²

So Seneca: "Non est Æthiopis inter suos insignitus color, nec rufus crinis et coactus in nodum apud Ger- manos."³

Originally, all the slaves of Rome were personal slaves. None were attached to the soil. All were the subject of removal and sale. When slavery, subsequently, gradu- ally changed into serfdom, the contrary was true. There were, in Rome, public and private slaves. The former belonged to the state, and their condition was rather better than the other class. They possessed the privilege of willing one-half of their *peculium*. They were em- ployed about the public buildings, and as attendants of the various officers. And also as lictors, jailors, execu-

¹ Curculio, IV, Sc. I; Smith's Dict. "Servus" (Rom.); Wallon, ii, 50, 51.
² Quoted in Types of Mankind, 255; see also reference in same place to Virgil's description of field slaves.
³ De Irâ, cap. iii.

tioners, watermen, &c.[1]   There were also convict-slaves (*servi pœnae*), whose servitude was the penalty of some crime.   These were treated with great rigor; and it is probable, much of the recorded cruelty to slaves was to this class.[2]

The private slaves were again distinguished into two classes, the rustic and the city slaves; any number of them, owned by the same master, were called *familia*. Hence, every master had the *familia rustica*, and the *familia urbana*.   The private slaves were still farther subdivided, according to their occupations, and from these occupations they derived their names: such as *ordinarii, vulgares, mediastini,* and *quales quales.*   The *literati,* were literary slaves.[3]

The number of Roman slaves, at any period, cannot be accurately ascertained.   That they were very numerous, and more numerous than the free population, is indisputable, and that the numbers increased rapidly during the latter days of the republic and under the emperors.   The numbers owned by a single individual are almost incredible.[4]   They were chiefly employed in agricultural pursuits, or the mechanic arts.[5]   Many, however, were, in these days, used as personal attendants; it being considered discreditable for a person of rank to be seen without a train of them.[6]   From the moment a stranger entered the vestibule of a Roman house, through the hall, in the reception-room, at the table, everywhere

[1] Smith's Dict. "Servus;" So. Quart. Rev. xiv, 427; see Livy, xxvi, 47; Copley's Hist. of Slav. 45; Wallon, ii, 89, et seq.

[2] For a full inquiry into the penal slavery of the Romans, see Stephens's W. I. Slavery, i, 337, et seq.

[3] Wallon, ii, 95; Smith's Dict. "Servus;" Becker's Gallus, Exc. III to Sc. I.

[4] So. Quart. Rev. xiv, 396–7; Wallon, ii, 72, et seq.; Becker's Gallus, Exc. III, Sc. I; Athenæus says as many as 20,000, vi, p. 272; see Pliny, xxxiii, vi, 9–10; Juvenal, xiv, 305; Hor. Sat. Bk. I, iii, 11.

[5] Cic. de Off. i, 42; Liv. vi, 12.

[6] Cic. in Piso, 27; Hor. Sat. i, 3, 12.

he was attended by different servants, each taking their name from their particular occupation. The same system was developed in every part of the household. The female slaves were, in like manner, so distinguished; every conceivable want being attended by a separate slave. The nursery, especially, being furnished with midwife (*obstetrix*), guard, nurse, porters, &c. &c. The smallest service had its appropriate slave. Thus, the holding of the umbrella (*umbelliferæ*), the fan (*flabelliferæ*), the sandal (*sandaligerulæ*), gave names to particular slaves. So the arranging the dress, the setting of the teeth, and the painting of the eyebrows, required distinct attendants.[1] Seneca says, "Infelix qui huic rei vivit ut altilia secet decenter."[2]

The wife, upon her marriage, received always a confidential slave (*dotalis*). He belonged to her, the master having no control over him. He frequently had the confidence of the wife more than her own husband. He was sometimes called "*servus recepticius*," because, perhaps, he received and took charge of the paraphernalia of the wife.[3] For her footmen and couriers, the wife preferred always the negroes; and one reason given was because of the contrast of the skin and the silver plate suspended upon the breast, upon which was inscribed the name and titles of the mistress.[4]

Even the schoolboy was followed by his little slave (*vernula*, born in the house), to bear his satchel to the school.[5] The old and luxurious were borne in sedans or

---

[1] So. Quart. Rev. xiv, 400; Wallon, ii, 113, 145. It is probable that the same slave performed several of these offices though bearing different names: Ibid. 140, and authorities cited.

[2] Epist. xl, vii, 4.

[3] Plautus, Asin. Act I, Sc. i; Aul. Gell. Bk. XVII, vi; Wallon, ii, 116.

[4] Sen. Epis. lxxxvii, 8; Wallon, ii, 120; Mart. vii, 201; Becker's Gallus, Exc. III to Sc. i, 201.

[5] Juv. Sat. x.

chairs, by stout Mesian slaves; while the wealthy made
an ostentatious display of their means, by multiplying
the number of their bearers (*lecticarii*).[1]

In addition to the common employments of slaves,
they were frequently used in other spheres, where the
labor was more or less intellectual. The literary slaves,
those used as librarians and amanuenses, were of this
class. So all the professions, now termed " learned,"
were not free from slave competition. " Physic" certainly was not. In every branch of trade and commerce
slaves were employed by their masters as agents, and in
many cases, sole managers and controllers.[2]

The Roman sports, corresponding to their tastes, were
always rough and violent. The combat of the gladiators
was more exciting and attractive than the pathos of
tragedy, or the wit of the comic muse, though Terence
and Plautus catered to their taste. To rear and prepare
slaves for these dangerous and murderous conflicts, as
well as for the fighting of wild beasts, became a common
practice, especially under the emperors; who encouraged
these sports in the people, in order to disengage their
thoughts from their own bondage. We should not,
however, judge them too harshly for this cruelty, as
frequently freemen, knights, senators, and even emperors, descended into the arena, and engaged in the fatal
encounter.[3] Sometimes even women joined in the conflict.[4] Juvenal gives a graphic idea of the passion for
this cruel sport, in the description of the horrid-looking

---

[1] Juv. Sat. vii, ix, 190, 200.

[2] Wallon, ii, 124; Plautus, Menæchmi, Act V, Sc. iii; C. Nep. Pomp.
Att. 13; So. Quart. Rev. xiv, 398–9. See Becker's Gallus, Exc. III to
Sc. i, for a full and learned disquisition upon the various classes of slaves,
their names, and occupation. It would seem as if, in the earlier days,
medicine was not considered an honorable avocation with the Romans.
Plautus does not hesitate to ridicule the whole fraternity (Menæchmi,
Act V, Sc. i).

[3] Wallon, ii, 126–139; Smith's Dict. " Gladiatores ;" Livy, xxviii, 21 ;
Suet. Jul. Cæs. xxxix.                    [4] Suet. Dom. iv.

gladiator, for whose bed, simply on account of his profession, Hippia, the wife of a senator, abandoned her husband and her home.[1]

This training of the slave, rendered him indomitable and intractable. Hence, we find this particular class frequently in insurrections. In Sicily the servile wars assumed a more alarming aspect.[2]

The price of slaves in Rome varied very much at different times, and according to the qualities of the slave.[3] Under the empire, immense sums were paid for beautiful slaves, and such as attracted the whim of the purchaser. We have accounts of their selling from 100,000 to 200,000 sesterces (say five to ten thousand dollars).[4] In the time of Horace, 500 drachmæ (about one hundred dollars) was a fair price for an ordinary slave.[5] Eunuchs, clowns, or jesters, and pretty females, brought high prices.[6] Females generally sold for less than males.[7] Hannibal, after the battle of Cannæ, being burdened with his prisoners, suffered the knights (*equites*) to be ransomed at seventy-five dollars, the legionary soldier at fifty dollars, the slaves at twenty dollars.[8] Negroes, being generally slaves of luxury, commanded a very high price.[9] Juvenal declares, that a rich man could not enjoy his dinner unless surrounded by the dusky and active Moor, and the more dusky Indian.[10]

The status of the slave, in the Roman law, was literally as a thing and not as a person. Some, apparently paradoxical, rights were given to him, which we cannot here specifically repeat. His general status was "pro

---

[1] Satire, vi, 110.                    [2] Smith's Dict. "Servus."

[3] For the prices in the time of Justinian, see Codex, L. vi, tit. 44, § 3; Wallon, ii, 160.

[4] Martial, iii, 62; xi, 70; Pliny, vii, x, 5, 6.          [5] Sat. ii, 7, 43.

[6] Martial, viii, 13; Plaut. Pers. Act IV, Sc. iv, 113.

[7] Smith's Dict. "Servus" (Roman).

[8] So. Quart. Rev. xiv, 398.                    [9] Juvenal, v, 73.

[10] Sat. xi, 211.

quadrupedibus." He consequently could not be a party nor a witness in court, except in extreme cases, and then under torture.[1] He could acquire no property; his *peculium* being held only at the will of the master. Whatever he received, by gift or bequest from others, became immediately the property of his master. He lived, as it were, in the shadow of his master. To him, all his gains, his acts, and the very current of his life, tended. From him, he received support and protection. He was, like the son and all the household of the Roman, swallowed up in the master. The state recognized the citizen, and addressed its laws and its requirements to him. The master controlled, as he listed, the household of which he was the head and representative. Hence, the power to kill the son and the slave with impunity; a power recognized, as to the latter, until the days of Antoninus, when it was abolished.[2] By the same constitution, for cruel treatment, the master might be compelled to sell the slave, and the slave was empowered to make his complaint to the proper authority.[3]

Notwithstanding this unlimited power of the master, and the fact that there are recorded many instances of its cruel abuse,[4] yet other facts and circumstances impress

[1] Dig. xxii, § 5, De Testibus; Terence, Phorm. Act II, Sc. i, 292; Plaut. Curcul. Act V, Sc. ii, 630; Juvenal, x, 100. It would seem from this passage that they testified with a halter around their necks.

[2] Wallon, Part II, ch. v, vi; Gaius, i, 52; Smith's Dict. " Servus." A constitution of Claudius also made the homicide of a slave murder. It farther provided that the exposure of an infirm slave gave him freedom; Sueton. Claud. xxv.

[3] Seneca, de Benef. iii, 22. According to Bodin, in commenting on this passage in Seneca, Nero was the first emperor who required of magistrates to receive the complaints of slaves against their masters. It would be a curious fact if the tyrant of the citizen was indeed the defender of the slave. Troplong, Influence du Christianisme, &c., 148.

[4] The cases of Flaminius, who killed a slave to gratify a guest who had never seen a man killed (Plutarch's Life of Flaminius), and of Polio, who fed his enormous fish upon the bodies of his slaves (Seneca, de Irâ, Lib. iii, ch. xl), are familiar to all who have read or heard of Roman slavery.

the belief that, as a general rule, the relation of master and slave was one of kindness and mutual regard.[1] This was peculiarly true of the urban slave, he that was always near his master.[2] The rustics, controlled by the villicus, and often unseen, for years, by the master, were doubtless more frequently subjected to oppression.[3] The claims of humanity were not entirely forgotten, nor overwhelmed by the more practical calls of interest. Hence, we find their moralists discussing clearly and fully such questions, as whether, in a famine, the master should abandon his slave? Whether, in the case of distress at sea, where the vessel must be lightened, should valuable property or valueless slaves be cast overboard?[4] It is true, that the elder Cato, in giving advice and directions as to the management of a farm, recommends the sale of old and infirm slaves.[5] Yet this is only the opinion of one man, and one noted for avarice—a passion which withers and blights the principle of humanity in any soul, and in any age of the world.[6] Certain it is, that we find the corpse of the deceased slave frequently interred in the same tomb with that of his master.[7] And the Roman satirist declares his preference to be a slave, and dig some great man's land, than to be the satiated votary of pleasure.[8]

---

[1] Plutarch tells of a faithful slave of Octavius whose eyes were torn out while he was defending his master from an incensed mob; Tib. Gracchus. Many such instances of fidelity and affection are recorded. See especially Seneca, De Benef. ch. iii; Valer. Max. Lib. vi, 8; Macrob. Sat. i, 11.

[2] Juvenal, describing the happy condition of a man "contented with little," compares it to that of the household slave. Sat. ix, 5.

[3] Quart. Rev. xiv, 401; Wallon, ii, 204, et seq. 213; Copley's Hist. of Slavery, 45; Smith's Dict. "Servus."

[4] Cic. De Offic. iii, 23.                      [5] De Re Rust. ii.

[6] Plut. Cato, the Censor, passim.

[7] Wallon, ii, 213. He refers to the work of Gruter, Sect. "Affectus dominorum et patronorum erga servos et libertos." I regret that this work is not within my reach. See also Smith's Dict. "Servus;" Dig Lib. xi, tit. 7, § 31.                      [8] Juvenal, ix, 25.

According to Horace, they joined their masters in offering up prayers and thanksgivings to the Gods.[1] In the earlier days, they partook of their meals in common with their masters, though not at the same table, but upon little benches (*subsellia*), placed at the foot of the *lectus*.[2] This habit was probably continued in such portions of the republic, where the proprietors of small farms overlooked and managed them for themselves.

While the law recognized no property of the slave, yet his *peculium*, as well as all property he acquired by gift or by finding, were secured to him by public opinion and natural justice.[3] Hence, we find slaves frequently purchasing their freedom ; nor was a Roman audience shocked in hearing a master entreat his own slave for a loan of money, and finally to secure his end, hoist him upon his back, and submit to be kicked and jeered at by his own slave.[4] Frequently they became very rich. Juvenal scourges the respect paid to money, by referring to the fact that a freeman felt honored by the company of a slave *if only* rich.[5]

The Romans, in later days, had no asylums, or places of refuge, for slaves flying from the cruelty of their masters ; and such fugitives were harshly treated, being branded and forced to work in chains. The master could pursue him anywhere, and all officers and authorities were required to give him aid. A class of persons called Fugitivarii, made it their business to recover runaway slaves.[6] We have already noticed the provisions

---

[1] Epist. Bk. II, i, 142.

[2] Plut. Coriol. 24 ; Smith's Dict. "Servus ;" Sen. de Tranquil. ii, 15 ; Plaut. Captivi, iii, i, 11.

[3] Terent. Phorm. Act I, Sc. i, 9 ; Seneca, Ep. 80 ; Plaut. Rudens, Aulularia.

[4] Plaut. Asinaria, Act III, Sc. ii, iii.          [5] Sat. iii, 150.

[6] Wallon, ii, 243 ; Smith's Dict. " Servus ;" Plautus, Most. Act. IV, Sc. i. Death was sometimes the punishment of fugitives. They were sometimes thrown among wild beasts. Polybius, Lib. i ; Lactantius, Lib. v, cap. 18 ; Val. Max. Lib. ii, cap. 6.

of the Constitution of Antoninus to protect the slave from the cruelty of the master.

There were certain feasts during which the slaves were abandoned to perfect liberty; of these the most remarkable were the Saturnalia, when such perfect equality existed that the master waited on the slave at the table. This feast was in the latter part of December, and lasted seven days.[1] Another was the feasts in honor of Servius Tullius, the sixth king of Rome, he being himself the son of Ocrisia, a captive and a slave. These lasted from the Ides of March, the date of his birth, to the Ides of April, the date of his inauguration of the temple of Diana.[2]

The Compitalia, a feast in honor of the Lares, or Household Gods, was also a season of liberty to the slaves. Augustus established an order of priests, to attend to their worship, called Augustales. These were selected from the *libertini*, or freedmen.[3]

The intimate relation between the slaves and their masters, may be gathered from many other allusions in the Roman authors. Juvenal gives, as the especial reason for leading an upright life, " that you may be able to despise your servants' tongues. For bad as your slave may be, his tongue is the worst part about him. Yet worse are you when you place yourself in his power."[4] The too intimate relation between the slave and the mistress, which sometimes existed, did not escape his observing eye, or his lashing pen.[5] A gilded bed, he said, seldom witnessed childbirth; but he consoles the childless husband with the reflection, that if

[1] Macrob. Saturnal.; Niebuhr, Hist. of Rome, vol. i, p. 319. Horace gives an amusing account of an interview between himself and one of his slaves on the occasion of the Saturnalia. Satires, Bk. II, Sat. vii.

[2] Wallon, ii, 235-6. The origin of the name " Servus" is attributed by some to " Servius."

[3] Dion. iv, 14; Macr. Sat. i, 7 ; Smith's Dict. " Compitalia."

[4] Sat. ix, 86.                    [5] Sat. vi, 300.

the child was allowed to be born, he would be "the sire perchance of an Ethiopian—a blackamoor would be his sole heir."[1]

There were, doubtless, instances of great cruelty exhibited towards slaves—such as justified partially the picture drawn by the satirist of the haughty and overbearing wife compelling her husband to crucify an innocent slave : " Crucify that slave !" "What is the charge, to call for such a punishment ? What witness can you produce ? Who gave the information ? Hark ! where man's life is at stake, no deliberation can be too long." " Idiot ! so a slave is a man then ! Let it be that he has done nothing. I *will* it!—I *insist* on it ! Let my will stand instead of reason."[2] Nevertheless, with the humane at least, the assurance of Trimalchio to his guests was believed and observed. " Amici et servi homines sunt, et æque unum lacten bibunt." Hence, we find the great moralist announcing, " Cum in servum omnia liceant, est aliquid, quod in hominem licere, commune jus vetet."[3]

[1] Sat. vi, 700.

[2] Juvenal, Sat. vi, 219, rendered thus by Gifford :

> " ' Go crucify that slave !' ' For what offence ?
> Who the accuser ? Where the evidence ?
> For when the life of man is in debate,
> No time can be too long, no care too great.
> Hear all, weigh all with caution, I advise.'
> 'Thou sniveller ! Is a slave a man ?' she cries.
> ' He's innocent—be't so—'tis my command,
> My will—let that, sir, for a reason stand ' "

All the descriptions of Juvenal are exaggerated of course. Satire deals in hyperbole, and requires only a substratum of truth. The descriptions he gives of the lewdness and corruption of the Roman women, if literally true, would be a more awful picture than that of the slaves. Sat. vi, passim.

This cruelty on the part of the master frequently and usually rebounded on himself in the vengeance of the slaves. Pliny gives a striking instance of this. Epis. iii, 14.

[3] Sen. de Clem. i, 18.

The punishments inflicted upon slaves for offences were various, and some very severe. They necessarily differed from those prescribed for the same offences when committed by freemen. Minor misdemeanors were submitted to the correction of the master.[1] The courts took cognizance only of graver charges, and even of these the master seems to have had concurrent jurisdiction.[2] The removal of the urban slave into the *familia rustica*, was a mild and yet a much-dreaded penalty. In such cases they worked in chains.[3] The handmill (*mola pistrinum*) was also a place of punishment, and its constant working became sometimes severe. Thus asks the slave in the Asinaria, "Will you send me there where stone grinds stone?"[4] Sometimes they were scourged, after being suspended with manacles to the hands and weights fastened to the feet.[5] Another mode of punishment was a wooden yoke (*furca*) upon the neck, and bound to the arms on either side.[6] Upon every Roman farm was a private prison (*ergastulum*), in which refractory slaves were confined. A trustworthy slave was the keeper. They were abolished in the time of Hadrian.[7] Sometimes extraordinary and cruel punishments were resorted to; such as cutting off the hand for thefts, and death by the cross. These, however, were very rare.[8]

---

[1] Cato, the Censor, upon his farm, instituted a kind of jury trial among the slaves themselves, and submitted to them the guilt and the punishment. Copley's Hist. of Slavery, 44.

[2] This is inferrible from a passage in Horace, where he represents himself as the judge of his slaves, even in cases of theft or murder. See Stephens on West India Slavery, 341. Dig. Lib. xi, tit. 4, sect. 5.

[3] Plautus, Mostel, Act I, Sc. i.

[4] Plaut. Asin., Act I, Sc. i. See also Odyssey, vii, 104. Cato, De re rust. 56; Matthew 24 : 41.

[5] Asinaria, Act II, Sc. ii.

[6] Plautus, Casina, Act II, Sc. ii; Mil. Act II, Sc. iv; Mostel. Act I, Sc. i; Dig. Lib. 48, tit. 13, § 6.

[7] Columel. i, 8; Gaius, i, 53; Juv. viii, 180.

[8] Plaut. Epid. Act I, Sc. i, ii; Hor. Ep. i, 16, 17; Senec. De Irâ, iii, 40.

In every slaveholding state, the intimate terms of companionship of the master and slave necessarily give the slave frequent opportunity for committing violence upon the master unknown to any other person. To protect the master, the Roman law was very stringent, and provided that, where the master was found murdered in his house, and no discovery of the perpetrator, *all the domestic slaves* should be put to death. This law necessarily could be enforced very rarely, as the slaves would discover themselves the murderer in their midst. However, we find that on some occasions, it was enforced rigorously—we might almost say barbarously.[1]

Instances of *manumission* were very frequent among the Romans. This could be effected in various ways, and the effects of it differed under different circumstances. In all cases, the enfranchised slave continued to serve his former master, who became his patron. Thus, in the Menæchmi, the freedman addresses his former master, "My patron, I do entreat that you won't command me any the less now, than when I was your slave. With you will I dwell, and when you go, I'll go home with you."[2]

Liberty was sometimes granted the slave by way of reward for discovering the perpetrators of certain crimes.[3] The enjoyment of liberty for a certain time barred the master's right, it being included within the *præscriptio temporis.*[4] On the contrary, no length of illegal bondage deprived the slave of the privilege of asserting his right to liberty.[5]

If the freedman conducted himself ungratefully towards his patron, he was reduced to his former state of slavery.[6]

---

[1] Tac. Ann. xiv, 41 ; Cic. ad Fam. iv, 12.

[2] Plautus, Menæchmi, Act IV, Sc. vi.    [3] Code Theod. tit 21, § 2.

[4] Code Theod. tit. 14 ; Bk. VII, tit. 39, § 3.        [5] Gaius, ii, 48.

[6] Sueton. Claudius, xxv. This rule seems not to have obtained in the time of Nero (see Tac. Ann. xiii, 27), but was restored under the later emperors. Dig. Lib. xi ; tit. 9, § 30.

He was bound to support his patron, and the children of his patron if necessary; and to undertake the management of his property and the guardianship of the children.[1] *E converso*, the patron lost all of his rights, if he failed to support his freedman, in case of necessity. These patronal rights were very considerable, especially in relation to the succession to the property of the freedman.[2] By a decree of the emperor declaring the *libertus* to be *ingenuus*, the patronal rights were not destroyed. This change was denominated "jus annuli aurei," from the fact that the *ingenui* alone had the right of wearing the gold seal-ring. That of the *liberti* being of silver, and the slaves of iron.[3] If, however, the form of proceeding, entitled *natalibus restitutio*, was adopted to confer perfect freedom on the *libertus*, this took away the patronal rights, because, by the fiction, the freedman was restored to his natural rights of liberty.[4]

In some cases, by the act of *manumission*, the slave became a Roman citizen at the same time that he became a freedman. In other cases he became only a *Latinus* or *Latinus Junianus*, so called from the fact that the *Lex Junia* declared and defined the rights of such persons, and placed them on the same footing with colonized citizens—*Latini coloniarii*.[5] In various ways the *Latinus* could obtain the rights of citizenship. The *Lex Aelia Sentia*, prescribed the formalities necessary to effect this object.[6] There was still a lower class of freedmen, but a little elevated above slaves, termed *Dedititii*. They took the name, and their status was the same with the *peregrini dedititii*, or persons subdued by the Roman

---

[1] Dig. Lib. xxxvii, tit. 14, ? 19.　　[2] Smith's Dict. "Patronus."

[3] Smith's Dict. "Annulus;" Isidorus, xix, 32; Dig. Lib. xl, tit. 10, ? 5. St. James alludes to this in ch. ii, v. 2.

[4] Dig. Lib. xl, tit. 11.

[5] Smith's Dict. "Libertus;" Gaius, iii, 56. The Latinus had not the power of making a will, nor of taking under a will. Gaius, i, 24.

[6] Gaius, i, 28.

arms, and submitting to their conquerors unconditionally.
They were not slaves, but had not political existence.
The *Lex Aelia Sentia*, adopted in the time of Augustus,
declared all manumitted slaves to be *Dedititii*, who, previous to manumission, had been in bonds, or branded,
or put to torture, or fought with wild beasts, or as gladiators.[1] This law seems to have been framed to protect
the state from the too frequent and unlimited use of the
power of manumission in the master.  Hence, one of its
provisions, that slaves manumitted under the age of
thirty years became Roman citizens only when a legal
ground (*justa causa*) for such manumission had been
made to appear before the *Consilium*, a tribunal appointed especially for this purpose, and which held sessions at stated times, in the provinces and at Rome.[2]
Other restrictions on manumission were prescribed
by this law, as to masters under the age of twenty
years; and where the act was done with a view to defraud creditors.[3]  Constantine abolished almost all the
formalities necessary for manumission, and gave to the
freedman in every case the privileges of Roman citizenship.  What was left undone by him Justinian com-
pleted, and opened wide the doors and added greatly
to the inducements for general emancipation.[4]

The condition of the freedman in the earlier days of
Rome differed but little from that of the slave.  "Liber-
tis, quibus illi non multum secus ac servis imperabant."[5]

There were instances, however, of freedmen and their

---

[1] Gaius, i, 13 ; Smith's Dict. "Dedititii."

[2] Gaius, i, 19, 20.

[3] Ibid.  Smith's Dict. "Lex Aelia Sentia."

[4] Constitutions of Constantine.  Justinian's Institutes.  See Troplong,
Influence du Christianisme, &c., 159, et sq.

[5] Cic. ad Quint.  The suit to obtain freedom, was called "proclamare
ad libertatem."  Cicero is related by Plutarch to have perpetrated a
pun upon this word.  A person suspected of having been once a slave,
was speaking boisterously in the Senate.  "Nolite mirari," said Cicero
to the bystanders, "quia unus est ex iis, qui olim *proclamaverunt*."

descendants attaining eminence and distinction among the Romans. Servius Tullius, "the last of the good kings," was the son of a bondmaid.[1] Vindicius, who gave to the Conscript Fathers notice of a secret treason, himself a slave, was mourned publicly by the Roman matrons at his death, as Brutus had been.[2] Terence, a captive slave, born near Carthage, became the delight of Roman audiences, through his graceful comedies.[3] And Horace was not ashamed to acknowledge himself the son of a freedman.[4]

There existed no reason why this result should not follow. The captives brought to Rome were of races intellectually equal; in cultivation, superior to their Roman masters. Slavery was, to them, an unnatural condition. The inferior should serve the superior, and the reverse is a violation of nature.

The precise time when slavery, property in the person, ceased to exist among the Romans, cannot be fixed with certainty. It was never abolished *formally*, by statute or decree. Circumstances combined to work a gradual change in the system, from slavery to serfdom.[5] Rome entered into the turbid flood of the dark ages weighted with slavery. When she emerged again, so that history

[1] Liv. i, 39; Juvenal, Sat. viii. Thus rendered by Gifford:

"And he who graced the purple which he wore,
The last good King of Rome, a bondmaid bore."

[2] Juv. viii, ad finem; Liv. ii, 7. Livy derives from his name "*vindicta*," the rod of manumission—used on occasions of manumitting slaves.

[3] Life, &c., Terence, prefixed to his plays.

[4] Sat. vi. He did not hesitate, however, to speak scornfully of the low birth of a freedman, who was made a military tribune. Carmina, Lib. v, Ode iv.

[5] M. Wallon, speaking of slavery under the empire, says: "L'homme libre devient moins libre, il est moins maitre de lui et des siens; et par contre-coup, l'esclave n'a pas changé en droit: il n'a pas plus de liberté, mais il a moins de dépendance; et le même mot finira par couvrir deux états fort diffe'rents, l'esclave et le serf, servus." Part iii, ch. iii, 121.

could mark her appearance, serfdom was substituted in
its place. The causes which produced this result, are
matters mostly of speculation. A few we may clearly
perceive. The supremacy of the barbarian conquerors,
unused to luxury, and eschewing even the comforts of
civilized life. The common bondage into which their
conquest threw both master and slave. The stagnation
of commerce, and all other channels of industry. These,
and concurrent causes, rendered the slave valueless in
the market, and a burthen to the master. The support
of the aged and infirm and infants, was without corresponding benefit, when the labor of the strong and
healthy barely provided for his own necessities. The
renunciation, by the master, of his rights and power,
became therefore a matter of *interest*,—a much stronger
motive, according to man's history, than *humanity* and
*charity*.

Many have sought to discover in Christianity, and its
pure and holy precepts, a sufficient explanation for the
extinction of slavery. That it contributed to this object
is undoubtedly true; and many masters felicitated themselves upon the charitable act of manumitting their
slaves, when those slaves had ceased to be useful. Habit
possibly would have continued the system a while longer,
and Christianity, to this extent, shortened its duration.
To the truly pious and zealous, imbued with the doctrine
of the equality of all men before the bar of God, who is
no respecter of persons, and that every man is a brother,
to whom we should act as we would have him, under
similar circumstances, to act towards us, the slavery of
Rome must have appeared sinful, and inconsistent with
their professions of universal charity. Alexander Severus caused this golden rule to be inscribed not only upon
the walls of his own palace, but also upon all the public
edifices.[1] Constantine, by taking away the restraints

[1] Lamp. in Vitâ Alex. Sev. 350; Troplong, Influence du Christianisme,
&c., 87.

upon manumission, and giving additional privileges to
those manumitted *in ecclesia*, by enforcing, with stern
penalties, the humane treatment of slaves, and adopting
in his laws the Christian principle of brotherhood, has
received from M. de Chateaubriand the praise of having
" affranchi tout d'un coup une nombreuse partie de
l'espèce humaine."[1]

Yet the same Emperor forbade the marriage of the
*curiales* with slaves, under penalty of the woman's being
condemned to the mines, and the man to perpetual
banishment, with confiscation of all his movable goods
and city slaves to the public, and all his lands and
country slaves to the city of which he was a member.[2]

The true agency of Christianity in effecting the destruction of Roman slavery, is more accurately described
by M. Troplong: "It is the feudal age, which, at a later
period, has had the eternal honor of having restored to
liberty the lower classes, oppressed with the yoke of
slavery. To arrive at this great result, it was necessary
that Christianity, penetrating profoundly the heart, had
humanized the masters to a high degree; and that the
*general interests* had been brought, by a happy combination of circumstances, to agree with these ideas. Great
revolutions are not accomplished by a sudden virtue.
Ages of preparation are necessary before they arrive at
their maturity. Slavery, though ameliorated by Christian morality and reforms full of humanity, continued to
exist legally, and to be fed from the impure sources,
trade and conquest."[3]

In Rome, as in Athens, the morality and expediency
of slavery did not fail to attract the attention of her
statesmen and philosophers, and as great diversity of
opinion existed in the former place as the latter. "Our

[1] Essais hist., tom. i, p. 308.

[2] Bingham's Antiquities of the Christian Church, Bk. XXII, ch. ii, § 6.

[3] Influence du Christianisme sur le droit civil des Romains, 162, 3. See
also Sismondi, tom. i, pp. 85  104.

slaves are our enemies," said Censor Cato. "Slaves truly, but men,"—"fortasse liberi animo," preached the almost Christian Seneca. "The old and infirm slaves are a nuisance on the farm, and should be sold," said Cato. "In servos superbissimi, crudelissimi, contume-liosissimi sumus," responded the conscientious Seneca. And in another place, either from inspiration or Christian teaching, adds the golden rule, "Sic cum inferiore vivas, quemadmodum tecum superiorem velles vivere."[1]

Cicero, the greatest of Roman philosophers as well as orators, seems to have been imbued with the same views concerning slavery as Plato and Aristotle. He even justified the cruelty with which some of them were treated. "Iis, qui vi oppressos imperio coercent, est sane adhibenda sævitia, ut heris in famulos."[2] Varro adopted, to its full extent, the doctrine of Aristotle.[3] Florus speaks of slaves as an inferior species of men.[4] And Pliny compares them to the drones among the bees, to be forced to labor, even as the drones are compelled.[5]

A different opinion prevailed among the later writers, and hence we find but one voice in the Digest and Code: "Jure naturali omnes liberi nascuntur."[6] "Servitus est constitutio gentium contra naturam."

So Quintillian: "Quid non liberum natura genuit? Taceo de servis, quos bellorum iniquitas in prædam victoribus dedit, iisdem legibus, eâdem fortunâ, eâdem necessitate natos. Ex eodem cœlo spiritum trahunt; nec natura ullis, sed fortuna dominum dedit."[7]

---

[1] Let. 47: "Quid est eques Romanus, aut libertinus, aut servus? Nomina ex ambitione aut ex injuria nata." Let. 32.

[2] De Off. Lib. II, 7. See also his oration against Verres, V. 3, De rep. iii.    [3] De re rustica, lxvii, 1.

[4] Florus, iii, c. xx, 2.    [5] Pliny, xi, c. xi, 1.

[6] Dig. Lib. IV, De Just. et Jure.    [7] Declam. iii.

# CHAPTER VII.

" In every age and country, until times comparatively recent," says Mr. Hallam, "personal servitude appears to have been the lot of a large, perhaps the greater portion of mankind."[1] Certainly during the middle ages, upon the continent of Europe, it was universal. So much oppressed and deprived of so many privileges were even the freemen of the lower classes, that it is with some difficulty that we are enabled to distinguish the slave, the serf, and the freeman. A term which, in one nation, indicated slavery, in an adjoining one represented a class of freemen. Thus, the *collibert* of France was a slave : "Libertate carens colibertus dicitur esse;" but among the Lombards, the *collibert* was ranked among freemen.[2] The truth seems to be, that all the classes below the nobles or lords, were in a state of actual servitude. In the absence of well-ordered government, the small proprietors of lands were the constant subjects of depredation by the lawless and warlike. Their only recourse was the protection of some more powerful neighbor. For that protection they yielded their liberty, frequently voluntarily, becoming thus the serfs or *coloni*

[1] Hist. Middle Ages, ch. ii, pt. ii, p. 89. "In the infancy of society," says M. Guizot, "liberty is the portion of strength. It belongs to whoever can defend it. In the absence of personal power in the individual, it possesses no other guarantee."—Essais sur l'Histoire de France, 126.

[2] See Appendix to Michelet's History of France.

so universal in these ages.[1]   In seasons of famine, also, many freemen sold themselves as slaves.   Their redemption, at equitable prices, is provided for in a Capitulary of Charles the Bald.[2]   Others surrendered themselves and their property to churches and monasteries, and became, with their posterity, their perpetual bondmen.[3] To these, extraordinary, were added the usual and universal sources of slavery, viz., war, debt, crime, birth, and sale of themselves and of children.[4]

Slavery existed in these countries long before their subjection to the Roman yoke.   The number of domestic slaves, previous to that period, was small; but the prædial or agrestic slaves were numerous.   Of the slavery in Gaul and Germany, previous to that time, we have some accounts.[5]   After the Roman subjugation, the laws of Roman slavery were extended more or less to every nation, modified necessarily by their previous customs.

Frequently, the *status* of slavery attached to every inhabitant of a particular district, so that it became a maxim, "Aer efficit servilem statum;' a different atmosphere it must have been from that which fans the British shores, according to the boasts of some of their judges.   It is a little curious that, by an ordinance of Philip, Landgrave of Hesse, the air of Wales was declared to be of the infected species.[6]

---

[1] Guizot's Hist. of Civilization in France, § 8, citing Salvianus de Guberu. Dei. Lib. v.   Bishop England gives us this quotation from Salvianus at large, in Letter VI, to Jno. Forsyth, p. 53.   See also Michelet, Origines du Droit Français, p. 274.

[2] Hallam, as above.   See also Muratori, Annali d'Italia.

[3] Beaumanoir, ch. 45.   In a charter granted by the Emperor, Otto I, to a monastery, are these words : "Si vero aliquis ex liberis voluerit litus fieri, aut etiam colonis, ad monasteria supra dicta, cum consensu suorum hæredum, non prohibeatur a quâlibet potestate." Potg. i, 5.

[4] See Du Cange v. Heribannum.

[5] Cæsar, De Bel. Gall. Lib. VI, cap. xiii; Tacitus, cap. xxiv; Potg. Lib. I, cap. i; Giraud, Histoire du Droit Français au Moyen-Age, art. v.

[6] Hertius, Lib. II, p. xii; Potgiesser, De Stat. &c., Lib. I, cap. i, § 15.

The names given to slaves differed in the several states, and at different times. Among the French, they were called *hommes de pooste*.[1] In some of their authors, *coustumiers*.[2] In the Salique laws and the Capitularies, they were called *servi, tributarii, lidi, coloni, liti*, and *lasinæ*.[3] In the formulas of Marculf, they are distinguished as *mansionarii* and *servientes*. In the Bavarian law, *lazi*. In the German law, *homines proprii, genetiariæ, ancillæ*, &c. These names varied in different centuries, indicating a change in their employments, and a melioration of their condition. In the twelfth century they were first called "*rustici;*" and not until the fourteenth were they called *glebarii*, indicating their permanent attachment to the soil. In the fourteenth century, also, we first find them called *slavi*.[4]

Of slavery in the German states, we have the most full and accurate account. The works of Heineccius and Potgiesser, and especially the treatise by the latter, "De Statu Servorum," answer every inquiry we could desire to make. From them we learn, that the early German slavery was mild in its character, differing widely from the Roman. The master and the slave were equal in education, tended upon the same flocks, and

---

[1] Hallam, as above ; derived from the Latin Homines in potestate. Bonnemère.          [2] Du Cange v. Potestas.

[3] Hallam, Potg., Lib. I, cap. iii, § iv; Guizot, Essais sur l'Histoire de France, 134; Giraud, as above.

[4] Potg., as above.

St. Augustine defines Colonus thus : " Coloni dicuntur, qui conditionem debebant genitali solo propter agriculturam sub dominio possessorum." De Civ. Dei. Lib. X, cap. i.

Guizot, in his Hist. of Civilization in France, Lect. vii, distinguishes, at length, the condition of the Colonus from the absolute slave. In his Essais sur l'Histoire de France, he says, that these names varied according to the extent of the liberty and the right of property which they possessed. p. 134.

Giraud traces the Colonus to the times of Augustus, vol. i, p. 155.

See Bonnemère, Histoire des Paysans, Introduction.

rested upon the same pillow. The invention of the one
was not taxed to provide tortures for the other; nor did
his cruelty excite the latter to devise schemes for his
destruction. The master sometimes did kill the slave,
not from cruelty and severity, but from anger and impulse, as an enemy, and for his own protection. In
Celtic Gaul, a custom existed at one time of burning
the slaves upon the funeral pyre of their master.[1] Cæsar
notices this custom in Gaul;[2] and Peter Dusbergensis
states its existence among the Prussians. The latter
gives the reason for it, in the popular belief of the trans-
migration of souls: that, in another world, the soul of
the slave entered into the master's body, and that of the
master into the body of the slave.[3] A similar superstition is frequently found among the negro slaves in the
United States at this day.

This state of things was of short duration, and the
condition of the slave became worse. The power of the
master over him was very extensive subsequently. Thus,
in an ancient deed, by which a sale of a freeman into
slavery was made by himself, it was covenanted that
the master should have power, "Ad disciplinandum,
tenendum, imperandum, et quicquid ei placuerit facien-
dum, tam de rebus, quam de peculio."[4] Slaves could
be sold, pawned, or otherwise disposed of, and were the
subject of inheritance at the death of the owner. If,
however, the master left no heir, the slave became free
immediately.[5] The master's power seems sometimes to
have been abused, as an edict of Charles, in the year
864, directs that slaves guilty of a fault, should be
beaten naked with rods, and not with huge clubs.[6]
Fugitives were arrested and returned to their owners,

[1] Potgiesser, Prolegomena, § xlviii.      [2] De Bel. Gall. Lib. VI.
[3] Chron. Pruss. Part III, ch. v, cited in Potg.
[4] Quoted in Potg. Lib. I, cap. i, § v.
[5] Potg. Proleg. L. Lib. I, cap. iii, §§ v, x ; Heinec. Elem. Jur. Germ.
Lib I, tit. i.                              Potg. § xiv.

and if no owner claimed them, were, nevertheless, retained in slavery. Even shipwrecked persons were reduced to slavery, for many centuries, notwithstanding the anathemas of the Church.[1]

We may judge of the extent of the master's power by a German proverb, which has been preserved: "He is mine: I can boil him or roast him." So, also, we read of a German custom: "If a master does not wish to place his slave in irons, he can put him under a cask, and place above a piece of cheese, a small loaf of bread, and a pot of water, and leave him thus till the third day."[2]

The slaves were distinguished in their dress from freemen. "After a battle, in the year 711, one could distinguish," says an old chronicler, "the corpses of the Goths, by their rings." Those of the nobles were of gold, those of the freemen of silver, and those of the slaves of copper.[3]

The sources of slavery among the Germans were the same as with the Romans. Tacitus mentions one peculiar to them, viz., gaming, the loser becoming the slave of the winner.[4]

The punishment of slaves differed from that prescribed for freemen, for the same offence. Thus, where a freeman was fined, the slave was stripped naked and publicly whipped. The testimony of slaves was not allowed against a freeman, nor were they permitted to bring accusations against their masters. They were excluded from all offices, nor could they receive ecclesiastical orders, except by the consent of their master.[5] Marriage was not allowed among them until the ninth cen-

---

[1] Potg. Lib. I, c. ii and iii.

[2] Cited by Michelet, Origines du Droit Français, 272.

[3] Capit. v, 247, vi, 271, cited by Michelet, as above, p. 273.

[4] Ea est in re prava pervicacia: ipsi fidem vacant. Tac. de Mor. Germ.                                                        [5] Potg. § xi.

tury, and then, if celebrated without the master's consent, it was void.[1]

The punishment of fugitives varied; none was specified among the early Germans. Among the Franks it was left purely to the discretion of the master. In the Capitularies we frequently find directions to the presbyters of churches to deliver up fugitives seeking refuge therein.[2] The laws were more specific as to the punishment of those who harbored or concealed them. By the Bavarian law it was a fine and the restitution of another slave. By the law of the Visigoths the restitution of *three* slaves. The law of the Frisians agreed with the Bavarian. The Burgundian law provided for a fine only.[3]

Long hair, being the badge of a freeman, was prohibited to slaves. Hence, one, that permitted a fugitive's hair to grow long, was subject to a fine. The Burgundian law forbade the giving of a loaf of bread to a fugitive. The law of the Visigoths forbade the showing him the way,—*ostendere viam.*

Escapes into a neighboring state were frequent. They were always unhesitatingly delivered to their owners. Marculf has preserved the form of a letter of demand for a fugitive. Potgiesser, who wrote about the first year of the eighteenth century, says the same form in substance was used in his day for the demand of *homines proprii.*[4]

Various modes of manumission were recognized. After the days of Constantine, manumission *in ecclesiâ* or *circa altare,* was the most common. Something in-

---

[1] Ibid. § xiv; Heinec. El. Jur. Ger. Lib. I, tit. i.

[2] In one of the Capitularies it is provided that slaves taking refuge in a church are to be delivered up, on promise of a light punishment. A fine was imposed on the master for violently abstracting his slave from the church, and for violating his promise, the master was excommunicated. Potg. Lib. II, cap. viii, §§ 10, 11.

[3] Potg. Lib. II, cap. viii.    [4] Potg. Lib. II, cap. viii.

dicating a renunciation of dominion by the master is all that, in the earlier nations, was required. Hence, the striking of a penny from the hand, among the Franks, the leading a servant to an open door, or to where two roads cross, and speaking these words, "De quatuor viis, ubi volueris ambulare, liberam habeas potestatem," adopted among the.Lombards, the delivery to the slave of the arms of a freeman,[1] and various other modes, were considered sufficient.[2]

The depriving a slave of an eye *ipso facto* manumitted him.[3] For other cruelties the master was sometimes compelled to sell him.[4]

The manumitted slaves, according to Heineccius, differed but little from their former associates, " Quod ad reliqua attinet, eorum status a servorum vel hominum propriorum conditione parum differt."[5]

Towards the fifteenth century the condition of slaves became ameliorated in many parts of Germany. This seems to have been attributed to various causes. One cause assigned, was the introduction of the Roman law and rule; under which the *coloni* were recognized in the census among freemen, because they possessed, in a modified manner, the right to marry, to contract, and to make a testament, whereas under the Saxon law they were ranked as slaves. Another cause assigned, was the numerous intestine wars among the German states, which necessarily relaxed for the time the domestic discipline over their slaves. Another cause was the indulgence and negligence of masters, especially the religious communities, who owned large numbers and demanded of them only a yearly rent or hire.[6] Occasionally, how-

---

[1] The use of these arms being forbidden to slaves. Thus, in Capitularies, Lib. V, cap. 247, " Et ut servi lanceas non portent."

[2] Heinec. El. Jur. Germ. Lib. I, tit. ii ; Potg. Lib. IV.

[3] Ducange v. Servus.          [4] Potg. Lib. I, cap. ii.

[5] Heinec. as above, § 57.

[6] Potg. Lib. I, cap. iii, §§ 35, 36, and 37.

ever, the immediate tithe-gatherers became very oppressive, and demanded more than was required by their
superiors.  The Pope himself interfered frequently on
such occasions.[1]

Another cause may be traced in the effects of the Crusades.  In these holy wars, the vassal and his lord had
fought side by side, stimulated by the same religious
enthusiasm, rejoicing in the same victory, and suffering
from the same defeat.  The idea of equality among men
became an admitted dogma, and the friendships originating in common toils and sufferings added another reason for admitting this equality.  Commerce, between
nations, springing up from this common intercourse and
common end, tended to enlarge and liberalize the
opinions of masters as well as men.[2]

In addition to these, were the mild and humanizing
influences of Christianity, which, while it did not forbid
the control of the master over his slave, for their mutual
benefit, exhorted him to remember that his slave was
"the Lord's freeman," and joint heir with him in Christ
of the promises held out to the faithful.  At the same
time, teaching the slave obedience to his master under
the law, all earthly authority being by permission of
God.  That bond or free, on earth, is a matter of no
moment, so that *heavenly freedom* is obtained.  Tertullian thus developed this idea to the early Christians:
"In the world they who have received their freedom are
crowned.  But thou art ransomed already by Christ, and
indeed bought with a price.  How can the world give
freedom to him who is already the servant of another?
All is mere show in the world, and nothing truth.  For
even then, thou wast free in relation to man, being redeemed by Christ, and now thou art a servant of Christ,

[1] See the Letters of Gregory the Great to the Subdeacon Peter, as to
the administration of the property of the Church in Sicily, given by Guizot, in Sect. 8, on Hist. of Civil. in Europe.

[2] See Michelet, Hist. &c. Bk. IV, ch. iv.

although made free by a man. If thou deemest *that* the true freedom which the world can give thee, thou art, for that very reason, become once more the servant of man, and the freedom which Christ bestows thou hast lost, because thou thinkest it bondage."[1]

So Ignatius, of Antioch, writes to the Bishop Polycarp, of Smyrna: "Be not proud towards servants and maids; but neither must they exalt themselves; but they must serve the more zealously for the honor of God, so that they may receive from God the higher freedom. Let them not be eager to be redeemed at the expense of the Church, lest they be found slaves of their own lusts."[2]

Such was not only the teaching of the early Christians, but we may well believe their works were in accordance with their faith. Thus, when a fatal pestilence devastated Carthage, we find the Bishop Cyprian writing to his flock: "How necessary is it, my dearest brethren, that this pestilence which appears among us, bringing with it death and destruction, should try men's souls; should show whether the healthy will take care of the sick; whether relations have a tender regard for each other; *whether masters will take home their sick servants.*"[3]

Thus, also, we find in the Apostolical Constitutions (which is of very early date in the Church, though not probably of apostolic origin), that the slave of a believing master was not to be received except upon the good report of the master himself, and not until he was approved by the master. Bingham adds, that "Experience proved it to be a useful rule; for it both made the mas-

[1] De Coronâ Militis, c. xiii, quoted in Neander's Hist. of Church, vol. i, 269. (2d Amer. Ed.)          [2] Quoted by Neander, as above.
[3] Lib. de Mortalitate, quoted by Neander, p. 258. Locenius, a commentator on Swedish law, speaking of the cessation of slavery, about the year 1295, says, "Hanc que id suasisse inter alios, rationem quod servatore nostro vendito, omnes redempti fuerint Christiani, et liberti facti." Quoted by Potg. Lib. I, cap. iii, § 39.

ters zealous for the salvation of their slaves, as we have
seen in the African negro mentioned in Fulgentius, and
also made the slaves sincere in their professions and pre-
tences to ᛐeligion, when they knew they could not be
accepted as real converts, worthy of baptism, without
the corroborating testimony of their masters.[1]  The same
Constitutions provided that no slave should be ordained
among the clergy, except by the consent of his master;
and the canons of several councils reiterated the same
injunction.  The Council of Eliberis went further, and
provided that the slave of a heathen master should not
be ordained even if he was manumitted.[2]  So St. Basil
forbade the marriage of slaves without the consent of
their masters, ᴈnd declared it to be fornication; and if
a woman, that she differed nothing from a harlot."[3]

That the true "heavenly freedom" was open to all,
bond or free, was inculcated by all the Fathers.  St.
Justin illustrates this idea by the history of Jacob:
"Jacob served Laban for the spotted and particolored
of the flock, and so Christ submitted to the vilest servitude for every form and variety of the human race, purchasing them with his divine blood, by the mystery of
the cross."[4]  St. Jerome declares "that we are all born
alike, kings and paupers; we all die alike—the same is
the condition of all;"[5] but that "enfranchisement exists
in the knowledge of the truth, so that there will be no
perfect liberty until the truth shall appear unclouded at
the judgment day."[6]  St. Ambrose develops this thought
more at large: "He is a slave who has not a pure conscience, who is cast down by fear, entangled by pleasure, governed by passions, excited by anger, over-

---

[1] Antiquities of Christian Church, vol. i, 502.  A full exposition of
these Constitutions can be found in Chevalier Bunsen's work, Hippo-
lytus and his Age, vol. ii.

[2] Bingham's Antiquities, &c., vol. i, 147.   [3] Ibid. vol. ii, 985.

[4] Dial. cum Trupho. 134.          [5] Hieron. in Ps. lxxxi, ₴ 4.

[6] Hieron. Comm. in Ps. clvi.

whelmed by grief. ... The man bound by his vices has many masters in himself. . . He who has power over his own conduct is perfectly free, for he does everything with prudence, and lives as he ought *o live—he alone is free."[1] So, in another place, "Servile est omne pecatum, libera est innocentia."[2] St. Augustine exhorts the slave to serve his master according to the flesh, for in so doing for Christ's sake, he serves God, and to serve God is true liberty.[3]

St. Chrysostom goes still farther, and exhorts servants not to seek temporal liberty, even if they could obtain it, as their bodily bondage caused their spiritual liberty to be more pre-eminent and shining.[4]

The Popes of subsequent days enforced the same views, both by precept, as is fully seen in Gregory the Great's book, Pastoralis Curæ, Admonition VI, and by their acts, holding and buying and transferring slaves.[5]

M. Wallon justly observes, that the Christian Fathers and Church did not pretend to undertake the labor of working out the abolition of slavery: "Another graver and more urgent labor in every respect, in their view, was the enfranchisement of their souls. In the short journey of life, where we take and leave our bodies matters not. The soul alone, born for eternity, gives interest to the question of liberty and slavery." Such was their view of Christian duty.[6]

---

[1] De Jacob. et vita beata, Lib. II, c. iii, § 12.

[2] De Joseph, IV, §§ 19, 20.

[3] "Servire Deo regnare est." Cited, with many others, by Wallon, Part III, ch. viii. Speaking of the liberation of the Jewish servants, he says, "Ne servi Christiani hoc flagitarent a dominis suis, apostolica auctoritas jubet servos dominis suis esse subditos, ne nomen Dei blasphemetur." Quæst. in Ex. lxxvii.      [4] In Genes. Serm. v.

[5] Bishop England's Letters to John Forsyth, tracing the whole history of the Catholic Church, in reference to slavery.

[6] Hist. de l'Escl. dans l'Ant. Part III, ch. viii. As late as the seventeenth century, Bossuet, the great pulpit orator of the world, declared that to condemn slavery "was to condemn the Holy Spirit, who com-

While this was the teaching of the Fathers, and such
was the effect of the principles of Christianity, yet it does
not appear that the Church was at all forward in manumitting her slaves. The villains upon the Church lands
were among the last emancipated.[1]

Villanage has never been entirely extinct in Germany.
The distinction between the villain and the ordinary
peasant is more in name than in fact. Indeed, the situation of the peasantry of the present day, differs but
little from their condition when they were *coloni* and
*rustici*. Mr. Hallam, speaking of the latter, says:
" Even where they had no legal title to property, it was
accounted inhuman to divest them of their little possession (the peculium of the Roman law); nor was
their poverty perhaps less tolerable upon the whole, than
that of the modern peasantry in most countries of Europe."[2]

In Gaul, the feudal system had a more extensive and
general sway, and continued for a longer time, than in
Germany. Under that system, the mass of the people
were bondmen—not absolute slaves, perhaps, but far
from exercising the privileges of freemen. Prior to
that system the bondmen in Gaul were numerous.
After the invasion of the Goths, the Burgundians and
Franks, who possessed themselves of different portions
of Gaul, the feudal system with its servitudes became
permanently fixed. The frequent conquests of Gaul,
and the consequent number of captives, swelled greatly
the list of bondmen, and the subsequent intestine wars
among the conquering hordes themselves, rendered servitudes more general in France than in any other of the
European countries.[3] As these conquering nations were

manded all slaves, by the mouth of St. Paul, to remain in their estate,
and did not force their masters to enfranchise them." Cinquième Aver-
tiss. aux Protestants, § 50.

[1] Hallam's Mid. Ages, Pt. II, ch. ii.                    [2] Ibid.

[3] Montesq. Esp. des Lois, Lib. XXX, ch. ii ; Histoire des Paysans, by
Eugène Bonnemère.

of Germanic origin, and carried with them their laws and customs, it is unnecessary to enter into a detailed view of the condition of the bondmen of Gaul.   Michelet, speaking of the days of Charlemagne, says : " Slavery, mitigated it is true, is greatly increased.   Charlemagne gratifies his master, Alcuin, with a farm of 20,000 slaves.   The nobles daily forced the poor to give themselves up to them, body and goods.   Slavery is an asylum where the freeman daily takes refuge."[1]

The condition of the bondmen in France was more onerous than in Germany.   In both, the burthen of raising the revenue for the support of government, fell upon them ; one of the privileges of a freeman, was freedom from taxation.[2]   Gibbon says, " The Goth, the Burgundian, or the Frank, who returned from a successful expedition, dragged after him a long train of sheep, of oxen, and of human captives, whom he treated with the same brutal contempt.   The youths of an elegant form and ingenuous aspect, were set apart for the domestic service ; a doubtful situation, which alternately exposed them to the favorable or cruel impulse of passion. The useful mechanics and servants employed their skill for the use or profit of their master.   But the Roman captives who were destitute of art, but capable of labor, were condemned, without regard to their former rank, to tend the cattle and cultivate the land of the barbarians." " An absolute power of life and death was exercised by these lords ; and when they married their daughters, a train of useful servants, chained on the wagons to prevent their escape, was sent as a nuptial present into a distant country."   He adds : " From the reign of Clovis, during five successive centuries, the laws and manners of Gaul uniformly tended to promote the increase and to confirm the duration of personal servitude.   Time and

[1] Hist. of France, vol. i, ch. ii ; see also Gibbon's Decline, &c., ch. xxxviii.    [2] Montesq. Lib. XXX, ch. 15.

violence almost obliterated the intermediate ranks of society, and left an obscure and narrow interval between the noble and the slave. This arbitrary and recent division has been transformed by pride and prejudice, into a national distinction, universally established by the arms and the laws of the Merovingians. The nobles, who claim their genuine or fabulous descent from the independent and victorious Franks, have asserted and abused the indefeasible right of conquest, over a prostrate crowd of slaves and plebeians, to whom they imputed the imaginary disgrace of a Gallic or Roman origin."[1] Michelet, describing the peasants of the fourteenth century, says: " It did not take long to make an inventory of the peasant's property : meagre cattle, wretched harness, plough, cart, and some iron tools. *Household goods he had none.* He had no stock, save a small quantity of seed-corn. These things taken and sold, what remained for the lord to lay his hands upon ?—the poor devil's body, his skin. Something more was tried to be squeezed out of him. The boor must have some secret store in a hiding-place. To make him discover it, *they did not spare his carcass ;* his feet were warmed for him. At any rate they had no mercy on the fire and iron."[2]

The rustic serf differed somewhat from the slave. He could not be sold for his master's debt, nor could he be separated from the land to which he was attached. He had a peculium, or rather the right to have one. If, however, he sought to fly from the rigors of his situation, the reclaimed fugitive became a pure slave.[3] The cruelty of the lord's treatment equalled anything related of the Roman masters. The Duc de Soissons caused to be buried alive a male and a female serf, who intermarried

---

[1] Decline and Fall of Roman Emp. ch. xxxviii.

[2] Hist. of France, Bk. VI, ch. iii ; see also Dr. Robertson's " View of the Progress of Society in Europe;" Edwards's Ecclesiastical Jurisdiction, § 36 ; Bonnemère's Histoire des Paysans, Introduction.

[3] Bonnemère, p. 5.

without his consent.  At his feasts he amused himself by forcing a naked serf to hold between his legs a flaming torch until it should be extinguished, repressing his cries and his moving by threatening death with a sword.[1]  The low estimate placed upon their value, may be inferred from the fact that the Bishop of Avranches gave five women and two men for a spirited horse, on which to enter his diocese.[2]  The slaves were bought and sold as other choses; and there are manuscripts in existence, showing the exchange of the half of a woman for the half of a man.[3]

The *mainmorte* of the French had its origin in the custom of the master to cut off the right hand of the deceased serf and presenting it to the lord, which evidence of dominion entitled him to the goods and effects of the deceased, to the exclusion of his children.  Even the religious lords sometimes nailed these hands over the doors of their towers, by the side of the heads of wild animals taken in the chase.[4]  The miserable condition of the people, combined with a superstitious piety, multiplied largely the slaves of the religious houses. The formulas of the ceremony, on receiving such voluntary slaves, are still extant.  The Church encouraged this practice, and in A. D. 847, procured a capitulary, by which every freeman was required to select a lord, under whose protection to place himself.[5]  The serfs bore around their necks a collar, upon which was inscribed the master's name.[6]

The children of slaves were frequently divided between the owners of the husband and wife; sometimes the former taking the males, and the latter the females. Some curious agreements, in reference to the division of

---

[1] Bonnemère, p. 37, citing Greg. de Tours, for his authority, who adds, that the Christian masters were equally cruel; naming a Bishop of Mans, Bertram, whose acts were of the same character.

[2] Bonnemère, 37.                [3] Ibid. 38.

[4] Ibid. 39.                [5] Ibid. 51.                [6] Ibid.

H

the children are still in existence.  The most abominable
feature of this state of slavery, was what was called the
" right of prelibation," which was the lord's privilege of
lying with the female vassal on the first night after her
marriage.  This custom seems to have prevailed, at one
time, in Scotland, England, Germany, Piedmont, and
most parts of Europe.[1]  To make this custom more horrible, the husband was required to carry his espoused to
her bed of dishonor.[2]  The remains of this custom are
still seen in certain gifts required of the villain on his
marriage, in various countries in Europe, being originally a composition for this right.[3]

The art of tormenting was carried to a degree of re-
finement seldom equalled, even in the imagination of
those depicting the horrors of the Inquisition.  " The
fire, the sword, the pit, the quartering, the wheel, the
sack, the axe, the fork, the gibbet, had no secrets from
him (the lord).  He knew how to draw, to prick, to rack,
to break the teeth, to burn the eyes, to cut off the hands,
the feet, nose, ears.  He knew how to castrate, to dis-
member, to lash, to break on a wheel, to castigate, to
flay alive, to boil, to roast, and with wise deliberation."[4]

That people, thus oppressed, should frequently revolt
and inflict vengeance upon their tyrants, is not surprising.  Their desperation compensated for their want of
discipline, and hence we are not surprised at their success for a season.  The Bagaudan conspiracy was a most
remarkable instance.  They became masters of several
of the rural districts, burnt several towns, and committed
other depredations.[5]  Almost the same scenes were re-

[1] Bonnemère, 57, et seq.

[2] " Maritus ipse femora nuptæ aperiet, ut dictus dominus primum flo-
rem primitiasque delibet facilius."  Ibid.        [3] Ibid.

[4] Bonnemère, 63.

[5] Michelet's Hist. of France, Bk. I, ch. iii.  A full history may be
found in Bonnemère's Histoire des Paysans. Introduction, ch. ii.

enacted in the fourteenth century, in the celebrated revolt of the peasants, known as the "*Jacquerie*."[1]

The names of the servile classes in France varied
according to their grades from the *seneschal* and *mareschal*,
the chief slaves, down to the *gens de corps*, who were
classed with the cattle, as *levant et couchant*. The intermediate grades, between absolute liberty and absolute
slavery, were infinite.[2]

The wars of the Christians and Moors in France and
the Peninsula, increased largely the number of slaves.
France and Italy were filled with Saracen slaves. At
the same time, the Jews of Lyons and Verdun were furnishing Christian slaves to their Saracen customers.[3]

On the other side, the wars of the German and Slavonic tribes gave to the slave-trade its greatest activity,
and filled the neighboring nations with so many of the
Slavonic captives, as to transfer their name "slaves," to
servitude itself.[4]

From the sixth to the fourteenth centuries there was
very little improvement in the condition of the serfs of
France. In 1315, Louis le Hutin, to render famous his
reign, promulgated a celebrated ordinance for the enfranchisement of royal serfs; wherein, after declaring,
by the law of nature, all men are born free, and that the
kingdom of the Franks should comport with its name
and be a kingdom of freemen, as an example to other
seigneurs, he ordered his officers to grant freedom to his
serfs, "upon certain composition, whereby sufficient
compensation shall be made to us for the emoluments

. [1] See a graphic description of this, by Michelet, Hist. of France, Bk.
VI, ch. iii.

[2] For a full and accurate view of this subject, see Michelet, Origines du
droit français, 276; Du Cange Gloss. v. Colonus, Mancipia, Accola, &c.
Guizot, Essais sur l'Histoire de France, p. 105; Giraud, Histoire du droit
français, tom. i, art. v; Bonnemère, Histoire des Paysans, Introduction.

[3] Bancroft's United States, i, 162, 164, and authorities there cited.

[4] Bancroft's United States, i, 162.

arising to us and our successors from their said servitude." The result, as might have been expected, was
much honor to the royal munificence and justice, and
but little amelioration to the serf.[1]

With very considerable abatement in rigor, the feudal
system, and the consequent oppression of the peasant,
continued in France until the revolution of 1789. "Fiefs
and the feudal system," says M. Troplong, "had introduced in France a *noblesse*, the members of which have,
even to the latest times, preserved privileges very onerous to the people, and unjust prerogatives very humilia-
ting to the balance of the nation."[2] One can almost
excuse the horrors of the revolution, when it is remembered, to use the figure of Macaulay, that the Devil of
Tyranny always tears and rends the body which it leaves.
Certain it is, that a people unjustly enslaved by masters,
in nowise their superiors, acquired thereby for the first
time their enfranchisement. The great Napoleon, it is
true, after the Empire, established a new and even an
hereditary nobility. But he exhibited the sagacious
wisdom of his master mind even in this; for while he
rewarded the brave and virtuous, and stimulated the
pride and emulation of their posterity, he withheld from
the new *noblesse* those prerogatives and powers which
oppressed the people. The French people objected not
to the display and pageantry attendant upon a titled
aristocracy; and when unaccompanied by oppression,
they were not distasteful to them.

Sicily, Italy, and Venice, for many ages furnished
marts to the slave-dealer. Venetian ships were engaged
in the commerce long after Venetian laws had prohibited
it; and never did the trade therein fully cease, until
treading the deck of an argosy of Venice was declared
by law to be itself freedom.[3]

[1] Guizot's History of Civilization, Lecture viii.
[2] Droit civil français, Liv. I, Int. § 195.
[3] Bancroft's United States, i, 163, and authorities there cited.

Slavery continued in Poland so long as it remained an independent state; the slaves were mostly prædial, living upon their master's land, furnished by him with agricultural implements and cattle, and bound to labor for him a specified portion of their time. They were allowed, by their lords, to own and possess personal property, and thus acquired occasionally a comfortable competency.[1]

When Russia became master of most of her soil, the condition of the serfs was not improved, as the slavery of Russia is as arbitrary and oppressive as that of any portion of the world. It has existed there ever since the Muscovite Empire has been known, and has undergone, in the progress of time, but little amelioration. It includes the vast majority of the population of this extensive domain, and presents but little prospect of change or improvement. Besides yielding passive obedience, the Russian slave must uncover himself in the presence of his master; must succor him when attacked; must not marry without his permission; must make no complaint against his master, except under the severest penalties, if it be decided against him; and must submit to any labor or punishment which his master may inflict upon him. The master may dispose of his serf in any manner he pleases, sell or mortgage him, transfer him from one estate to another, or to his household, or transport him to Siberia. May inflict any punishment he pleases upon him. May seize all of his earnings, and appropriate to his own use. However, by the indulgence of their masters, some of the serfs acquire considerable estates.

Emancipation is allowed by law; and one article provides, that " an emancipated serf can never again become a slave, but he may be compelled to serve as a soldier all his life." But emancipation is no blessing to the

[1] See Dickens's Household Words, i, 342.

Russian serf. There exists no intermediate grades between the nobles and the serfs. There is no opening for
rewarding industry and probity; no stimulus for energy
and integrity. The serf, bond or free, is still a serf, confined to the occupation of a serf, without hope of a
better condition. As free, he is liable to starvation,
while otherwise his master must provide food for him:
and hunger and famine are *realities* among the Russian
serfs. It is not surprising then, that they are contented
with their lot and seek no change. They are indolent,
constitutionally, and indulge it at their master's expense.
They are mendacious, beyond the negro perhaps, and
feel no shame at detection. Like him, too, they have
no providence for the future, and no anxiety about it.
They are filthy in their persons, and in their rude huts;
exhibiting, in all their handiworks, the ignorance of a
savage and the stupidity of a dolt.[1]

In Turkey, and wherever Islamism prevails, slavery is
a part of the religion of the people. The slave-market
at Constantinople is always crowded with both blacks
and whites; and in the same stall may be seen the negro
from Sennaar or Abyssinia, and the beautiful Circassian
girl, sold by her parents to avoid poverty and misery.
Except to the Christian slave, the Turk is not in practice
a cruel master, though his power is almost absolute. It
is said that other Europeans, residing in Turkey, are invariably more cruel masters than the Turks themselves.
Young and promising boys are frequently purchased by
the sovereign, to be reared and educated for officers of
state; and the Circassian beauties usually find a home
in the harem of a wealthy proprietor. The right of redemption, too, is strictly enjoined by the Koran; for all
slaves who properly conduct themselves, a writing is

---

[1] In this description of Russian serfdom, I have followed, chiefly, the
work of Germain de Ligny, "The Knout and the Russians," Art. viii,
"Slavery."

given to them fixing their value, and when the sum is tendered, the master is bound to accept it.[1]

A few remarks as to the condition of the peasantry at the present time, will properly close our view of slavery on the continent of Europe. Except in Turkey and Russia, slavery in name does not exist at this day. In these we have already noticed the present condition of the servile classes. It is due to the Emperor Nicholas of Russia to say, that he emancipated many of his serfs, as an experiment to test the success of freedom granted to them. The present Emperor is seeking to extend the experiment. Without a radical change in the constitution of the state, offering greater inducements for effort on the part of the people; and perhaps also a change still more difficult to produce, that of the character of the serf himself, no bright hopes need be cherished of any material improvement in the condition of Russian slavery.

In Hungary and Transylvania, the serfs rise but little above a state of slavery. *Involuntary* and *vile* personal services to their lords are still enforced; corporal punishment, at the will of the lord, is still allowed in the latter country, and existed in the former till the year 1835. The Urbarium of Maria Theresa, the Magna Charta of the peasantry, with all its boasted reform, did not elevate them to the position of *base* villanage in England.[2]

While slavery in name is extinct, slavery in fact exists on the continent, and must continue to exist, until enlightenment shall have driven intellectual darkness from the earth, and religion shall have changed so completely the heart of man, that every one shall be con-

---

[1] See Stephens's Travels in Greece, Turkey, &c., vol. i, ch. xiii; Copley's Hist. of Slavery, p. 92. For description of slave-market, see Byron's Don Juan, Canto iv and v.

[2] For an interesting and graphic view of the peasantry of Hungary and Transylvania, see Paget's work, i, 178, et seq.; ii, 143, et seq.

tented to occupy that sphere for which his nature fits
him.

The labor performed by the lower classes, is servile
labor.   In name, it is *voluntary*, in reality, it is *involuntary*, forced by a master more relentless than their feudal
lords,—stern necessity.   The female slavery described
by Professor Silliman in his Second Visit to Europe, as
witnessed by himself in Saxony,[1] had no parallel among
the ancient Germans, whose slavery we have been examining.   When population becomes dense, and the numbers depending upon their labor for their food increase,
the price of labor can have but one standard, to which
it of necessity comes : that is, the smallest possible
amount upon which the laborer can feed and clothe himself and such of his family as are absolutely helpless.
Another result is, that, as the price of labor decreases,
the age at which the child shall be considered capable
to toil for his own support correspondingly decreases ;
and the age at which the old shall be considered exempt
from labor, in the same ratio increases.   Necessity, too,
forces the laborer to submit to an amount of labor to
which his physical frame is incompetent, and hence, laws
are necessary to protect him from such exactions.   Another result is, that, despairing of an honest support, or
yielding to natural indolence, the number of paupers
frightfully increases, and with it the number of thefts
and offences of that character.   Michaelis, a learned
German writer, after considering the question, " whether
it be better to have slavery or not?" sums up thus : " To
strike a balance, then, between the advantages and dis-
advantages of slavery, is a difficult matter ; but upon
the whole, when I consider the severity of our numerous
capital condemnations for thefts, and our insecurity after
all against its artifices; when I consider that the punishment of our culprits only serves to make them a burden

[1] Vol. ii, p. 341.

to our neighbors, who in return land theirs upon us, and
that it thus becomes a sort of nursery for robbers, or, at
any rate, for vagabonds and beggars, who are the pest
of every country, I am often led to think that the establishment of slavery under certain limitations would
prove a profitable plan."[1]

[1] Commentaries on the Laws of Moses, Art. cxxii; see also Silliman's
Second Visit, vol. i, p. 233; vol. ii, p. 7, 9, 11; Prime's Travels in Europe
and the East, i, 361, 394; ii, 8, 47.

# CHAPTER VIII.

A GLANCE at the history of slavery in Great Britain must suffice us.

. The ocean-bound isle has not been exempt from the common fate of the nations of the world.

Of the ancient Britons and their social system but little is known. They were a simple, rude, and warlike people; "satisfied with a frugal sustenance and avoiding the luxuries of wealth."[1] They were governed by a large number of petty chiefs or lords, by whom the people were not oppressed; "for," says an old writer, "it is a certain maxim, that though great nations may be upholden by *power*, small territories must be maintained by *justice*."[2] In fact, they seemed unusually free, for Dion, in the Life of the Emperor Severus, says, " that, in Britain, *the people* held the helm of government in their own power."[3] Their wealth consisted of cattle, and they might almost be termed a nomadic race, their towns consisting of mere huts, temporary in their structure and occupation.[4] Among such a people it is more than probable slavery, if it existed at all, was mild, and similar to that of the Jewish patriarchs.

The Romans, with their invasion, introduced their system of slavery. Many of the conquered Britons were

[1] Diodorus, Lib. V, p. 301.
[2] Discourse on Government, by Nath'l Bacon, p. 2.
[3] Cited by Bacon, as above.
[4] Turner's Anglo-Saxons, Bk. I, ch. v, pp. 63, 64.

exposed in the slave-market of Rome.[1]  The rule of the Saxons did not change the social system of Britain in this respect.  Among no people were the orders or classes more distinctly divided.  The *edhiling*, or nobility; the *frilingi*, or freed slaves; and the *lazzi*, or slaves, were among their earliest distinctions.[2]  The slaves are mentioned by other names, in the ancient laws, such as *theow*, *thræl*, *men*, and *esne*.[3]  There were great numbers of these slaves, being a large majority of the population. Single individuals owned large numbers.  Alcuin, an Anglo-Saxon abbot, had ten thousand.

The usual sources of slavery were recognized among the Saxon laws.  Birth, sale, captivity in war, the penalty for crime, are all mentioned as legitimate sources of slavery.  From the laws of Henry I, it would appear that a great variety of causes of slavery were recognized at that time : "Servi alii naturâ, alii facto, et alii empcione, et alii redempcione, alii, suâ vel alterius dacione servi, et si qui sunt aliæ species hujusmodi."  He reduced them all to two, "servi, alii casu, alii geniturâ."[4]

The condition of the Saxon slave was that of pure slavery.  His very existence was merged in the master, so that the maxim of their law was, "omne damnum quod servus fecerit, dominus emendet."  The master could inflict corporal punishment *ad libitum;* and while their laws prescribed the "*wegreaf*," or "*weregild*," of a *theow*, when slain by a stranger, no punishment was affixed for his homicide by his master.[5]  He was the

[1] They were considered, in Rome, as stupid.  Thus Cicero, speaking of the captive Britons, "Ex quibus nullos puto te literis aut musicis eruditos expectare."  Ad Art. Lib. IV, 16.

[2] Turner's Anglo-Saxons, Bk. VII, ch. ix; Nithard's Hist. Lib. IV. From lazzi, comes the English word lazy, so often applied to servants. See Rees's Cyclopædia, "Lazzi."

[3] Turner, as above; Ancient Laws and Institutes of England, *passim.*

[4] Leg. Hen. I, § 76.

[5] Laws of Kings Hlothheare and Eadric, § 1, and note thereto.  Wihtr. ch. xxiii.  The slayer of a slave, by the law of Aethelbert, paid three

subject of sale and of gift. Some of the later kings
forbade the sale of a Christian slave to be sent beyond
the realm.[1] He could not appear in court except through
his lord; nor was he allowed his oath, that privilege
being one of the characteristics of a freeman.[2] The
slaves were conveyed both by deed and by will, and in
juxtaposition with cattle and other personalty.[3] Branding was a common punishment with them; and it would
seem, from one expression, that they were sometimes
yoked: "Let every man know his teams of men, of
horses, and oxen."[4]

It is very certain that the slaves wore around their
necks brazen collars, having their own and their masters'
names inscribed thereon.[5]

The freedmen were allowed, by the laws of Alfred, as
holidays, "xii days at Yule (Christmas), and the day on
which Christ overcame the Devil, and the commemora-
tion day of St. Gregory, vii days before and vii days
after; one day at St. Peter's tide and St. Paul's; and in
harvest, the whole week before St. Mary mass; and one
day at the celebration of All-Hallows, and the iv Wed-
nesdays in the iv Ember weeks. To all *theow* men be
given to those to whom it may be most desirable to give,

shillings. By the law of Ethelred, the slayer paid one pound. By the
same law, the slayer of a freeman paid thirty pounds. Laws of Ethelred,
ii, § 5. See also Bacon's Discourse, 35. Alfred procured the passage
of the Jewish law, as to the homicide of a slave, or the maiming by loss
of eyes or teeth, by the master. Laws, § 17.

[1] Laws of King Cnut (secular), § 3. Laws of Etheldred, viii, § 5,
which adds, "Si quis hoc presumat, sit præter benedictionem Dei, et
omnium sanctorum, et præter omnem Christianitatem, nisi pœniteat et
emendet, sicut episcopus suus edocebit." Laws of William the Conqueror, § 41.                         [2] Laws of King Withraed, §§ 22, 23.

[3] Some curious instances are collected in Turner's Anglo-Sax., Bk. VII,
ch. ix.                            [4] Wilk. Leg. Sax. p. 47.

[5] In Ivanhoe, ch. i, Sir Walter Scott introduces a slave, with his collar
on his neck, with the inscription—"Gurth, the son of Beowulph, is the
born thrall of Cedric, of Rotherwood."

whatever any man shall give them in God's name, or they, at any of their moments, may deserve."[1]

The working of slaves on the Sabbath, however, was expressly forbidden, and the penalty therefor was the freedom of the slave. If a freedman worked on that day, without his lord's command, he forfeited his freedom. If a slave worked on that day, without his lord's command, "let him suffer on his hide."[2]

The harborer of a fugitive slave was required to pay the owner the value of the slave.[3] The slaves themselves were not allowed admittance into sacred orders, "ante legitimam libertatem."[4]

The written contracts of that day, which have been preserved, enable us to give accurately the prices of slaves. A half pound was the average price.[5] They were purchased for exportation, until that was forbidden; and Henry states, that at Bristol a brisk slave-trade was carried on, in purchasing Englishmen and exporting them to Ireland for sale.[6] And William of Malmsbury states, that it seems to be a natural custom with the people of Northumberland, to sell their nearest relations.[7]

It would seem, from the fact that slaves purchased their freedom sometimes, that the indulgence of masters allowed them something similar to the Roman *peculium*. Theft appears to have been a common offence with them, and the master was made responsible therefor, unless he showed, by his oath and compurgators, that it was done without his command. In the event of their committing homicide, they were required to be delivered to the avengers of blood; and for other offences, branding was

---

[1] Laws of King Alfred, ch. xliii.          [2] Dooms of King Ina, § 3.
[3] Laws of King Ina, § 30.          [4] Laws of Henry I, ch. lxviii.
[5] Turner has collected several; Bk. VII, ch. ix.
[6] Hist. vol. iv, p. 238; Barrington on Statutes, 274; Bancroft's United States, i, 162.
[7] Lib. I, ch. iii; consult also Strabo, Lib. IV, p. 199 (ed. Paris, 1620).

a common punishment.[1]  We have already mentioned
the punishment for the homicide of a slave.  The rape
of a female slave was also punished by a fine.[2]

Manumission *at the altar*, is mentioned as early as the
laws of King Wihtraed (about the year 700), as an existing and established custom.[3]  The laws of William the
Conqueror prescribe other modes of manumission, evidently borrowed from the continent, viz., the declaration
of freedom before the County Court, the "ostendens ei
liberas vias et portas," the giving to him of the arms of
a freeman, a lance and a sword.[4]  The laws of Henry I
are very full in prescribing additional modes of effecting
manumission.[5]

The records of ancient wills exhibit a number of cases
of emancipation by will.  The causes operating upon
the testator were usually gratitude and benevolence.
One instance is given of two Irishmen who were freed
for the sake of an abbot's soul.[6]

The effect of manumission was simply to release the
slave from the bondage of the master.  It did not place
him upon the footing of a free citizen.  "Thus," says
Bacon, "though they had escaped the depth of bondage,
yet attained they not to the full pitch of freemen; for
the lord might acquit his own title of bondage, but no
man could be made *free* without the act of the whole
body.  And therefore the historian (Tacitus) saith, that
they are not *multum supra servos*, or scarce not servants.
. . . . Those are, nowadays, amongst the number and
rank of such as are called *copyholders*, who have the privilege of *protection* from the laws, but no privilege of
*vote* in the making of laws."[7]

---

[1] Laws of King Ina, ch. lxxiv; Laws of King Aethelstan, Ordinance
3; Laws of King Ethelred, ch. ii; Laws of King Cnut, ch. xxxii.

[2] Laws of King Alfred, ch. xxv.

[3] Ibid. ch. viii.          [4] Ibid. ch. xv.          [5] Ibid. ch. lxxviii.

[6] See Turner, Bk. VII, ch. ix.

[7] Discourse of the Laws and Government of England, by Nath'l Bacon
(1739), p. 35; see also Glanville, Lib. V, ch. v.

The Christian religion, and other causes, combined both to promote manumission and to ameliorate the condition of the Saxon slaves.[1] King Alfred procured the adoption of the Jewish law, that whosoever bought a Christian slave, the time of his servitude should be limited to six years, and on the seventh he should go free, with his wife, if he brought her with him. But if the master had given him a wife, she and her children remained. If he chose to continue a slave he might do so.[2] So Edward the Confessor ordained: "That the lords should so demean themselves towards their men, that they neither incur guilt against God, nor offence against the king: or which is all one, to respect them as God's people and the king's subjects."[3]

The invasion of the Normans had considerable effect upon the Saxon slavery. The followers of the Conqueror were accustomed to the feudal system. In accordance with it, they reduced to a state of vassalage, indiscriminately, both masters and men.[4] The most ruinous oppressions were resorted to, to extort the last cent, from which "neither the poor man's poverty, nor the rich man's abundance, protected them."[5] The very existence of a common oppressor, and of a common hatred, produced a feeling of kindness and sympathy, lessening the distance between the master and his villain. When the fruits of the slave's industry were taken from the master by oppressive taxation, and the slave ceased therefore to be valuable, the lord either manumitted him, or by disuse lost his absolute control. Thus by degrees villan-

[1] Edwards's Ecclesiastical Jurisdiction, § 37.

[2] Wilk. Leg. Sax. 29; Alfred, in his will, "In the name of the living God," forbade his heirs to invade the liberty of those men whom he had set free. Edwards's Ec. Jur. § 55.

[3] Bacon's Discourse, as above.

[4] Fitzherbert gives this account of it; see Bar. on Statutes, 307; see Black. Comm. Bk. II, p. 92.

[5] William of Malmsbury, Bk. IV, ch. i. Roger of Wendover's Chronicle, A.D. 1085.

age, with its acknowledged rights to the villain, was substituted for the ancient Saxon slavery.

Pure or base villanage, however, was only a modified slavery. Their service was uncertain, and entirely within the discretion of the lord. They were liable to corporal chastisement and imprisonment.[1] They were incapable of acquiring property, except by the lord's permission; the rule of law being "quicquid acquiritur servo, acquiritur domino." They could not purchase their own liberty, because, says Glanville, "omnia catalla nativi intelliguntur esse in potestate domini sui."[2] They could be sold and transferred, if *vileins in gross*, ad libitum; if *vileins regardant*, with the land. They descended as chattels real to the heir, and their condition was transmitted to their posterity; the *status* of the father determining their condition, contrary to the rule of the civil law.[3] They could not be heard as witnesses or suitors against their lord; nor were they allowed their oath in any case, the privilege of being sworn being the privilege of a freeman.[4] If the villain ran away, or was purloined from the lord, he might be retaken or re-

[1] The Stat. of 1 Rich. II, recites, that the villeyns had assembled riotously, and endeavored to withdraw their services from their lords; not only those by which they held their lands, but likewise the services of their body; and provides for their imprisonment at the will of the lord, without bail or mainprise. Barrington on Stat. 299. This oppression was the occasion of the insurrection under Wat Tyler and Jack Straw. Ib. 300.

[2] Lib. V, ch. 5. Bracton describes a villain as one, "ubi scire non poterit vespere quale servitium fieri debet mane." Lib. IV, fol. 208.

[3] Glanville, Lib. V, ch. vi; Bracton, fol. 4; Fleta, Lib. I, ch. iii; and The Mirror, ch. ii, sect. 28; all declare that the villanage of either parent makes the issue bond.

[4] Black. Comm. Bk. II, p. 93; Glanville, Bk. V, ch. v. Some of the rights exercised by the lord are hardly to be credited; such as the "jus laxandæ coxæ sponsarum vassallorum." The same author informs us, "In dominum peccat vassallus, si dominum cucurbitaverit, sive ejus uxore concubiverit vel etiam conatus fuerit, turpiter contrectando, vel osculando." Struvii Jur. Feud. p. 541, cited Bar. on Stat. 306, 307.

covered by action, "like beasts or other chattels."[1]  As
to persons other than the lord, the villain had some
recognized rights.  He could sue if his lord did not interfere.  'He could be executor.  He could purchase and
sell, if done before his lord took possession.[2]

The lord could not kill or maim his villain, and an
appeal of murder lay at the instance of the relatives of
a murdered serf.[3]

Base villanage gradually gave place to privileged villanage, by which the services due the lord were made
fixed and determinate, and generally payable in money.
The latter have still their relics in Britain, in the *copy-
hold* tenures.[4]  The last instance of a claim of base villanage in the courts of justice, is said to be found in the
fifteenth year of James I.[5]  Edward III, when in need
of funds, gave to a manumitted villain, John Simondson,
a general power to go through the royal manors, and
grant manumission to all the vassals thereon for a certain composition in money.  This example of the sovereign was followed by many other lords in similar need,
and to this, among other causes, may be attributed the
extinction of villanage.[6]  In 1574, we find a commission
issued by Queen Elizabeth, for inquiry into the condition
of " all her bondmen and bondwomen in the counties of
Cornwall, &c., such as were, *by blood*, in a *slavish* condition, and to compound with them for their manumission
and freedom."[7]  The benevolence and negligence of
lords, and the unfruitfulness of villain services (especially

---

[1] Black. Comm. Bk. II, p. 93.

[2] Co. Lit. Bk. II, ch. xiii.                                    [3] Ibid.

[4] So says Coke and Blackstone, Comm. Bk. II, 96.  But Lord Lough-
borough questions the correctness of this opinion as to the origin of copy-
holds. Dougl. 698.

[5] See Mr. Hargraves's argument, and Lord Mansfield's decision, in
Somersett case, 20 Howell's State Trials.

[6] Barr. on Statutes, 304, 305.

[7] Rymer, quoted in Barr. on Stat. 308.

when confined to the land), may be added as principal causes of the gradual extinction of villanage. It is true, however, in Britain as on the Continent, that the religious houses were the last to grant freedom to their villains.[1]

About the middle of the fourteenth century we find the first of a number of statutes passed by Parliament, the object of which was to compel laborers and servants to work at reasonable wages, and also to regulate their diet, their apparel, and their games.[2] Other acts gave to the justices of the peace the power to rate wages, and fix prices of work.[3] When the employers ceased to be dependent on laborers, and the provision as to justices rating wages, would work beneficially to the laborer, Parliament repealed the act; and when, in 1824, the Arbitration Act was passed, a provision was inserted, prohibiting the justices from establishing wages, without the consent of both master and workmen.[4]

In Scotland, the colliers, coalbearers, and salters continued in a state of actual personal bondage to a much later period than we find villains in gross in England. In fact, freedom was not acquired by them till the passage of the Act of 39 Geo. 3, c. 56. Nearly a quarter of

[1] Black. Comm. Bk. II, 95, 96; Barr. on Stat. 309; Sir Thom. Smith, Comm. Bk. III, ch. x.

[2] The curious will be amused with some of these provisions. "No servant nor common laborer shall wear, nor suffer their wives to wear in their clothing, any cloth, whereof the broad yard shall pass the price of two shillings. Nor shall they suffer their wives to wear any veile or kercheffe, whose price exceedeth twenty pence; nor any hosen, whereof the paire shall pass eighteen pence." No valet, or under that degree, "shall use, nor wear in array for his body, any bolsters, nor stuffs of cotton, wool, or cadas, nor other stuffing in his parer point," &c. &c. 3 Edw. IV, c. v; 22 Edw. IV, c. i. Sampson on Codes and Common Law, pp. 131, 132, 133; Smith on Master and Servant, Introd. p. 29, &c.

[3] 5 Eliz. c. iv; 29 Geo. 2, c. xxxiii; 20 Geo. 2, c. xix.

[4] Smith on Master and Servant, Introd. p. 30.

a century before that time an act was passed for the same purpose, but was disregarded by those for whose benefit it was intended.[1]   In fact, they esteemed the interest taken in their freedom, to be a mere device on the part of the proprietors to get rid of what they called head or harigald money, payable to them when a female, by bearing a child, added to the live stock of their master's property.[2]

The villains in Ireland were termed *Betaghii* or *Tœagua*.[3]   The Irish do not seem ever to have been fond of slaveholding.[4]   Their early slaves were Englishmen, all of whom, in 1172, they emancipated by a decree of a national synod.[5]   Their subsequent history has been a succession of efforts to rid themselves of political bondage.

The present condition of the laboring classes in Great Britain differs from personal bondage chiefly in the name. Necessity and hunger are more relentless masters than the old Saxon lords.   The power of life and death, and the use of corporal chastisement are the mere attendants of slavery; neither are necessary to constitute perfect bondage.[6]   When the time and labor of one person are by any means not purely voluntary, the property of an other, the former is a slave and the latter is a master.   And it makes no change in their condition, whether the food and clothing of the laborer be furnished him from the obligation to support and clothe

[1] Hargraves's argument, Somersett case, 20 Howell's State Trials; Smith on Master and Servant, Int. xxviii, note 2.

[2] See note to Red Gauntlet, ch. xxi, p. 265 (Abbotsford edition).

[3] Hence the Irish term of reproach, *Teague.*   Barr. on Stat. 303, 306.

[4] Fancy might suggest as the reason for this, the fact that St. Patrick was himself sold, by his father, into slavery, to a Scotchman, whom he served as a swineherd; see Roger of Wendover's Chronicle, A.D. 491.

[5] Copley, on Slavery, 82.

[6] Yet the most cruel corporal punishment is used in the English mines. See Cobden's White Slaves of England, 33, 34.

one's property, or from the scanty return of nominal wages.

As to food, clothing, residences, and the amount and character of the labor required, the working classes of Britain compare unfavorably with many slaveholding countries.[1] The earnings of the agricultural peasant will barely furnish a support, when he is in health and employment. When out of employment or diseased, he becomes necessarily a pauper. The parliamentary reports give a view of wretchedness, destitution, ignorance and cruelty, in connection with the men, women, and children, engaged in the English mines, which from any less reliable source would be incredible.

From the same reliable evidence we are informed of degradation, poverty, and cruel oppression under which the poor laborers, of every age and sex, groan and exist in the factories and workshops of the United Kingdom. The use of the lash is no uncommon resort of the bosses, and the fear of starvation bars up the door of justice.

The menial and liveried servants of Britain share a fate not much superior. Actual, corporal cruelty is not so frequent, and detection and punishment more certain; yet, the abject submission required, and the contemptuous treatment received, break the spirit of the slave, and give food to the insolence of the master.

A prominent evil to which the poor of Britain are subjected, is their miserable homes. Crowded into a single

---

[1] Says M. De Beaumont, "J'ai vu l'Indien dans ses forêts; j'ai vu le noir dans l'esclavage, mais je n'ai vu aucune misère qui puisse être comparée à celle de l'Irlandais." Quoted by M. Levavasseur, who adds, "Nous avons vu à Dublin même des hommes qu'on eut pris pour des spectres, et à leur approche nous détournions involontairement les regards, car ils avaient l'aspect du cadavre." Esclavage de la race noire, pp. 40, 41. Carlyle compares the condition of the Saxon slave with the modern peasant; and, aft showing its preferableness, concludes, "Liberty, I am told, is a divi thing. Liberty, when it becomes the liberty to die by starvation, is not so divine." Past and Present, Bk. III, ch xiii.

room, of all sexes and ages, filth, disease, vice, and crime, are the inevitable consequences. To this, add a degree of ignorance appalling, in so old and civilized a nation; and the result is not astonishing that so many of the children should be thieves, and the women prostitutes, and the men paupers.[1]

The Parliament of Great Britain, at the instance of great and good men, have not been backward in striving, by legislation, to stay the oppressor's hand; to give air and light, and food and clothing to the caged children; to encourage all improvement in the lodging-houses for the poor; in fact, to remedy every evil within the reach of their legislation, without giving too violent a shock to the great agricultural, mechanical, and commercial interests. Nor has the philanthropy of England been exclusively extended abroad. Private and associated charity have done much to relieve suffering humanity. Yet after all that charity enlightened by religion, and legislation guided by humanity, can do, the picture we have drawn is not overcolored, when applied to the actual condition of many of their poor. How these evils shall be remedied is a problem yet unsolved, and to-day taxing the thoughts and burdening the hearts of the wise and good of the land.

---

[1] In addition to the Reports to Parliament, I have relied upon the following authorities: Mayhew's London Labor and London Poor; Cobden's White Slaves of England; Dickens's Household Words, ix, 398; Silliman's Second Visit to Europe, i, 31; Dr. Durbin's Observations in Europe, ii, 120, 170, 171, ch. xii, at large; The Glory and Shame of England; Prime's Travels in Europe and the East, i, 149, 173, 182; Chartism, by Thomas Carlyle.

# CHAPTER IX.

## NEGRO SLAVERY AND THE SLAVE-TRADE.

WE cannot go back to the origin of negro slavery.[1] We have seen that the earliest authentic histories and monuments exhibit the negro in a state of bondage.[2] From that time to the present he has in greater or less numbers ever been a slave. Whether this condition is the curse on Canaan, the son of Ham, as many religiously believe, and plausibly argue, it is not our province to decide. The investigation would lead us into tempting but too extensive fields for our purpose. The fact exists undeniably, be the cause what it may. Nor is it our purpose to describe the oppressive slavery to which the negro is subjected in his own land and at the hand of his fellows. Both master and slave being barbarians, we could expect to find only the most savage and cruel forms of slavery. The ingenuity of an enlightened intellect could scarcely, by effort, devise the numerous and skilful and horrid cruelties of these barbarian masters.[3]

[1] Herodotus, the oldest Greek historian, commemorates the traffic in slaves, Lib. IV, c. clxxxi.

[2] "We have effigies of negroes, drawn by six different nations of antiquity: Egyptians, Assyrians, Persians, Greeks, Etruscans, and Romans, from about the eighteenth century before Christ, to the first centuries of our own era." See Indigenous Races of Man, 190.

[3] To those disposed to pursue this inquiry, the following works will give most ample information: Travels of Park, Clapperton, Saunders, and others, *passim;* Capt. Canot, or, Twenty Years of an African Slaver; Bayard Taylor's Journey into Central Africa; Buxton's Slave-Trade and its Remedy, Pt. I, ch. iv; Edwards's West Indies, vol. ii, ch. xvii.

In the ecclesiastical annals of Ortiz de Zuniga it is mentioned, that a traffic in negro slaves to the city of Seville existed as early as A.D. 1399. There certainly were large numbers in Seville at the time he wrote (1474); but the former statement seems doubtful. In 1442, some Moors who had been captured by the Portuguese, proposed to purchase their liberty by a ransom of negro slaves. Prince Henry of Portugal instructed Gonsalvez to accept the ransom, for whatever negroes he should get "he would gain souls, because they might be converted to the faith, which could not be managed with the Moors."[1] Ten negro slaves were obtained; and around this nucleus, thus commenced, either from true or pretended religious zeal, was gathered that immense trade, for which Spain, Portugal, and England, for centuries, contended, and which has since been branded as piracy by almost every civilized nation of the world.

The horrors of the trade seem to have commenced with its beginning, and there were generous hearts to weep over them then, as there were in after years. The good chronicler, Azurara, thus opens his description of a division of captive slaves, in the year 1444: " O thou heavenly Father! I implore thee that my tears may not condemn my conscience, for not its law but our common humanity constrains my humanity to lament piteously the sufferings of these people." The good man, after describing the scene, thus concludes, " And I, who have made this history, have seen in the town of Lagos, young men and young women, the sons and grandsons of those very captives born in this land, as good and as true Christians as if they had lineally descended since the commencement of the law of Christ, from those who were first baptized."[2]

[1] The Conquerors of the New World and their Bondsmen, i, 28, 29 ; Edwards's West Indies, ii, c. xv.  La traite et son origine, par M. Schœlcher.
[2] The Conquerors, &c. i, 33, 36.

The success of the first expeditions encouraged the Portuguese, and they sent out, in successive years, numerous expeditions, each with instructions "to convert the natives to the faith." This, and discovery, were the paramount objects with the early Portuguese expeditions. The slaves obtained by them, were in exchange for merchandise with slave-dealers, who brought them from the interior; and until the discovery and colonization of America, there was no market for the slaves sufficient to excite the covetousness and other evil passions of men.[1]

The discovery of America in 1492 was an event, the effect of which upon the civilized world can never be calculated, and perhaps is seldom fully apprehended. Upon the subject we are now considering, it was both the forcing-bed, and yet the broad field. It stimulated enterprise and discovery. It furnished a receptacle for the innumerable slaves which the African petty kings offered in exchange for the manufacture and gaudy trinkets of Europe. The demand necessarily increased the supply, and of course gave stimulus to the petty wars and marauding expeditions by which that supply was effected; and thus we might travel from cause to effect almost *ad infinitum*.

The same religious fervor which governed and controlled the action of the Portuguese, in their early conduct towards the negro slaves, seems to have been the ruling passion with the Spaniards in their discoveries in the New World. Hence, we find the pious Herrera chronicling the death of the first baptized Indian, as the pioneer of that nation in his entry into heaven.[2] The

[1] Ibid. 37 to 75. Expedition of Ca da Mosta, Astley's Voyages, i, 574. He places the exportation at seven to eight hundred per annum. But this was evidently more than the truth.

[2] Dec. I, Lib. II, cap. 5. The proclamation made by the voyagers to the Indians, is a curious picture of the notions of those times. After telling them of the creation of the world, it traced title thereto to

same spirit is breathed in all the early instructions of the
government to Columbus.   The prime object is to bring
all the dwellers in the Indies to a knowledge of the
sacred Catholic faith, and to that end he is charged to
deal *lovingly* with the Indians.[1]   The Admiral, fully ap-
preciating his instructions, in 1494, sent home some
Indians, "as slaves, to be taught Castilian, and to serve
afterwards as interpreters, so that the work of conversion
may go on."[2]   It was not a difficult task for the Spaniards
to convince themselves, that in enslaving the Indians
they were doing God's service; and hence, we find their
captives first, and afterwards the unoffending neighboring natives,[3] by thousands, reduced to the most abject
slavery.   The fields and the mines of their conquerors
were soon filled to overflowing with these easily acquired
laborers; and so different a life was this from the indolent habits of a people, whose generous land had ever
supplied their scanty wants without toil or care, that it
is not strange that we should hear piteous tales of their
sufferings under their new masters.   It would be aside
from our subject to give a minute detailed account of

St. Peter, and thence to the reigning Pope.   It then recited the grant of
the Indies, by the Pope, to the sovereigns of Castile; and after urging
the Indians to acknowledge their fealty to these sovereigns, it threatened
them with war and slavery if they refused.   The historian adds: "We may
fancy what ideas the reading of the document conveyed to a number of
Indians sitting in a circle, squatting on their hams."   The Conquerors, &c.,
vol. ii, 117.

The question of the legality of the Indian enslavement was frequently
discussed in Spain, and submitted by the King to both learned lawyers
and divines.   Their various opinions, and the reasons given for them,
are curious and amusing.   See Conquerors of the New World and their
Bondsmen, vol. i, passim.

[1] The Conquerors, &c., i, pp. 118, 119.                    [2] Ibid. 121.

[3] Isabella seems, at first, to have been much horrified at the enslavement of Indians not captives in war, and has been much applauded for
proclamations she caused to be made, ordering.all such to be restored to
freedom.   Herrera, Dec. I, Lib. IV, cap. vii; quoted in The Conquerors,
&c., i, 155.                    •

these sufferings. Suffice it to say, that they broke the spirit of a people so long accustomed to freedom, and constitutionally so little qualified for slavery, and that they sickened and died under the restraint. The race dwindled away, both in physical capacity and numbers, and the fact was soon demonstrated, that though morally heathen, and intellectually the inferior race, still the Indian was not by nature qualified and capacitated for bondage. It was this fact, and the observation of these sufferings, which induced the good Las Casas, the early friend of the red man, to remonstrate with his government against this system, and to urge the importation of negroes, accustomed in their native land to a state of bondage, and whose physical and intellectual development improved while in slavery. The wisdom and the piety of the good man have both been severely censured for this advice, by which, it is said, he enfranchised one race by enslaving another. But the subsequent history of the races, and the observation of the world, will eventually vindicate both his far-seeing wisdom and his broad benevolence.[1]

The first mention made of negroes carried to the New World, we find in the instructions given by the Spanish court to Ovando, in the year 1501, by which negro slaves, "born in the power of Christians," were allowed to be sent to the Indies.[2] In 1510 and 1511, we find frequent mention of negro slaves sent by the mother country, although the numbers did not increase very fast up to the

---

[1] Las Casas, though much censured, was not alone in his recommendation of this policy. Herrera says, "This project was rather that of the Cardinal Tortosa." Dec. II, Liv. II, ch. xx. This cardinal afterwards occupied the Holy See, as Adrian V. In 1516, a proposition similar to that of Las Casas, was made by the Three Fathers of the Order of St. Jerome. So also the orders of Ferdinand, dated in 1512 and 1513, refer to representations of like import, from the Franciscan friars. La traite et son origine; Colonies Etrangères, par M. Schœlcher, i, 373.

[2] The Conquerors, &c., i, 170; Irving's Columbus, Bk. XIV, ch. iii.

death of Ferdinand, in 1516.  The last notice we have
of this trade during his reign, was a reply of his to a
request from the Bishop of Conception, in Hispaniola,
for more negro slaves, in which he says, that there are
already many negroes, and it may bring inconvenience
if more male negroes should be introduced into the
island.[1]  It would seem from this, that up to that time
none but grown males had been sent over; and it is true,
that up to his death no private enterprise was engaged
in this traffic.  All the negroes were sent by order of the
government.[2]  To his successor, Charles V, it was left to
grant the first license to De Bresa, one of his Flemish
favorites, for the importation of negroes into the West
Indies.  This license or patent was sold to some Genoese
merchants for 25,000 ducats, and here may be properly
dated the commencement of the slave-trade proper.[3]

By this time, the Indian population of Hispaniola had
decreased from 3,000,000, the number at the date of its
discovery, according to Las Casas, and 1,130,000, according to Tuazo, to about ten to twelve thousand.  Such
mortality is almost incredible.[4]  The result, however,
was a still more urgent cry for negro laborers.  From
the governors, the priests, and the people, one united

[1] The Conquerors, &c., vol. ii, 214, 215.

[2] Bancroft states the opposite, and says, "Herrera is explicit."  I have
not access to this book.  Irving, who wrote from the same sources, viz.,
the MS. of Las Casas, from which Herrera compiled this portion of his
work, gives a synopsis of the ordinances of Ferdinand, which agree with
the text; see Irving's Columbus, Appendix, No. 28; Bancroft's United
States, i, 170.

[3] Ibid. 230, 231; Robertson's America, i, 163 (Harper's Ed.); Irving's
Columbus, as above.

[4] Ibid. ii, 206, 207.  We are told that whole villages of Indians committed suicide, to escape this bondage.  Some villages invited others to
join them in the dreadful work (198, 199).  The free Indians had no
better fate.  Wishing to starve out the Spaniards, they agreed to plant
no crops for a year.  The result was, numbers of them died of starvation (vol. i, 137, 138).  Prescott's Ferdinand and Isabella, Pt. II, c. xxvi,
and the authorities referred to by him.

voice demanded negro slaves. The Genoese merchants who had purchased the patent, sent over cargoes of slaves, but the prices were so high that the people refused to purchase. Las Casas and the Jeronimite priests, whose business it was to protect the Indians remaining from oppression, joined in suggesting to the King to pay back to the Genoese merchants their 25,000 ducats, and allow the free importation of negroes by the Spaniards, paying De Bresa the custom duties.[1] So great was the demand for labor at this time, that the colonists fitted out vessels to cruise on the coast of the mainland, and by traffic and by force made slaves of the Indians, whom they took back to Hispaniola.[2]

The superiority of negroes as slaves over Indians was early demonstrated by the Spaniards. Vasco Nunez, wishing to explore the sea beyond the Isthmus, cut his wood and prepared his timbers for four brigantines on the Atlantic side, and thence carried them across the Isthmus until he reached the waters flowing into the Pacific. In this work he employed numerous Indians, thirty negroes, and a few Spaniards. Five hundred Indians perished in executing this terrible labor. Not a single negro died.[3] "The Africans,' says Herrera, "prospered so much in the island of Hispaniola, that it was the opinion, unless a negro should happen to be hanged, he would never die; for, as yet, none had been known to perish from infirmity. Like oranges, they found their proper soil in Hispaniola, and it seemed even more na-

---

[1] Ibid. ii, 268, 270, 271, 273. This was very different from the remonstrance of Ovando, in 1503, at the number of negroes in the colony. Irving's Columbus, Appendix, No. 28, p. 418.

[2] Robertson's America, i, 167, 168. It appears that there was slavery among the Indians on the Continent, along the present coast of Mexico and Central America; as we find slaves among the subjects of their sacrifices, and also presents of slaves to the early explorers. The Conquerors, &c., ii, 8, 73.

[3] The Conquerors, &c., vol. i, 150, 151.

tural to them than their native Guinea."[1] An ordinance of the Spanish Court, in 1511, gives the secret of the slave-trade, wherein it was decreed that " a large number of negroes should be transported to the colonies, because *one negro does more work than four Indians.*"[2]

Cardinal Ximenes has received undeserved praise for his opposition to the patents granted by Charles V, for the furnishing of negro slaves to the Indies, the praise being based upon his supposed benevolence and spirit of justice.[3]  The reasons assigned by the historians for this opposition vary, but the more plausible one is, that his sagacity foresaw that the numbers of negroes would be greatly multiplied in a climate so favorable to their race, and that revolt would be the inevitable result.[4] This result was hastened beyond the expectation of the statesman, for as early as 1522 there was a revolt among the negroes of Hispaniola.  The number engaged in it was small, and their punishment exemplary, and their example was not followed for many years.[5]  This revolt was doubtless the effect of cruel treatment; yet, we must admit that while the Spaniards were brutal in their conduct, both to the Indians and the negroes, yet their government, as exhibited through their ordinances and instructions, was ever anxious to mitigate these evils, having the care of souls and the conversion of the heathen as the paramount objects, and the discovery of gold as a secondary but eagerly desired consummation.  The latter object was obtained, but in the words of an elo-

---

[1] Hist. Ind. Lib. II, Dec. III, c. iv.

[2] La traite et son origine, par M. Schœlcher; found in Colonies Etran-gères, i, 369.

[3] Robertson's America, i, 163; Copley, on Slavery, 3.

[4] Irving's Columbus, Appendix, No. 28, p. 418; The Conquerors, &c., ii, 231, et not.; Colonies Etrangères, par M. Schœlcher, i, p. 367; Histoire du Cardinal Ximenes, par Marsollier, Liv. VI.

[5] Irving's Columbus, App. No. 2, p. 303; Herrera, Dec. III, Liv. IV, ch. ix.  He mentions a previous attempt in 1518.  Dec. II, Liv. III, ch. xiv.

quent historian, "the nation, like the Phrygian monarch who turned all he touched to gold, cursed by the very consummation of its wishes, was poor in the midst of its treasures."[1]

No religious zeal prompted the English nation in their participation in the African slave-trade. In 1553, we are informed by Hakluyt, twenty-four negro slaves were brought to England from the coast of Africa. The virtuous indignation of the people seems not to have been aroused, but the slaves were quietly sold as in other markets. The introduction of negro slaves into that country continued without question as to its legality, until the trial of the celebrated Somersett case, in 1771, when it was discovered that even as far back as the eleventh year of Elizabeth's reign, in the case of the Russian slave, it had been solemnly adjudged that the air of England was *too pure for a slave to breathe in*. And yet strange to say, in 1 Edward VI, c. iii, certain vagabonds and idle servants were by Parliament declared to be *slaves* to their masters; and still stranger, while the Russian slave was thus enjoying the pure air of England, the virtuous Elizabeth was sharing the profits and participating in the crimes of the African slave-trade.[2]

Sir John Hawkins has the unenviable distinction of being the first English captain of a slave-ship, about the year 1562. His first cargo, landed in Hispaniola, yielded a rich return in the tropical production with which his ships returned laden to England. The news of his success attracted the notice of the reigning sovereign Eliza-

---

[1] Prescott's Ferdinand and Isabella, Pt. II, ch. xxvi.

[2] Barrington, on Statutes, 312, and N. S. The present philanthropists of Britain are greatly horrified at the advertisements in American newspapers, carefully collated by American abolitionists. To such we commend the files of old English journals, in the British Museum; where they will find negro runaways and negro sales advertised, with as much naïveté as their virtuous ancestors could assume. See London Quarterly Review, 1855, Art. Advertising.

beth, and in the subsequent expeditions of this most heartless manstealer, she was a partner and protector. The account given by an eye-witness of one of these expeditions, exhibits an amount of brutal atrocity and heartless cruelty but seldom equalled and never surpassed in the subsequent history of the slave-trade.[1] During the reign of James I (1618), a charter was granted to Sir Robert Rich and his associates, merchants of London, for the exclusive privilege of carrying on the slave-trade from the coast of Guinea. A second charter was granted to a company during the reign of Charles I (1631), and so extensive were their operations, that at vast expense they erected numerous forts and warehouses on the coast of the West Indies for the defence of their commerce. During the reign of Charles H (1662), a third company with exclusive privileges was chartered. The Duke of York, the King's brother, was at the head of this company. They engaged to furnish the West Indian colonies with three thousand slaves annually.

In 1672, the fourth and last exclusive company was chartered, under the name of the Royal African Company, including among its stockholders, the King, his brother, the Duke of York, and others of distinguished rank. This Company continued its existence until the Revolution in 1688, when Parliament abolished all exclusive charters. They continued their operations, however, seizing the ships of private traders. In 1698, the trade to the African coast was by Act of Parliament made free to all persons, upon the payment of certain duties; negroes and gold, however, were exported free of duty. This act operating hardly upon the " Royal African Company," Parliament voted them annually from 1739 to 1746, £10,000.[2]

---

[1] Edwards's West Indies, ii, 355, et seq.; Bancroft's United States, i, 173. Rev. John Newton, in his Thoughts upon the African Slave-Trade, p. 33, bears testimony to the humanity of the Portuguese traders, and to the contrary and cruel and selfish policy of the English traders.

[2] Edwards's West Indies, ii, 359–363. The magnitude of the trade

But while the monopoly of the Company was destroyed, the monopoly of British subjects in furnishing slaves to British colonies was strictly secured. Ten judges (among them Holt and Pollexfen), declared that "negroes are merchandise," and hence, within the Navigation Acts.[1]

France was not blind to the vast profits arising from the trade, nor remiss in taking measures for supplying her colonies with slaves, the source of their wealth, and also in protecting the trade with the African coast, and by proper regulations.[2]

Portuguese and French companies, at sundry times, procured *assientoes* from the Spanish government, granting to them the privilege of furnishing slaves to the Spanish colonies. At the conclusion of that granted to the Royal Guinea Company of France, in 1713, a treaty was entered into between Philip V, King of Spain, and Anne, Queen of Great Britain, by which the privilege of furnishing negro slaves to the Spanish West Indies, Buenos Ayres, and other Spanish colonies, was secured to British subjects. This treaty was to last for thirty years, within which time at least 144,000 negroes were to be imported. The Spanish sovereign reserved to himself a duty *per capita* on the negroes, and also *one-fourth* the net profits, as well as five per cent. upon the remaining *three-fourths*. He bound himself to furnish one vessel of five hundred tons burthen. Her Britannic Majesty's share of the profits is recognized by the treaty (Sec. 29), but the exact amount is not specified.[3] A distinct tribunal is established for the ascertainment and settle-

with Africa, at this time, is hardly appreciated by those who have not made it a subject of inquiry. The curious are referred to a very full table, showing the amount of merchandise sent in British vessels, from 1701 to 1787, in McPherson's Annals of Commerce, iv, 153.

[1] 3 Bancroft's United States, 414.

[2] Valin, tom. i, 411; cited in 2 Mason Rep. 420.

[3] Bancroft says one-fourth, and this seems to be the intention; vol. ii, p. 232.

ment of the shares of these high contracting parties, and
extraordinary privileges are granted for the collection
from the purchasers, of the price of the slaves.[1]  Her
Majesty, in her speech to Parliament announcing this
treaty, boasted of her success in securing to Englishmen
a new market for slaves.

Not only the fact of the making of this treaty, and of
the royal partners in the enterprise, but the contents of
the paper itself, show the sentiment of the day in relation to this subject.  The eighth section declares, that
experience has shown the prohibition to import negroes
into certain provinces to be very prejudicial to the interest of his Catholic Majesty; "it being certain that the
provinces which have not had them, endured great hard-
ships for want of having their lands and their estates
cultivated, from which arose the necessity of using all
imaginable ways of getting them, even though it were
fraudulently."

The provisions of this treaty also indicate the care
taken for the health and comfort of the slaves during
the passage.  Twelve hundred being required for Buenos
Ayres and Chili, it is provided, that four large vessels
shall be used in their transportation.  Other sanitary
regulations were prescribed.  While the trade was thus
regulated by law, the "horrors of the middle passage"
were not enacted, at least to the extent which was subsequently developed.

The non-payment to Spain of the amounts due her
under this treaty, was the principal cause of the war
declared in 1739, and ended by the peace at Aix-la-Cha-
pelle, in 1748.[2]

By various acts of Parliament, the trade in slaves was
regulated and encouraged.  As late as 23d George II
(1749–50), we find indirect encouragement given to the

[1] This treaty may be found in full, in Collection of Treaties, vol. iii,
375, London, 1782.          [2] Smollett's.Hist. Bk. II, ch. vi.

traffic, in the "Act for extending and improving the trade to Africa;" and the fact is spread upon the statute-book, that "the slave-trade is very advantageous to Great Britain." The last act regulating the trade was passed in 1788.[1]

In the meantime large numbers of negro slaves were introduced into the British Isles, and were held in sub-jection without question as to their master's title. At one time, the negro page was indispensable to the English lady on her daily walks through the city thorough-fares; and for fear "the pure air of Britain" might engender beneath his thick skull some idea of liberty, the collar, known to the Roman slave, was fastened around his neck, with the name and residence of his mistress neatly engraved thereon.[2]

The other nations of Europe did not, as we have seen, leave this profitable trade entirely in the hands of the English. The Portuguese furnished not only their West Indian colonies, but also their East Indian possessions, the latter trade being supplied from Mozambique. To insure humane treatment, they used negro seamen, and offered premiums for every slave transported safely.[3] The Dutch carried on a similar trade to their colonies, confining the privilege to their own vessels.[4] The French government, to encourage the trade, in the year 1784, gave a bounty of forty livres upon every ton of the vessels employed therein, and a premium of sixty to one hundred livres for every negro carried to their different colonies.[5]

---

[1] Anderson's Hist. of Commerce, vi, 905.

[2] See London Quarterly Review, 1855, Art. Advertising. The following is from the London Gazette, 1694: " A black boy, an Indian, about 13 years old, run away on the 8th inst., from Putney, with a collar about his neck, with this inscription, 'The Lady Bromfield's black, in Lincoln's Inn Fields.' Whoever brings him to Sir Edward Bromfield's, at Putney, shall have a guinea reward." See a similar statement in Granville Sharp's Just Limitation of Slavery, p. 34.

[3] McPherson's Annals of Commerce, iv, 164.

[4] Ibid. 165.                                    [5] Ibid.

In 1607, the first successful English colony was landed at Jamestown, in Virginia. Thirteen years thereafter (1620), a Dutch man-of-war landed twenty negro slaves for sale. This was the germ of negro slaveholding in the territory now occupied by the United States of America.[1] The Spaniards may have introduced them at an earlier day in Florida, but of this we have no certain knowledge. During the next year (1621), the cotton plant was first cultivated in the new province.[2] The negro and the cotton plant seem to be natural allies, and there was something ominous in their almost simultaneous introduction into the New World. For many years, the number of negroes in Virginia was comparatively small; the introduction of the cultivation of tobacco increased the demand, and finally impressed upon Virginia and Maryland the position of slaveholding States.

The enterprise of New England was not tardy in availing itself of the prospect for gain, held out in the cheap labor of negro slaves, and the rich returns of the slave-trade.[3] Among the "fundamentals," or body of liberties adopted in Massachusetts, as early as 1641, we find the distinct recognition of the lawfulness of Indian and negro slavery, as well as an approval of the African slave-trade.[4] The Puritans, however, insisted that the traffic should be confined to those who were captives in war and slaves in Africa. Hence, when, in 1644 or 1645, a Boston ship returned with two negroes captured by

---

[1] Beverly's Virginia, 35; 1 Bancroft's United States, 176; Cooper's Naval History, 25.

[2] 1 Bancroft, 179. The coffee-tree was introduced in the West Indies, about the beginning of the eighteenth century. There is a species of coffee indigenous to these islands, but not the one cultivated. Du Tour says, that a tree, sent by the magistrates of Amsterdam to Louis XIV, in 1714, is the parent of all those subsequently introduced into the West Indies. See Rees's Encyc. "Coffee."

[3] See Remarks of Goodall, Slavery and Anti-Slavery, p. 11. He thinks "the scent of the roses hangs round it still." [4] 1 Hild. Hist. 278.

the crew, in a pretended quarrel with the natives, the General Court ordered them to be restored to their native land.[1]  In 1754, by an official census, there appears to have been 2448 negro slaves over sixteen years of age in Massachusetts—about 1000 of them in the town of Boston.  Manumission was allowed, but only upon security that the freed negroes should not become a burden upon the parish.[2]

Connecticut was not free from the "sin of slavery." In 1650, Indians who failed to make satisfaction for injuries were ordered to be seized and delivered to the injured party, " either to serve or to be shipped out and exchanged for negroes, as the case will justly bear." Insolvent debtors also were authorized to be sold to English purchasers, and the proceeds applied to their debts. Negro slavery had been abolished in Connecticut many years before the latter provision was expunged from the statute-book.[3]  The proportion of slaves to freemen was greater in Connecticut than in Massachusetts.[4]

Rhode Island joined in the general habit of the day, with the exception of the town of Providence.  The community of the heretical Roger Williams, alone placed the services of the black and the white races on the same footing and limitation.[5]  In the plantations generally, slaves abounded to a greater extent than in any other portion of New England, and in Newport, the second commercial town of New England, there was a greater proportion of slaves than in Boston.[6]

As early as 1626, the West India Company imported negro slaves among the quiet burghers of New Amsterdam.  The city itself owned shares in a slave-ship, advanced money for its outfit, and participated in the profits.  The slaves were sold at public auction to the

---

[1] 1 Hild. 282.          [2] 2 Hild. 419.          [3] 1 Hild. 372.
[4] 2 Hild. 419.  Goodall gives some instances of cruel rigor in this State, Slavery and Anti-Slavery, pp. 11–13.  I do not vouch for him as reliable authority.          [5] 1 Hild. 373.          [6] 2 Hild. 419.

highest bidder, and the average price was less than $140. Stuyvesant was instructed to use every exertion to promote the sale of negroes. "That New York is not a slave State like Carolina," says a distinguished historian, "is due to climate and not to the superior humanity of its founders."[1] In New Netherlands, negroes were employed as agricultural laborers as well as domestics. In the city of New York, about the year 1750, the slaves constituted one-sixth of the population. The slave code differed but little from that of Virginia.[2]

New Jersey, it is known, was dismembered from New York when New Netherlands was conquered by England in 1664. In the next year, a bounty of seventy-five acres of land was offered by the proprietaries for the importation of each able-bodied slave. This was doubtless done in part to gain favor with the Duke of York, then President of the African Company.[3]

The Quakers of Pennsylvania did not entirely eschew the holding of negro slaves. It is a mooted question whether William Penn himself did or did not die a slaveholder.[4] In 1712, to a general petition for the emancipation of negro slaves by law, the response of the Legislature of Pennsylvania was, "It is neither just nor convenient to set them at liberty."[5] As early as 1699, Penn had proposed to provide by law for the marriage, religious instruction, and kind treatment of slaves, but there was no response from the legislature. Slaves, however, were never numerous in Pennsylvania, and manumissions were frequent. The larger portion were to be found in Philadelphia, one-fourth of the population of which, about the year 1750, are supposed to have been of African descent.[6]

The Swedish and German colony of Gustavus Adolphus, who formed the nucleus of the subsequent State

---

[1] 2 Bancroft, 303.    [2] 2 Hild. 419.    [3] 2 Bancroft, 316.
[4] 2 Bancroft, 401, and n. 1; 1 Stephens's Hist. of Georgia, 286.
[5] 3 Bancroft, 408.    [6] 2 Hild. 420.

of Delaware, was designed to rest on free labor; and
although negro slavery crept in among them, as early as
1688, the German friends resolved that it was not lawful
for Christians to buy or keep negro slaves.[1]  Yet slavery
retained its foothold, and to this day Delaware is ranked
among the slaveholding States.

North Carolina, from its climate and soil, became an
inviting field for slave labor, and though many of its
early settlers were Quakers, negro slavery soon obtained
a sure foothold.

In South Carolina slavery was planted simultaneously
with the colony.  Sir John Yeamans brought African
slaves with him from Barbadoes in 1671.  The climate
was congenial to the negro, while the miasma of the
swamps was fatal to the white laborer.  The prosperity
and wealth of the planter was in proportion to the number of his slaves, and hence, at a very early day, "to buy
more slaves" was the great object of his desire.[2]  It is
not astonishing, therefore, that the race multiplied so
rapidly by importations, that in a few years the whites
constituted but little over one-third of the population.[3]

Georgia, on the other hand, is the only colony in
which slavery was positively prohibited by its organic
law.  Rum, Papists, and negroes, were all excluded from
the new colony; the former because experience had
proved it to be the bane of the colonist, and the destruction of his neighbor, the Indian; the last, not from
any principles of humanity to the negro,[4] but as a matter purely of policy; to stimulate the colonists to personal
exertions; to provide a home for the poor and starving
population of the mother country; to create a colony
densely populated with whites, to serve as a barrier

[1] 2 Bancroft, 401.          [2] Wilson's Carolina, 17.
[3] 2 Bancroft, 171.
[4] Oglethorpe himself was Deputy-Governor of the Royal African Company, and owned a plantation and slaves, in South Carolina.  1 Stephens,
287, 288.

against incursions from the Spanish settlements in Florida, and also to promote the cultivation of silk and wine, to which the negro was by no means adapted. The trustees provided laborers in indented white servants, in their judgment better adapted to the wants of the colonists. Experience soon proved the fallacy of their reasoning. The contests between them and the colonists were unceasing and stubborn on this point. The best and wisest of the latter joined in the universal demand for slave labor. The Salzburghers of Ebenezer, accustomed to the labors and exposures of husbandry at home, for a time maintained the policy of the trustees. But the white servants imported, for more than half the year (from March till October), were utterly unable to do service, and to so deplorable a state did the colony arrive, that at last the pastor of these hardy Germans (Mr. Bolzius), beseeched the trustees "not to regard any more our or our friends' petitions against negroes." The great and good Habersham, and the Rev. George White-field, the celebrated divine, were the most efficient advocates, in behalf of the colonists, in obtaining a removal of this restriction. The purity of their motives, and their opportunities for personal observation, convinced those who had been deaf to the clamors of the people. The latter distinguished man was himself a planter and a slaveholder, within the borders of South Carolina, the proceeds of his farm being devoted to his darling charity, the orphan-house at Bethesda. In 1749, the restriction was finally removed, after a struggle of fifteen years. At this time Georgia numbered only fifteen hundred inhabitants, and the condition of "her borders" was anything but "blest." Her climate and her soil demanded negro laborers, and her resources began to be developed when this demand was supplied.[1]

The negroes thus introduced into America, were gross

---

[1] 1 Stephens's Hist. of Georgia, ch. ix.

and stupid, lazy and superstitious. With an occasional exception of a captive warrior, they were only trans-ferred from the slavery of a savage to that of a civilized and Christian master.[1] It is true that their enslavement was justified on the plea that they were heathen, and that, for a time, the idea prevailed extensively, that upon baptism they were enfranchised; but the opinions of Talbot and Yorke, the attorney and solicitor general of England, in 1729, in reply to the inquiry of the planters, satisfied their minds that this proposition was *legally* untrue; while the declaration of Gibson, the Bishop of London, about the same time, that "Christianity and the embracing of the Gospel does not make the least alteration in civil property," quieted their consciences as to the moral question. To make "assurance doubly sure," however, the Legislature of South Carolina, in 1712, of Maryland, in 1692 and 1715, and of Virginia, at sundry times from 1667 to 1748, denied to baptism the supposed effect.[2] To the fact of their improved condi-tion, as well as their natural constitution and habit, the want of a common language, a common sympathy, and a common grief, may be attributed the absence of any concerted attempt at rebellion, even in those colonies where they outnumbered the white population.

We cannot determine, with accuracy, the number of negroes imported into the Colonies prior to their inde-pendence. Bancroft, the historian, estimates the num-ber, up to 1740, at 130,000; and prior to 1776, at 300,000. His estimate is as reliable as any we can make.[3] The colonies to which the largest number were brought,

---

[1] As an evidence of the early attention paid to their Christian teaching, see the provisions made, when first admitted in Georgia. 1 Stephens, 312.

[2] 3 Bancroft, 408, 409; 2 Hild. 426; Plantation Laws (1704), Mary-land, p. 50.

[3] Vol. iii, p. 407. Mr. Carey's estimate is 333,000 for the entire impor-tation. See his "Slave Trade," ch. 3.

were not unmindful spectators of this continual influx
of barbarians; and hence, we find Virginia, Maryland,
and Carolina, not only remonstrating, but passing laws,
designed to restrict their importation. But the trade
was profitable to the mother country. Every slave added
to the treasury. British capital and British commerce
were too deeply engaged in the traffic for the voice of
the Colonies to be heard, or their interests to prevail;
and hence the veto of royal governors, and the withholding of the royal assent, which continually frustrated
the will of the people.[1] The Continental Congress of
1776 resolved, that "no slaves be imported into any of
the thirteen United Colonies."[2] After the recognition of
the independence of the States, the Convention which
framed the Constitution of the United States were
unanimous in putting a limit upon the introduction of
negroes. Massachusetts, whose merchants were engaged
in the slave-trade, joined with Georgia and South Carolina in demanding a few more years ere the final prohibition.[3] The year 1808 was agreed upon. Yet, in 1798,
Georgia, of her own accord, incorporated into her organic law a prohibition of the slave-trade. It may not
be amiss here to allude to the fact, that this action of
America, in her Convention, in 1789, was *eighteen* years
in advance of the British government; and that it required a struggle of *twenty* years, the last throes of which
were felt in 1807, to enable British philanthropy to rise
to the point to which Georgia attained in 1798 l

---

[1] Another reason given by "A British Merchant," in a pamphlet issued
at the time, was, that white emigrants became freemen, and might become
troublesome. The increase of slaves increased dependence on the mother
country.

[2] Journals of Congress, i, 307. The original frame of the Declaration
of Independence, contained, as one of the grievances of the Colonies, this
withholding of the royal assent.

[3] The State of Rhode Island alone numbered fifty-four vessels engaged
in the slave-trade, at the period when the Act of Prohibition took effect.

The entire number of slaves exported from Africa
prior to 1776, has been variously estimated. Raynal
adopts the large sum of nine millions. The German
historian, Albert Hune, considers this estimate too small.
The lowest is three and a quarter millions. More than
one-half of these were carried in English ships; and the
profits from this traffic, to English merchants, is supposed to have been at least four hundred millions of
dollars.[1]

Since 1776, the numbers exported from Africa have
been variously estimated. Notwithstanding the efforts
of Great Britain, France, and the United States, to repress the trade, the demand for the slaves has caused a
supply of a larger annual exportation than there ever
was while the trade was free. It is estimated, that
during the whole continuance of the traffic, legal and
illegal, full forty millions of negroes have been exported
from Africa.[2]

The immense supply of slaves (near 75,000 annually),
necessarily caused most wretched cruelties to be practised by the petty kings and slave-dealers on the African
coast. From the great river Senegal to the farther limits
of Angola, a distance of many thousand miles, the entire
coast was visited to furnish this supply. The interior,
especially along the banks of the rivers, yielded its
quota to the general demand. Numerous tribes in-
habited this vast extent of country, and consequently
great differences existed in the color, nature, habits, and
dispositions of the negroes exported. Prominent among
these were the Mandingoes, Koromantyns, Whidahs or
Fidahs, Eboes, and Congoes. The first were considered
the most elevated and farthest removed from the pure
negro type. The second, from the Gold Coast, were

[1] 3 Bancroft, 411, 412; see Edwards's West Indies, vol. ii, p. 368, et
seq. In the year 1771, there sailed from England alone, 192 ships, provided for the exportation of 47,146 slaves. Copley's Hist. of Slavery,
114.        [2] M. Schœlcher, Colonies Etrangères, i, 386.

the most stubborn, unruly, rebellious, and intrepid. The Whidahs were the most thievish; and the Eboes from Benin, the most timid and dejected. Their peculiarities were soon discovered; and hence, upon the arrival of a slave-ship, the advertisement always gave notice of the tribes from which they were purchased.[1]

The passage from Africa to the Colonies was the most trying period in the sufferings of the slaves. The "horrors of the middle passage" have been sung by poets, and minutely described by eye-witnesses. Nothing aided so much to the final prohibition of the trade. Yet doubtless these "horrors" have been exaggerated. The cupidity and avarice of the dealer tempted him to over-load his small vessel. Yet experience soon taught that the consequent pestilence and decimation of his cargo, more than overbalanced his gains. Self-interest co-operated with humanity in demanding a proper regard to the health and comfort of the victims. The slaves were transported naked. Yet clothing was, to them, an unknown and unnecessary luxury. The males were secured with irons when put on board, but these were removed, unless they proved unruly and rebellious. The decks, between which they were stowed side by side like bales of goods, were only high enough to allow a sitting posture. Yet the day was spent on the upper deck, and ample provision made for ventilation; while cleanliness was enforced as a matter of necessity. Wholesome and bountiful food was provided, as a matter of calculation for the improvement of their appearance. While bathing and other sanitary regulations were of universal practice.[2]

[1] Edwards's West Indies, ii, ch. xvi.

[2] Edwards's West Indies, ii, ch. xvii; Capt. Canot, &c., ch. xi; Buxton's Slave-Trade and Remedy, Pt. I, ch. ii. The great and good John Newton was once engaged in the trade, and was captain of a slave-ship. His Thoughts upon the African Slave-Trade give a candid, and doubtless, truthful account of the trade, as he knew it. They will be found to agree substantially with the text. See also McPherson's Annals of Commerce, vol. iv, 140–149.

While this is the general truth, instances existed of great wretchedness experienced during the voyage. And even with all these precautions, disease frequently made sad havoc among the poor creatures. Avarice and cupidity too frequently drowned the voice of experience; and hence we find the British Parliament, by statute, restricting the number of slaves to be carried to *five* for every *three* tons, up to 201 tons, and to *one* for every additional ton. By the same act, a well-qualified surgeon was required on every vessel; and as an inducement to efficiency, fifty pounds sterling was allowed him, and double that sum to the master, if the mortality during the voyage did not exceed two per cent.[1]

Of the slaves exported to the West Indies two-thirds were males. Various causes conspired to bring about this result. A more even proportion of females were found in the cargoes intended for the American colonies. The prices varied, but seldom exceeded forty pounds sterling for females and fifty pounds for males.[2] The cost on the African coast varied from three pounds to twenty pounds sterling.[3] The profits of such a trade, notwithstanding the large percentage of deaths, are manifest.

The negroes thus imported were generally contented and happy. The lamentations placed in their mouths by sentimental poets, were for the most part without foundation in fact. In truth their situation when properly treated was improved by the change. Careless and mirthful by nature, they were eager to find a master when they reached the shore, and the cruel separations to which they were sometimes exposed, and which for the moment gave them excruciating agony, were

[1] Edwards, 413.

[2] Edwards, 427; McPherson's Annals of Commerce, vol. iv, p. 153, makes the prices much lower. The tables there given show £10 as the minimum and £35 as the maximum. Average, £20.

[3] McPherson's Annals, &c., iv, 153.

forgotten at the sound of their rude musical instruments and in the midst of their noisy dances. The great Architect had framed them both physically and mentally to fill the sphere in which they were thrown, and His wisdom and mercy combined in constituting them thus suited to the degraded position they were destined to occupy. Hence, their submissiveness, their obedience, and their contentment.

Some of the more turbulent occasionally instigated rebellion; for their treatment in the West India Islands, and especially while the Spaniards were almost exclusive owners, was harsh in the extreme. Newton records the candid confession of a planter at Antigua, in 1751, that the owners had calculated with exactness to determine whether it was most to their interest to treat the slaves in such manner as to protract their lives, or to wear them out before they became old and decrepid, and to supply their places with new ones. The latter was found to be most profitable, and was their settled policy, and hence, nine years was considered the limit of a slave's life on many plantations.[1] That such rigor should produce rebellion in the most abject slave would be a natural result. Hence, the early disturbances in 1518 and 1522, already alluded to. In 1551, Charles V interdicted the carrying of arms to all negroes, free and bond, and in 1561, Philip IV renewed the ordinance and extended it to the slaves of the viceroys themselves, even in their master's presence.[2] When Jamaica was ceded to the English, in 1655, the mountains were infested with fugitive and rebellious negroes, known as the Maroons, who made frequent incursions on the plains. These continued at intervals till 1796, when, by the aid of bloodhounds, they were effectually repressed.

[1] Thoughts upon the African Slave-Trade, p. 38.
[2] La traite et son origine, par M. Schœlcher, 368.

The captives were transported to Lower Canada and afterwards to Sierra Leone.[1]

The treatment of the English colonists on the American continent towards their slaves was very different. In fact, the relation between the master and slave in the West Indies and in the English colonies was totally different. In the former, slaves were merely articles of merchandise, a commercial institution worked in large numbers, upon vast plantations, under the care of agents frequently, and for the benefit of masters whose homes were in many cases in the mother country. Bought from the slave-ship, their language was an unknown tongue to the master, and the only communication between them was to learn to understand the orders to work and to enforce obedience thereto. It being more profitable to buy than to breed,[2] instead of servants " born in his house," the West India planter continually was surrounded with new supplies of untutored Africans. Having the sanction of the Holy See to the traffic, his religion left his conscience unexcited to the duties he owed to his fellow-man, farther than to require the occasional visit of a priest or the distribution of mass. The bountiful productions of a generous soil, in a region of perpetual spring, stimulated his avarice to give no rest to the laborer where no rest was required by the land. Hence, despite the humane laws, inhuman treatment never ceased, though the government of some of the islands passed into other hands; and notwithstanding the trade has been declared piracy, and the bristling guns of ships of war have striven to clear the

[1] Dallas's Wars of the Maroons; Schœlcher, Colonies Françaises, i, ch. viii. The term *maroon* was applied to all fugitive slaves. It seems to have originated with the Spaniards, where it was called *cimarron*. Schœlcher, as above, 102.

[2] See Statistics of M. Puynode, as to rate of increase in the French and English West Indies, De l'Esclavage, p. 35; Carey's Slave-Trade, Domestic and Foreign, 8.

seas of the slave-dealers, yet the ports of the West India Islands ever afforded a ready market for slaves so long as slavery was permitted to exist.

On the contrary, the English colonists on the continent were generally men of moderate means, who had sought a home in the New World. The slave bought from the slave-ship wielded his axe side by side with his master in felling the forest around his rude home. He was his companion in wild hunts through the pathless woods. A common danger made them defend a common home from the wild beast and the more cruel savage. The field cultivated by their common labor furnished to each his daily bread, of which they frequently partook at a common board. The more wealthy master lived generally in the midst of his farm. No tempting market enticed him to forget humanity in his search for gain. The return of the labor of his slaves was generally in grain, consumed mostly in reproducing more. Even tobacco was exported but in small quantities. Cotton was reared almost exclusively to furnish employment for the females in extricating the seed, and then by the flax-wheel and the hand-loom, in providing clothing for the slaves themselves. The culture of rice required but moderate labor, except at harvest. The vine, and the olive, and the silk-worm, were all sought to be introduced in the more Southern colonies, to furnish employment for the slaves. With all, the labor was light. The master was not therefore tempted to overwork his slave. Even upon the score of interest it was with him more profitable to breed than to buy. Hence, at an early day the females were brought to the Colonies in numbers far beyond those carried to the islands. To take care of the sick, to shelter and provide for the children, to feed bountifully and clothe warmly, became the interest of the planter, and soon his pride. The natural result of all these causes was a

sympathy between the master and slave unknown upon
the islands.

They stood to each other as the protector and the protected. The relation became patriarchal. The children
of the planter and the children of his slaves hunted,
fished, and played together. An almost perfect equality
existed, in their sports, between the future master and
his future slave. To dispense exact justice to all was
the office of the planter. Obedience and respect from
all was his reward. Such a state of society made slavery, in the Colonies, a *social institution*. It was upheld
and maintained, not for gain solely, but because it had
become, as it were, a part of the social system, a social
necessity.

It is not strange, therefore, that the treatment of slaves
upon the continent, differed widely from their treatment
upon the islands. The result of this difference is to be
seen in the great and steady increase of the negroes
within the Colonies, as exhibited by the census, and their
astounding decrease in the islands, notwithstanding the
constant influx from the African coast.[1]

The slave-trade was not confined to America as a
market. Though to a much more limited extent, England, Spain, and perhaps France, received a part of the
cargoes prepared for the Indies.[2] At the time of the
decision of the Somersett case, Lord Mansfield supposed
there were 15,000 slaves in the British Isles; and Lord
Stowell, in the case of the slave Grace, says, "The personal traffic in slaves, resident in England, had been as
public and as authorized in London, as in any of our

[1] See the instructive and conclusive statistics and comparison, given
by Carey, in his Slave-Trade, Domestic and Foreign.

[2] Hume, in his Essay on National Characters, asserts that negro slaves
were "dispersed all over Europe;" and Granville Sharp, in his Essay
on the Just Limitation of Slavery, quotes the passage from Hume, and
admits the fact, pp. 29, 30. Dr. Beattie does the same, Essay on Truth,
p. 459.

West India Islands.   They were sold on the Exchange and other places of public resort, by parties themselves resident in London, and with as little reserve as they would have been in any of our West India possessions. Such a state of things continued from a very early period up to nearly the end of the last century.[1]

Long before this trade commenced upon the western coast of Africa, the Mohammedan markets of Morocco, Tunis, Tripoli, Egypt, Turkey, Persia, Arabia, and other portions of Asia, had been supplied with slaves from the great hive of Africa.   When it commenced we cannot say.   Before the days of Abraham doubtless.   It has continued to the present time.   It is carried on, partly by means of Arab vessels on the northeast coast, and partly by caravans across the desert.   The number thus exported is probably 50,000 annually, if not more.[2]

[1] 2 Hagg. Adm. Rep. 105 ; Granville Sharp states, in his Essay on the Just Limitation of Slavery, that three married women were torn violently from their husbands, in London, and quotes an advertisement for a negro boy, "having round his neck a brass collar, with a direction upon it, to a house in Charlotte Street, Bloomsbury Square," p. 34.

[2] The reader disposed to examine this branch of the trade more fully, is referred to Buxton's Slave-Trade and Remedy, p. 59, et seq.; Levavasseur's Esclavage de la race noire, 84.

# CHAPTER X.

THAT the slave-trade should have been prosecuted so long by Christian nations, is a matter of greater surprise than the united efforts subsequently made for its abolition. In the meantime, there were not wanting those who not only deprecated the trade, but denied the lawfulness of the relation of master and slave. Milton embodied his protest in his immortal poem:

> " But man over man
> He made not lord, such title to himself
> Reserving, human left from human free."

Pope, Cowper, Savage, Thomson, Shenstone, and many others of less reputation, continued the strain thus commenced, and Montgomery devoted an epic poem to the descriptions of the wrongs of " Afric's sons."

The prose writers of England, during this period, are equally numerous. And America was not behind in furnishing her voice against the trade. Among the former may be mentioned Baxter, Steele, John Wesley, and Warburton. Among the Americans, Dr. Franklin, Dr. Rush, and William Dillwyn, were among the most prominent. Montesquieu and the Abbé Raynal, awakened the French nation to the importance of the same question.

As a body the Quakers, or Society of Friends, were the first to take bold position as to the sinfulness both of the trade and the system.   George Fox, and his co-workers on either shore of the Atlantic, early recognized the fact that God was no respecter of persons, and that the souls of Africans were redeemed by a Saviour's blood, as well as those of the descendants of Japhet.   It was not surprising then that their zeal should become a fanaticism upon this subject, that has continued to the present day.[1]

As already observed, the American colonists were the first people, through their legislative bodies, to seek to put an end to the trade with the colonies.   No religious zeal, nor Quixotic crusades for universal liberty, prompted them to act; but a sincere self-interest, which dictated this policy, as a preventive against an overflowing black population.   The trade, however, was too valuable to British merchants, and too profitable to the British treasury, and hence the royal assent was repeatedly refused.[2]

We have already seen the action of the Continental Congress, in 1776, and the subsequent adoption into the Constitution of the United States, of the clause limiting the importation to the year 1808, if Congress should see proper.   Before the time arrived, viz., in 1807, Congress availed itself of the power granted, and passed an act prohibiting the farther importation of slaves.   Before that time, however, Georgia, in 1798, by virtue of her own State sovereignty, incorporated into her State Constitution, a prohibition of future importation into that

[1] By the laws of Barbadoes, passed 1696, negroes were prohibited from attending the meeting of Quakers, under a penalty of 10l., to be recovered of any Quaker present.   If the negro belonged to the Quaker, he was forfeited.   See Plantation Laws (1704), p. 249.   In 1663, Virginia prohibited the introduction of Quakers, under a penalty of 5000 lbs. of tobacco upon the captain of the vessel.   Ibid. 52.

[2] This was inserted in the original draft of the Declaration of Independence, as one of the grievances of the Colonies, but was stricken out, at the instance of the delegation from Georgia.

State. South Carolina had preceded her, by a legislative enactment to the same effect.

To bring the British mind to such a sense of the evils and sin of the trade, as to induce the nation to forego the benefits arising therefrom, was a much more difficult task; and the fervid zeal of Granville Sharp, the unwearying exertions of Thomas Clarkson, and the powerful appeals and touching eloquence of Wilberforce, but barely effected this object, after a parliamentary struggle continuing through nineteen years. After spending months in preparing the public mind for the effort, the first motion was made in Parliament on the 9th May, 1788 (the year subsequent to the adoption of the Constitution of the United States). Defeat attended that, and a similar effort in 1789. The accession of both Pitt and Fox to their ranks in 1790, did· not change the result. In 1791, there were arrayed in behalf of the movers, Pitt, Fox, Burke, Grey, Sheridan, Wyndham, Whitbread, Courtnay, Francis, and others; but defeat still awaited them. In the meantime, pamphlets and books had been written. Pictures of slave-ships, delineating the decks and the close confinement, and other "horrors of the middle passage," had been distributed throughout the kingdom. The people had become excited, and voluntarily abandoned, in many places, the uses of sugar and rum. In almost every part of the kingdom, public meetings gave vent to the public voice, demanding the prohibition of the trade.[1]

In 1793, the Commons yielded to the public voice, and passed an act for the gradual abolition of the trade. It was lost in the Lords, by a motion to hear farther evidence, which postponed action till the next session. In 1794, the Commons receded from their position, and left the battle to be fought over again. In 1795, it was again carried in the Commons, and lost in the Lords. The

[1] See Stuart's Memoir, pp. 51, 52.

sessions of 1796, 1798, 1799, still brought defeat to the cause. The years 1797 and 1800, 1801, 1802, and 1803, were allowed to pass without effort in Parliament. In 1804, the bill again passed the Commons, but was lost in the Lords. In 1805, it was again lost in the Commons. In 1806, the measure was brought forward under the auspices of the government, being then under the administration of Lord Grenville and Mr. Fox. During that session an act was passed prohibiting British vessels and British capital from being employed in the foreign slave-trade; and, in 1807, the last struggle was ended by the "Act for the abolition of the slave-trade."[1]

It is worthy of remark, that that which Parliament denied to the voice of the excited public, was yielded when that excitement had passed away, and then on the motion of government. When we remember that Fox was the devoted friend of the East India Company, and the fact that, at that time, the project was rife of growing sugar in the East Indies at a less cost than in the West Indies, we may surmise a reason for the final success of the measure, not based either upon philanthropy or justice.[2]

In France, Napoleon Bonaparte, upon his return from Elba, in 1815, passed an order for the immediate abolition of the trade. And in the same year, the Congress at Vienna, representing Great Britain, Austria, Russia, Prussia, and France, declared the slave-trade to be "repugnant to the principles of humanity and of universal morality; and that it was the earnest desire of their sovereigns to put an end to a scourge which had so long desolated Africa, degraded Europe, and afflicted humanity." After the restoration of the Bourbons, the decree of Napoleon was re-enacted, and the year 1819

[1] See Clarkson's History of the Abolition of the Slave-Trade. A concise history may be found in Rees's Cyclop., Slave-Trade.

[2] See Remarks of Bryan Edwards, published in 1794, in History of West Indies, vol. ii, p. 637.

witnessed the legal abolition of the trade by France. No active measures, however, were taken to enforce this edict until 1831, when the right of search was granted to English cruisers.

The treaty of 1814, between Spain and Great Britain, provided for the cessation of the trade under the flag of the former in 1820. The violations of the law, however, have continued ever since, notwithstanding the efforts of a mixed commission of British and Spanish judges, established at Havana, for the condemnation of slavers.[1]

A quintuple treaty for the suppression of the trade, signed at London, December 20, 1841, by representatives of Great Britain, France, Austria, Russia, and Prussia, allowed a mutual right of search. Previous to that time a treaty with the Netherlands in 1818, and with Brazil in 1826, provided for the cessation of the trade by the citizens of those nations. The trade with Brazil, however, continued to be carried on without any effort on the part of the Brazilian Government to prevent it effectually until about the year 1850.

The Act of 5 Geo. IV, c. 113, declared the slave-trade to be piracy in British subjects. Five years before that date (1820), the United States had passed a statute to the same effect. Before these statutes the trade was held to be legitimate by the subjects of all countries not expressly forbidding it,[2] and these statutes do not and cannot make the offence piracy, except in citizens of these respective nations.[3]

[1] See Buxton's Slave-Trade, &c., 212 et seq. In a despatch from Lord Palmerston to Lord Howden, dated Oct. 17th, 1851, with reference to this matter, he says, " During the last fourteen or fifteen years, those treaty engagements have been flagrantly violated, and those laws have been notoriously and systematically broken through in Cuba and Puerto Rico."

[2] Judge Story held to the contrary, in the case Le Jeune—Eugène, 2 Mason, 409; but this decision, in the words of Mr. Wildman, in his work on International Law, is " elaborately incorrect."

[3] See 2 Mason, p. 417. The sweeping provisions of these acts, show

Notwithstanding these several treaties and statutes, and notwithstanding both Britain and the United States have for many years kept a naval force cruising upon the western shores of Africa along the Slave Coast; yet the trade remains unsuppressed to this day, and for a series of years the number of slaves shipped for transportation was greater than it had ever been while the trade was legal and fostered by the legislation of France, Britain, and Spain. Its illicit character, however, has added much to its enormity and horrors. The slave-marts have ceased to be markets overt, and the victims of the trade are hidden in prisons and dens from the time they are brought to the coast. The transfer to the slave-ship is by night, and attended with much danger. The ship itself, instead of the large commodious vessels formerly used, is of the narrow clipper-built style, prepared with a view to a chase from the English or American cruiser. The slave decks are no longer ventilated with a view to health, but placed below the hatches, to escape detection, closely confined and of much diminished proportions. The numbers crowded into these narrow cells are much increased, being no longer regulated by law, and the increased risk and increased expense requiring increased profits to the adventurous owners. The persons engaged in the trade, of necessity, are no longer the enlarged and liberal merchant, with his humane master and crew, but the most desperate of buccaneers, who being declared pirates by law, become pirates in fact. The horrors of the middle passage are necessarily increased, and the difficulties of

another instance of the object of legislation defeated by its own vindictiveness. The bonâ fide purchaser of slaves, in a slave country, who seeks to transport them to another slave country, is not a pirate. The kidnapper of free negroes might be properly so declared. The acts are justified upon the difficulty of making proof of kidnapping, &c. This is an unfortunate truth, but does not justify the severity of the proposed remedy. The result is, that convictions under the act are very rare.

landing the cargoes add to the sufferings of the slaves, already more than decimated by disease.[1]

This trade is not carried on with the United States. But few slaves have been landed on their coast since the trade was prohibited. All the West Indies for a time, and subsequently the Spanish and Portuguese West Indies and Brazil, furnished the markets for this illicit trade.[2] As already remarked, the policy has been to buy rather than to breed negroes. And so long as slave labor in the West Indies remains so profitable, the price of slaves will continue to hold out inducements to lawless adventurers to violate all treaties and laws, in order to reap the immense profits of this trade. The abolition of slavery, in the English, French, Danish, Dutch, and Swedish West Indies, as we shall directly show, have only increased the profits of slave labor in the Spanish and Portuguese colonies, and thus increased the value of slaves and the temptation for the trade.

[1] Mr. Buxton estimates that seven-tenths of the captured slaves die in the process. Thus, of 1000 victims of the trade,

One-half perish in the seizure, march, and detention on the coast, . . . . . . 500
One-fourth of those embarked, die in the middle passage, 125
One-fifth of the remainder die in being climatized, . 75

700

Slave-Trade and Remedy, 199, et seq.

[2] See Wilkes's Exp. Exp. i, pp. 36, 55, 88. He states that the eastern coast of Africa furnishes most of the slaves. Zanzibar is a great slave-mart. The slaves are carried across the Island of Madagascar, to be sold on the eastern coast to Europeans, ix, pp. 184, 190, 272, 273. The slaves in the captured vessels are treated but little better by the English than by the traders; i, 55, 88.

# CHAPTER XI.

As the first efforts for the prohibition of the slave-trade were made in America, so the first movement for the abolition of negro slavery had its origin there. To trace all the efforts that have been made, their origin and end, would be a task we have neither time nor space to enter upon. A mere glance at results is all that we can do.

The American Revolution was in a remarkable degree a struggle for political liberty. The grievances of the Colonies, though existing in fact, were not sufficiently aggravated to have aroused a whole people to throw off the government of their fathers. The war was undertaken for a principle, was fought upon principle, and the success of their arms was deemed by the colonists as the triumph of the principle. That principle was the right of a people to the enjoyment of political liberty. But the investigation and assertion of this right by a nation for a series of years necessarily imbued their minds with an ardent love of personal liberty, and hence, the very declaration of their political liberty announced as a self-evident truth, that *all* men were created *free* and equal.

This announcement was not a formal incorporation of an abstract truth into a diplomatic paper. It was the reflection of the feelings of the ardent espousers of the cause. It was the natural result of the excited state of the public mind. We should expect to find such a declaration from men about to engage in such a struggle.

And knowing as we do, and rejoicing as we should, in the honesty and purity of their motives, we should expect to find such men prosecuting their principles to their legitimate results, and proclaiming *all* involuntary servitude to be opposed to the natural rights of man. It is not surprising, then, that Franklin should have been the president of the first abolition society in Pennsylvania, as early as 1787; nor that Henry, and Jefferson, and Jay, should avow their hostility to the system, and their hopes for its overthrow; nor that even the wise, and good, and great Washington, should, by his will emancipating his own slaves, acknowledge that his own mind was at least wavering as to the propriety of their bondage. In fact, at that day, Virginia was much more earnest in the wish for general emancipation than were New York, Massachusetts, or Rhode Island. So general was the feeling, that the Ordinance of 1787, which excluded slavery from the Northwest Territory (out of which the present populous and thriving Northwestern States are formed), was ratified by the first Congress of the United States, with but one dissenting voice, and that from a delegate from New York; the entire Southern vote being cast in its favor.

Neither the climate nor the productions of the northern and eastern portions of the United States are adapted to negro slavery. The sun is as necessary to negro perfection as it is to the cotton plant. The labor of the slave is only valuable where that labor can be applied to a routine of business which requires no reflection or judgment upon the part of the laborer, and which continues throughout the year. Hence, the number of slaves in these older and more flourishing portions of the States, by the census of 1790, amounted only to 40,370, while the southern and more feeble colonies (Virginia excepted), embraced in their territory 567,527. It required, therefore, no sacrifice of interest upon the part of these States, to provide for the extinction of slavery. It checked not their growth; did not make it necessary for them to seek out new channels for labor and the acquisition of wealth; and required no great sacrifice of property at their hands. Vermont claims the honor of having first excluded slavery, by her Bill of Rights, adopted in 1777. The census of 1790 shows but *seventeen slaves* in the whole State. It required no great measure of philanthropy to sacrifice the value of seventeen slaves.

Massachusetts never did, by statute, abolish slavery; and as late as 1833, her Supreme Court left it an open question, when slavery was abolished in that State.[1] Certain it is, that the census of 1790 gives no enumeration of slaves in that State.

The statute-book of New Hampshire also seems to be silent upon this subject, and the census of 1790 gives to this State 158 slaves; *one* of these was still reported in 1840.

Rhode Island adopted a plan of gradual emancipation by declaring that all blacks born in that State after March, 1784, should be free. *Five* of the old stock seems to have survived to have their names registered in the census of 1840.

Connecticut adopted a similar plan of emancipation, and *seventeen* of her slaves, it seems by the census, were surviving in 1840. Connecticut held 2759 slaves in 1790. The interest was too great for immediate emancipation.

Pennsylvania was in the same situation, having 3737 slaves in 1790. This State also provided for gradual emancipation, by an act passed in 1780, by which it was provided, that all slaves born after that time should serve as slaves until they reached the age of twenty-

[1] Commonwealth v. Aves, Pick. 209.

eight, after which time they were free.   The census of
1840 shows sixty-four still in slavery.[1]

In New York a similar act was passed in 1799, emancipating the future issue of slaves, males at the age of
twenty-eight, females twenty-five years.   In 1817, another act was passed, declaring all slaves free on the
4th July, 1827.   In 1790, there were 21,324 slaves in
this State.   In 1800 (before the emancipating act could
take effect), there were only 20,343.   In 1840, four only
remained.

New Jersey, in 1790, held 11,423 slaves.   In 1804,
the prospective extinction of slavery was provided for
by a similar statute to those of New York and Pennsylvania.   The process, however, must have been slower,
as the census of 1840 gives her 674 slaves, and that of
1850, 236.

Notwithstanding the ardent temperament of the
Southern people, and their early zealous advocacy of
universal liberty, practical emancipation with them was
a much more momentous question.   Virginia alone in
1790 contained 293,427 slaves, more than seven times
as many as *all* the foregoing States combined.   Her productions were almost exclusively the result of slave
labor.   Her white population exceeded her slaves only
about twenty-five per cent.   Her soil and climate and (in
a much greater degree), those of the more Southern
States, were not only peculiarly fitted for negro labor,
but almost excluded white labor from agricultural pursuits.   The problem was one of no easy solution, how
this " great evil," as it was then called, was to be removed with safety to the master and benefit to the
slave.   It would have doubtless remained a problem
perplexing the thoughts and paining the hearts of the

[1] A negro woman slave was sold by the sheriff, in Fayette County,
Pennsylvania, to pay debts, in the year 1823.   Lynch v. The Commonwealth, 6 Watts, 495.

good and wise to this day, had not the Northern and foreign fanaticism forced upon the South an investigation back of the stand-point which was then occupied, and with it the conviction that the Omnipotent Ruler of the universe has not permitted this " great evil" to accumulate until it is beyond control, but has exhibited in this, as in all his dealings with man, that overruling wisdom and providence which causes man's wrath to praise Him.

# CHAPTER XII.

WE will refer hereafter to the subsequent history of the abolition struggle in the United States. We turn now to the West Indies, to trace hurriedly the progress of emancipation there.

Prominent among them stands Hayti, or St. Domingo. Originally belonging to Spain, by gradual encroachment it became partially under the French dominion, until, in 1789, the latter nation owned about one-third of the island. Voluntary manumission, granted generally to the half-breed or mulattoes, the fruit of the illicit intercourse of the whites with the slaves, had, at the time of the French Revolution, placed in the French portion of the island a population of 21,808. At that time the whites numbered only 27,717, while the slaves amounted to 405,564.[1] The cry of "Liberty and Equality" of the French metropolis was taken up and echoed by the whites of Domingo, especially the poorer classes, who looked with envy and hatred upon the immense estates of the landed proprietors. The free mulattoes also (many of whom were possessed of slaves and other property), rejoiced in the cry, for though free they had never been admitted to any political privileges, and the " prejudice of color" existed to a remarkable degree,

---

[1] These are the estimates of M. Barbé-Marbois, in 1788. See Rees's Cyclopædia, Domingo. Others estimate the slaves at 700,000. Schœlcher, Colonies Etrangères, tom. ii, p. 86.

where nothing but color and these political privileges distinguished the one class from the other.

The first outburst of the French Revolution found three distinct parties in Domingo : the wealthy landed proprietors, who were averse to change, and desired at least to act in subordination to the Government of the metropolis; Les Blancs, or the white Republicans, who desired to set up an independent government in the island; and the mulattoes, who were clamorous for equality, whatever might be the extent of the privileges gained. The first dissension arose between the two former classes, and so great was the prejudice of color, that neither would accept of the aid of the mulattoes unless they would wear a badge, of a color different from the whites.[1] The latter petitioned the National Assembly for a recognition of their rights, and the reply was, that "no part of the nation should appeal in vain for its rights before the assembled representatives of the French people,"[2] and on the 8th March, 1790, a decree was passed, granting political privileges to all free persons of the age of twenty-five years, and who were proprietors of land. Both factions of the whites combined to defeat this decree, and succeeded in inducing the Governor of the island to construe it as applying only to white persons. The fraud was subsequently discovered by a young mulatto, Vincent Ogé, while in France, and upon his return home he assembled eighty or ninety of his class, and boldly demanded the execution of the decree. He was routed by the chief of the National Guard, and he and his followers taken prisoners and executed. But the "prejudice of color" would not allow the scaffold to be erected where the whites were usually executed.[3]

In the meantime each party of the whites were at-

---

[1] Schœlcher, Colonies Etrangères, tom. ii, 95.      [2] Ibid. p. 91.
[3] Schœlcher, tom. ii, pp 95, 96.

tempting to set up a government. The Governor, Peynier, at St. Domingo, represented the metropolitan party. The Assembly of the Reformers was held at St. Mark.

Pending these difficulties, the slaves in the north began to talk of liberty.[1] The 24th of August, 1791, witnessed a formidable insurrection among them. They carried fire and devastation in their route. The National Guard, however, soon dispersed them, and the head of their leader, Boakmann, was placed on a pike in the midst of the public square. The punishment inflicted by the whites was excessive. They confined it not to those engaged in the revolt, but considering every black an enemy, massacred without distinction all that fell in their way.[2] In this insurrection it is supposed that two thousand white persons perished; twelve hundred families were reduced to indigence; one hundred and eighty sugar and nine hundred cotton plantations destroyed, and the buildings consumed by fire.[3]

About this time, there reached the island the decree of the National Assembly of the 15th May, 1791, which, in plain terms, granted equal political privileges to all freemen born of free parents, without regard to color. The whites resolved that they would not submit to its provisions; the mulattoes to obtain, by force, their legal rights. Each party armed themselves, and each party armed also a body of their faithful slaves, to do

---

[1] Insurrectionary pamphlets had been previously distributed among them, issued by the abolitionists of Paris (Amis des Noirs), who counted among their numbers, Mirabeau, Robespierre, Abbé Grégoire, and other leaders of the Revolution. See Speech of the Deputies, before the National Assembly, Nov. 3d, 1791, in which the insurrection is attributed entirely to this cause.

[2] See Schœlcher, pp. 99–101. Some palliation for this is found in the barbarous cruelty of the revolting negroes. Their standard was the body of a white child, elevated on a pole. Their murders and rapes were brutal in the extreme. See Speech of Deputies, as above.

[3] Rees's Cyclopædia, Domingo.

battle for them.   On the 2d September, an engagement was had near Port au Prince, in which the mulattoes obtained the advantage.   On 23d October, a treaty of peace was signed, acknowledging the political equality of the mulattoes.   Their armed slaves, however, were banished from the island and sold in Jamaica.   They were driven thence by the English governor, who sent them back to St. Domingo, where they were executed, and their bodies cast into the bay.[1]   This peace was of short duration, as the Provincial Assembly declared the treaty to be subversive of the colonial system. The whites, being in open violation of the decree of the Home Government, proposed to deliver the island to the English Governor of Jamaica, which proposal he declined to accept.

In the meantime, the National Assembly, by the fickleness of their policy, only aggravated the state of anarchy in the island.   By a decree of the 24th September, that of the 15th May was annulled, and power was given to the Colonial Assembly to regulate the political *status* of the free persons of color.   This they exercised on 2d November, by postponing indefinitely their political emancipation.

Hostilities soon recommenced, and on 29th November one-half of Port au Prince was reduced to ashes.   The whites accused the mulattoes of the deed, and to avenge themselves massacred indiscriminately their women and children who were within their reach.[2]   With varying success, this civil war continued until the Governor, Blanchelande, joined his forces to the mulattoes, and thus subdued the whites.   This step of his was in consequence of another decree of the vacillating National Assembly, who, on the 4th April, 1792, revoked the decree of 24th September, and declared all freemen to be equal.   To enforce this decree, they sent out three

[1] Schœlcher, 102, 103.          [2] Pamphile La Croix, tom. i, ch. 4.

commissioners, Sonthonax, Polverel, and Alliand, and six thousand troops. These commissioners took part with the colored men, and heaped upon them honors and arms. For a time peace seemed to have been established, but the equality of the mulattoes was too galling for the whites, and they again endeavored to right themselves by an appeal to arms. Fortifying themselves in Port au Prince, they again offered to deliver the island to the English, if they would re-establish the ancient order of things.[1]

After considerable skirmishing, this rebellion was repressed, and peace seemed again to be restored; but mutual hatred was still rankling in the bosoms of both classes, and an opportunity soon offered for the recommencement of hostilities. A difficulty between a mulatto and an officer of marine was sufficient, and the battle was fought in the streets of Port au Prince. In the *mêlée*, a parcel of revolted negroes placed fire to the jail, to release four or five hundred negro prisoners. The flames spread, and reduced to ashes the most beautiful city of the Antilles. The government troops and the mulattoes again triumphed over the whites, and one thousand of the latter, the flower of the island, condemned themselves to voluntary exile.

In the meantime, Spain had declared war against the French Republic. The close proximity of their possessions in Domingo, gave the Spaniards a fine opportunity of harassing the already distracted French colony. The slaves of the latter were encouraged to take refuge among the Spaniards, and many of them were enrolled in their army, under the lead of two of their fellows, Jean François and Biassou. Under these generals, continued attacks were made upon the French province. About August, 1793, a desperate attack was made by them. They were about to take possession of Fort

---

[1] See Schœlcher, 105, et seq., and authorities cited by him.

Liberty, and menaced even the town of the Cape. Sonthonax occupied it alone, with about one thousand
troops, and five or six hundred mulattoes, and without
the munitions of war. Moreover, the rebellious whites
had called upon the English of Jamaica to come to
their assistance, and they themselves occupied much of
the country. Under these circumstances, Sonthonax
proclaimed, on 29th August, liberty to all slaves who
would enrol themselves under the banner of the Republic. His colleague, Polverel, condemned this act as
an abuse, or rather a stretch of power. But when the
English at length came to take part with the rebels, he
admitted the necessity of the act, and obtained the consent of the proprietors thereto. Malenfant, who gives
this account, adds, that he himself was the only proprietor
who refused to subscribe to this consent.[1] This was the
formal beginning of the emancipation of the blacks of
Domingo.

On 3d September, 1793, a treaty was signed by the
English and the colonists in Jamaica. On 19th September, the British soldiers, eight hundred and seventy in
number, were introduced into one of the towns where
the rebels were in power, and five others were successively delivered up to them. On 4th June, 1794, Port
au Prince surrendered to the British arms. But the
fatal *black vomit* appeared among the troops, and forty of
the officers and six hundred of the rank and file fell victims to the scourge.[2]

On 4th February, 1794, the National Convention not
only confirmed the offer of liberty made by Sonthonax,
but by decree abolished slavery in all of the French
colonies. To maintain some kind of order, Polverel,
one of the commissioners, in May, 1794, published agricultural regulations, by which the enfranchised slaves

---

[1] See Schœlcher, tom. ii, p. 114.
[2] Schœlcher, ii, 115 et seq.; Rees's Cyclop. Domingo.

were to have one-fourth of the gross products of their labor. This arrangement for a time seemed to be satisfactory.

Previous to this time there appeared upon the stage the most remarkable person in this eventful drama. A negro of middle age, the coachman of a rich planter, fled from his master and took refuge with the Spaniards. Having learned to read and write, and knowing something of simple medicines, he was placed under Biasson, the negro General, and honored with the titles of Surgeon and Colonel. He continued to serve in the Spanish army until the news arrived of the decree of February 4th, 1794, when he immediately deserted. The time was propitious. The French General Lavaux had been appointed Governor *ad interim*, while the commissioners went to Paris to answer charges made against them by the colonists. The troops had been left under the directions of three mulatto officers, Beauvais, at Jacmel; Rigaud, at Cayes; and Villatte, at the Cape. The Governor, Lavaux, made the latter his headquarters and took command. Villatte, dissatisfied with being in a subordinate position, fomented a sedition, and placed the Governor in prison, under the pretence of saving him from the fury of the populace. In this conduct he was but following the example of Montbrun, another mulatto, who a short time previously had forced Sonthonax to fly from Port au Prince. Toussaint, the negro alluded to, placing himself at the head of five thousand men, marched upon the Cape, defeated Villatte, released the Governor, and placed himself subject to his orders. It must be remarked in passing, that there was no more sympathy between the blacks and mulattoes, than between them and the whites, for the mixed race were equally as averse to an equality with the negro as the whites. Lavaux, from gratitude, nominated Toussaint general-of-brigade, and placed him at the head of his administration. In his zeal he pronounced him " the liberator of the blacks."

The knowledge which Toussaint had of the country, and especially of the situation of his old protectors, the Spaniards, enabled him very soon to drive them out from the French possessions. The enfeebled condition of the English forces gave him a good opportunity of at least holding them from any aggressive movements. At the same time he forced the blacks to enrol themselves in the army, or else return to their work upon the plan of Polverel, before alluded to. The commissioner, Sonthonax, upon his return to the island, appointed him general-of-division.

About this time Rigaud, another of the mulatto generals, placed himself in an attitude of independence in the South. He oppressed indiscriminately both blacks and whites, and his command, almost exclusively mulattoes, sustained him in his position. The government was too feeble to resist him, and Toussaint had no disposition to aid them in it, for the design had already formed itself in his breast of setting aside this exhausted government and taking possession of the island for the colored race exclusively. The commissioner soon penetrated this design, and hastened to return to France to make it known. Toussaint, suspecting his intention, sent with him two of his sons as hostages for his devotion to the Republic.

After his departure Toussaint drove the English from Port au Prince, Jeremy, and the Mole. They sought in vain to bribe him to deliver the island to them. His scheme was independence. Failing in this last resort, the English finally evacuated the island, where disease and defeat had added nothing to the glory of their arms.

Both Toussaint and Rigaud endeavored to force the negroes to continue their work. They were required to remain upon the farms and not to leave them without

permits.   Notwithstanding, many of them fled and became highway robbers. Rigaud erected a prison in
which he incarcerated all such.

The French Directory sent out General Hedouville,
as their agent, to supervise Toussaint and to arrest
Rigaud.   He arrived 21st April, 1798.   Toussaint refused to aid in the arrest of Rigaud, pleading as an excuse his great services to the Republic.   At the same
time he proposed to Rigaud to combine against Hedon-
ville and declare the island independent.   The prejudice
of color, however, extended even to the mulattoes, and
a combination with the negroes was repugnant to their
feelings.   Rigaud rejected these overtures and preferred
to combine with Hedouville against the blacks.

This combination was an expiation for his offences,
and when Hedouville, in October following, was forced
to leave the island, he released Rigaud from all obligation to obey the general-of-division, and appointed
him commander-in-chief of the army in the South.
Thus commenced the war between the blacks and
mulattoes.   The whites were already virtually driven
from the island.   The contest for the mastery was now
between the other colors.   The mulattoes in Toussaint's
army deserted and joined their own color.   A bitter and
bloody contest ensued.   But the blacks were too numerous for the small band of mulattoes.   After several
desperate conflicts, on 29th July, 1800, Rigaud, Pétion,
Boyer, and their followers, abandoned the island and
left the old negro Toussaint sole master thereof.

The Consular Government confirmed Toussaint in his
plenary powers, and ordered him to take possession of
the Spanish portion of the island ceded to the French
by the Treaty of Basle in 1795, which order he executed
with but little opposition.

In June, 1801, Toussaint called together such of the
white inhabitants as were subject to his will, under the

name of the Central Assembly of St. Domingo, and published a constitution by which slavery was forever abolished in the island, and he was nominated as governor for life. This constitution he formally presented to the French government for their sanction; but, at the same time, made every preparation to maintain it by force. He endeavored, also, to reconstruct the social condition of the island; opened a court around himself; encouraged luxury in his favorites; and sought, by rigorous decrees, to enforce upon the agricultural slaves, a continuance of their labors. Idleness in them was punished by death. In short, he established an iron despotism that knew no law but his will. In this manner he alienated from himself the affections of those whose gratitude for his services would have bound them to him.

In 1801 was signed the Peace of Amiens. The First Consul of France had time now to turn his attention to her colonies. He reviewed the scenes in St. Domingo, and his great intellect soon detected the fatal mistake which the National Assembly had made. That mistake was, in seeking to make equal those whom the Almighty had made unequal. The white colonists, who had fled to Paris, urged him to restore the former order of things. His wife, Josephine, herself a West India creole, doubt-less as an eyewitness, gave him a true picture of the condition and capacity of the negro. He resolved to restore the old *régime*. Le Clerc, his brother-in-law, with 23,000 troops, embarked; and on 5th February, 1802, appeared at the Cape. He demanded possession of the city of the negro commandant, Christophe. He refused; and following the instructions formerly given him by Toussaint, reduced the town to ashes. Leogane, Port de Paix, and Saint Marc, shared the same fate at the hands of their commandants. Other cities were de-livered into the hands of the French general.

Le Clerc endeavored to induce Toussaint to acquiesce

in the views of the First Consul, and with this view, sent his two sons (formerly sent to France as hostages) to persuade him to this course. But the old negro's ambition could not be thus restrained. Several engagements were had. In the attempt to take a fort called Crète-à-Pierrot, the French suffered considerably. Le Clerc changed his tactics, and published that there was no intention, on the part of the First Consul, to enslave the negroes; that they should continue to enjoy their liberty. The despotic conduct of Toussaint was now avenged. All of his officers, with but few exceptions, accepted of this overture, and yielded to the terms of the French General. Toussaint was forced at last to treat. He made two conditions: the liberty of his fellow-citizens, and that he should retire to his own estate, retaining his title as General, and his staff. Being subsequently detected in a conspiracy (as it was alleged) against the government, he was arrested and sent to Paris. He was there cast into prison, and soon ended his life in a dungeon.[1]

After the departure of Toussaint, Le Clerc disarmed many of the negro and mulatto soldiers, removed their officers, put to death several, under various accusations, and then, throwing off the mask, announced the Consular decree restoring slavery. Dessalines, and others of the old negro officers, deserted, and raised the standard of revolt. The mulattoes and negroes now cordially united against the whites, their common foe. They had enjoyed their liberty too long to submit quietly to a re-enslavement. Thus commenced the bloody war between

---

[1] In giving this brief account of this remarkable negro, I have followed chiefly M. Schœlcher, a French abolitionist. There is great conflict among authors in respect to him. Some laud him as the model upon which Napoleon endeavored to improve; others treat him as a traitor and weak tool in the hands of others. I have taken the middle, and I believe the true ground.

the whites and the colored races.    The yellow fever, the negro's ally, came to their assistance.    The French army were decimated in numbers, and the remainder enfeebled by disease.    Le Clerc himself fell a victim to the *vomito*.

The war was bloody and desperate; no quarter was given on either side.    The negroes devastated the country, destroying the crops, and even cutting down the trees.    Famine then came to add to the difficulties of the French.    Great Britain having declared war against the Consular government, neutral nations could furnish provisions only by stealth.

Rochambeau, the successor to Le Clerc, was an unfortunate appointment.    Cruel and despotic, he exercised his unlimited power so as to drive from the French all sympathy.    In fact, his exactions upon the French themselves made them his enemies.    Besieged and confined in the Cape, he exacted from the inhabitants enormous taxes, to pay for provisions introduced by American vessels.    A merchant, who refused to pay 33,000 francs, was shot down in the national palace.

Dessalines finally carried on his siege so successfully, that the French General was forced to capitulate.    He and his soldiers were permitted to embark, and thus evacuate the island, with the exception of a small garrison in St. Domingo, under General Ferrand.    These bravely maintained themselves until they were expelled in 1809.    The treaty of Paris, in 1814, re-ceded that portion of the island to Spain.

On 1st January, 1804, the officers of the army met in convention and declared the independence of Hayti (resuming the aboriginal name).    At this time, the civil wars had reduced the population to about 400,000.    Dessalines was declared Governor-general, and signalized his entry into office by a proclamation written in blood, justifying and ordering the massacre of the whites remaining in their midst.

On 8th October, 1804, Dessalines was declared emperor. He ruled with a rod of iron. His hatred of the
whites was intense. In May, 1805, a constitution was
published, by which a white man was prohibited from
emigrating thither to purchase land or acquire any other
property. In 1806, Pétion, a mulatto general, headed a
conspiracy against him, and caused him to be assassi-
nated.

The war of races again commenced between the mulattoes and blacks; Pétion heading the former, and
having control of the South and West; Christophe, a
black, controlling the North. The latter was nominated
President of the Republic by the Assembly at Port au
Prince, on 27th December, 1806. On 9th January, 1807,
he was deposed by the same Assembly, and Pétion
named in his stead. Hence the claim of each.

Pétion continued, in name, President of the Republic.
Christophe soon had himself declared King, under the
name of Henry I. He established a court, and granted
vast numbers of titles and orders of nobility, and of the
grand cross. He maintained, essentially, a military
government. He compelled the laborers to continue at
their posts with an iron arm; and required his soldiers
to furnish their own equipments, under pain of death.
Two of his mulatto officers having deserted at St. Marc,
he butchered, in cold blood, every mulatto man, woman,
and child, in the city.

A deliverer appeared about the year 1820, in a negro,
Richard, Duke of Marmelade, who led a conspiracy of
the principal officers of the army, and delivered the
North to Boyer, then President of the South. The two
sons of the King were massacred, after he himself committed suicide.

Pétion took a different course. He encouraged idleness. He was faithless to the constitution under which
he was elected, and dispersed the Senate, who sought to

limit his powers.   He put to death many of the senators, and alienated all of his friends.   About 1810, Rigaud returned from France, and assuming the title of Restorer of Liberty, headed an army in the South to put down Pétion.   They met, and agreed to hold separate dominions; a small part of the island being set apart for Rigaud, as General-in-chief of the South.   He died suddenly, shortly thereafter, and a mulatto, General Borghella, was named as his successor.   On the approach of Pétion he surrendered.   In 1816, Pétion was nominated President for life; and on 29th March, 1818, he died, having, during his long exercise of power, done no act to entitle him to a higher commendation than that he was an ambitious sluggard.   Boyer, a French mulatto, who accompanied Le Clerc, was elected President in his stead.

We have seen how he was indebted to Richard for the possession of the North.   Upon a false charge of conspiracy he caused him to be shot, on 28th February, 1821.   Five or six others of the most prominent of his subjects shared a similar fate.

About this date, the Spanish colony of Domingo revolted from the mother country and set up an independent republic.   This fell an early prey to Boyer, who thus became master of the whole island.   .

Upon the restoration of the Bourbons, negotiations were opened, and efforts made to restore this most prized colony to the French throne.   It would be tedious to pursue the details.   In April, 1827, Charles X sent his last propositions, and accompanied them with a fleet of thirty sail.   Boyer, intimidated by the fleet, accepted of the terms proposed.   By these, the independence of Hayti was acknowledged upon the payment of an indemnity of 150,000,000 francs.   Thus was effected the first great effort of liberating the slaves of the West Indies.[1]   We will consider its consequences hereafter.

[1] Colonies Françaises, par M. Schœlcher.

# CHAPTER XIII.

In the year 1823, a society, was formed " for the miti-
gation and gradual abolition of slavery throughout the
British dominions." Clarkson, who had been so instru-
mental in calling public attention to the slave-trade,
devoted his time and pen to this consummation of his
work. During the same year, the subject was brought
before Parliament by Mr. Buxton, and immediate abolition urged by him, Wilberforce, and others. Compromise resolutions, recommending judicious reforms, were
proposed by government and finally passed. In 1826,
the same gentlemen renewed the subject in Parliament,
and numberless petitions were presented from various
portions of the kingdom, especially from the manufac-
turing cities; the latter praying particularly that equal
facilities be afforded for commerce to the East Indies,
with those extended to the West Indies. The motion
was renewed in various shapes from year to year. Commissioners were appointed by the government to inquire
into the state of affairs in the colonies, and especially
into the administration of civil and criminal justice; and
their elaborate reports gave minute information as to
the condition of the islands.[1] From forfeitures and es-
cheats sundry slaves had become the property of the

---

[1] See substance of the three reports, published in 1827. London.
The reports, complete, make a dozen folio volumes.

government.   These were termed "crown slaves."   In 1830, these were liberated by an order in council.   The number, however, was very small, not exceeding a few thousand.

The efforts being made for their liberation could not be concealed from the slaves.   The colonists charged that it was not only industriously circulated, but that the slaves were incited to insurrection by various Baptist and Methodist missionaries, who were sent out among them from the mother country.   Certain it is, that insurrection and rebellion did follow, and that numbers of the slaves lost their lives in consequence thereof.   The missionaries were arrested, imprisoned, and some of them. driven from the islands.

In 1832, committees were appointed in both Houses of Parliament to inquire and report such measures as were expedient on the subject of emancipation.   These spent some time in examining witnesses, and reported their investigations.   In 1833, was finally passed the act providing for the abolition of slavery.   Fearing the result of immediate abolition, the act postponed its operation for one year (till 1st August, 1834), and then substituted a system of apprenticeships, varying from four to six years, prescribing the number of hours per week the apprentices should labor for their former masters, allowing one-third of their time for themselves, restricting the infliction of corporal punishment, except by order of special justices of the peace, and giving minute specifications of the powers and rights both of the masters and the apprentices.   The sum of £20,000,000 was appropriated to make compensation to the owners for the loss of their property.

This act was the result of the wisdom and philanthropy of the British nation, and great expectations were entertained of the beneficial results to flow from this tutelage of the slave, before investing him with perfect liberty. That it failed of its object is universally admitted, and the emancipationists attributed to this apprentice system the many evils growing out of this violent uprooting of an entire social system. The colonists complained bitterly, and their opponents (perhaps not without cause), accused them of seeking to evade all of its provisions. They again accused the negroes of miserable evasions under pretence of sickness and otherwise. On the day before perfect liberty was granted, the infirmaries of Jamaica, says an intelligent French writer, were crowded with negroes professing to be sick. The next day they were all cured. What worked this miracle? The arrival of liberty.[1] The English abolitionists appealed to Parliament to cut the Gordian knot and grant immediate freedom. The rights of the proprietors were laughed to scorn. It is possible that this movement would have succeeded, but it was rendered unnecessary by the colonies themselves, who, sick of their apprentices, granted entire freedom before the day appointed. Antigua led in this movement contemporaneously with the commencement of the system. Bermuda and other smaller islands followed the example soon thereafter. Barbadoes came next early in 1838, others followed, and on 1st August of that year, the apprentice system ended in Jamaica. Some insignificant outbreaks had attended its workings, but on the whole it was effected peaceably.[2]

In another place we will examine the results of this abolition in its effects upon these colonies. It may be well here to remark, that the character of the slavery of the negro in the British West Indies and in the United States, differs widely. That the negroes were not improving *physically* in the former, is proven conclusively by the fact, that instead of increasing in numbers, they

---

[1] Cassagnac's Voyage aux Antilles, i, 275.
[2] Report of Duc de Broglie, p. 10.

were rapidly decreasing. Before the abolition of the trade, twenty years were estimated as the average labor of a healthy negro. It is estimated, that at least 700,000 negroes were imported and retained in Jamaica before the trade was checked. Yet, in 1834, there were liberated only 311,000, showing a destruction of life almost unparalleled. That this annual decrease continued to the last days of slavery, is evident from the registry of deaths and births kept by requisition of law. These show a plurality of deaths for almost every year. The same results are shown from the statistics of Barbadoes, St. Vincents, British Guiana, Trinidad, and Grenada. The whole number of slaves imported into the British West Indies is estimated at 1,700,000. There were emancipated 660,000, a little over *one-third* of the importations. The decrease for the last five years, before emancipation, was nearly *one per cent.* per annum.

On the other hand, for 333,500, estimated as imported into the United States, there were, in 1850, 3,800,000; showing a steady increase of population itself almost unparalleled. Had the negroes imported into the British West Indies increased in the same ratio as they increased here, instead of the sum paid, it would have required from the British treasury the enormous sum of £500,000,000 to have compensated the masters at the same prices. And so, had the negroes decreased with us as they did in the British colonies, every master could now be compensated, at the same rates paid there, with the small sum of £4,000,000.[1]

Sweden and Denmark, by various provisions, ameliorated greatly the condition of the slaves in their respective colonies. The hours of work were prescribed, their food and clothing, the amount of chastisement, and the instrument. The right of the slave to his *peculium*, and to make complaint against his master, was secured by

[1] See Carey's Slave-Trade, Foreign and Domestic, ch. ii, iii.

law, and also the right to purchase his own freedom.[1] These regulations were not followed by the elevation of the slaves, but were followed by a diminution of the products of the colonies.[2] Sweden finally, in 1846, determined on the abolition of slavery in her only island, St. Bartholomew. There were only 578 slaves, and to purchase these there was appropriated about $50,000, payable in five instalments. On 9th October, 1847, the work of emancipation was completed.[3] Denmark followed the next year (1848), and by indemnifying the masters, gave liberty to the slaves in her colonies.

Martinique, Guadalupe, Bourbon, and French Guiana, had slavery restored under Napoleon, although he failed in his efforts to restore it in Hayti. After British emancipation, the French abolitionists renewed the agitation of the question in France. It was argued with great zeal and learning by its advocates and opponents, and many volumes were written on either side.[4] On 26th May, 1840, a commission was appointed by a royal edict, to examine into and report upon the state of the Colonies. The mass of material and evidence laid before this commission almost defy analysis. The reports to the Duc de Broglie upon colonial questions, by M. J. Lechevalier alone, are embodied in three huge folio volumes.[5] From these, we learn that the condition of the French colonies was wretched in the extreme. The abolitionists at Paris were threatening, and urging emancipatioǹ. The colonists were protesting, and yet

[1] Schœlcher, Histoire de l'Esclavage, i, 532; Gurney's Letters on the West Indies, 19.

[2] Gurney's Letters on the West Indies, 17 et seq.

[3] Schœlcher, as above, 534.

[4] It is a little curious that Voltaire, who painted so vividly the miseries of the slave and the slave-trade, in Candide, took an interest in a slave-ship, and rejoiced, in a letter to his partner, in having "made a good speculation and done a good action." Levavasseur, pp. 75, 76.

[5] The curious can find a list of these documents prefixed to the report of the Duc de Broglie.

in continual suspense. The slaves were discontented and rebellious, causing frequent insurrections, with much loss of life. Once in the enjoyment of freedom, of which they were again deprived, surrounded by the English colonies, where abolition had not only granted liberty to the slaves, but a refuge and asylum for all fugitives from the French colonies, with the hopes of abolition ever held out before them, it is not at all strange that two hundred and fifty thousand negroes should resist the domination of the few constituting their masters. The report of this Commission shows, that all parties agreed as to the necessity of some action on the part of the home government. The abolitionists insisted on immediate freedom. The colonists insisted that an end be put to this state of suspense, by perpetuating the old régime.[1] The Commission, after examining both sides with apparent candor, recommended as the most salutary plan the apprentice system adopted by the English government. The evils flowing from it were admitted, but the Commission looked hopefully to time; which, by replacing the old generation of slaves with a new of freeborn men educated to liberty, would do away with the idleness, vice, and superstition, which they attributed to the former state of bondage.[2] Time has shown that this hope was ill-founded. The secret of the error was the ignorance of European statesmen of the negro character. The result of this Commission was the law of 18th July, 1843, which sought to ameliorate the condition of the slaves, and to regulate the relation of master and slave. It provided for the punishment of the slaves, for their marriage, for their mental and religious instruction, and for the protection and security of their *pecu-*

[1] See the Report of Duc de Broglie to the Colonial Secretary, March, 1843.

[2] There was much plausibility in this hope. Moses, under Divine direction, kept the Israelites in the wilderness until the generation of Egyptian slaves was extinct. These were not the conquerors of Canaan.

M

*lium.* It regulated the number of hours of labor to be required of the slaves, provided for their holidays, and required that one day in each week should be allowed them to labor for themselves; and that land should be provided for their cultivation on their own account, with various other similar provisions, calculated to insure humane treatment.

It gave also to every slave the privilege of purchasing himself, his parents, or his descendants, and provided a mode of ascertaining the price where the master and slave could not agree. This law was followed by another, of 19th July, 1845, to encourage the introduction of free laborers from Europe into the colonies, by which 930,000 francs were appropriated, 400,000 of which were to be used in aiding slaves in the purchase of themselves.[1] That these laws failed of their desired effect seems to be acknowledged. The abolitionists complained that the colonial officers joined with the colonists in having them evaded. In January, 1846, no part of the 400,000 francs had been used in effecting the purchase of slaves. In March, 1846, 3,900,000 francs had been expended for establishing schools, to which the young negroes were gratuitously admitted, and yet only *twelve* such scholars had ever partaken of their benefits. Whipping having been virtually abolished by the act, cudgelling was substituted in its place. It is useless to multiply the details.[2]

The French Government were not prepared to pay the requisite indemnity of the purchase of 250,000 slaves, though constantly urged thereto by the abolitionists. In June, 1846, 140,000 francs were appropriated for the purchase of the royal slaves (*esclaves du domaine*), and this was the only appropriation ever made for this purpose. In 1847, petitions signed as was said by one of

[1] Schœlcher, Histoire de l'Esclavage, i, 33–38.
[2] Schœlcher, i, passim.

the orators, by " tous les Français," were again presented, demanding the complete and immediate emancipation of the slaves.  A law to that effect is proposed in the Chamber of Deputies, and ably advocated among others by M. Ledru Rollin, but it could not be passed.[1]

What could not be effected by the Kingdom of France, was soon accomplished by the Revolutionary Republic. One of the first acts of the Provisional Government of 1848, was to declare freedom to *all* held in bondage throughout the French dominions.  No pretence of in- demnity was attempted at the time.  In the mad zeal for new-born liberty, justice was forgotten.  We shall hereafter examine the effects of this emancipation.  Sub- sequently, a mere nominal indemnity has been paid to the planters.

[1] Schœlcher, ii, 135–146.

My intention was to have examined minutely the effects of abolition upon Hayti and the British West Indies, to have followed the history of the transition, to have noted the tendency and gradual return to barbarism, of a race rescued from that condition only by slavery, and to have sought in the character of the negro for the reasons of this decline; but the extent of this prefatory sketch forbids so minute a detail. It is unquestionably true, that from the ancient kingdom of Meroe, in which, centuries before Christ, the experiment of a negro government of a nation far advanced in civilization, was attended with retrogradation and final extinction, down to the latest abolition in the West Indies, however varying the circumstances, however cautious and wise the provisions, the result has been uniformly and invariably disastrous to every element of civilization. The fact is admitted; the difference of opinion exists only as to causes.

" From 1804 downwards, the history of the unfortunate island (Hayti), has been little or nothing else than the history of rapine—one black rising up to contest the sovereignty with another, and filling the island with scenes of confusion and misery, which go far to prove the theory of those who maintain that the negro race is by natural incapacity unfitted for self-government." Such is the testimony of an intelligent Englishman, who visited St. Domingo in 1849, and whose prejudices are all in favor of the negro race.[1] The statistics of the commerce of the islands show a continual retrocession. Every visitor, whatever be his opinions as to negro capacity, notes and admits the evidences of decay in every mark of advancement and civilization, and to-day the mock empire of Hayti, the subject of ridicule and regret, is but a transfer of an African despotism from Ethiopia to the West Indies.[2]

The history of Hayti and its present condition show the results of an abolition effected by insurrection and revolution. In these causes, the abolitionists of England and France found reasons for all the savage barbarity, the miserable idleness, the continual outbreaks, the ruined cities, the abandoned agriculture, in short, for the dark mantle of heathenism which settled upon this once beautiful and fertile island.[3] A peaceable emancipation, with proper guards against the natural outbreaks of too sudden liberty, with judicious provision for educating and training the rising generation, whose spirits had never been crushed by the galling chains of slavery: this was the true philosophy and philanthropy, and from such a course, results very different from those witnessed in Hayti, were confidently predicted and sincerely anticipated. As we have seen, Great Britain took the first steps in this new experiment. A gradual emancipation, during which an apprentice system and ample educational privileges were provided, was the result of the best statesmanship and philanthropy of the wisest and best of the nations of the Old World. Its

[1] Impressions and Experiences of the West Indies and North America, in 1849, by Robert Baird, A.M., 82.

[2] Franklin's Present State of Hayti; Levavasseur's Esclavage de la race noire, 22, et seq.

[3] Colonies Etrangères, by Schœlcher, vol. ii, pp. 171–320, gives a minute history of this period; pp. 321–331, give the excuses of the abolitionists.

first fruits differed so widely from prophecy, that new causes had to be sought to explain the result. These were found in this tardy system of gradual emancipation. Immediate and unconditional manumission was the only panacea. We have seen how soon it followed. The world knows its results, and none are more ready to acknowledge the utter failure of the entire scheme, than the enlightened statesmen and patriots of England. This is not attributable to their want of statesmanship or foresight. The whole secret of the failure was their utter ignorance of the negro character. The same legislation for a body of oppressed Saxons or Celts, would have been productive of blessings commensurate with the sacrifices made. But for the negro, they labored not only in vain but to his injury.

There is but one testimony as to the present condition of the British West Indies. " Magnas inter opes inops," is the lamentable condition of them all, and " daily they are sinking deeper and deeper into the utter helplessness of abject want." Taking Jamaica, the largest and most visited, as a standard (ex uno, disce omnes) : " Shipping has deserted her ports; her magnificent plantations of sugar and coffee are running to weeds; her private dwellings are falling to decay; the comforts and luxuries which belong to industrial prosperity have been cut off, one by one, from her inhabitants; and the day is at hand when there will be none left to represent the wealth, intelligence, and hospitality, for which the Jamaica planter was once so distinguished."[1]

The condition of the Colonies has been frequently the subject of investigation by committees of the British Parliament; and huge volumes are filled with the evi-

---

[1] Bigelow's Notes on Jamaica (1850); The West Indies and North America, by Robert Baird (1849); The State and Prospects of Jamaica, by Dr. King; Colonies Etrangères, by Schœlcher; Gurney, on the West Indies; Cassagnac, Voyage aux Antilles; Negromania, by Campbell, and opinions of Knox, Franklin, and others, cited by him.

dence taken before such commissions. Legislative pal-
liatives and cures have been exhausted in seeking to
restore prosperity to these rich dependents of the crown.
Despairing of ever infusing industry and thrift, where
nature implanted idleness and improvidence, resort has
been and is now being had to the introduction of Coolies
from East India, to supply the labor necessary for an
island amply supplied, could it be brought into requisition; and even a modified resumption of the importation from Africa meets with favor from British statesmen, substituting (nominally, as it must be) voluntary
for involuntary emigration.

Not alone in material wealth has been the decline of
these once flourishing colonies. The condition of the
negroes physically, intellectually, and morally, keeps
pace with this downward tendency. Their numbers are
annually decreasing from disease, the result of unclean-
liness, and from want, the result of improvidence. Increase of crime is proportionate with the spread of
misery. Chapels and schools are abandoned, and faithful
teachers and missionaries have returned in despair to
Europe.[1]

If the reports of travellers and the local newspapers
can be relied on, these islands have not yet reached the
lowest depth of degradation and misery to which they
are doomed. Every year but adds to the desolation,
physical and moral.[2]

The other British possessions upon which the decree

[1] See Reports of Missionaries, made in 1849, quoted by Dr. King, p.
111; The Slave-Trade, Foreign and Domestic, by Carey, p. 27.

[2] See numerous quotations, in Mr. Carey's work, pp. 25–35; also an
instructive statement, by the West India Association of Glasgow, made
April 14th, 1853; and found in New York Herald, May 31, 1853. From
the official documents attached, it appears that from 1832 to 1847, 605
sugar and coffee plantations, containing 356,432 acres of land, and afford-
ing employment to 49,383 laborers, had been entirely abandoned. From
1848 to 1853, 513 more, containing 391,187 acres, were totally or partially abandoned.

of emancipation took effect, have experienced the same
results.  A graphic account of Guiana is given in the
report of a commission, appointed in 1850, to inquire
into its state and prosperity.  "The most ordinary marks
of civilization are fast disappearing," and the prediction
is made of "its slow but sure approximation to the condition in which civilized men first found it."[1]

In Southern Africa the effects have been equally disastrous.  Though the British residents at the Cape keep
up a flourishing trade, the agricultural interests have
suffered for want of laborers, and the farms have run to
waste.[2]  The same effects followed the Emancipation Act
at Mauritius, and Coolies have been introduced to supply
the place of former laborers.  The free blacks everywhere were idle, unreliable, vicious, and thievish.[3]

The same results have followed the experiments of
abolition made in the West Indies by other European
nations.  In the Danish colonies, where the slaves were
well treated, the free negroes are described as living in
"the greatest poverty, filth, and wretchedness."[4]  The
prosperity of the island is in the same degree diminished.

We shall see hereafter that the results in South America, Mexico, and Central America, exhibit a negro population in the same abject condition.[5]

[1] Lord Stanley's Letters to Mr. Gladstone.

[2] United States Japan Expedition, i, pp. 99–101, 103 ; The Cape and
the Kaffirs, by Harriet Ward.

[3] United States Japan Expedition, 103, 109.

[4] Cor. of N. Y. Herald, Nov. 9th, 1855 ; Brougham's Colonial Policy,
Bk. IV, Sect. 1.

[5] Dunn's Sketches of Guatemala.

# CHAPTER XV.

THE number of negroes emancipated in the United States was comparatively small, but the effects do not vary materially as to their condition, from those already noticed. The fact of their limited number, as well as the additional facts, that previous to their emancipation they were employed but little in agricultural pursuits, and that the nature of the agriculture of the Northern States of the Union was illy suited to this species of labor, protected the prosperity of those States from the depressing influences experienced elsewhere from the abolition of slavery. That their physical condition does not compare favorably with that of the slaves of the South is evident from the decennial census of the United States, showing a much larger increase in the latter than in the former. No surer test can be applied.[1]

[1] In order to obtain accurate information, I sent a circular to the Governors and leading politicians of the non-slaveholding States. I received answers as follows:

Maine, Hon. I. J. D. Fuller.
Vermont, Hon. J. Meacham.
Connecticut, Gov. Pond, and Hon. O. S. Seymour.
Rhode Island, Hon. B. B. Thurston.
New Jersey, Gov. Foot.
New York, Hon. S. G. Haven.
Pennsylvania, Hon. E. D. Ingraham.
Indiana, Gov. Wright.
Illinois, Gov. Matteson, Hon. W. A. Richardson.
Iowa, Judge Mason, Hon. Mr. Hern.
Michigan, Gov. Parsons.

Notwithstanding the very labored efforts made for their intellectual improvement, taken as a body they have made no advancement. Averse to physical labor, they are equally averse to intellectual effort. The young negro acquires readily the first rudiments of education, where memory and imitation are chiefly brought into action, but for any higher effort of reason and judgment he is, as a general rule, utterly incapable.[1]

I extract from their answers:

*Maine.*—"The condition of the negro population varies; but is very far below the whites."

*Vermont.*—"Their condition and character have great varieties. They are not in as good condition as the whites."

*Connecticut.*—Gov. Pond says: "The condition of the negro population, as a class, is not thrifty, and does not compare favorably with the whites. There are many, comparatively speaking, who are industrious."

*Rhode Island.*—"They are, generally, industrious and frugal."

*New Jersey.*—"Their condition is debased; with few exceptions very poor; generally indolent."

*New York.*—"The condition of the negro population is diversified,— some prosperous, some industrious. They have no social relations with the whites. Generally on about the same level that whites would occupy with like antecedents."

*Pennsylvania.*—"I deem the condition of the negro population, in this State, to be that of a degraded class, much deteriorated by freedom. They are not industrious."

*Indiana.*—"They are not prosperous. The majority of them are not doing well. We have sent off thirty or forty this year to Liberia, and hope to send off one hundred or more, next year, and finally to get rid of all we have in the State, and do not intend to have another negro or mulatto come into the State."

*Illinois.*—"As a class, they are thriftless and idle. Their condition far inferior to that of the whites." (Gov.)   "About the towns and cities, idle and dissolute, with exceptions. In the rural districts, many are in-dustrious and prosperous." (Mr. Richardson.)

*Iowa.*—"Very few negroes in Iowa. Far above the condition of those met with in our Eastern cities."

*Michigan.*—"Tolerably prosperous. Far behind the white popula-tion."

[1] *Maine.*—"Admitted into the public schools with the whites. Very far below them in education."

His moral condition compares unfavorably with that of the slave of the South. He seeks the cities and towns, and indulges freely in those vices to which his nature inclines him. His friends inveigh against "the prejudice of color," but he rises no higher in Mexico, Central America, New Grenada, or Brazil, where no such prejudice exists. The cause lies deeper: in the nature and constitution of the negro race.[1]

*Vermont.*—"Generally able to read and write; a few are liberally educated; not like the whites."

*Connecticut.*—"Fall much below the whites in education."

*Rhode Island.*—"Some are educated in the district schools. Compare well with the whites of their condition."

*New Jersey.*—"Generally ignorant. Far below the whites in intelligence."

*New York.*—"Generally very poorly, or but little educated."

*Pennsylvania.*—"Not educated. It is remarkable, that almost all the decent and respectable negroes we have, have been household slaves in some Southern State."

*Indiana.*—"Not educated."

*Illinois.*—"Ignorant." (Gov.)

*Michigan.*—"Not generally educated. Far below the whites."

[1] *Maine.*—"Far below the whites."

*Vermont.*—"Not as good as the whites."

*Connecticut.*—"Does not compare favorably with the whites." (Gov.) "They are, with us, an inferior caste; and in morality fall much below the whites." (Seymour.)

*New Jersey.*—"Immoral; vicious animal propensities; drunkenness, theft, and promiscuous sexual intercourse quite common. One-fourth of the criminals in the State prison are colored persons; while they constitute only one twenty-fifth of the population."

*New York.*—"Diversified; some moral."

*Pennsylvania.*—"Immoral. I am satisfied, from forty years' attention to the subject, that the removal of the wholesome restraint of slavery, and the consequent absence of the stimulus of the coercion to labor of that condition, have materially affected their condition for the worse. They exhibit all the characteristics of an inferior race, to whose personal comfort, happiness, and morality, the supervision, restraint, and coercion of a superior race seem absolutely necessary."

*Indiana.*—"In many instances very immoral."

*Illinois.*—"Thriftless, idle, ignorant, and vicious." (Gov.) "In towns and cities dissolute, with exceptions." (Richardson.)

The emancipated negroes do not enjoy full and equal civil and political rights in any State in the Union, except the State of Vermont. In several of the States they are not permitted to vote,[1] in some under peculiar restrictions.[2] In almost every State where the matter has been made a subject of legislation, intermarriages with the whites are forbidden.[3] In none are such marriages at all common.[4] In many they are forbidden to serve as jurors, or to be sworn as witnesses against a white person,[5] or hold any elective office.[6]

The criminal statistics of the slaveholding and non-slaveholding States show that the proportion of crime committed by negroes in the former does not reach the ratio of this population as compared with the whites,[7] while in the latter the ratio is much greater. The same is true of the statistics of mortality and disease. The apparent disproportion in the former case is greater than the truth, as many petty crimes by slaves do not reach the courts; and in the latter, it may be truly said that the southern climate is more favorable to the health and longevity of the negro. But making due allowances in both cases for these causes, it is still true, that the ne-

*Iowa.*—" Of a fair character."

*Michigan.*—" Tolerably moral. Far below the whites."

[1] Connecticut, New Jersey, Pennsylvania, Indiana, Illinois, Iowa, Michigan.                                          [2] New York.

[3] Maine, Rhode Island, Indiana, Illinois, Michigan.

[4] *Connecticut.*—Issue cannot vote.

*New Jersey.*—No legislation; and no cases of such marriage.

*New York.*—Issue considered as blacks.

*Pennsylvania.*—Issue considered as blacks.

*Iowa.*—No such cases.

[5] Connecticut, New Jersey, Indiana, Illinois, Iowa.

[6] Connecticut, New Jersey, Pennsylvania, Indiana, Illinois, Michigan.

[7] Judge Starnes, of Georgia, published several articles, giving statistics on this point, worthy of a more lasting existence, than derived from the columns of a newspaper.

groes are less addicted to crime, and are more healthy and longlived, in a state of slavery than of freedom.[1]

[1] In giving my conclusions, as to the free negroes of the North, I have relied on numberless authorities, combined with personal observation. I subjoin only a few. Paulding, on Slavery; Abolition a Sedition, by A Northern Man; Bishop Hopkins's American Citizen, 135; Seaboard Slave States, p. 125; Reports of American Colonization Society; Report of Naval Committee of H. of R., on establishing a line of Mail Steamships to Liberia (1850); Negromania, by John Campbell, being a collection of papers by distinguished men.

# CHAPTER XVI.

THE slave-trade was kept open by the Brazilian Government to a very late period. The number of negroes and persons of mixed blood within the territory is estimated as bearing the proportion of five to one of the white population. All of these are not slaves; the bond being estimated as only two-fifths of the whole. The number of free negroes, mulattoes, &c., is hence very considerable. There is probably no state in the world where there is less "prejudice of color" than in Brazil, though a slaveholding state. At court, in the army, in the haunts of business, everywhere may be found freely mingling together persons of every hue. The free negroes are frequently the owners of numbers of slaves, and are reported to be the most cruel masters. The slaves generally are kindly treated by, and are attached to their masters, though destitute in a great measure of the sense of gratitude. They are "indolent, thoughtless, and licentious," but not rebellious.[1]

New Grenada, with all other Spanish provinces, inherited negro slavery. The numbers were never very great, nor have they increased as in the United States; while the mixed and copper-colored constitute nearly

[1] For these facts, I rely principally on Wilkes's Exploring Expedition, vol. i, pp. 36, 56–68, 89, and Brazil and La Plata, by C. S. Stewart, U. S. N. In Brazil, as in other slaveholding states, there seem to be no beggars.

one-third of the entire population. The negroes were estimated, in 1853, at only 80,000, which is scarcely one-
thirtieth. In 1821, just after the Revolution, a law was
passed by the Republic of Colombia, for the gradual
manumission of slaves, and all born after that date were
declared free at the age of eighteen. By a law of 1851,
slavery was entirely abolished in New Grenada, by
giving liberty to all who remained slaves, on the 1st of
January, 1852, provision being made for the payment
of the owners.[1] The results of this emancipation have
been the same with similar efforts elsewhere. The negroes, as a class, are idle, immoral, vicious, preferring to
beg and steal rather than work. The destruction and
desolation in some of the finest agricultural districts,
consequent upon the Act of 1821, are described as deplorable in the extreme. The want and destitution of
the poorer classes are pitiable. "Their morals can sink
no lower, and their religion can raise them no higher."[2]

Slavery exists in other portions of South America. In
Chili and Peru there seem to be but few negroes. In
the latter the slaves are treated with great kindness. It
is no unusual sight to see a mistress and her slave kneel-

---

[1] Memoir on the Physical and Political Geography of New Grenada,
by General De Mosquera, ex-President of the same.

[2] New Grenada, by Isaac F. Holton, pp. 173, 269, 527, 533. I am
indebted for some of the facts stated, to letters from Col. King and Judge
Bowlin, late ministers of the United States to New Grenada. The latter
says, "The universally admitted characteristics of the negro, when unrestrained,—of indigence, improvidence, and indolence,—are strikingly
exemplified in New Grenada, where every avenue is equally open to
him as to the white man, to elevate his condition; yet, if he does not
recede, he certainly makes no advance in the progress to a higher civilization." Living on tropical fruits, and indulging in intoxicating drinks,
he adds, "He generally goes in a state of nudity; and when he does not,
he merely wears a coarse shirt, or a shirt and pantaloons made of coarse
cotton." "Take them all in all, they are a miserable race, encumber-
ing the earth, whose vicious qualities civilization seems only to develop
more strongly."

ing in a cathedral, side by side, on the same piece of cloth.[1]

The negroes in La Plata are more numerous. Commodore Stewart saw more than one thousand negro washerwomen at one time on the shores of the river. In the late Revolution the negroes were offered their liberty, without compensation to their masters, on condition of enlisting as soldiers for the war. Many availed themselves of this privilege.[2]

[1] Wilkes's Exp. Exp. vol. i, 257 ; vol. ix, Races of Man, by Dr. Pickering.

[2] Brazil and La Plata, by C. S. Stewart.

# CHAPTER XVII.

. SLAVERY IN THE UNITED STATES.

NEGRO slavery continues to exist in fifteen of the United States of America. In Virginia, Kentucky, and Missouri, attempts have been made to bring about emancipation by the State governments; it being admitted by all that the Federal Government has no power to interfere with or seek to regulate the institution within the States. In 1787, the first abolition society was formed, since which time they have greatly increased, their object being to bring to bear upon the slaveholding States the powerful public sentiment of the other States; to bring into action the powers of Congress, wherever legitimately to be exercised, against the continuance of the institution, and thus indirectly to effect what could not be done directly. The infatuated zeal of many fanatics has carried them farther, and induced them to endeavor, by incendiary publications and agents, to excite insurrections among the slaves, and in other ways to force the masters to consent to their emancipation. In later years, some of the more excited have inveighed against the Constitution of the United States, as a "league with hell," because its provisions limited the powers of the general government on this subject. In fact, the history of abolitionism in the United States has been the history of fanaticism everywhere, whose later deeds are not even shadowed forth in its earlier years; and with whom obstacles and impediments, the more insurmountable they are in fact,

N

but feed the flame of zeal, and more effectually dethrone
the reason. This class of abolitionists, however, have
ever been comparatively few in number; while those who
sympathize with the objects above-mentioned (the legitimate use of means to extinguish slavery), have ever been,
in the non-slaveholding States, numerous and respectable. The points of conflict in our national assemblies,
upon which difficulties have arisen between the advocates of these doctrines and their opponents, are based
upon the question, what powers were given by the Constitution to Congress, and at what time and in what way
they could be exercised? Such have been the questions
as to the admission of new States into the Union, where
slavery was recognized; the abolition of slavery and the
slave-trade in the District of Columbia, and in the forts
and arsenals, and other public property belonging to the
United States, and situated within the slaveholding
States; the prohibition of slavery within the territories
of the United States, before their application for admission as States, and the regulation of the domestic slave-
trade between the slaveholding States.

It is not my purpose to extend this sketch, by giving
the history of the conflicts upon each of these questions.
They have threatened, seriously, the existence of the
government. Suffice it to say, that the right of each
State to regulate for itself its domestic relations, so far
as this question is concerned, seems now to be acknowledged by the statesmen of the country; and that, hence,
the existence of slavery in a State is no ground for re-
jecting its admission into the Union. The slave-trade
in the District of Columbia has been properly abolished;
and slavery therein, and in the public forts, &c., is left,
as required by good faith, to abide the fate of the institution in the adjacent States by which they were ceded.
The right to prohibit slavery in the territories of the
United States has been denied by the Supreme Court, in

a late and most elaborate decision.[1]  And the same Court long since decided, that an attempt to regulate the domestic slave-trade between the States, would give virtually to Congress the right to abolish or establish slavery in every State of the Union.[2]  That these questions may be allowed here to rest, and be no longer used as hobbies by interested demagogues to excite sectional strifes for personal advancement, should be the sincere wish of every true American citizen.[3]

Having been generally well-treated, the slaves have never exhibited that disposition to revolt so frequently seen in the West Indies.  No Maroons have infested our mountains; no wars of the Maroons stain our annals. But one insurrection, worthy the name, has ever occurred, and that was in Virginia in the year 1800.  The plot (as all others will be) was made known by faithful slaves to their masters, and effectual measures taken for its suppression.  Several negroes, leaders in the rebellion, were tried and executed.  The evidence on their trial showed that they were instigated by a white man, and that their whole plans manifested a weakness in conception unequalled except by the history of the negro.[4]

Cases of individual manumission have been frequent in all the States.  In many of them, the idle and lazy habits of the free negroes, and the continual agitation of the question of abolition by Northern fanatics, have

[1] Dred Scott v. Sandford, 19 Howard.  The other and interesting question decided in this case, whether a negro can become a citizen of the United States, will be considered at another place.

[2] Groves v. Slaughter, 15 Peters, 449.

[3] M. Levavasseur exposes, in a masterly manner, the policy of Great Britain, in fomenting the abolition excitement in the United States; hoping thereby, to retard their march towards universal empire on the American Continent.  I would that every citizen of the Union could read the remarks of this disinterested philosopher.  Esclavage de la race noire, p. 31, et suiv.

[4] See the documents, respecting the insurrection, published in the Richmond Recorder, April 3d, 6th, and 9th, 1803.

induced the legislatures to prohibit domestic emancipation, and thereby compelled masters, thus disposed, to
send their slaves either to other States or to Africa in
order to receive their freedom.  This influx of free
negroes has not been acceptable to the non-slaveholding
States, especially the new States of the West, to which
they were principally sent.  Hence most, if not all of
them, some by their constitution, and some by legislative acts, have prohibited the introduction of free negroes
into their territory.  Liberia is therefore left as the only
home of the emancipated negro.  Africa gave birth to
the negro.  Africa alone offers him, as a freeman, a
grave.

The work to which this sketch is an introduction, is
intended to exhibit the exact *status* of the slave in the
United States; a repetition here upon these points
would be inappropriate.  That their bondage has been
mild is evidenced by their great and rapid increase.  For
about 333,000 slaves imported, there are now more than
4,000,000.  Their physical development is unquestionably
much superior to that of the negro in his native country.
Their longevity is remarkable.  Their mental development has advanced very considerably, still retaining,
however, the negro characteristics, except in the case of
the mulattoes, where the traits of the white parents are
sometimes developed.  But above all, their moral improvement is most evident.  Though still inclined to
superstition, they are frequently exemplary Christians,
and generally inclined to be religious.  An avowed infidel is a *rara avis* among the negroes.  The statistics of
the different churches in the slaveholding States show
a greater number of negroes converted, and admitted
into the Church than all the conversions which have
crowned the missionary efforts of the world.  The improved negro, however, exhibits still the moral weak-
nesses of the native Ebo; his sins, if any, are theft, lust,
and falsehood.

Both politically and socially negro slavery has its benefits and its evils. To the negro himself the former greatly preponderate. To the owners, the masters, the question is a greater problem, and there is more room for honest differences of opinion.

Politically, slavery is a *conservative* institution. The mass of laborers not being recognized among citizens, every citizen feels that he belongs to an elevated class. It matters not that he is no slaveholder; he is not of the inferior race; he is a freeborn citizen; he engages in no menial occupation. The poorest meets the richest as an equal; sits at his table with him; salutes him as a neighbor; meets him in every public assembly, and stands on the same social platform. Hence, there is no war of classes. There is truthfully republican equality in the ruling class.

The laborers being slaves, there is not the same danger of conflicts between labor and capital, nor the same liability to other excitements in crowded masses, which end in riots. These are unknown in pure slaveholding communities.

Raising their own laborers, there is no inducement for foreign immigration into slaveholding communities. Their citizens imbibe freedom with their mother's milk.

The leisure allowed to the slaveholder gives him an opportunity of informing himself upon current questions of politics, and his interest being identical with his neighbors, in preserving existing institutions, the Southern politician addresses always a body of men having a common sentiment, and not to be influenced to so great an extent by the "humbugs" of demagogues. This is an influential element in forming public opinion, and acts thus *conservatively* upon the public men of the South.

Official position is not very consistent with the interest of the slaveholder, and hence is never sought for its

pecuniary emoluments.   It is coveted only by those
ambitious of distinction.   Hence, the public men of the
South do not find themselves supplanted by unprovided
aspirants, but their services are frequently gratefully
received by their constituents.   Born to command, and
habituated to rule, they frequently commend themselves
to the nation by their firmness, their independence, and
their fearlessness.   These are important elements in the
character of a statesman.

Slavery is a protection from *pauperism*, the bane for
which the wisdom of civilized man has not yet prepared
an antidote.   In America, affliction, old age, and idleness,
are the only sources of pauperism.   Where the laborers
are slaves the master is compelled by law to provide
against the former, and is authorized to protect himself
against the latter.   The poorhouse, therefore, is almost
unknown.[1]

The severities of winter and the depression of finan-
cial crises, bring no horrors to the laborers of the South.
The interest of the master as well as the law of the
land protect the negro against the former, while a change
of masters is the worst result which can befall him from
the latter.

As already intimated, there is perhaps no solution of
the great problem of reconciling the interests of labor
and capital, so as to protect each from the encroachments
and oppressions of the other, so simple and effective as
negro slavery.   By making the laborer himself capital,
the conflict ceases, and the interests become identical.

On the other hand, a slaveholding State can never be
densely populated.   The slaves, moreover, occupying

[1] See a very instructive and interesting table, on this subject, in the
Abstract of the Seventh Census, p. 28, by which it appears that the
small State of Rhode Island returned 2560 paupers, as receiving support
during the year ending 1st June, 1850, while in Georgia there were only
1036.

the places of free laborers, and three-fifths only of their number being estimated under the Constitution of the United States, for representative purposes, the result is inevitable that the slaveholding States must ever have a smaller voice, politically, than the same territory would command with free labor. To this extent slavery destroys their political equality in the nation.

Another result of a sparse population is, that a perfect system of thorough common school education is almost an impossibility. Extensive plantations, occupied by slaves only, independent of the exhausting crops cultivated and annually adding to barren fields, render a perfect system of common schools impossible.

In a slaveholding State, the greatest evidence of wealth in the planter is the number of his slaves. The most desirable property for a remunerative income, is slaves. The best property to leave to his children, and from which they will part with greatest reluctance, is slaves. Hence, the planter invests his surplus income in slaves. The natural result is, that lands are a secondary consideration. No surplus is left for their improvement. The homestead is valued only so long as the adjacent lands are profitable for cultivation. The planter himself, having no local attachments, his children inherit none. On the contrary, he encourages in them a disposition to seek new lands. His valuable property (his slaves) are easily removed to fresh lands; much more easily than to bring the fertilizing materials to the old. The result is that they, as a class, are never settled. Such a population is almost nomadic. It is useless to seek to excite patriotic emotions in behalf of the land of birth, when self-interest speaks so loudly. On the other hand, where no slavery exists, and the planter's surplus cannot be invested in laborers, it is appropriated to the improvement or extension of his farm, the beautifying of the homestead where his fathers are buried, and where he hopes to lie.   Of course we speak of classes, not of individuals. The result is the withdrawal of all investments from the improvement of the lands, another deleterious effect of slavery to the State.

It has been asserted that slave labor is exhausting to lands.   So far as the cause already alluded to withdraws the planter from the improvement of his land, it is true. But the more satisfactory explanation of the exhausting cultivation of Southern lands, is the nature of the crops planted.   Being "clean" crops, the exposure of the naked ploughed lands to the long-continued heat of the summer sun, would be followed by sterility, partial or complete, whether free or slave labor was used in their cultivation.

It has often been asserted that free labor is cheaper than slave, and evidence has been industriously sought in the British colonies to show that the labor of the emancipated negro there, is cheaper than that of the slave.[1]  In dense populations, where the question is labor or hunger, the assertion is generally true ; for the amount invested, either in the purchase or rearing of the laborer, is necessarily that much more than the cost of food and raiment, which both free and bond must have, and which is all that, under such circumstances, competition and necessity leave to the free laborer.   If either one of two facts existed, the assertion might be true of the Southern slaveholding States, viz., the successful introduction of a dense white population to take the place of the slaves ; or, the introduction into the negro nature of some principle to counteract that sloth which abhors work, and that absence of pride and principle which prefers theft and beggary to industry and thrift.   To the possibility of the former two great obstacles arise, in the first place, climate and disease, which bring death to the Saxon, and health and immunity to the African ; in the second,

---

[1] See Gurney's West Indies.

the impossibility of cultivating extensively the staple productions of the South, rice, sugar, cotton, and to-bacco, except by associated labor, not subject to the contingencies of "strikes" or caprices.

The possibility of the latter contingency is shown not to exist, by the examples of the negro character wherever and whenever emancipated. The free negroes of the United States, North and South, of the West Indies, and of Liberia, show an indisposition to labor, except from absolute necessity, which manifests a characteristic of the race.[1] The introduction of Coolies, by both Great Britain and France, into their colonies, is upon the avowed allegation of the idleness of the negro.

While, then, the general proposition, that free labor is cheaper than slave, may be true, it would seem that slave labor is the only effectual, and therefore cheapest, labor which the Southern States can use in the production of their staples. Experience, at the South, has shown this to be true in the building of railroads. Slave labor must be used successfully on uniform work, requiring physical strength, without judgment or discretion. Wherever such work in large quantity can be found in the Southern climate, slave labor is the cheapest that can be applied.

As a social relation, negro slavery has its benefits and its evils. That the slave is incorporated into and becomes a part of the family, that a tie is thus formed between the master and slave, almost unknown to the relation of master and hireling, that in consequence even the young spendthrift experiences a pang in sundering a relation he has recognized from his infancy, that the old and infirm are thus cared for, and the young

[1] Antigua is frequently referred to as an example of voluntary free labor by negroes. The island is small, the inhabitants few; but at the same time, fully occupying the whole territory. The whites have been wise and humane, and the experiment, on this small scale, has been more successful than elsewhere.

protected and reared, are indisputable facts. Interest joins with affection in promoting this unity of feeling. To the negro, it insures food, fuel, and clothing, medical attendance, and in most cases religious instruction. The young child is seldom removed from the parent's protection, and beyond doubt, the institution prevents the separation of families, to an extent unknown among the laboring poor of the world.[1] It provides him with a protector, whose interest and feeling combine in demanding such protection.

To the master, it gives a servant whose interests are identical with his own, who has indeed no other interest, except the gratification of a few animal passions, for which purpose he considers it no robbery to purloin his master's goods.

In short, the Southern slavery is a patriarchal, social system. The master is the head of his family. Next to wife and children, he cares for his slaves. He avenges their injuries, protects their persons, provides for their wants, and guides their labors. In return, he is revered and held as protector and master. Nine-tenths of the Southern masters would be defended by their slaves, at the peril of their own lives.

The evils of the system are equally unquestionable. That it engenders in the youth of the South that overbearing and despotic spirit, ascribed to the relation by Mr. Jefferson, is not true to the extent he alleges. The fact, that Northern men are sometimes the most exacting masters, is well known. The reason of this is that they expect from the slave the amount of work which they have received from a hireling. *This he never will do*, and the Southern-bred master does not look for it. The security of his place, as well as the indolence of his

[1] On my father's plantation, an aged negro woman could call together more than one hundred of her lineal descendants. I saw this old negro dance at the wedding of her great granddaughter. She did no labor for my father for more than forty years before her death.

nature, do not furnish the necessary stimulus. It is true, however, that the young man of the South *is accustomed to rule*, and even the son of a poor man, without a slave, to a certain extent, commands obedience from the negro population. The result is a spirit of independence, which brooks not opposition. Within a proper limit this is not an evil. Indulgence makes it a sin.

A good consequence of this is, a more perfect equality in social life, among the rich and poor, than can be had where the menial servants are of the same color. An evil consequence is a too great sensitiveness on questions of personal honor, and a corresponding disposition to settle them "by wager of battle."

An evil attributed to slavery, and frequently alluded to, is the want of chastity in female slaves, and a corresponding immorality in the white males. To a certain extent this is true; and to the extent that the slave is under the control and subject to the order of the master, the condition of slavery is responsible.

Every well-informed person at the South, however, knows that the exercise of such power for such a purpose is almost unknown. The prevalence of the evil is attributable to other causes. The most prominent of these is the natural lewdness of the negro. It is not the consequence of slavery. The free negro in Africa, in the West Indies, in America, exhibits the same disposition, perhaps not to the same degree when living in a Christian community.[1] Another cause is the fact that the negress knows that the offspring of such intercourse, the mulatto, having greater intelligence, and being in-

---

[1] The ratio of mulattoes to blacks, among the free colored population of the Northern States, shows this to be true among them. In Maine, 51; New Hampshire, 54; Vermont, 40; Massachusetts, 34; Connecticut, 30; and Rhode Island, 24, out of every 100 were mulattoes, in 1850. See Mortality Statistics of the Census of 1850, p. 35. Bowen alludes to this vice in Liberia, but hopes it is not so prevalent, "if report may be trusted, as with the people of Sierra Leone, or of France." Central Africa, p. 32.

deed a superior race, has a better opportunity of enjoying the privileges of domestics; in other words, *is elevated* by the mixture of blood. Her sin does not entail mis fortune but good fortune on her children. Nor does she lose any social position even with her own race. Under such circumstances the prevalence of this sin is not surprising.

It is undoubtedly true, that from this cause the poor white females of the slaveholding States are not subject to as great temptations and importunities as they would be under other circumstances. That the ignorant poor, under the heating Southern sun, would compare unfavorably with those of colder climates in this particular, except for this institution, is manifested by the immorality of some ignorant districts in slaveholding States, where but few negroes are found. How far such a result counterbalances the evil admitted, can be weighed only by the great Arbiter of the universe.

A social evil of no small magnitude, arising from this condition, is the imbibing by children of the superstitions, fears, and habits, of the negroes, with whom they are necessarily, to some extent, reared. The negro is not yet more than semi-civilized. The marvellous and the unearthly, ghosts, witches, and charmings, are mingled even with his religion. Great caution is necessary, on the part of the Southern mother, to protect the young child from such influences.

The inability of the slave parents to control and govern their own children from the intervention of another power, the master's, has been considered an evil of this social system. Theoretically it is; practically it is not, for two reasons: first, the master never interferes with but rather encourages such government; it is an aid to him. And, second, unless the child in some way interferes with the comfort or wishes of the parent, the negro has no disposition to control his waywardness or his vices.

That the marriage relation between slaves is not recognized or protected by the law, is another evil to the
negro attending the system, and to a qualified extent it
is an evil. In practice, public opinion protects the relation. The unfeeling separation of husband and wife, is
a rare occurrence. It never happens when both belong
to the same master. To regulate properly this relation
by legislation, so as to prevent inhumanity on the one
hand, and not to bind too much the owner's power of
selling an unworthy or unruly slave on the other, requires
great sagacity and prudence.

It would require a prophetic vision to foretell the
future of the American negro slaves. Emancipation, in
their present location, can never be peacefully effected.
Until the white race of the South is exterminated or
driven off, it can never be forcibly effected. Amalgamation, to any great extent, is a moral impossibility.
Colonization on the coast of Africa could be effected
only at immense cost, and at the sacrifice of the lives of
at least one-fourth of the emigrants. So long as climate
and disease, and the profitable planting of cotton, rice,
tobacco, and cane, make the negro the only laborer inhabiting safely our Southern savannas and prairies,
just so long will he remain a slave to the white man.
Whenever the white laborer can successfully compete
with him in these productions and occupy this soil, the
negro will either be driven slowly through the Isthmus,
to become amalgamated with the races of South America,
or he will fall a victim to disease and neglect, begging
bread at the white man's door.

# CHAPTER XVIII.

Two attempts have been made to colonize the negro in Africa. During the American war of revolution, Great Britain, to induce the slaves to join her standard, promised to all such freedom. At the close of the war, such negroes as had accepted the offer were carried temporarily to Nova Scotia, and finally colonized at Sierra Leone, on the coast of Africa. To these have been added large numbers of captured Africans found on board of slavers, which have fallen into the hands of British cruisers. No special attention has been aroused in the mother country, among the benevolent and Christians, to this colony; and so far as the same may be considered as an effort to evidence the capacity of the negro for self-elevation, it is an admitted failure. Without dwelling longer on its history, we turn to Liberia, where everything has been done which philanthropy or religion could suggest, to develop to its fullest capacity the moral and intellectual growth of the negro.

Satisfied that the only condition in which the white and black races could live together, to their mutual advantage, was that of slavery to the latter, and looking to Africa, the birthplace of the negro, for a home and a grave, the friends of the negro in the United States inaugurated an effort, in 1816, to test his capacity for a self-sustaining civilization upon its shores. The philanthropists of the entire Union joined heartily in this enterprise, some of the noblest names of the Republic being recorded as its earliest friends. The legislatures of the States, North and South, with great unanimity, approved of the movement, and earnest, zealous, active friends have devoted time, talents, wealth, health, and life, to insure its success. Never in the history of the world has a colony been planted from purer philanthropy, nor cherished with greater munificence, nor followed by more ardent prayers. Liberia is the child of philanthropy and religion. The sympathies of the civilized world have been with her. She has had no human enemies, save the savages of her own race, surrounding her borders, and a few fanatical abolitionists in our own country.

It is not necessary to our purpose to trace minutely its history. A few facts will present its inception and its present position. The first emigrants were sent out in 1820. In April, 1822, the American flag was first hoisted at the spot now occupied by Monrovia, the capital of the Republic. From that date to 1847, white Governors, appointed by the American Colonization Society, presided over its destinies. During that year steps were taken to declare its independence, and on the 3d of January, 1848, Governor Roberts was inaugurated President of the Republic. From that time to the present it has maintained its separate existence, although the Colonization Society has continued, not only its friendly advice and sympathy, but has annually sent out, at its own expense, large numbers of emigrants, besides frequent direct contributions of money for various purposes. The British Government presented to the young Republic " a man-of-war." The French Government presented her a supply of arms. Their and the American cruisers have been ever ready to extend to her their assistance and protection.[1] Her entire

---

[1] Africa and the American Flag, by Com. Foote, 181, 182.

territory, extending along the coast seven hundred miles, has been purchased and paid for by the contributions of friends.   These and similar facts only show the favorable circumstances which have attended the new Republic.

Too much should not be expected from an infant colony; but remembering that these emigrants, in the main, represent the most worthy and most energetic of the negro and mixed race of the United States; that they have annually received a fresh supply of similar emigrants from the States; that they have been fostered as before stated; and that *thirty-seven* years have elapsed since the planting of the colony, we are permitted to look, to some extent, for the evidence of their capacity for a self-sustaining civilization.

From this view, we will not say that the effort is a failure.   The prospect of the negro being used as the instrument of civilizing his birthplace; and that, torn away a savage from his native land by the cupidity and avarice of his fellow-man, he shall be restored, a Christian, by the philanthropy of his brother man, has in it something of that sublimity which would evidence the purpose of God.   We should be slow to disbelieve such a purpose, though "his ways are not as our ways."

In 1845, a census of the colony, with several interesting statistical tables, was published.   From these we learn that the total number of emigrants sent out up to that date was 4454.   Of these there were left in the colony only 1736.   Of the remainder, 2198 had died, and 520 had removed.   The Thirty-fifth Annual Report of the Society shows that, in 1851, the number of emigrants sent out had increased to 8636.   In 1852 and 1853, there were sent out 1449 more, making 10,085 emigrants to that date.   Estimating 700 for the four last years each, would give us 12,885.   How many of these survive and remain in the colony, I have no means of deciding.   The total civilized population of the Republic does not now amount to exceeding 8000 souls.[1] The increase of population does not show physical improvements. I am aware of the numbers who fall victims to the acclimating fever, greater, I doubt not, than publications admit. I am aware also of Dr. Lugenbeel's account of the diseases of the colony, the most troublesome and fatal of which, according to him, have their origin in a want of cleanliness, precisely what one would fear, at all acquainted with negro character.[2]

Another striking fact to be deduced from the tables alluded to, is the congregation of all the emigrants in the towns and villages, and their adherence to traffic, rather than agricultural or mechanical employments.[3] The love of a negro for a town, and his aversion to regular labor, which are proverbial,[4] he seems to retain in Liberia, where, with a rich and productive soil, agriculture seems confined to the natives. Hence, the current report of the emigrants holding slaves, so often contradicted.[5] That many of the emigrants have amassed considerable property by their industry, is a gratifying fact; although it would be more satisfactory did we

[1] Commander Foote, U. S. N., estimates them at 7500, in 1854. Africa and the American Flag, 198. Bowen estimates them, from the best authorities, at 7792, in 1857. Central Africa, 35.

[2] Sketches of Liberia, ch. vii (published by Am. Col. Soc.).

[3] Bowen estimates those devoted to agriculture, at 8 per cent.; mechanics, 5 per cent., p. 35.

[4] Mr. Gerrit Smith gives a striking illustration of this fact in a letter, stating the number of free negroes to whom he has donated farms, in Western New York, and the very small number who have cultivated them.

[5] Dr. Lugenbeel says, "that comparatively few of the present citizens of Liberia are regularly and systematically engaged in the cultivation of the soil." Again, "A more *regular, systematic*, and *persevering* course of farming operations must be introduced." The italics are his own. Foote says, "The want of agricultural industry has been the difficulty with the Liberians." 194. Bowen says, "A majority of the colonists appear to be, more or less, engaged in traffic." p. 35.

o

know how much they carried with them, and also how many of these successful traders were pure negroes. That there are very many idlers and some *beggars* in the Republic, is an admitted fact.[1]

It is not easy to arrive at a satisfactory opinion as to the intellectual progress of the Liberians. Their Constitution was framed, to a great extent, for them.[2] The addresses of Governor Roberts (a mulatto), and the productions of the pens of others, indicate thinking minds, and some considerable education. These, however, were trained in America. In the census referred to, the name of every child *born in the colony* is given, and the extent of the education of each. The highest specified was, "can read and write," though many had reached twenty years of age. Not one is reported as having a *liberal* or classical education. It does not speak well for the appreciation of education by the Liberians, that every school in the Republic is maintained by the charity of religious sects in the United States;[3] nor the additional fact, that the "classical school," established by the Presbyterians, the only one in the Republic, numbered, in 1852, only *eight* scholars, out of the entire population.

As to the moral progress of the Liberians, we cannot

---

[1] "It is said that the young people are too much addicted to idleness." Bowen's Central Africa, 33 (1857). "Indolence is the only just reason why beef, milk, and butter are not abundant in this country, where they are now almost unknown." p. 45.

"Some are rich, some are doing well, and some are just able to get along in the world; others are poor, and there are those that beg." "We see farms and lots of many grown over with bushes, and not a single potato planted in them. In the very countenance of some, we see industry and enterprise depicted, but with others, we discover the reverse." Fuller and Janifer's Reports to Maryland Col. Soc. "If they exerted themselves a little more, and depended not so much on the natives, they would have no complaints to make." Ibid.

[2] Report of R. R. Gurley, p. 21.

[3] Bowen's Central Africa, p. 32 (1857); School Reports, attached to census of Africa's Redemption, 203.

speak with any degree of certainty. They seem to retain many of the characteristics of the negroes in the United States. Foote speaks of their disposition to deal in superstition and the supernatural.[1] Their religious teaching is almost exclusively confined to the labors of missionaries, sent from and supported by American Christians. From the tables accompanying the census, above referred to, it appears that the crimes to which they are addicted in Liberia, partake much of the same character with those committed by the negroes of America. Of 373 reported trials for offences, 308 were for larceny of different degrees. Kidnapping, rioting, rape, and murder, complete the list. Lust, the besetting sin of the negro, seems to accompany him to Liberia, and a want of chastity in the female.[2] The proportion of the population, who are professing Christians, is perhaps larger than that of the slaves in the United States.

The emigrants have waged several wars successfully against neighboring tribes, with great disparity of numbers. They have rendered some efficient service in repressing the slave-trade along their coasts.[3] They have not been guilty of the excesses, the turbulence, nor the restlessness of the emancipated negroes of the West Indies. All these facts speak in favor of their civilization. How far they may be accounted for, on other grounds, it is unnecessary to discuss. Let us hope that they indicate a developing civilization. For the present, African colonization is an experiment. Its disinterested and not too zealous friends, are not prepared to announce its success. Foote says, "In devising measures for the benefit of Liberia, one thing was pre-eminently to be

[1] Africa and the American Flag, 197.

[2] Bowen's Central Africa, p. 32.

[3] The abolitionists deny this, and say that the trade was carried on in the Colony. No reliance, however, can be placed on these statements. See Slavery and Anti-Slavery, by Goodell, 352, and note.

kept in view, which was, that the people be prevented from sinking back to become mere Africans." Dr. Lugenbeel, who resided long in Liberia, speaks with hesitation of its future: "I am quite satisfied that if the Republic of Liberia shall ingloriously fall, and her institutions be demolished, the result will indubitably exhibit the melancholy fact, that the maintenance of an independent government, by the colored race, is at least a subject of doubtful practicability."

I have referred only to a few facts admitted by the best friends of colonization, which seem to indicate that the negro has undergone no radical change by removal to his native shores. The danger is, that as the generation of emigrants becomes extinct, their descendants will relapse gradually into the heathenism and barbarism which surround them. So long as annual exportations from the United States, of the most energetic and intelligent of our free colored population continue, an appearance of activity and life will be exhibited. But to prove the capacity of the negro for a self-evolving civilization, he must be left to himself for a few generations. Good men and wise men differ as to the final result. I must confess my own incredulity.

THE

LAW OF NEGRO SLAVERY.

THE

# LAW OF NEGRO SLAVERY.

---

I PROPOSE to consider the Law of Negro Slavery as it exists in the United States of America; to examine into its origin, its foundation, and its present condition; to note the striking differences in the legislation of the various slaveholding States, and occasionally to suggest amendments to the existing laws.

---

## CHAPTER I.

### WHAT IS SLAVERY, AND ITS FOUNDATION IN THE NATURAL LAW.

§ 1. *Absolute or Pure Slavery* is the condition of that individual, over whose life, liberty, and property another has the unlimited control. The former is termed a slave; the latter is termed the master. Slavery, in its more usual and limited signification, is applied to all involuntary servitude, which is not inflicted as a punishment for crime.[1] The former exists at this day in none of the civilized nations of the world; the latter has, at some time, been incorporated into the social system of every nation whose history has been deemed worthy of record.[2] In the former condition the slave loses all *personality*, and is viewed merely as *property;* in the latter, while treated under the general class of *things*, he possesses various rights as a person, and is treated as such by the law.[3]

§ 2. A preliminary inquiry presents itself, and demands our first consideration, viz.: By what law or authority does this dominion of one man over another exist? by the law of nature, or by municipal law? And a satisfactory reply to this inquiry is absolutely necessary to the true resolution of many

[1] The definitions of slavery have been various. According to the Institutes it was " constitutio juris gentium, quâ quis domino alieno, contra naturam subjicitur." This definition was adopted *verbatim* from the Stoic philosophers. See Heinec. Opera V, p. 20.

Heineccius defines slavery as follows: " Servi sunt personæ; qui ad dominorum utilitatem operis suis, vel pro certâ mercede alimentisque, vel pro solis alimentis promovendam obstricti sunt." Jus Nat. et Gent. cap. iv, § 77.

The Civil Code of Louisiana defines a slave to be " one who is in the power of a master, to whom he belongs." Arts. 35 and 173.

[2] See Preliminary Sketch, &c.

[3] Among the Romans, the slave was classed as a thing: Res. He was "Homo sed non persona." Heinec. Elem. Jur. Lib. I, § 75. He was considered "pro nullo et mortuo, quia nec statu familiæ nec civitatis nec libertatis gaudet." Ibid. § 77. See also Kaufmann's Mackeldey; State v. Edmund, 4 Dev. 340; Neal v. Farmer, 9 Ga. Rep. 582.

of the perplexing questions which arise from that relation. In the laws of Henry I, we find the declaration, "servi alii naturâ, alii facto, alii empcione, alii redempcione, alii suâ vel alterius dacione servi."[1] The Institutes, on the contrary, declared all slavery to be " contra naturam," and this declaration, which might be true of a system which ignored entirely the existence of the slave as a person, has been almost universally adopted by courts and jurists.[2] Upon the investigation of the truth of this proposition we propose to enter.

§ 3. That slavery is contrary to the law of nature, has been so confidently and so often asserted, that slaveholders themselves have most generally permitted their own minds to acknowledge its truth unquestioned.) [Hence, even learned judges in slaveholding States, adopting the language of Lord Mansfield, in Somerset's case, have announced gravely, that slavery being contrary to the law of nature, can exist only by force of positive law.[3]] The course of reasoning, by which this conclusion is attained, is very much this: That in a state of nature all men are free. That one man is at birth entitled by nature to no higher rights or privileges than another, nor does nature specify any particular time or circumstances under which the one shall begin to rule and the other to obey. Hence, by the law of nature,

---

[1] Ancient Laws and Institutes of England; Leges Henr. I, ch. lxxvi, § 3.

[2] For the modification or explanation of this expression in the Institutes, see post: § 12.

[3] Case of the Antelope, 10 Wheat. 120; State v. Jones, Walker's Miss. Rep. 83.

no man is the slave of another, and hence all slavery is contrary to the law of nature.

§ 4. For a proper inquiry into the truth of this proposition, it becomes very important that we should have a definite understanding of what is meant by the *law of nature*. Jurists have declared it to be the only true foundation of all law. International law is defined to be but the law of nature as applied to the conduct and affairs of nations. Philosophers have vied with each other in pronouncing encomiums upon its pure morality and unadulterated justice; and in the prophetic vision of the greatest of Roman orators, it was calculated to bind the world in one great bond of justice, when, in process of time, there should be "non alia lex Romæ, alia Athenis, alia nunc, alia posthac, sed una lex et sempiterna prevalebit." Hooker, in strains no less sublime, has said, " Of this law, no less can be said than that her seat is the bosom of God, her voice the harmony of the world; all things in heaven and earth do her homage, the very least as feeling her care, the greatest as not exempted from her power; both angels and men, and creatures of what condition soever, though each in different sort and manner, yet all, with uniform consent, admiring her as the mother of their peace and joy."[1]

§ 5. Yet we find it very difficult to cull from them all, a clear, concise, tangible definition of what is meant by the *law of nature*. The Roman lawyers and others applied the term to that "law which nature teaches *all living creatures*," thereby causing

---

[1] Ecclesiastical Polity, conclusion of Book I.

it to include all animals, beasts as well as men.[1]
To this others have demurred, and insist that *law*
can be applied only to creatures who have *reason*
and *will*, to perceive an obligation and to adapt their
acts accordingly.[2] And Potgiesseri very properly
observes, that even when applied to men it assumes
a double aspect: " Vel, ut concipiuntur omnes et
singuli homines in naturali libertate, nullique imperio subjecti vivere; vel, ut intelliguntur cum ali-
quibus tantum in societatem civilem coivisse, cum
reliquis autem nullo, nisi communi humanitatis
vinculo colligari."[3]

§ 6. As great diversity exists when we come to
examine the rules deduced from this law. Hobbes
found one of its fundamental rules to be, that war
was the natural condition of mankind. Montesquieu,
on the contrary, declares peace to be the first law of
nature.[4] Cicero, as we have seen, supposed its obligations to be sufficient to be a rule of conduct for all

---

[1] Just. Lib. I, tit. 2. " Jus naturale," says Ulpian, "est quod
natura omnia animalia docuit." Puff. Bk. II, ch. iii, §§ 2, 3;
Ward's Law of Nat. vol. i, 41. St. Ambrose, upon this principle,
declared the copulation of asses and mares, by which mules are
produced, forbidden, the same being an unnatural connection.
Hexæmeri, Lib. V, c. 3, quoted by Puff.

[2] Puffendorf, Bk. II, ch. iii, § 2; Rutherforth's Just. I;
Ayliffe's Civil Law, Bk. I, tit. 2.

Thus Hesiod, Op. & Dier. Lib. I:

> " This law did Jove for human race ordain;
> The beasts, the fishes, and the feathered train,
> He left to mutual spoil and mutual prey,
> But justice gave to man."

[3] De Statu Servorum, Proleg. § 3.

[4] Montesquieu, Spirit of Laws, Bk. I, ch. ii.

nations. Yet Ward, after examining its claims with great attention, is forced to conclude, in the language of another writer, that "To speak of one fixed, immutable, and universal law of nature, is framing an imaginary scheme, without the least foundation in the nature of things, directly contrary to the present order of the whole creation."[1]

§ 7. The expression "law of nature" is sometimes, though unphilosophically, used to express those deductions which may be drawn from a careful examination of the operations of the natural world. Hence, it is said that slavery is contrary to the law of nature, because we find no counterpart or analogous operation in the natural world. To this we may say, in the first place, that by such a definition of the law of nature, cannibalism and every other horrid crime of savage or natural man would be justified. Among lower animals, the destruction of their own species is of frequent occurrence. In the second place, that the fact does not exist as stated, for not only is slavery found to coexist with the human race, but even among the lower animals and insects, servitude, in every respect the counterpart of negro slavery, is found to exist. It is a fact, well known to entomologists, and too well established to admit of contradiction, that the red ant will issue in regular battle array, to conquer and subjugate the black or negro ant, as he is called by entomologists. And, that

[1] Ward's Law of Nations, vol. i, ch. ii, p. 119. In the fourteenth century, Bartholus, the most famous civilian of his day, contended gravely, that the Emperor of Germany was the Emperor of the world; and Dante, another civilian, gave as the reason for it, because it was for their good. Ibid. 77.

these negro slaves perform all the labor of the communities into which they are thus brought, with a
patience and an aptitude almost incredible. These
facts, originally noticed and published by Huber,
have subsequently been verified by many observers;
and M. Latreille has demonstrated, that the rufescent
ants, on account of the form of their jaws and the
accessory parts of their mouth, have not the physical'
ability either to prepare habitations for their family,
to procure food, or to feed them.[1] Upon this definition, therefore, of the law of nature, negro slavery
would seem to be perfectly consistent with that
law.

§ 8. With other writers, the law of nature is held
to be the general conduct of mankind under any given
state of circumstances. Thus, " the whole of this
interesting question resolves itself, at last, into the
history of man. For, in vain do we pursue the
matter through all the subtleties of intellect, in vain
are the profoundest metaphysics made use of to prove
anything concerning the nature of man *a priori*. Of
that nature I can obtain no knowledge, except
through the same channel by which I become acquainted with the nature of any other animal; nor
can I tell what it is that nature demands of man to
do, except by inquiring what he has actually done."[2]
If this be the test, the answer is easily given to the

[1] Considérations nouvelles, &c., p. 408. For very interesting
accounts of the facts here stated, and many others equally as remarkable, see Spence & Kirby's Entomology, vol. ii, pp. 68–88;
Silliman's Journal, vol. xiii, pp. 177, 178; Natural History of
Insects, vol. viii, Harper's Family Library, pp. 130, et seq.

[2] Ward's Law of Nations, vol. i, 67.

inquiry as to the consistency of slavery with the law of nature. Its universality through every age of the world, since Noah announced the curse of Canaan, is too well established to require argument.

§ 9. What then is the law of nature? Grotius, the father of modern natural law, defines it to be "the dictate of reason, by which we discover whether an action be good or evil, by its agreement or disagreement with the rational social nature of man."[1] Blackstone and many other writers define it to be "the will of the Creator."[2] The Roman law made it synonymous with "natural justice and equity, and the rules of abstract propriety;" and a late English writer (Wildman), adopts this as the more simple and tangible definition.[3] Cicero defines this law to be "right reason, implanted in man by nature, commanding those things which ought to be done, and forbidding the contrary."[4] The object of this law he declares to be "God, our neighbor, and ourselves."[5] Erskine, the Scotch commentator, adopts the definition of Grotius.[6] Ayliffe, in his Pandects of the civil law, approves best that of Cicero.[7] Rutherford says, "Natural laws are those which mankind are obliged

---

[1] In another place, he says, "Bonum et æquum, id est rerum naturæ jus." Lib. II, 18, § 3.

[2] Comm. vol. i, p. 39. The writers on the common law, generally, have adopted this definition. See Kent's Comm. vol. i, pp. 2, 4, and notes; Manning's Comm. Law of Nations, Bk. II, ch. i; see also Heineccius, De Jur. Nat. & Gent. Lib. I, cap. i, § 12.

[3] Wildman's International Law, ch. i, p. 3.

[4] De Legibus, Lib. I. 　　　[5] Tusc. Quæst. Lib. I, c. 26.

[6] Institutes, &c., Bk. I, tit. i, § 7.

[7] Book I, tit. 2, § 1.

to observe from their nature and constitution."[1]
Similar is the exposition of Puffendorf, that it is
"that most general and universal rule of human
actions, to which every man is obliged to conform,
as he is a reasonable creature."[2] Vattel says, "The
general law of natural society is, that each individual
should do for the others everything which their
necessities require, and which he can perform without neglecting the duty which he owes to himself."[3]
The editor of the English translation of this author
(ed. 1797), defines the law of nature to be those
"rules which man must follow in order to attain
the great end of his being, viz., the most perfect
happiness of which he is susceptible."[4] Ward adopts
the same idea, when he declares the fundamental
principles of this law to be "the desire of happiness,
the pursuit of good, and the rejection of evil."[5] The
same view is taken by Chancellor d'Aguesseau,
when he says, that "for a man to live according to
nature, is to follow in all things that course, which
conducts most surely to his true end, which is to be
as perfect and happy as is consistent with his
nature."[6] Similar is the definition of Burlamaqui:
"Those rules which nature alone prescribes to man,
in order to conduct him safely to the end which
every one has, and indeed ought to have, in view,

---

[1] Institutes of Natural Law, Bk. I, ch. i, § 5.
[2] Law of Nature and Nations, Bk. II, ch. iii, § 1.
[3] Law of Nations, Bel. Bk. p. 9.
[4] Note to page lviii.     [5] Law of Nations, vol. i, p. 71.
[6] Méditations Métaphysiques, xix; Oeuvres, tom. xiv, p. 460.

namely, true and solid happiness."[1] Carlyle, speaking in reference to negro slavery, says, " This is the eternal law of nature for a man, that he shall be permitted, encouraged, and *if need be compelled*, to do what work the Maker of him-has intended, by the making of him for this world."[2]

§ 10. These varying definitions might be multiplied to almost any extent.[3] Sufficient have been adduced for our purpose, viz.: first, to show that as a general rule, men have very indefinite ideas, when they speak of the law of nature, and would many times be puzzled to explain their own meaning; second, to deduce from these the most satisfactory idea of this law, for the investigation which we undertake. From what has been said, it is evident that whatever definition we adopt, the nature of man enters as a very important element, and if that nature is subject to any variation, from race, or climate, or history, to that extent the consequences of the law of nature must vary when applied to him.[4]

[1] The Principles of Natural Law, Pt. I, ch. i.

[2] Letter on Rights of Negroes. So, again, "If thou do know better than I, which is good and right, I conjure you, in the name of God, force me to do it; were it by never such brass collars, whips, and handcuffs, leave me not to walk over precipices." Past and Present, Bk. III, ch. xiii. So again, "It is the everlasting privilege of the foolish to be governed by the wise, to be guided in the right path by those who know it better than they. This is the 'first right of man.'" Latter Day Pamphlets, No. 1.

[3] See Burrill's Law Dictionary; Bouvier's Law Dictionary; Webster's Dictionary; Jacob's Law Dictionary; Holthouse's Law Dictionary; Wheaton's Law of Nations, ch. i.

[4] Sir James Mackintosh recognizes this fact, in his Introductory Discourse on the Law of Nature and Nations. Essays, p. 29, 35.

To illustrate. The German student, immersed for years amid the ponderous tomes of some university library, finds nothing in his voluntary imprisonment uncongenial to his nature. But the American Indian submitting to the same fate, would do violence to the law of his nature, because his pursuit tends nothing to the great end of his existence, the greatest happiness of which he is susceptible. And hence slavery may be utterly inconsistent with the law of nature when applied to one race of men, and yet be perfectly consistent with the nature of others.[1]

§ 11. Again. We must be careful to distinguish between the state of nature and the law of nature. Many things are contrary to the state of nature, which are not contrary to the law of nature. Marriage, government, all civilization is adverse to a state of nature, yet it would be hardly asserted, that thereby violence was done to the law of nature. A celebrated Scotch commentator applies this distinction clearly and philosophically to the subject of slavery: " It is indeed contrary to the state of nature, by which all men were equal and free; but it is not repugnant to the law of nature, which does not command men to remain in their native freedom, nor forbid the preserving persons at the expense of their liberty," &c.[2] Heineccius points out clearly the same distinction, for while with all writers on the

So also Cicero, " Natura enim juris explicanda est nobis, eaque ab hominis repetendâ naturâ." De Leg. Lib. I, c. v.

[1] Montesquieu, Spirit of Laws, Bk. XV, ch. viii.

[2] McDouall's Institutes, Bk. I, tit. 2, § 77, p. 66. Burlamaqui seems to favor this distinction, though not pointedly, in his Principles of Natural Law, Pt. I, ch. iv, § 11.

civil law, he declares the natural freedom of all men, he adds : " Posset videri servitus juri naturæ repugnare; sed id, meritò negatur; servitus enim, in se nihil aliud est, quam obligatio ad perpetuas operas. Si non injustum est obligari ad annuas operas, quidni et ad perpetuas ?"[1] " It may appear that slavery is repugnant to the law of nature; but that may be properly denied. For slavery in itself is nothing but an obligation for perpetual service. If it be not wrong to be bound to serve for a year, why not also for life ?"[2] And again, " Juri naturæ, hujus modi servitus non repugnant, sed tamen non est juris naturæ; quæ sæpe auctores confundunt."[3] " This kind of slavery is not repugnant to the law of nature, but yet is not of natural right, which oftentimes authors confound." The admission therefore of the proposition that " all men are created free," or are free in a state of nature, does not carry with it as a consequence that slavery is inconsistent with the law of nature. " Jus naturæ tamen id non impedit."[4]

§ 12. So the Roman law defined slavery to be a condition, "quâ quis dominio altero contra naturam,

---

[1] Prælec. Ac. in H. Grot. Lib. II, cap. v, § 27.

[2] Heinec. Prælec. Ac. in H. Grot. Lib. II, cap. v, § 27.

[3] Ibid. § 32.

[4] Heinec. Prælec. Ac. in H. Grot. Lib. II, cap. v, § 27. So also Potgiesseri, speaking of slavery by captivity, " Tametsi—servitus ex captivitate orta sit contra naturam, id est, libertatem naturalem, non tamen, hoc ipso, contra jus naturæ erit." De statu serv. prol. § 25. After stating the arguments, pro and con, he comes to the same conclusion as to slaves by birth, §§ 26, 27, 29. And as to slaves by penalty of the law, § 31.

subjicitur."[1] But the commentators upon that law
warn us, " Id non intelligi debere ac si juri naturæ
adversetur, sed tantum statui naturali sive primævo,
in quo quilibet liber nascitur."[2] " This is not to be
understood as if it was opposed to the law of nature,
but only to that natural or primeval condition, in
which every one is born free." So Vinnius : " Hoc
est contra communem illam omnium hominum conditionem, quam ab initio habuerunt a naturâ, quanquam justitiæ naturali non repugnat, ex pactione aut
delicto servum fieri."[3] " This is contrary to that
common condition of all men, which they had, by
nature, from the beginning, although it is not repugnant to natural justice to become a slave, either by
contract or by crime." So Huberi : "Dicitur contra
naturam et contra jus naturæ. Hoc est contra
statum naturæ primævum ut jus pro facultate accipi-
atur, non contra dictamen rectæ rationis : vel est contra jus naturæ permittens non præcipiens."[4] And
again, "servitutem cum ratione non pugnare, diximus
modò."[5] It is said to be contrary to nature and contrary to the law of nature. This is contrary to the
original state of nature, that right should be derived
from power, but it is not opposed to the dictates of
right reason, nor is it contrary to the law of nature,
which permits, but does not enjoin it, and we have
said above, that servitude does not conflict with reason.

§ 13. The same distinction was taken by the

[1] Just. Lib. I, tit. 2, § 2.
[2] Potgiesseri, De statu servorum, proleg. XIII.
[3] Vinnius, Comm. Lib. I, tit. 3, § 2.
[4] Prælect. Lib. I, tit. 3, § 3.          [5] Ibid. § 6.

Fathers of the Church, on the subject of slavery. Bishop England, reviewing them at length, says: "Thus, a state of voluntary slavery is not prohibited by the law of nature." "All our theologians have, from the earliest epoch, sustained, that though in a state of pure nature all men are equal, yet the natural law does not prohibit one man from having dominion over the useful actions of another, as his slave." The following, quoted by him from St. Thomas of Aquin, makes the point clearly: "This man is a slave, absolutely speaking, rather a son, not by any natural cause, but by reason of the benefits which are produced; for it is more beneficial to this one to be governed by one who has more wisdom, and to the other to be helped by the labor of the former."[1] Cassagnac, pursuing the same idea, gives us the views of other Fathers, to the same effect. Thus, Saint Basil says: "He who, by the weakness of the intellect, has not in him that which nature requires, finds it to his interest to become the slave of another, the experience of his master being to him what the pilot is to the vessel."[2]

§ 14. With these preliminary remarks, we adopt, as the law of nature, when applied to man in his intercourse with his fellow-man, that obligation which reason and conscience impose, so to shape his course as to attain the greatest happiness, and arrive at the greatest perfection of which his nature

[1] Letters of Bishop England to Hon. John Forsyth, pp. 22, 23. He quotes from St. Augustine, St. Ambrose, St. John Chrysostom, Pope Gelasius I, &c. For the opinions of other Christian Fathers on the subject of slavery, see ante, Preliminary Sketch.

[2] Cassagnac, Voyage aux Antilles, tom. ii, p. 413. He quotes also from St. Bernard.

is susceptible. Consequently, whatever interferes with the attainment of this happiness and perfection does violence to the law of his nature, and whatever promotes or is consistent therewith is sanctioned by the law of his nature. In this view, *natural rights* depend entirely upon the nature of the possessor, not of the right; for, it is the former and not the latter that determines the question of right. Hence, to speak of the natural right to personal liberty is unphilosophical, until the previous question is settled, that such liberty will conduce to the happiness and perfection of the possessor.

§ 15. In this view, is Negro Slavery consistent with the Law of Nature? We confine the inquiry to negro slavery, because, upon the principles already established, it is undoubtedly true, that the enslavement, by one man or one race, of another man or another race, physically, intellectually, and morally, their equals, is contrary to the law of nature, because it promotes not their happiness, and tends not to their perfection. Much of the confusion upon this subject has arisen from a failure to notice this very palpable distinction. The ancient Greeks were so far the superiors of their contemporaries, that it did no violence to the existing state of things for their philosophers to declare their pre-eminence, and draw thence the conclusions which legitimately followed. Hence, Aristotle declared that some men were slaves by nature, and that slavery was absolutely necessary to a perfect society.[1]

! Polit. Lib. I, cap. i.   Hence Euripides, Iphig. :

    " 'Tis fit barbarians own the Grecian sway,
      And not that Greece should serve a barbarous lord.

§ 16. On the contrary, the slaves of Europe during
the middle ages, and of Britain prior to the Norman
invasion, were many of the same race with their
masters, their equals in intelligence and in strength,
and nothing but the accidents of their birth distinguished them apart.    It is not strange, therefore,
that their philosophers and jurists should see in such
slavery palpable violations of the law of nature,
and should have proclaimed that nature made them
all free and equal.[1]   Montesquieu perceived this distinction and the different conclusions to which these
different states of fact gave rise, and hence, whilst
he says all slavery must be accounted unnatural,
yet he admits, that " in some countries it is founded
on natural reason," viz., " countries where the excess of heat enervates the body, and renders men so
slothful and dispirited, that nothing but the fear of
chastisement can oblige them to perform any laborious duty."[2]   Hence, he says, that " natural slavery
must be limited to some particular parts of the
world."[3]   So Puffendorf says : " It is most evident
that some men are endued with such a happiness of
wit and parts, as enables them not only to provide

> Wise nature made the law ; 'twas nature formed
> Them to obey, and us to be obeyed."

It is a curious fact, that Sir Thomas More, one of England's
purest and wisest judges, in his celebrated creation of fancy, Uto-
pia, provided each of his families, in this imaginary perfect world,
with *two slaves* to perform the menial offices, thereby confirming
Aristotle's opinion of the necessity of slavery to a perfect society.

[1] Puffendorf, Bk. III, ch. ii; Montesquieu, Esprit des Lois,
Liv. XV, ch. viii.

[2] Spirit of Laws, Bk. XV, ch. vii.            [3] Ibid. ch. viii.

for themselvés and their own affairs, but to direct
and govern others. And that some again are so
extremely stupid and heavy, as to be unfit to
govern themselves, so that they either do mischief
or do nothing, unless others guide and compel them.
And farther, that these last being commonly furnished by nature with strong and hardy bodies, are
capable of bringing many notable advantages to
others by their labor and service. Now, when these
have the fortune to live in subjection to a wise
director, they are without doubt fixed in such a
state of life as is most agreeable to their genius and
capacity."[1]

§ 17. So Heineccius: "Ipsa quorundam natura ad
servitutem aptissima et tota comparata est, ita ut
nec actiones suas dirigere nec victum et amictum sibi
lucrari possint."[2] "The nature itself of some is so
fitted and prepared for servitude, that they can
neither direct their own actions nor furnish food and
clothing for themselves." Potgiesseri advances the
same opinion: "Ita enim societas humana comparata
est, ut alii licet se pacto, ad operas adhibendas
obstrinxerint, eas tamen, segniter et perfidiose per-

---

[1] Law of Nature and Nations, Bk. III, ch. ii, § 8; see also Bk.
VI, ch. iii, § 2. He quotes from Apuleius as follows: "It is
most agreeable that a man who is neither by nature or industry
prepared for a right way of living, should not govern, but be
governed; should be a servant, not a master; should, upon account
of his own weakness and incapacity, be under the control of others;
should sustain the part of obeying, not of commanding." Carlyle
adopts the same reasoning, Latter Day Pamphlets, No. 1. Potgiesseri advances the same opinion.

[2] Praelec. Ac. ad H. Grop. Lib. II, cap. v, § 27.

ficiant, adeo, ut 'eos castigationibus ad officium sui
cogi necessum sit; alii vero, a præstatione mutuæ
opis sint alienissimi, et libertatem effrenam præfer-
ant honestæ et tolerabili addictioni, atque malint,
ex rapto et latrociniis vivere, et in furcam agi quam
licitis mediis inopiæ suæ consulere."[1] "For human
society is so constituted, that it is lawful for some
to bind themselves by contract to the performance
of duty, so that it may be necessary to compel them
to its performance by stripes." So another learned
writer, in speaking of the slavery among the Turks,
says, "Non omnium ingenia inopem ferunt libertatem, nec omnes ita nati sunt, ut se regere et suo
arbitrio recte uti sciant." "The natural temperament of all will not suffer helpless liberty, nor are
all so born that they know how to govern themselves, and rightly to use their own power." He
says, "Ceteroquin qui apud nos mendicant, apud
eos (the Turks) serviunt." "Otherwise, those who
beg with us, serve among them." And concludes,
"At nescio, an optime rebus nostris consuluit qui
servitutem primus sustulit." "And, I doubt whether
he consulted best our interests, who first abolished
slavery."[2] So Hertius, quoting Aristides: "Legem
esse naturæ a potentioribus plane clariorem factam,
ut majoribus, minora pareant." "That this is the
law of nature, clearly is made to appear by the most
eminent, that the less should obey the greater." And
also Halicarnassus: "Naturæ legem esse omnibus

---

[1] De Statu Servorum, Proleg. § 32.
[2] Busheq. In Epistol. Turcic, Epist. III.

insitam, quam nullum tempus dissolvat, deterioribus semper imperare meliores." That this law of nature is engrafted upon all, which no time destroys; that the noble always govern the ignoble. Also Plutarch: "Naturæ legem semper velle potiorem imperare deterioribus." "That the law of nature always prefers that the nobler should govern the ignoble." Hertius adds: "Quanquam, ut dixi, hoc non sit proprie, stricteque dicendum jus naturale, quoniam jus exigendi nullum tribuit." "Though, as I have said, this cannot be properly and strictly called a natural right, since it gives no right of exaction."[1]

§ 18. Resuming then the inquiry as to the consistency of negro slavery with the law of nature, the first question which demands our attention, and necessarily is preliminary to all other investigation, is, what is the nature of the negro? Were this question asked of a mere animal, our inquiry would be confined to his physical nature alone, and could we show that, like the horse and the cow, the domestication and subjection to service did not impair, but on the contrary improved his physical condition, the conclusion would be inevitable, that such subjection was consistent with his natural development, and therefore not contrary to his nature. But we recognize in the negro a man, endowed with reason, will, and accountability, and in order to justify his subjection we must inquire of his intellectual and moral nature, and must be satisfied that its development is thereby promoted. If this be true, if the physical, intellectual, and moral development of the African

---

[1] De Coll. Leg. I, § 3.

race are promoted by a state of slavery, and their happiness secured to a greater extent than if left at liberty, then their enslavement is consistent with the law of nature, and violative of none of its provisions. Is the negro's own happiness thereby best promoted? Is he therein most useful to his fellow-man? Is he thereby more surely led to the discharge of his duty to God? These, as we have seen, are the great objects of the law of nature, " God, our neighbor, and ourselves."

§ 19. In this investigation, we should understand distinctly the meaning to be attached to " Negro." The black color alone does not constitute the negro, nor does the fact of a residence and origin in Africa. Agassiz very properly remarks, that " in Africa, we have the Hottentot and Negro races in the south and central portions respectively, while the people of Northern Africa are allied to their neighbors in Europe, just as we have seen to be the case with the zoological fauna in general."[1] The language and history of the nations of Northern Africa show them to have a different and Asiatic origin. The people we are inquiring of are thus described by Cuvier : " The negro race is marked by a black complexion, crisped or woolly hair, compressed cranium, and a flat nose. The projection of the lower parts of the face and the thick lips evidently approximate it to the monkey tribe. The hordes of which it consists have always remained in the most complete state of utter barbarism."[2] And even of this very extensive

---

[1] Principles of Zoology, by Agassiz and Gould, 180; see also Martin's Natural History of Man and Monkeys, p. 279.

[2] Animal Kingdom, McMurtrie's translation of Bimana, p. 50.

negro race, there are a great number of tribes, differing not so much in their physical as moral nature,
and adapting them more or less for a state of servitude. This difference was well known among the
native tribes long before the Dutch, Portuguese, and
English vied with each other in extending the slave-
trade ; and the Mandingo slave-dealer had determined this question long before a mart was opened
for him by European enterprise.[1] Our inquiry, therefore, is properly confined to those tribes of negroes
who were in a state of servitude in their native
land, viz.: the Fantis, Ashantis, Krumen, Quaquas,
Congos, Ibos or Eboes, Whydah or Fidohs, Coro-
mantines, Mandingoes, &c., and their descendants in
America.

§ 20. *First* then is the inquiry as to the physical
adaptation of the negro to a state of servitude. His
black color peculiarly fits him for the endurance of
the heat of long-continued summers.[2] The arched
leg and receding heel seem to indicate a natural preparation for strength and endurance.[3] The absence
of nervous irritability gives to him a complete ex-

---

[1] See an interesting paper on this subject, by R. G. Latham, and
read in a course of Lectures, before the Royal Institution, Manchester, in " Ethnology of the British Colonies," pp. 33 to 75.
The planters in America soon discovered this difference, and hence
a Caffre or Cafir negro was never a favorite in their markets. See
upon this subject, also, Martin's Nat. Hist. of Man and Monkeys,
220, 280, 299. Cassagnac's Voyage aux Antilles, vol. ii, p. 129;
Levavasseur, Esclavage de la race noire, 77, n.

[2] Copland's Dict. of Pract. Medicine, Article "Climate," A
Tribute for the Negro, p. 70; Chambers's Information for the
People, Art. "Physical History of Man."

[3] Cassagnac, Voyage aux Antilles, tom. i, p. 130.

emption from those inflammatory diseases so destructive in hot and damp atmospheres, and hence the remarkable fact, that the ravages of that scourge of the tropics, the yellow fever, never reach the negro race.[1]  In other portions of the body, especially the formation of the pelvis, naturalists have discovered a well-defined deterioration in the negro which, a late learned observer, Vrolik, of Amsterdam, has declared, shows "a degradation in type, and an approach towards the lower form of animals."[2]  So the arched dome of the head and the perpendicularity of the vertebral column are said, by an observant writer, to be characteristic, and to fit the negro peculiarly for the bearing of burdens upon the head.[3]

[1] Types of Mankind, by Nott & Gliddon, 68; Dr. Mosely's Treatise on Tropical Diseases. He says: "What would be the cause of insupportable pain to a white man, a negro would almost disregard.  I have amputated the legs of many negroes, who have held the upper part of the limbs themselves."  See also, on the peculiar diseases of negroes, Guenebault's Nat. Hist. of Negro Race, 76; White's Regular Gradation in Man, 73–79; see also Indigenous Races of Man, p. 380, et seq.  No case of yellow fever has ever occurred in Liberia.

[2] I am indebted for this fact to Prichard's Nat. Hist. of Man, p. 123.

[3] Smith's Nat. History of Human Race, 191.  Professor Soemmering enumerates forty-six distinct differences in the anatomy of the Negro from the European race.  Ueber die koerperliche Verschiedenheit des Negers, v. d. Europ., 1785, referred to in Guenebault's Natural History of the Negro Race, p. 57.

Lawrence (p. 246), describing the negro variety, says, "1. Narrow and depressed forehead, the entire cranium contracted anteriorly; the cavity less, both in its circumference and transverse measurements.  2. Occipital foramen and condyles placed further back.  3. Large space for the temporal muscles.  4. Great development of the face.  5. Prominence of the jaws altogether, and

§ 21. As a connecting link between the physical and mental capacity of the negro, we may consider

particularly of their alveolar margins and teeth; consequent obliquity of the facial line. 6. Superior incisors slanting. 7. Chin receding. 8. Very large and strong zygomatic arch, projecting towards the front. 9. Large nasal cavity. 10. Small and flattened *ossa nasi;* sometimes consolidated and running into a point above. In all the particulars just enumerated, the negro structure unequivocally approximates to that of the monkey. It not only differs from the Caucasian model, but is distinguished from it in two respects: the intellectual characters are reduced; the animal features enlarged and exaggerated. . . . This inferiority of organization is attended with corresponding inferiority of faculties, which may be proved, not so much by the unfortunate beings who are degraded by slavery, as by every fact in the past history and present condition of Africa."

Nott & Gliddon say, "A man must be blind not to be struck by similitudes between some of the lower races of mankind, viewed as connecting links in the animal kingdom, nor can it be rationally affirmed that the ourang-outang and chimpanzee are more widely separated from certain African and Oceanic negroes, than are the latter from the Teutonic or Pelasgic types." Types of Mankind, 457.

Dr. Wyman, of Harvard University, after pointing out clearly the difference between the negro and ourang-outang, adds: "Yet it cannot be denied, however wide the separation, that the negro and ourang-outang do afford the points where man and the brute —when the totality of their organization is considered—most nearly approach each other."[1]

Charles White, a naturalist of Manchester, as early as 1795, published a work, in which he pointed out twenty-eight distinct points of difference between the African and European, and in all of which the latter approached the brute creation.[2]

I am indebted to the Indigenous Races of Man, and the Arti-

[1] Troglodytes Gorillæ, Boston Jour. of Nat. Hist. 1847, p. 27. Quoted by Dr. Nott, p. 457.
[2] An Account of the Regular Gradation in Man (London), 83.

the osteological formation of his head, and comparative size of the brain. The opinion of Cuvier we have already noticed. Good, in describing the negro, says : " The head is narrow; the face narrow, projecting to the lower part. The countenance, in this variety, recedes farther than in any other from the European, and approaches much nearer than in any other that of the monkey."[1]  Camper, Soemmering, Lawrence, Virey, Ebel, and Blumenbach, agree that the brain is smaller; and Gall, Spurzheim, and Combe, that it is so distributed as to denote less capacity for reasoning and judging.[2]  On the contrary, Prof. Tiedemann, in a paper giving the result of his investigations and experiments on a large number of skulls, concludes that in mere bulk the brain of the negro is very nearly equal that of the European.[3]  Dr. Morton's experiments and observa-

cle by F. Pulszky, for the following anecdote, taken from Petronius, who wrote in the days of Nero, going to show that the distinctive features of the negro were well known in his day : Three vagrants, having taken passage on a vessel, discovered that the merchant owner was a person formerly robbed by them.  One proposes to black their faces with ink, and pass as Ethiopians; but the other exclaims, in reply, " As if color alone could transform our shape! for many things have to conspire that the lie might be maintained, under any circumstances; or can we fill our lips with an ugly swelling? can we crisp our hair with an iron? and mark our forehead with scars? and distend our shanks into a curve? and draw our heels down to the earth ?" p. 191.

[1] Book of Nature, p. 214.

[2] Martin's Nat. Hist. of Man and Monkeys, 301; Bachman on the Unity of the Race, 224; Guenebault's Nat. Hist. of Negro Race, 33; Types of Mankind, 403.

[3] Philosophical Transactions of the Royal Society in 1836, p. 479.

tions seem to have led him to the conclusion that the brain of the negro was somewhat smaller.[1] Without seeking to hold the balance between these authorities, we may remark, that it is too well settled now to be a matter of doubt, that the size of the brain is not the only criterion for deciding upon the mental capacity of the possessor; and philosophers least disposed to profess faith in phrenology as a science, are forced to admit that the arrangement and location of the brain, by some mysterious law, are, as a general rule, indicative of the mental power.[2] The application of Camper's facial line and facial angle demonstrated the inferiority of the negro in this particular, and Prof. Tiedemann does not seek to deny the correctness of the result thus tested.[3]

§ 22. *Second.* The mental inferiority of the negro has been often asserted and never successfully denied. An inviting field for digression is offered here, in the much-mooted question of the unity of the human race. It is unnecessary for our purposes to enter these lists. The law deals with men and things as they are, and whether the negro was originally a different species, or is a degeneration of the

[1] Germanic nations, 92 cubic inches; negroes, 83; Types of Mankind, p. 454; see Tables prepared by Dr. Meigs, in Indigenous Races of Man, p. 257; Bachman on Unity of Race, 227.

[2] Consult, directly on this point, Combe's Review of Morton's Crania Americana; Amer. Journal of Science and Art, vol. xxxviii, No. 2.

[3] Phil. Trans. of Royal Soc. 1836; see also Prichard's Nat. Hist. of Man, 111, 112; and the Natural History of the Human Species, by Lieut. Charles H. Smith, p. 190; Martin's Nat. Hist. of Man and Monkeys, p. 296.

same, is a matter indifferent in the inquiry as to his
proper status in his present condition. We deal
with him as we find him, and according to the measure of his capacity, it is our duty to cultivate and
improve him, leaving to time to solve the problem,
whether he is capable of restoration to that pristine
equality, from which his admirers maintain that he
has fallen.[1]

§ 23. Mentally inferior, now, certainly he is.
Says Lawrence: "The mind of the negro is inferior
to that of the European, and his organization also is
less perfect."[2] And this he proves, "not so much
by the unfortunate beings who are degraded by
slavery, as by every fact in the past history and
present condition of Africa."[3] Says Charles Hamilton Smith—whose opportunities for observing and
judging, for ten years, on the Coast of Africa and in
the West Indies (1797 to 1807), were unsurpassed,
and whose sympathies he confesses are with the
negro,—"The typical woolly-haired races have
never invented a reasoned theological system, discovered an alphabet, framed a grammatical language, nor made the least step in science or art.[4]

---

[1] The following curious fable is translated from the Arabic, by
Rosenmüller: "Niger in die quodam exuit vestas suas, incipit
que capere nivem et fricare cum eâ corpus suum. Dictum autem
ei fuit: quare fricas corpus tuum nive? Et dixit ille, fortasse
albescam. Venitque vir quidam sapiens qui dixit ei: O tu, ne
afflige te ipsum: fieri enim potest ut corpus tuum nigram faciat
nivem, ipsum autem non amittet nigredinem." Locmanni, Fabula
XXIII.

As to the probability of time effecting a radical change, see
Types of Mankind, p. 260, et seq.

[2] Lectures on Slavery, p. 74.          [3] Page 246.

[4] F. Pulszky, in his Iconographic Researches, furnished

They have never comprehended what they have learned, or retained a civilization taught them by contact with more refined nations, as soon as that contact had ceased. They have at no time formed great political states, nor commenced a self-evolving civilization; conquest with them has been confined to kindred tribes and produced only slaughter. Even Christianity, of more than three centuries duration in Congo, has scarcely excited a progressive civilization."[1] Says Knox: "The grand qualities which distinguish man from the animal; the generalizing powers of pure reason; the love of perfectibility; the desire to know the unknown; and last and greatest, the ability to observe new phenomena and new relations,—these mental faculties are deficient or seem to be so in all dark races. But if it be so, how can they become civilized? What hopes for their progress?"[2] These questions are

Messrs. Nott & Gliddon, for their late work on the Indigenous Races of Man, speaking of the black race, says, "Long as history has made mention of negroes, they have never had any art of their own. Their features are recorded by their ancient enemies, not by themselves." p. 188.

Hume, in his Essay on National Characters, after arguing for the superiority of the whites over all other races, and attributing to them all civilization, says, "There are negro slaves dispersed all over Europe, of which none ever discovered any symptoms of ingenuity."

[1] The Natural History of the Human Species, its Typical Forms, &c. (Edinburgh), p. 196. "In no part of this extended region (Negro Africa) is there an alphabet, a hieroglyphic, or even a picture, or symbol of any description." Murray's Encyclopædia of Geography, vol. iii, p. 38; see also Chambers's Information for the People, Art. Physical History of Man.

[2] Lectures on the Races of Men, 190.

answered by a most observant and intelligent French traveller in the West Indies : " The friends of useful and moral liberty should strive to maintain the supremacy of the white race, until the black race understands, loves, and practises the duties and obligations of civilized life."[1]

§ 24. Carlyle places this question in an eccentric but plain view, addressing himself to the emancipated negroes of the West Indies : " You are not slaves now ! nor do I wish, if it can be avoided, to see you slaves again ; but decidedly you will have to be servants to those that are born wiser than you, that are born lords of you ; servants to the whites if they are (as what mortal man can doubt they are?) born wiser than you. That, you may depend on it, my obscure black friends, is and was always the law of the world for you and for all men to be servants, the more foolish of us to the more wise. . . . . Heaven's laws are not repealable by earth, however earth may try ?"[2]

§ 25. The intelligent, unprejudiced writers of the non-slaveholding States of America, are constrained to admit the inferiority of the negro mind. Paulding, speaking of amalgamation, says : " It is a scheme for lowering the standard of our nature, by approximating the highest grade of human beings to the lowest."[3] And, " We have a right to conclude, from all history and experience, that there is an equal disparity of mental organization." " The experience

[1] Cassagnac, Voyage aux Antilles, tom. ii, p. 291.
[2] Letter on Rights of Negroes ; inserted, at length, in Negromania, 502, et seq.
[3] Paulding, on Slavery in the United States, 61.

of years stands arrayed against the principle of
equality between the white man and the black."
"All that the black man has ever done is to approach to the lowest scale of intellectual eminence,
and the world has demonstrated its settled opinion
of his inferiority by pronouncing even this a wonder."[1]
Dr. Morton, impartial and scientific as he is acknowledged to be, says: "It makes little difference whether
the mental inferiority of the negro, the Samoyede,
or the Indian, is natural or acquired; for if they ever
possessed equal intelligence with the Caucasian, they
have lost it, and if they never had it, they had
nothing to lose. One party would arraign Providence
for creating them originally different, another for
placing them in circumstances by which they inevitably became so. Let us search out the truth, and
reconcile it afterwards."[2] Judge Conrad says: " The
negro in the North has equal, if not superior, advantages to the mass of poor white men. .... It cannot,
however, be boasted that his intellectual character
has been materially elevated, or his moral nature
greatly improved."[3] George H. Calvert says: " At
one end of the human scale is the black man, at the
other the white; between them the brown and the
yellow. The white man never comes into contact
and conflict with the others, that he does not conquer them."[4] We might add the names of Browne,
the triumphant opponent of Prichard, on the sub-

[1] Pages 66 and 67.
[2] Letter to Mr. Gliddon, quoted in Types of Mankind, p. lii
of Memoir. [3] Plea for the South, 230.
[4] Scenes and Thoughts in Europe, 2d Series, p. 72.

ject of the hair of the negro, English,[1] Van Am-
bridge,[2] and others.

§ 26. Puynode, a French philanthropist, says:
"We no longer consider negroes as devoted to the
hatred of God, but we hold them generally, almost
universally, as our inferiors by their own nature."[3]
Levavasseur, another, says: "In times past, as now,
it seems that the negro race, left to themselves, cannot arrive at civilization."[4]

§ 27. In this opinion of the mental inferiority of
the negro, every distinguished naturalist agrees.
We have already seen that most of them agree as
to their physical inferiority in the size of the brain.
To those already named, we might add White, Bory
St. Vincent, Long, and last, in order of time, Count
A. de Gobineau, whose much-praised "Essai sur
l'Inégalité des races humaines," I regret I have not
been able to examine.    Prichard, it is true, who, in
maintaining the unity of the race, sees fit to become,
very unnecessarily, the defender and apologist of the
negro, yet even he is forced to admit that, " by the
animality or degradation of the forms of the pelvis,
peculiar to the negress and the Bushman or Hottentot, is implied an approach towards the forms of
these latter species" (the chimpantsi and ourang-
outang).[5] The great Humboldt, in his late "Cosmos,"
while declining virtually to enter the lists on the
question of monogeny, without discussing the ques-

[1] See Types of Mankind, 50 ; Negromania, 430.
[2] On Nat. Hist. of Man (Negromania, 369).
[3] De l'Esclavage et des Colonies, 12.
[4] L'Esclavage de la race noire, 77, 80, 84.
[5] Nat. Hist. of Man, 125.

tion, "repels the assumption of superior and inferior races of men."[1] Even so great an authority must yield to stubborn facts.

§ 28. Even the champions of the negro's freedom, who have distinguished themselves by their zeal, both in England and America, are forced to admit the apparent inferiority, and to ascribe the same to the degradation of slavery and other causes, which, in their opinion, if removed, would enable the negro to assert and prove his equality. Says Buxton : " I beg to call attention to certain indications, faint no doubt, but, considering the difficulties and impediments to improvement in Africa, encouraging indications, of a capability for better things."[2] Says Armistead, in a late elaborate " Tribute for the Negro :" " The present apparent inferiority of the negro race is undoubtedly attributable, in a great measure, to the existence of the slave-traffic in Africa."[3] Wilberforce admitted the same fact, and referred it to the same cause.[4]

§ 29. The American philanthropists have been equally constrained to acknowledge the apparent inferiority, and equally industrious in accounting therefor.[5] " The Caucasian," says Theodore Parker,

[1] Vol. i, p. 358 (Harper's edition). As to the correctness of this translation, see Indigenous Races of Man, 405, et seq.

[2] The Slave-Trade and Remedy, by T. F. Buxton, p. 459.

[3] A Tribute for the Negro, by Wilson Armistead, Manchester, 1848, p. 19.

[4] Appeal in behalf of the Negro Slaves of the West Indies.

[5] Channing on Slavery, ii, 66 ; Bacon on Slavery, p. 171 ; Miss Beecher on the Slave Question, 143 ; Godwin's Lectures on Slavery, 153–156 ; Freeman's Plea for Africa, 18 ; Andrews on Slavery and the Slave-Trade, in the United States, 21 ; Mrs. Childs's

"differs from all other races. He is humane, he is civilized, he progresses. He conquers with his head as well as with his hand. It is intellect, after all, that conquers, not the strength of a man's arm. The Caucasian has often been the master of other races, never their slave. Republics are Caucasian. All the great sciences are of Caucasian origin. All inventions are Caucasian. Literature and romance come of the same stock."[1] It will be noticed, that among these names, cited and quoted, no slaveholder appears, not even that of Mr. Jefferson, who is so often quoted as authority against the slaveholder.[2] We might add the names of many men whose intellects were too bright to be dimmed by interest, and whose hearts were too pure to be closed to the claims of humanity. We refer to Dew, Harper, Campbell, Calhoun, Simms, Hammond, Fletcher, Priest, and others.

§ 30. Our conclusion from this investigation must be, that the negro race is inferior mentally to the Caucasian. Whether or not this inferiority is the result of centuries of barbarism or of the degrading effects of a state of slavery, we will presently briefly inquire. Certain it is that the negro, as we now find

Appeal, 155. She says, p. 189, "The opinion that negroes are naturally inferior in intellect, is almost universal among white men." See also Second Annual Rep. of New England Anti-Slavery Society, pp. 18, 19, 22, 23; and Fourth Annual Rep. of Mass. Anti-Slavery Society, p. 28.

[1] Quoted by Nott, Types of Mankind, 462.

[2] See his Notes on Virginia, where he says, "Never yet could I find that a black had uttered a thought above the level of plain narration; never saw even an elementary trait of painting or sculpture."

him, whether in a state of bondage or in his native wilds, exhibits such a weakness of intellect that, in the words of Puffendorf, " when he has the fortune to live in subjection to a wise director, he is, without doubt, fixed in such a state of life as is most agreeable to his genius and capacity."[1]

§ 31. The prominent defect in the mental organization of the negro, is a want of judgment. He forms no definite idea of effects from causes. He cannot comprehend, so as to execute the simplest orders, unless they refresh his memory as to some previous knowledge.[2] He is imitative, sometimes eminently so, but his mind is never inventive or suggestive.[3] Improvement never enters into his imagination. A trodden path, he will travel for years, without the idea ever suggesting itself to his brain, that a nearer and better way is present before him ; what he has seen another do, he can do also, and practice will make him perfect in its execution, but the discovery of a better, easier, or cheaper pro-

---

[1] Law of Nature and Nations, Bk. III, ch. ii, § 8.

[2] Ca. da Mosto, the earliest of modern European travellers in Africa (1454), says, "Although very ignorant and awkward in going about anything which they have not been accustomed to, yet in their own business which they are acquainted with, they are as expert as any Europeans can be." Astley's Voyages, vol. i, p. 582.

[3] The following is from the Report of one of the visitors to the schools, including white and negro children : "I have uniformly found the blacks inferior to the whites, in every branch of education requiring mental effort. In writing and painting they bear a tolerable comparison ; but in reading, grammar, geography, and more particularly arithmetic, requiring the greatest mental effort, they are vastly below the level of a comparison." Extracted from Paulding, on Slavery in the United States, 279, 280.

cess never engages his thoughts. Faustin I, can imitate with ludicrous nicety all the pageantry of the Grand Emperor, but when his model ceases, his genius has executed its utmost.[1] This mental defect, connected with the indolence and want of foresight of the negro, is the secret of his degradation. The imitative faculty makes the negro a good musician, yet he never originates a single air, nor invents a musical instrument.[2] This faculty, combined with memory, sometimes might distinguish him in the acquisition of language, yet he never would originate an alphabet or distinguish the parts of speech.[3] The earlier training of the child at school exercises largely and depends much upon memory and imitation. Hence negro children would learn with equal facility with the white, during the first essays in the school-room, but so soon as education reaches the point where reason and judgment and reflection are brought into action, the Caucasian leaves the negro groping hopelessly in the rear.[4]

§ 32. Our next inquiry is as to the moral character of the negro race, and how far that character adapts them for a state of slavery. The degraded situation of the barbarous tribes of Africa is well attested by every observer. So debased is their

---

[1] Travellers inform us that everything in Liberia is a mere transcript of American ideas. See Bowen's Central Africa.

[2] Nat. Hist. of Human Species, &c., by Lieut.-Col. Smith (London, 1848), p. 190.          [3] Types of Mankind, 456.

[4] Nat. Hist. of Human Species, by Lieut.-Col. Smith, 191; Lyell's Second Visit to United States, vol. i, p. 105. Mrs. Stowe admits this fact, but seeks to account for it on different principles. Key to Uncle Tom's Cabin, Pt. I, ch. xii.

condition generally, that their humanity has been even doubted. It is not of the negro in this state of barbarism alone, that we should inquire. The development of his moral character, when in contact with civilization, and under the fostering care of religious instruction, is also to be considered. Viewing him then in both these relations, we find, first, that the negro race are habitually indolent and indisposed to exertion, whether seen in their native country, according to the concurrent testimony of all travellers,[1] or in the condition of slavery in America, or as free negroes after emancipation.[2] With reference to the first fact, we are told that the hot climate and the free productions of the earth, on the one hand enervate, and on the other take away all stimulus for exertion. With reference to the second, that it is the degrading effect of slavery, leaving no hope to the slave. With reference to the third, that it is the prejudice of color that depresses the spirits of the free negro of America. We will not stop to inquire as to the truth of these apologies. One thing is certain, that the ingenuity of the philanthropist is severely taxed in behalf of the negro

[1] I am aware that some expressions may be found in the works of travellers, varying from the general current. These may serve well the purposes of fanatics; but to the mind of those accustomed to decide upon testimony, they make no impression.

[2] "The blacks living in London are generally profligate. . . . Being friendless and despised, on account of their complexion, and too many of them being really incapable of any useful occupation, they sink into abject poverty." Walstron's Essay on Colonization. As to the free blacks of the North, see Paulding, on Slavery in United States, p. 66. As to the Liberians, see Preliminary Sketch, ch. xvii.

race, for wherever found they exhibit the same characteristics, and the reasons are obliged to be varied
to suit the varying circumstances.    Perhaps it is
but right to remark, that this enervating effect of
climate has never proved so powerful upon the
white race, physically less prepared to withstand it;
that slavery did not to this extent destroy the spirit
of the Israelites in Egypt, nor of the villains in
England, nor of the homines proprii of Germany.[1]
And that in Hayti, in Jamaica, in Brazil, and New
Granada, no such prejudice of color exists, and yet
notwithstanding the variant testimony of prejudiced
observers, there can be no question that neither the
enjoyment of liberty, nor the ingenuity of British
statesmanship, has been sufficient to infuse energy
and activity, where the Maker stamped indolence
and sloth.[2]

§ 33. In connection with this indolent disposition,
may be mentioned the want of thrift and foresight
in the negro race.   When enslaved, there is no great
necessity for the development of this faculty, and
this may account for its absence, but unfortunately .
for the friends of negro equality, it displays itself
more palpably in the free negro than in the slave.[3]
We speak of course of the general character, admit-

[1] See remarks, on this point, of J. K. Paulding, in his Treatise
on Slavery in the United States, p. 69, et seq.

[2] See Wallon, de l'Esclavage dans les Colonies, 81.   For a faithful representation of the effects of liberty upon the Haytians, and
the inhabitants of French Guiana, see Levavasseur's Esclavage de la
race noire, p. 22, et seq. ; Schœlcher's Colonies Etrangères, vol. ii,
"Haiti."

[3] See Walstron's Essay on Colonization, as above; Paulding, on
Slavery in the United States, 59.

ting the existence of individual exceptions. In their native wilds, with a most productive soil, they have recourse to the "most revolting food, as frogs, lizards, serpents, spiders, the larvæ of insects, &c. &c."[1] In the free West India Islands, the same indolence appears, and is excused on account of climate, &c. And, even in the cold climate of the Northern States, where the apology fails to apply, the result of the labored efforts of philanthropists, aided by the sympathies of the whole community, is "idleness, insolence, and profligacy."[2]

§ 34. The negro is not malicious. His disposition is to forgive injuries, and to forget the past.[3] His gratitude is sometimes enduring, and his fidelity often remarkable. His passions and affections are seldom very strong, and are never very lasting. The dance will allay his most poignant grief,[4] and a few days blot out the memory of his most bitter bereavement. His natural affection is not strong, and consequently he is cruel to his own offspring, and suffers little by separation from them.[5] He is superstitious and reverential, and consequently is very susceptible of religious impressions, exhibiting, in many individual instances, a degree of faith unsurpassed, and a Christian deportment free from

[1] Lawrence's Lectures on Slavery, 324.

[2] Paulding, on Slavery in the United States, 66, et seq.

[3] Channing, on Slavery; Candler's Brief Notices of Hayti.

[4] It is a curious fact, that upon one of the monuments in Egypt, a company of negro slaves are represented in a dance, 1300 years before Christ.

[5] Lawrence, Lectures on Slavery, 325; Cassagnac's Voyage aux Antilles, vol. i, pp. 167, 169, 235.

blemish. He is passive and obedient, and conse-quently easily governed.[1]

§ 35. The negro is naturally mendacious, and as a concomitant, thievish.[2] His apologists have referred these traits to his bondage, and have in-stanced the Israelites borrowing the Egyptian gold, and the cases of Europeans enslaved by the barba-rians in Africa, to show that such is the effect of slavery. Unfortunately, however, the prisons and court records of the non-slaveholding States show that enfranchisement has not taught the negro race honesty, nor caused them to cease from petty pil-fering.[3] And the census of Liberia shows the same disposition, as exhibited by their criminal court calendar.[4]

§ 36. Another striking trait of negro character is lasciviousness. Lust is his strongest passion; and hence, rape is an offence of too frequent occurrence. Fidelity to the marriage relation they do not under-stand and do not expect, neither in their native country nor in a state of bondage.[5] The latter, to

[1] See A Tribute for the Negro, 163; Nat. Hist. of Human Species, Lieut.-Col. Smith, 196.

[2] Ca. da Mosto says, "They are liars and cheats;" Astley's Voy-ages, vol. i, p. 582.

[3] Paulding, on Slavery in the United States, 59. Judge Conrad, in his Plea for the South (1836), says, "The free blacks are, in the mass, the most ignorant, voluptuous, idle, vicious, impoverished, and degraded population of this country. . . . They have sunk lower than the Southern slaves, and constitute but a melancholy proof of the advantages of abolition." p. 230.

[4] Of 373 offences, 308 were for larceny of different degrees. See Census of 1845.

[5] See Lawrence's Lectures on Slavery, pp. 325, 326, for proofs as to their debauchery, sensuality and cruelty.

some extent, is the fault of the law. Yet, colonized on their native shores, the same disregard for the marriage tie is noticed, and regretted by their friends.

§ 37. Let us now briefly notice the positions of those who deny the inferiority of the negro race. When the fact is stated that, living for centuries in contact with civilization, yet the negro tribes of Africa have never received or exhibited its influences; that they never have produced a single example of organized government; that they have never exhibited the first evidence of a self-evolving civilization, not even in the formation of an alphabet, a hieroglyphic, or a symbol, much less a grammatical language, we are referred to Egypt, the cradle of literature and the sciences, and triumphantly asked if Africa was not the very fountain whence all the streams of enlightenment flow; and the authority of Herodotus is invoked, to show that the ancient Egyptians were of " a black complexion and woolly-haired." Cuvier, Morton, Gliddon, and others, versed in Egyptian antiquities, have proven so many errors in the account that the " Father of History" has given of the land of the Nile, as to discredit his testimony, and to cause doubts even as to his having ever visited the country.[1] That there were negroes in Egypt, as slaves, at that period, there can be no doubt, but, that the ruling castes of

[1] Types of Mankind; Morton's Crania Egyptiaca, 22–29; Industrial Resources of the South, vol. ii, p. 200, et seq. Dr. Prichard, himself, seems to have little confidence in the accuracy of Herodotus; see Analysis of Egyptian Mythology (London, 1838), p. 374; and Examination, &c., of Egyptian Chronology, p. 17.

the Egyptians were of the Caucasian race is equally free from difficulty.[1] Was there no other evidence? the ten thousand mummies, that have been exhumed and examined, and the numerous deeds, describing the persons of the contractor, are, every one, witnesses to disprove the assertion of the negro origin of the Egyptians.[2] The lower castes (herdsmen, agriculturists, and artisans), were very numerous, and many of these, doubtless, were negroes. In fact, it was the boast of one of the Pharaohs that no native Egyptians had placed a brick in one of the huge pyramids that he built. Herodotus being ignorant of the language of the Egyptians, and not very accurate in his observations, may have thus mistaken the numerous for the ruling caste. This interesting question opens an inviting field for digression. We must content ourselves with referring the curious to the authorities relied on for our conclusions.

§ 38. The uncertain and as yet unlocated Ethiopia of the ancients, is also referred to as an example of negro civilization.[3] When discovered, and its monuments, and people, and works of art, and records of history, are brought before the world, we will be called on to examine the witness, and determine his

[1] See Industrial Resources of the South, vol. ii, p. 200; Types of Mankind, passim, and Negromania, 108; Lawrence's Lectures on Slavery, 229–237; see Prichard's Analysis of Egyptian Mythology (London, 1838), p. 374.

[2] Authorities cited above.

[3] The first book of the Iliad comes as near locating as any other authority, where the mother of Achilles tells him that Jupiter is "not at home," having set off with all the gods "to feast with the excellent Ethiopians."

competency and credibility.   From the examination
I have been able to give this question, I am disposed
to believe, that with the ancients Ethiopia included
all unknown or little known and unexplored countries.  It certainly included India and Central Africa.

§ 39.  The ancient kingdom of Meroe has also
been referred to sometimes as evidence of a negro
self-sustaining and self-evolving civilization.   The
Zerah of the Bible (2 Chron. 14 : 9), is supposed to
have been one of its kings, and its high civilization
and great power are almost beyond question.   Its
situation, at the head of the Nile, in the midst of
Ethiopia, is referred to as positive proof of the negro
type of its inhabitants.  Much learning and research
have been exhibited in tracing its history and
fathoming its fate.[1]   Into this field we are forbidden
to go.   To conclusions alone we must address ourselves, and since the labors of the Prussian scientific
mission, many of the former opinions of scientific
men have been proven fallacious.   Chev. Lepsius
states the fact to be now undoubted, that the
Meroites, the people who built the Pyramids, and
left other undoubted traces of civilization, were a red
people, and of the Caucasian race.   He adds, that
there is not to be drawn from Meroe, the slightest
trace of an Ethiopian civilization properly so called.[2]
For many years, and during her prosperity, Meroe
was an Egyptian dependency.   So soon as she

[1] Cf. Heeren. Ideen. vol. i, p. 385, et seq. Oxford trans.; An-
thon's Class. Dict. "Meroe," and authorities there cited; Morton's
Crania Egyptiaca.

[2] Letter to John Pickering, translated in Types of Mankind, pp.
203, 204.

became independent, and was "cut off from Egyptian blood and civilization, the influx of negroes deteriorated her people, until, by the fifth century after Christ, she sank amid the billows of surrounding African barbarism, mentally and physically obliterated forever." Were these truths doubtful before, the bas-reliefs upon her monuments, and the inscriptions upon her pyramids, would dispel these doubts forever.[1]

§ 40. Few have the hardihood to refer to Hayti, Jamaica, or even Liberia, as successful experiments of negro civilization. Their apologists beg for time, that the baneful influences of former slavery may be removed. Be it so. The reaction may come, but the fate of Meroe checks the hope of the philanthropist.

§ 41. But passing from communities, when we ask for individual instances of superior intellect developed in the negro, we are referred to Origen, Cyprian, St. Augustine, Tertullian, Clemens Alexandrinus, and Cyril, among the fathers of the Church, to Hanno and Hannibal among warriors, and to Terence and Phædrus among poets, as examples of strongly marked genius in the negro race. The reference excites a smile, and the answer is already given in the fact, that the people inhabiting the northern portion of Africa, along the coast of the Mediterranean Sea, are as distinct from the negro proper, as the Caucasian origin of the one should make them different from the negro origin of the other. African and negro are not synonymous, a fact which these philanthropists seem to forget.

[1] Types of Mankind, pp. 259–264.

§ 42. In a work lately issued under the auspices of British abolitionists, entitled " A Tribute for the Negro,"[1] all the examples of negro intellect, which the research and industry of the author could collect, are brought together, and short memoirs are given of some threescore of the most remarkable. This collection is drawn from the entire negro family for eighteen hundred years, in all portions of the world, and the meagreness of the material could not be better proven, than by the book before us. Were it proper, we would be amused by a review of these lives, many of whose highest and only achievement was "moving in the first circles in society in Great Britain."[2] For excellence in poetry we have Phillis Wheatley, whose productions Mr. Jefferson pronounced to be "beneath criticism." In composition, is Gustavus Vasa, whose only work was a narrative of himself (by whom written, or revised we know not), which would hardly give credit to a schoolboy in his teens. Among warriors, is Toussaint L'Ouverture, who exhibited perhaps more energy, more treachery, and less principle, than any negro whose memoirs are included in the volume. Of the threescore selected for immortality in this negro Thesaurus, four-fifths were developed under the "baneful influences of slavery;" having been at some time, and generally for the most part of their lives, slaves. Of the remaining one-fifth, very few if any belong to those African tribes that have supplied the Ameri-

[1] By Wilson Armistead, 1848 (Manchester and London). This book is but an enlargement of a work published at Paris, by H. Grégoire, Bishop of Blois, in 1808, entitled "De la Littérature des Nègres," &c.      [2] Page 136.

cans with slaves. The inference would seem irresistible, from the testimony of this volume, that the most successful engine for the development of negro intellect is slavery.

§ 43. But were we without other witnesses to the inferiority of the negro, the instinct of the Caucasian would be of itself demonstration clear. It is called the "prejudice of color," but such a prejudice is never wholly unfounded. Intellect, energy, and moral worth, do not supplicate but demand respect.[1] It is said to arise from their state of bondage, yet strange to say, it exists where they were never known in bondage, and is strongest where no slavery exists. We find it in the capital of the British empire, among the courteous French, in the slaveholding States of America, and in those States where slavery has been abolished, but strongest than all, in those States where negro slavery never existed.[2]

§ 44. This inquiry into the physical, mental, and moral development of the negro race, seems to point them clearly, as peculiarly fitted for a laborious class. Their physical frame is capable of great and long-continued exertion. Their mental capacity renders them incapable of successful self-development, and yet adapts them for the direction of a wiser race. Their moral character renders them

[1] Paulding, speaking of a prudent free negro at the North, says, "There is every disposition to encourage and foster his efforts. He is looked upon as something remarkable, an exception to his kind, a minor miracle." Slavery in the United States, 67.

[2] De Tocqueville's Democracy in America; Levavasseur, Esclavage de la race noire, 89, et seq.

happy, peaceful, contented, and cheerful in a status that would break the spirit and destroy the energies of the Caucasian or the native American.[1]

§ 45. History and experience confirm this conclusion. Probably no better test could be adopted, to determine the adaptation of a system to a race, than their relative increase while living under it.[2] Nature has so constituted the animal creation, that when any portion of it is placed in a position doing violence to the law of their nature, it dwindles and becomes extinct. Thus domestication is destruction to many animals *feræ naturæ,* while it perfects the development of the horse, the cow, and others. So bondage has ever proved annihilation to the American Indian, whether under the Spanish Hidalgo,[3] or the New England Puritan, or the Virginia Cavalier. What has been its effect, in this respect, upon the negro? The answer to this question is, the voice of Nature, whether her law is violated in his enslavement.

§ 46. The census of the United States exhibits a

---

[1] For proof of their contentment and happiness, see Cassagnac's Voyage aux Antilles, vol. i, pp. 149, 155, 239.

[2] Puynode, a French abolitionist, feeling the importance of this view, strives to show that slavery diminishes the increase of the slave population. De l'Esclavage et des Colonies, p. 35.

[3] The Conquerors of the New World, and their Bondsmen, vol. ii, p. 151, gives a striking instance where several thousand Indians and fifty negroes were employed by the Spaniards in transporting the timbers for vessels across the Isthmus. The Indians perished by hundreds—not a single negro died. As early as 1511, the King of Spain directs his Colonial Governor "so to act, that the Indians may increase, and not diminish, as in Hispaniola." Ibid. vol. i, p. 232.

steady and remarkable increase in the slave population. From a few hundred thousand, they now number more than four millions; and, making allowance for emigration and other causes, the ratio of
increase is at least equal to that of the white population of the same States.[1] On the contrary, the
increase among the free black population of the
Northern States, notwithstanding the element of
fugitives from the South, and emancipated slaves,
shows a ratio of increase very inferior.[2] The Census of 1850 shows, also, the fact, that the duration
of life is greater among the slaves of the South,
than among the free negroes of the North.[3] The
same unerring testimony also shows, that there are
three times as many deaf mutes, four times as many
blind, more than three times as many idiots, and
more than ten times as many insane, in proportion
to numbers, among the free colored persons, than
among the slaves.[4] The same is true of the free
blacks of Liberia. Notwithstanding the constant
influx from America, the census of that colony

---

[1] The whole number imported is estimated at 333,000. In 1850,
they were 3,800,000; see Carey's Slave-Trade, Domestic and
Foreign, ch. iii; Census of the United States for 1850. The same
is true as to the increase of slaves in the French West Indies. See
Cassagnac's Voyage aux Antilles, vol. i, p. 183; Schœlcher, Colonies Françaises, p. 20.

[2] The increase of free colored persons, from 1840 to 1850, was
hardly 1¼ per cent. per annum; while that of the slaves was very
nearly 3 per cent. per annum. See Compendium of Seventh Census, pp. 68, 87.

[3] Abstract of Seventh Census, p. 13.

[4] Ibid. p. 26. The number of total afflicted is nearly four times
greater among the former than the latter.

shows no ratio of increase; but, on the contrary, for more than 12,000 emigrants, it contains now a civilized population of not exceeding 8000.

§ 47. From the same observation, we learn that the mere physical development of the negro is improved by his transport and enslavement. As an animal, in stature, in muscular energy, in activity, and strength, the negro has arrived at his greatest development while in slavery.[1]

§ 48. In mental and moral development, slavery, so far from retarding, has advanced the negro race.[2] The intelligence of the slaves of the South compares favorably with the negro race in any country, but more especially with their native tribes.[3] While, by means of this institution, the knowledge of God and his religion has been brought home, with practical effect, to a greater number of heathens than by all the combined missionary efforts of the Christian world. But remove the restraining and controlling power of the master, and the negro becomes, at once, the slave of his lust, and the victim of his indolence, relapsing, with wonderful rapidity, into his pristine barbarism. Hayti and Jamaica are living witnesses to this truth;[4] and Liberia would probably add her

[1] See notes to preceding section.

[2] See the pertinent remarks of Lawrence, in his Natural History of Man, pp. 325, 326. This fact is admitted, in A Tribute for the Negro, pp. 151, 152, 153; see also Cassagnac's Voyage aux Antilles, vol. i, pp. 240, 246.

[3] Levavasseur, Esclavage de la race noire, 77.

[4] See Cassagnac's Voyage aux Antilles, vol. ii, 283; Levavasseur, Esclavage de la race noire, p. 22, et seq., 43 et seq.; especially the extract from an eye-witness, in Jamaica, M. Mollien, both before and after the Act of Emancipation, pp. 46, 47, and 48;

testimony, were it not for the fostering care of philanthropy, and the annual leaven of emancipated
slaves.[1]

§ 49. The history of Africa is too well known to
require of us an argument or an extended notice, to
show, that left to themselves, the negro races would
never arrive at any high degree of civilization. In
the words of an intelligent French writer : " Ni les
sciences de l'Egypte, ni la puissance commerciale de
Carthage, ni la domination des Romains en Afrique,
n'ont pu faire pénétrer chez eux la civilisation."[2]
We have neither space nor inclination to prove the
fact, well known to naturalists and ethnologists, that
the Abyssinians and others, exhibiting some faint
efforts at civilization, are not of the true negro race,
but are the descendants of the Arabs and other Caucasian tribes.[3]

While this fact may be admitted, we are told that
after, by means of slavery and the slave-trade, the
germs of civilization are implanted in the negro, if
he is then admitted to the enjoyment of liberty, he
is capable of arriving at a respectable degree of enlightenment. Charles Hamilton Smith, an Englishman, and an acute observer, says, "They have
never comprehended what they have learned, nor

see also Southern Quarterly Review, vol. xii, p. 91, an able and
dispassionate article by Judge Campbell, of the Supreme Court of
the United States.

[1] Nott & Gliddon's Types of Mankind, 402, see Prel. Sketch.

[2] Levavasseur, Esclavage de la race noire, 77; see similar views
of Paulding, on Slavery in the United States, 70.

[3] Chas. H. Smith's Nat. History of Human Species, &c., 196;
Levavasseur, Esclavage de la race noire, 77.

retained a civilization taught them by contact with more refined nations, as soon as that contact had ceased."[1] The emancipated slaves of the French and English West Indies, have corroborated this statement. Hayti, once "la plus belle colonie" of France, despite the apologies made for her excesses is, to-day, fast retrograding to barbarism. Jamaica, and the other English islands, notwithstanding the care and deliberation to avoid the shock of too sudden liberty, have baffled the skill and ingenuity of the master minds of the British government. In a preliminary historical sketch, we have examined the facts in detail. The important truth is before us from history, that contact with the Caucasian is the only civilizer of the negro, and slavery the only condition on which that contact can be preserved.[2]

§ 50. The history of the negro race then confirms the conclusion to which an inquiry into the negro character had brought us: that a state of bondage, so far from doing violence to the law of his nature, develops and perfects it; and that, in that state, he enjoys the greatest amount of happiness, and arrives at the greatest degree of perfection of which his nature is capable. And, consequently, that negro slavery, as it exists in the United States, is not contrary to the law of nature. Whenever the laws regulating their condition and relations enforce or allow a rigor, or withdraw a privilege without a corresponding necessity, so far they violate the natural

[1] Nat. Hist. of Human Species, its Typical Forms, &c., 196.
[2] Paulding, on Slavery in the United States, 271, 272. " No two distinctly marked races can dwell together on equal terms." Types of Mankind, by Nott & Gliddon, p. 79.

law, and to removal of such evils should be directed
the efforts of justice and philanthropy.  Beyond
this, philanthropy becomes fanaticism, and justice
withdraws her shield.

That the system places the negro where his
natural rights may be abused, is true; yet this is no
reason why the system is in itself wrong.  In the
words of an enlightened cotemporary, "It becomes
us then to estimate the value of the declamations of
those who oppose the institution of slavery in the
Antilles and the United States, on account of the
partial abuses which sometimes happen.  Judicial
records are filled with processes for adultery; yet we
should not, for that, destroy marriage.  Every day
our tribunals visit with severity parents who abuse
their children, yet we would not, for that, abolish
the paternal power.  Every system has its abuses
and its excesses.  It becomes us to correct the excess, punish the abuse, and ameliorate the system.
If we should deliberately compare the evils of colonial slavery, with its beneficial effects, in civilization,
agriculture, and commerce, we would be quickly
convinced upon which side the balances would fall."[1]

---

[1] Cassagnac's Voyage aux Antilles, vol. ii, p. 292.

# CHAPTER II.

SLAVERY VIEWED IN THE LIGHT OF REVELATION.

§ 51. WE have examined the question of the consistency of negro slavery with the law of nature, outside of revelation. But the law of nature is the will of God, "summa ratio in Deo existens."[1] To be content, in searching for that will, without opening the book of His Revelation, would be unbecoming the Christian philosopher. I feel compelled, therefore, to enter upon the field, so much more fitting to the theologian, and to give a condensed statement of the Biblical argument on either side of this question. The necessity of the investigation does not require the extended and learned research which others have bestowed. I shall not, therefore, stop to inquire the true rendering of Greek and Hebrew words, but take the English Bible as a correct translation.[2]

§ 52. In a preliminary historical sketch of slavery, we have seen the nature of this institution among the Jews, and many of the rules by which it was governed. Was this evidence of the sanction and approval of God?

---

[1] Halm's Collegium Polemicum, Controv. IX.

[2] Of the denial that slavery existed among the Jews, Dr. Wayland says: "I wonder that any one should have had the hardihood to deny so plain a matter of record."—Letters to Dr. Fuller, IV.

The first great revelation of moral precepts was given upon Mount Sinai, and condensed in that most wonderful code, the Decalogue. Its precepts are not only pure, but " the law of the Lord is *perfect*."[1] Its general teachings are not only true, but, by no implication can sin find an apology or excuse therein. This law was not intended for any particular age or people. It is that universal law of God which Christ came "not to destroy, but to fulfil." When he was asked by the young man, What shall I do to inherit eternal life? his reply was, Keep the commandments. The last of these commandments is, " Thou shalt not covet thy neighbor's house, thou shalt not covet thy neighbor's wife, nor his *man-servant*, nor his *maid-servant*, nor his ox, nor his ass, nor anything *that is thy neighbor's*."[2] The right of property in the man-servant and maid-servant is not only here plainly recognized, but is protected even from covetousness.

§ 53. But again : God sought for a man in whose " seed shall all the nations of the earth be blessed;" who should be called " the friend of God,"[3] and " the father of all them that believe."[4] He found him in Abraham, a large slaveholder.[5] And God blessed him. How? By opening his eyes to the sin of slavery? No; but by " *giving* him flocks and herds, and silver and gold, and *men-servants* and *maid-servants*, and camels and asses."[6] And God made a covenant with him, and established a church with a sign of that covenant for every member of that

---

[1] Psalm 19 : 7.  [2] Ex. 20 : 18.

[3] James 2 : 23.  [4] Rom. 4 : 11.

[5] Gen. 14 : 14.  [6] Gen. 24 : 35.

church. To whom did that covenant extend, and
who were admitted into that church? Along with
the master Abraham was him "that is bought with
thy money," his slave;[1] thereby teaching his chosen
servant the great lesson upon this question to be
found throughout the sacred Scriptures, that while
God recognizes domestic slavery, in some cases, as a
necessary part of civil government, and would regulate it as such, the master and the slave are both
*alike* the subjects of his care, and the recipients of
his mercy.

§ 54. God not only *gave* slaves to Abraham, as
evidence of his blessing, but he commanded the Jews
to make slaves of the heathen round about them:
"Of them shall ye buy bondmen and bondmaids.
Moreover, of the children of the strangers that do
sojourn among you, of them shall ye buy, and of
their families that are with you, which they begat in
your land, and they shall be your possession; and
ye shall take them as an inheritance for your children after you to inherit them for a possession.
They shall be your bondmen forever."[2] This command being given very shortly after the escape of
the Israelites from Egypt, was probably before they
owned a slave, was the charter under which they
enslaved the Canaanites. At the same time, God
commanded them, that "if thy *brother* by thee be
waxen poor and be sold unto thee, thou shalt not
compel him to serve as a bond servant, but as a hired
servant and a sojourner."[3] Revelation here sustain-

---

[1] Gen. 17 : 12, 13.      [2] Lev. 25 : 44, 46.
[3] Ib. 39 : 40. See also Deut. 24 : 7; 1 Kings 9 : 22; Neh.
5 : 8; Joel 3 : 3; Jer. 34 : 9, et seq.

ing the conclusion to which the natural law points, that inferiority of race is necessary to make slavery consistent with the Divine will. The Jews understood thoroughly this distinction, and when the Saviour announced to them that this truth should make them free, they answered, "We be Abraham's seed, and were never in bondage to any man; how sayest thou ye shall be made free?"[1]

§ 55. It is unnecessary to follow the history of the Jews, and note the numerous instances in which they enslaved others, under the direct command of the Almighty; nor to refer to the various provisions of the Mosaic law, regulating the relation of master and slave. And yet, nowhere do we find it condemned. When the Jews failed to abide by the regulation, giving liberty to the Hebrew servant on the year of jubilee, Jehovah failed not to pronounce his anathema. "Ye have not hearkened unto me, in proclaiming liberty every one to his brother, and every man to his neighbor; behold, I proclaim a liberty for you, saith the Lord, to the sword, to the pestilence, and to the famine."[2] So, when they oppressed or defrauded the hireling of his wages, the prophets of the Almighty did not wink at the offence: "Thou shalt not oppress an hired servant that is poor and needy."[3] "And I will be a swift witness against those that oppress the hireling in his wages, the widow, and the fatherless, and that turn aside the stranger, and fear not me, saith the Lord of Hosts."[4] It is very strange that labor should

[1] John 8 : 32, 33.          [2] Jer. 34 : 17.
[3] Deut. 24 : 14.          [4] Mal. 3 : 5.

be robbed of its wages so long, in the persons of Jewish slaves, and yet the cry of the oppressed never reached the ears of the God of Sabaoth.

§ 56. It is argued, that the privilege of enslaving the heathen was granted only to the Hebrews, and for peculiar reasons, and hence is no argument in favor of other domestic slavery. The reply is, if slavery is sinful, morally wrong, *per se*, and under all circumstances, God could not in his nature have authorized or enjoined it.[1] If it was not sinful in the Jews, it is not sinful under all circumstances; and the question of its morality in every case depends upon its circumstances,—precisely the conclusion to which we have previously arrived.

§ 57. But it is said by others, that the same argument may be used to support polygamy as slavery. That both were practised by the patriarchs, and against neither did Jehovah pronounce his curse. The facts do not show the similarity. No such regulations can be found emanating from the Almighty, in reference to polygamy, as we have shown in reference to slavery. To say the least, the law was silent as to the former. Whenever the marriage relation is spoken of, man and wife, "they twain shall be one flesh," is the teaching of the law.[2] "Live joyfully with the *wife* whom thou lovest, all the days of thy vanity."[3] And "thy *wife* shall be as a fruitful vine by the sides of thine house, thy children like olive plants round about thy table.

---

[1] "O, mighty God, thou art of purer eyes than to behold evil, and canst not look on iniquity."—Habakkuk 1 : 12, 13.

[2] Gen. 2 : 20, 24; 7 : 9; Ex. 20 : 17; Deut. 5 : 21, 22; Matt. 19 : 4, 5; Eph. 5 : 31.      [3] Eccl. 9 : 9.

Behold, that thus shall the man be blessed that feareth the Lord."[1]

But suppose the analogy was complete, and that there is nothing in the Old Testament, either directly or indirectly, showing monogamy to be the will of God, or that polygamy in the Hebrews was disapproved by him. The conclusion is simply, that polygamy in the Jews was not sinful, "for sin is the transgression of the law,"[2] and hence that polygamy is not necessarily a sin, but becomes so so soon as it is the transgression of the law.

§ 58. But let us enter into the bright light of Christianity, as developed in the New Testament, and examine the question there. That there is no direct positive prohibition of slavery, nor even an intimation by Christ or his Apostles that its principle or practice was violative of the Divine will, is admitted. Various excuses are given for this want of fidelity in the Saviour, in his great duty and mission,—the rebuking of sin. The universality of its existence, the terrible results consequent upon the upheaving of the whole social system, his abstinence from all interference with civil institutions, have each been suggested as explanatory of his silence. Other sins went not unrebuked because of their prevalence. He hesitated not in any other call of duty from motives of expediency, trusting ever to the power of the truth to make its sure way over every human obstacle; and the suggestion that it was merely a *civil* institution, is an admission that it was not morally a sin. We must look farther for a satisfactory explanation.

[1] Ps. 128 : 3, 4.                    [2] 1 John 3 : 4.

§ 59. But first, how is slavery treated in the New Testament? It did not escape the notice of the Lord, for we find him illustrating the great truths that he taught, by references to the relation of master and slave. It is true that he used other human conduct, wrong in itself, such as the unjust steward, as the foundation of parables; yet, in every instance, he either at the time or on other occasions condemned the sin. On this sin he was silent. When the rich young man came to ask a blessing from him, though his heart yearned towards his loveliness, he saw the sinful love of wealth, and rebuked it. But when the Roman centurion came to ask his blessing upon a sick slave, one whom he commanded to do, and he was forced to obey, though he commended his humility and his faith, did not the Saviour perceive the great sin of slaveholding adhering to his skirts? Why did he not rebuke this sin, as he had rebuked the young man's love of gold?

§ 60. But Christ went farther: he recognized distinctly and approved the master's superiority: " But which of you having a servant ploughing, or feeding cattle, will say unto him, by and by, when he is come from the field, Go and sit down to meat, and will not rather say unto him, Make ready wherewith I may sup, and gird thyself and serve me, till I have eaten and drunken, and afterward thou shalt eat and drink? Doth he thank that servant because he did the things that were commanded him? I trow not."[1] " For whether is greater, he that sitteth

[1] Luke 17 : 7, 8, 9.

at meat, or he that serveth? Is not he that sitteth at meat?"[1] "Verily, verily, I say unto you, the
servant is not greater than his Lord."[2]

§ 61. The apostles went farther, and laid down in
express terms, rules regulating the relation of master and slaves. "Servants, be obedient to them that
are your masters according to the flesh, with fear
and trembling, in singleness of your heart, as unto
Christ. Not with eye-service, as men-pleasers, but
as the servants of Christ, doing the will of God from
the heart. . . . Knowing that whatsoever good thing
any man doeth, the same shall he receive of the
Lord, whether he be bond or free. And ye masters,
do the same things unto them, forbearing threatening; knowing that your Master also is in heaven.
Neither is there respect of persons with him."[3] "Let
as many servants as are under the yoke count their
own masters worthy of all honor, that the name of
God and his doctrine be not blasphemed. And
they that have believing masters, let them not despise them, because they are brethren; but rather
do them service, because they are faithful and be-
loved partakers of the benefit. These things teach
and exhort. If any man teach otherwise, and consent not to wholesome words, even the words of our
Lord Jesus Christ, and to the doctrine which is according to godliness, he is proud, knowing nothing,
but doting about questions and strifes of words."[4]
"Exhort servants to be obedient unto their own
masters, and to please them well in all things, not

[1] Luke 22 : 17.                    [2] John 13 : 16.
[3] Eph. 6 : 5, 6, 8, 9.   See also Col. 3 : 22, 23, 24.
[4] 1 Tim. 6 : 1, 2, 3, 4.

answering again, not purloining, but showing all good fidelity, that they may adorn the doctrine of God our Saviour in all things."[1] "Servants, be subject to your masters with all fear; not only to the good and gentle, but also to the froward."[2] "Let every man abide in the same calling wherein he was called. Art thou called, being a servant, care not for it, but if thou mayest be made free, use it rather; for he that is called in the Lord, being a servant, is the Lord's freeman; likewise also, he that is called, being free, is Christ's servant."[3]

§ 62. From these passages, it cannot be inferred that Christ and his apostles recommended slavery, such as they saw it; or that these precepts exhorted the establishment of the institution where it does not exist, or the continuance of it in all cases. They simply treated slavery as they did all other civil government, as of God, so long as in his providence he permitted it to exist; and regulated, by precepts, the relation, as they did that of ruler and subject. The only legitimate inference to be drawn is, that the relation is not necessarily and *per se* sinful. That it may or may not be, according to the circumstances of each particular case, thus harmonizing with the conclusion to which we were brought by an inquiry into the unrevealed law of nature.

§ 63. But it is said, that while the Saviour did not expressly prohibit the institution, he announced principles with which it is utterly inconsistent, and the legitimate fruits of which must be its extinction. These principles are, "Thou shalt love thy neighbor as thyself. And whatsoever ye would that men

---

[1] Tit. 2 : 9, 10.　　[2] 1 Pet. 2 : 18.　　[3] 1 Cor. 7 : 20, 21, 22.

should do unto you, do ye even so unto them." The argument is legitimate, if the conclusion is correctly drawn. Let us examine it. The analysis of the rule is, we should act towards others, not as they act towards us, not as the laws of the land allow us to act, but as we would have them to act towards us, were our respective situations reversed. How would we have them to act toward us in all cases? According to our whims or childish desires? If so, we must give free scope to the crude wishes of our children; we must release the condemned convict, for thus it is that we would have them to act toward us were our situations reversed. Such is not the rule. We would have them to act toward us, in all cases, in that manner which would tend most to promote our real good and happiness, even though we could not ourselves see it. Hence we should control the child, though its wishes be adverse, for its ultimate good. We should punish the criminal however he may regard it, for his interest as a citizen requires the execution of the laws. We should deal in the same way with the slaves. We should act towards them, in all cases, in that manner which tends most to promote their real good and happiness; in that manner which will most surely elevate them, physically, intellectually, and morally: for so, according to the golden rule, would we have them to act toward us. If the condition of bondage does actually promote their real good and happiness, then this precept sanctions and enjoins it. If, on the contrary, it diminishes their real good, and does not promote their true happiness, it runs counter to this great precept, and should cease to exist. The test then is, does the institution of negro slavery tend to promote the physical, intellectual, and moral growth of the negro race? The very test to which we arrived by our investigation of the unrevealed natural law.

§ 64. It is said, that were the great principles of Christianity perfectly implanted in every heart, so as to control every action, the institution of slavery would end. So far as that institution involves the idea of the control of the inferior by the will of the superior, this is true. And so would it be true of *all* government. Revelation teaches us, that God gave different gifts to different men. To one five talents, to another two, to another one. To one the gift of tongues. To another, government. It teaches us to repress every feeling of envy, strife, ambition; and whatever may be our situation in life suited to our capacity therewith to be content. If every man in the community thoroughly appreciated his own gifts, and was therewith content, then each would, unbidden, assume that position in the scale of life to which his talent fitted him. The rulers would be pointed out of God; the subjects would rejoice to obey. The master would recognize a brother in his servant; while the servant would take pleasure in the service of his Lord. Nothing would be of constraint. Everything would be of free-will. Such is the Apostle's idea of the perfect law of liberty in Christ.[1] To be such is to be Christ's freemen. "Where the spirit of the Lord is, there is liberty."[2] Such a man needs no restraint, whatever may be his situation. If " called, being a servant, he cares not

---

[1] James 1 : 25.   See Psalm 119 : 45.
[2] 2 Cor. 3 : 17; John 8 : 32.

for it." "For, brethren, ye have been called unto liberty; only use not liberty for an occasion to the flesh, but by love serve one another."[1] Such would be the glorious fruits of the complete triumph of the Gospel of Christ. In the present dispensation, it would seem that we need hardly expect it. For when the prophetic vision of St. John saw the "heaven departed as a scroll when it is rolled together," there were "bondmen" as well as "freemen," who "hid themselves in the dens and in the rocks of the mountains."[2]

§ 65. From this investigation into the law of nature, the will of God, our conclusion is, that until the nature of the African negro becomes by some means radically changed, there is nothing in his enslavement contrary to the law of his nature. In this, we speak of the limited or qualified slavery, such as exists at present in the United States, and not of absolute or pure slavery, as defined by us. For the latter includes the power over life, the *jus vitæ et necis;* and as it cannot be said that the physical, intellectual, or moral nature of the slave, can be improved, or his happiness promoted, by the existence or exercise of such a power as this, so we find in the law of nature no justification of or foundation for this power.[3]

[1] Gal. 5 : 13.  See also 1 Pet. 2 : 16.

[2] Rev. 6 : 14, 15.  In replying to the argument to show slavery a sin from the Bible, I have not referred to the authors by express reference.  The reader will perceive that I have examined the objections made by Sharp, Barnes, Channing, and Wayland, and repeated in varied forms by smaller imitators.

[3] This is the conclusion to which Grotius arrives.  De Jure Belli et Pacis, Lib. II, c. v.

# CHAPTER III.

§ 66. WE have seen in a preliminary sketch the history of the introduction of negro slavery into the United States. The origin of the system is found, therefore, in purchase, of persons already in a state of slavery in their own land. The law does not go back of that fact, to inquire into the foundation of that slavery there,[1] but recognizing the rights of the master there to sell, sustains the title of the purchaser from him.[2] It was alleged, and, doubtless, was true, that the slave-traders sometimes stimulated or were engaged in kidnapping free negroes on the coast of Africa, who were afterwards sold as slaves. Such a foundation could not sustain a legal claim to the bondage of the victim.

§ 67. A few of the slaves in America are the descendants of conquered Indians. The foundation of their enslavement is the right of conquest, which has been recognized in all countries as one of the

---

[1] Mary v. The Vestry, &c., 3 Harr. & McH. 501; Hudgins v. Wright, 1 Hen. & Munf. 134; Davis v. Curry, 2 Bibb. 238.

[2] The presumption is in favor of slavery there. 3 Harr. & Mc-Hen. 501.

sources of slavery.[1]   The presumption in relation to the Indian, is that he is free, and it is incumbent on the party alleging slavery to show his title.[2]

§ 68. White persons may not be enslaved or held as slaves, except by express statutory enactment.[3] The presumption of freedom arises from the color,

---

[1] State v. Van Waggoner, 1 Halsted, 374 ; Marguerite v. Chouteau, 2 Miss. 71 ; 3 Ib. 540 ; Seville v. Chretien, 5 Martin, 275 ; 1 Dallas, 167.

In Georgia, by the Act of 1770 (New Digest, 971), all Indians were declared slaves, " except free Indians in amity with this Government." In Virginia, since 1691, no American Indian could be reduced to slavery.  See Gregory v. Bough, 4 Rand. 611, for a full history.  See also note to Code of Virginia (1849), p. 456. In South Carolina, Indians, prisoners of war, were directed to be bought and sold as slaves.  2 Statutes at Large, 325.   And all theretofore bought and sold as slaves, declared slaves, 8 Ibid. 352, 371, 385.

Mr. Stroud, in his " Sketch of the Law of Slavery," has indulged in great indignation at the enslavement of Indians.  It certainly is in accordance with the law of nations, and was practised by all the colonies.  See " General Laws and Liberties of Massachusetts Bay," ch. xii, § 2.   And is preferable to the treatment in other places of conquered Indians, where " the old men, the women, and babes, perished by hundreds in the fire." Bancroft's King Philip's War, vol. ii, pp. 104, 105.

[2] Ulzire et al. v. P. Farra, 14 Martin, 504 ; Hudgins v. Wright, 1 Hen. & Munf. 134 ; Hook v. Nancy Pagee, 2 Munf. 379 ; Gregory v. Baugh, 2 Leigh, 686 ; S. C. 4 Rand. 632 ; Gatliffe's Admr. et al. v. Rose et al., 8 B. Monr. 632.

[3] Gentry v. McMinnis, 3 Dana, 382.

In Maryland, by the Act of 1663, a white woman marrying a slave, became with the issue slaves.  This act was repealed in 1681.  But the descendants of those marrying in the meanwhile have been held to be slaves.  Butler v. Boarman, 1 Har. & McHen. 371 ; Butler v. Craig, 2 Har. & McHen. 214.

and it is incumbent on the person claiming title to rebut that presumption.[1]

§ 69. As all the negroes introduced into America were brought as slaves, the black color of the race raises the presumption of slavery,[2] contrary to the principles of the common law, which would presume freedom until the contrary is shown.[3] This presumption is extended, in most of the States, to mulattoes or persons of mixed blood, casting upon them the onus of proving a free *maternal* ancestor.[4] In others, it is confined to the negroes.[5] In those States where slavery has been abolished, no such presumption would attach, except to persons proven to be fugitives from a slaveholding State.[6]

[1] Hook v. Nancy Pagee and her children, 2 Munf. 379; Gentry v. McMinnis, 3 Dana, 382 ; Gatliffe's Admr. v. Rose et al., 8 B. Monr. 632.

[2] Remick v. Chloe, 1 Miss. 197 ; Macon & W. R. R. Co. v. Holt, 8 Ga. 157 ; Davis v. Curry, 2 Bibb. 238; Gibbons v. Morse, 2 Hals. 253 ; 3 Ibid. 375 ; Kegler v. Miles, Mart. & Yerg. 427 ; Tritigot v. Byers, 5 Cowen, 480 ; Adele v. Beauregard, 1 Mart. 183 ; Gober v. Gober, 2 Hayw. 170 ; 3 Dana, 382 ; 6 Gill & J. 136 ; 1 Dev. 376 ; 5 Sm. & Mar. 609 ; 4 Har. & McH. 295.

[3] Coke Lit. 128 a; 3 Harrington, 551, 559; 3 Scammon, 232 ; 4 Har. & McHen. 295.

[4] In many of the States by statute, Georgia (New Dig. 971), Maryland (1 Dorsey's Laws, 28), South Carolina, 7 Stat. at Large, 352, 371, 385. In Virginia and Kentucky, one-fourth negro blood presumes slavery, less than that, freedom. Gentry v. McMinnis, 3 Dana, 385 ; Rev. Code Va. 1849, 457, note.

[5] 2 Haywood, 170 ; Scott v. Williams, 1 Dev. 376 ; State v. Muller, 7 Iredell, 275 ; State v. Cecil, 2 Martin, 208 ; Gober v. Gober, 1 Taylor (Lou.), 164.

[6] Kinney v. Cook, 3 Scammon, 232 ; Stoutenborough v. Haviland, 3 Green, 266.

§ 70. The issue and descendants of slaves, in the maternal line, are slaves. The rule, *partus sequitur ventrem,* has been adopted in all the States.[1] The

[1] 1 Hen. & Munf. 134; 1 Hayw. 234; 1 Cook, 381; 2 Bibb. 298; 5 Dana, 207; 2 Ib. 432; 2 Miss. 71; 3 Ib. 540; 8 Peters, 220; 15 Sergt. & Rawle, 18; 2 Brev. 307; 20 John. 1; 12 Wheat. 568. In several of the States this rule is adopted by statute. South Carolina, 7 Stat. at Large, 397; Georgia, New Dig. 971; Mississippi, Hutchinson's Code, 512; Virginia, Rev. Code (1849), 457; Louisiana, Civil Code, Art. 183; Maryland, semble, 1 Dorsey, 28; formerly otherwise, 1 Har. & McH. 370.

Mr. Stroud, in his "Sketch of the Laws regulating Slavery in the United States," has indulged in considerable abuse of the slaveholding States for the adoption, by their statutes and by their courts, of this principle of the civil law in preference to the doctrine of the common law. He calls it "a degrading principle" (p. 11), "a measure of cruelty and avarice" (p. 12), "a reproach to our republics" (p. 13), &c.; and urges, that the doctrine of the common law, coupled with the other principle, that all bastards are free, would have emancipated all mulattoes (p. 14). I have referred to these remarks more to show the spirit in which this sketch is written, than seriously to argue the question. I cannot refrain from remarking, however, that a moment's reflection would have shown Mr. Stroud that it is the latter principle, viz., the freedom of all bastards, that would effect the object so desirable in his eyes, the freedom of mulattoes; and that, independent of this principle, it is a matter of secondary importance as to the end he has in view, whether the civil or common law rule be adopted. In fact, were the common law rule adopted, the issue of a free white woman, by a slave, would be slaves. Such was the rule for a short period of time in Maryland and Pennsylvania, and most heartily does Mr. Stroud condemn the consequence (pp. 10, 19). The truth is, Mr. Stroud wrote to make slavery odious. In a note to p. 23, Mr. Stroud says, that "the *harsh features* of slavery were never known in New England." Yet this "degrading principle" of "cruelty and avarice," was adopted in all their courts! See Slavery as It Is, p. 191. The principle changes wonderfully in turpitude as comes south of the Potomac.

reason of this rule, as given by the civilians, was, " Ex juris principiis fœtus, tanquam accessio ventris, ad dominum ventris pertinet." " From principles of justice, the offspring, the increase of the womb, belongs to the master of the womb."[1] This rule has been almost universal among those nations recognizing slavery.[2] It was certainly the Levitical law, which provided, that when the Hebrew slave, at the end of six years, went free, " the wife and her chil-

[1] Heineccius, Elem. Jur. Lib. I, tit. iii, § 81; Potgiesser, De Statu Servorum, Proleg. § xxix; Domat, § 99. See also Rutherforth's Institutes, 247, for the reasons of the rule. Grotius says, that by the law of nature the issue should be the common property of the masters of both parents, " Quia uterque parens sit causa partus." Hein. Prælec, in H. Grot. Lib. II, c. v, § 29.

[2] Among all the German nations, Heinec. Elem. Jur. Lib. I, § 86. See also Vol. VI, oper. 13.

Among the Austrians and Swedes, Potg. De Statu Serv. Lib. I, c. i, § xi, note c. In Helvetia, Batavia, and Denmark, Ibid. L. II, c. ii, § 50.

Among the ancient Germans and Franks, the issue followed the condition of the most ignoble (deterior) parent, whether father or mother. Hence, if either was a slave, the issue were slaves. Ibid. Lib. I, cap. i, §§ xi, xii. The Bavarian law excepted cases where the mother was ignorant of the ignoble condition of the father. Ibid. All bastards and infants exposed were, on this principle, slaves. So also were hermaphrodites. Ibid. § xiii. This was the Roman law as to infants exposed. Ibid. By the custom of Ravensberg, the eldest child of a free woman, by a slave, was free; the remainder were slaves. Ibid. § 50.

Le Code Noir, for the regulation of slavery in the French colonies prescribes, that " Les enfans qui naissent d'un mariage entre esclaves, sont aussi esclaves, et appartiennent au maître de la femme esclave, et non à celui du mari, si le mari et la femme ont des maîtres différents." Merlin, Report de Juris, verbo Esclavage. " Et si le père est libre, et la mère esclave, les enfants sont pareillement esclaves." Ibid.

dren shall be her master's, and he (the Hebrew father) shall go out by himself."[1]

§ 71. Lord Coke announced the common law to be different, and subsequent writers have followed this high authority. The older authors, Bracton, Britton, and Fleta, announce the civil law rule as the law of England; except that they regulate the *status* by the condition of the mother at the time of conception and not of birth,[2] and this principle seems

[1] See Lev. 25 : 45, 46; Grotius, De Jure, &c., L. II, ch. v. To this there is this curious note: "Seneca has observed, that children belong equally to both father and mother." De Benefic. Lib. VII, cap. xii. In the laws of the Visigoths this question is asked: "If a son is produced by the concurrence of both parents, why should he share the condition of his mother only, since he could not have existed without a father?" From which it is concluded, that, "according to the law of nature, children born of two slaves, belonging to different masters, are to be divided equally between them both." Lib. X, tit. i, 17. The children of two Sclavonians followed their father, as appears from the Speculum Saxonicum, iii, 73. The same thing was practised in some parts of Italy. See the Decretals, Lib. IV, tit. ix, De Conjug. Servorum, cap. iii. Among the Lombards and Saxons, the children shared the fate of that parent whose condition was lowest. Speculum Saxonicum, i, 16. So also among the Visigoths in Spain, in Isidore's time, as appears from the canon law. Can. xxxii, Quest. iv, c. xv. The laws of the Visigoths formally declare, that a child born of a free father and a mother that is a slave, thereby became a slave. Lib. III, tit. ii. 3; Lib. IV, tit. v, 7; Lib. IX, tit. i, 16. Those that were born of two slaves, served the masters of both their parents equally. If there was but one son, he belonged to the father's master, on paying the mother's master half his value. In regard to those termed *originarii*, the father's master had two-thirds and the mother's master the other, according to the edict of King Theodoric, in Cassiodore, c. 67.

[2] Bracton, Lib. I, ch. 6, §§ 4, 5; Britton, ch. 31; Fleta, Lib. I, ch. 3, § 2; Glanville, Lib. V, ch. 6.

to be as old as the Penitentials of Theodore and Egbert.[1] The common law, as announced by Littleton, was, that "if a freeman married a niefe (slave), their issue shall be free."[2] Bracton gives the reason which Lord Coke adopts : " The niefe marrying the freeman is enfranchised during the coverture, and therefore, by the common law, the issue is free."[3] But without marriage, the bastard followed the condition of the mother.[4] Littleton, on the contrary, says, all bastards are free ; a deduction from the fact, that the father being unknown, the presumption is in favor of liberty. But this falls to the ground if the earlier writers were correct, that without marriage, the issue of a niefe followed the condition of the mother.[5] Upon this inference of Littleton, Lord Coke announced a rule for the common law, different from that of the civil law.[6]

§ 71 a. By the civil law rule, adopted as before stated, the *status* of the issue is determined by that of the mother at the time of the birth, and not at

[1] Ancient Laws and Institutes of England, 273.

[2] Lib. II, § 187.

[3] Fol. 78 b.  So if a freewoman married a niefe, she became a slave.  Bracton, Lib. IV, ch. 6, § 4.

[4] Bracton, Lib. I, p. 5 a; Britton, fol. 78, ch. 31; Fleta, Lib. I, ch. 4; The Mirror, ch. 2, § 28; Fortescue, ch. 42; Glanville, Lib. V, ch. 6.

[5] Potgiesser notices this disagreement of the English authorities.  Lib. II, cap. ii, § 50.

[6] As to all inferior animals, the English law follows the rule : " Vitulus autem matris est, cujuscumque taurus alluserit."  See Ancient Laws and Institutes of England, title Leges, R. Hen. I, art. lvii; De Solucione Liberi vel Servi, and notes thereto.

the time of conception.[1] Being fixed at the birth, it matters not how soon thereafter the condition of the mother may be changed, that of the issue is fixed. Hence, if a female slave is emancipated by will or deed, to take effect at a future period, and, before that period arrives, she has issue, the issue are slaves.[2]

§ 72. And so, if the mother is free at the time of the birth, the issue is free, and no subsequent enslavement of the mother will deprive the child of freedom.[3] Indeed, so unbending is the principle, that it has been held, that if a deed emancipating a female slave reserves her future increase as slaves, the reservation is void : the Court observing,

---

[1] Ned et al. v. Beal, 2 Bibb. 298; Rawlings v. Boston, 3 Har. & McH. 139; Adams v. Barrett, 2 Howard U. S. 496; Miller v. Dwilling, 14 S. & R. 446; 2 Rand. 246; 4 Rand. 600. By the Saxon law, the *status* was determined at the time of conception. Theod. Pen. xvi, 33, n. 2; Egb. Conf. c. 25; Ancient Laws, &c. 272; Glanv. Lib. V, ch. 6. A late law at Rome made the issue free, if the mother was free at any time during the pregnancy. Paulus, S. R. II, tit. xxiv; Dig. Lib. I, tit. i, § 5.

[2] McCutchen v. Marshall, 8 Pet. 220; 8 Martin, 218; 2 Rand. 228; 6 Har. & John. 526; 2 Bibb. 298; 3 Iredell, 224; 5 Dana, 207; 3 B. Monr. 60; 12 Ala. (N. S.) 728; 2 Harrington, 77. A different decision has been made in some of the courts, arising from their construing such cases to be an immediate emancipation, with a reservation only of services. Pleasants v. Pleasants, 2 Call. 206; Harris v. Clarissa, 6 Yerg. 227. This construction is now followed only by the courts of Tennessee. See decision of Ruffin, C. J., in Mayho v. Sears, 3 Ired. 226; Hartsell v. George, 3 Humph. 255. In some of the States, it has been declared by statute, that the issue of *statuliberi* shall be free when the mother becomes free.

[3] Barrington v. Logan's Admrs. 2 Dana, 432; Charles v. French, 6 J. J. Marsh. 331.

"A free mother cannot have children who are slaves. Such a birth would be monstrous, both in the eye of reason and of law."[1] So a female slave, emancipated by her owner, is subject to sale for indebtedness previously contracted, but her issue, born while she is enjoying her freedom, are not thus subject.[2]

§ 73. A more difficult question arises when the emancipation of the mother is to take effect upon the happening of some event in future—as, for instance, the assent of the Legislature to the act of manumission—whether the issue born pending the contingency are slave or free. Upon principle, the proper rule would seem to be, that where, upon the happening of the contingency, the act of manumission relates back to the period when it first became inchoate, the issue should be free, the mother's freedom dating from that period. And, on the contrary, where the mother's freedom dates only from the happening of the event, the issue are slaves.[3] Thus, should a testator, in one of the States where emancipation is not allowed, except with the assent of the Legislature, bequeath to a female slave her freedom, instructing his executors to procure the assent of the Legislature to the bequest, and such assent was subsequently obtained, it would seem

---

[1] Fulton v. Shaw, 4 Rand. 597; see also Maria et al. v. Surbaugh, 2 Rand. 240.

[2] Parks v. Hewlett, &c. 9 Leigh, 511.

[3] Maria et al. v. Surbaugh, 2 Rand. 234; Henry v. Bradford, 1 Robinson, 54; Black v. Meaux, 4 Dana, 188; Sydney v. White, 12 Ala. (N. S.) 728; Johnson's Admrs. v. Johnson's Heirs, 8 B. Monroe, 470.

that such assent would relate back to the death of
the testator, and the issue born since the death and
before the act of the Legislature would be free.[1] On
the contrary, if the bequest of a female slave be to
A. for life, and, at his death, to B., if he survive A.,
and if B. die before A., then the slave to be free.
Upon the happening of this contingency, issue born
during the life of A. would be slaves.[2]

§ 74. Another class of cases is, where the mother
is emancipated, to take effect at a future period,
and in the meantime remains in a state of slavery.[3] Such persons, by the civil law, were termed
*statuliberi*, and their issue, born prior to the time
when their freedom took effect, were slaves.[4] Thus,
where the testator devised to his wife all of his
slaves, " provided that at her death they should be
set free, with the exception of those who should not
be of age at the death of his wife, who were to re-

[1] See opinion of Roane, J., in Pleasants v. Pleasants, 2 Call. 286;
see also Donaldson v. Jude, 2 Bibb. 57; Lewis v. Simonton, 8
Humph. 189. So, where a female slave is emancipated by will,
and the probate thereof is caveated, and pending the litigation, a
child is born, upon the establishment of the will, the child is
held to be free, *a nativitate*. Black v. Meaux, 4 Dana, 188. And
where a testator gave to his slaves an election to go to Liberia, and
by his will "emancipated all such," on the slaves electing to go,
the emancipation related back to the death; and issue born since
were held to be free. Graham's Exr. v. Sam, 7 B. Monroe, 403.

[2] McCutchen et al. v. Marshall et al., 8 Peters, 220; Maria v.
Surbaugh, 2 Rand. 228.

[3] It has been held, in some of the States, that no such qualified
or middle state, between slavery and freedom, can exist. Thus in
Virginia, Wynn et al. v. Carrell et al., 2 Grattan, 227; see also
Henry v. Nunn, 11 B. Monroe, 239.

[4] Huberi, Præl. Lib. I, tit. iii, § 5.

main under the control of certain persons until they became of age, when they were to be set free." The females had issue pending the life estate. As to their *status*, Thompson, J., delivering the opinion of the Supreme Court of the United States, says : " If this was an open question, it might be urged with some force that the condition of the female slaves, during the life of the widow, was not that of absolute slavery, but was, by the will, converted into a modified servitude, to end upon the death of the widow or on their arrival at the age of twenty-one, should she die before that time. If the mothers were not absolute slaves, but held in the condition just mentioned, it would seem to follow that their children would stand in the same condition, and be entitled to their freedom on their arrival at the age of twenty-one years. But the course of decisions in the State of Tennessee, and some other States, where slavery is tolerated, goes strongly, if not conclusively, to establish the principle, that females thus situated are slaves ; that it is only a conditional manumission, and until the contingency happens upon which the freedom is to take effect, they remain, to all intents and purposes, absolute slaves, and the Court do not mean to disturb the principle."[1]

§ 75. So also, where a master made a deed, emancipating a female slave " with the qualification and condition, that she shall hold and enjoy freedom immediately after my death, but during my life, she is to remain in my service and power," &c. The

---

[1] McCutchen et al. v. Marshall et al., 8 Peters, 220; see also opinion of Ruffin, C. J., in Mayho v. Sears, 3 Ired. 224.

issue born during the lifetime of the master, were
held to be slaves by the Supreme Court of Louisiana,
the mother " being of that class of persons known
to the Roman law by the appellation of *statuliberi*."[1] Such also is the rule of the civil law, from
which we have adopted the principles controlling
the *status* of the issue of slaves.[2]

§ 76. It will be seen from the cases referred to
and other decisions of the courts, that while they
do not deny, that if the condition of slavery of the
mother becomes qualified, the condition of the issue
would be either the same[3] or absolute freedom, yet
they incline to hold the condition of the mother,
under the facts of each case, to be that of absolute
slavery.[4] This being established, the consequence

[1] Catin v. d'Orgenoy's Heirs, 8 Martin, 218. "Statuliber est
qui statutam et destinatam in tempus vel conditionem libertatem
habet." Dig. Lib. XL, tit. vii, § 1. By the civil law, if a female
were bequeathed to another, to be by him set free at a future time,
or upon a condition, and the time had come, or the condition been
performed, but the slave not actually manumitted, and thereafter,
before an actual emancipation, had a child born, the child was a
slave, belonging to the person bound to manumit. But in that
case he was bound to transfer the child to the mother, that he
might be, by that means, set free. Dig. Lib. XL, tit. v, § 13.
Cited by Green, J., 2 Rand. 242. In Maryland, by statute, the
person manumitting may prescribe, in such a case, whether the
issue shall be bond or free. If he fails to do so, they are slaves.
Dorsey's Laws, &c. 593.

[2] Just. Inst. Lib. I, tit. iii, § 14; Dig. Lib. XL, tit. vii, § 1.

[3] Pleasants v. Pleasants, 2 Call. 319; Harris v. Clarissa, 6 Yerger,
227.

[4] Henry v. Bradford, 1 Robinson (Va.), 53; Crawford v. Moses,
10 Leigh, 277; Ned v. Beal, 2 Bibb. 298; Jameson v. Emeline,
5 Dana, 207; 3 B. Monroe, 60. The conflict of the authorities

follows, that the issue are slaves. But, wherever the deed of manumission changes the condition of the mother from slavery to mere servitude, though the time of the enjoyment of perfect freedom be postponed, issue born subsequent to the deed, and pending the service of the mother, are free.[1] According to the civil law, in such a case the slave would be free immediately, and the condition annexed of servitude is nugatory. " Libertas ad tempus dari non potest. Ideoque, si ita scriptum sit, usque ad decem annos liber esto, temporis adjectio supervacua est."[2]

§ 77. The same principle applies, in those States where laws have been passed for the gradual abolition of slavery, whereby the condition of the slaves at certain times and under circumstances varying according to the provisions of the respective acts, is changed to a state of servitude or apprenticeship. The issue born during this state are free, subject only to such services as the respective acts may im-

upon this question, arises from the different views the courts take of the character of the bequest, or gift of freedom to the slave. See an elaborate review of the cases, by Ruffin, C. J., in Mayho v. Sears, 3 Ired. 226.

[1] McCutchen et al. v. Marshall et al., 8 Peters, 221; Isaac v. West, 6 Rand. 652; Scott v. Waugh, 15 Serg. & Rawle, 17; Harris v. Clarissa, 6 Yerger, 227; Hudgens v. Spencer, 4 Dana, 589; Charles v. French, 6 J. J. Marsh. 331; Johnson's Admrs. v. Johnson's Heirs, 8 B. Monroe, 471; O'Bryan, v. Goslee, 10 B. Monroe, 100; Civil Code, Louisiana, Art. 196. In some of the States, however, it has been held that there can be no middle condition between slavery and freedom, and that all deeds and bequests, seeking to create such a condition, are void. Wynn et al. v. Carrell, 2 Grattan, 227.

[2] Dig. Lib. XL, tit. iv, §§ 33, 34.

pose.[1] If, however, the act provides for the freedom
of children of slaves " born within the State," and
after the passage of the act, a female slave is sold
and removed into another State, where no such law
exists, issue born after her removal are not free.[2]

§ 78. If the instrument emancipating the mother,
declared that the mother " and her increase" shall
be free at a future period, children born after the
making of the deed, and before the time arrives, will
be free at that time.[3] So also, where a testator
bequeaths his negroes to A. for life, and " at her
death all his negroes to be free," the issue born,
pending the life estate, are entitled to their freedom
at the termination of the life estate.[4] So also, where
a testator emancipated "all his negroes," upon their
electing to go to Liberia, and to enable them to
transport themselves, fair wages were to be allowed
them, and pending the time of their service issue
was born, such issue have also the right of election.[5]

§ 79. Another question of importance arises where
the law of the place of the birth and the law of the
domicile of the mother are conflicting. By which

[1] Barrington v. Logan's Admrs. 2 Dana, 432; Gentry v.
McMinnis, 3 Dana, 382; Spotts v. Gillaspie, 6 Rand. 566; Miller v. Dwilling, 14 Serg. & Rawle, 442; Boon v. Juliet, 1 Scammon, 258.

[2] Spotts v. Gillespie, 6 Rand. 566; Frank v. Shannon's Exrs.
1 Bibb, 615.

[3] Fanny v. Bryant, 4 J. J. Marshall, 368.

[4] Erskine v. Henry and wife, 9 Leigh, 188; see also Campbell
v. Street, 1 Ired. 109; Hart v. Fanny, 6 Monroe, 49; Hamilton
v. Cragg, 6 Har. & John. 16.

[5] Adams v. Adams, 10 B. Monroe, 69.

law is the *status* of the issue to be decided? Where the mother is regularly domiciled at the time of the birth, the law of the place of the birth, will determine the *status* of the issue.[1]  But where a female slave, at the time of the birth of a child, is either temporarily or wrongfully within a different jurisdiction from that of her true residence and domicile, the law of her domicile and not the law of the place of the birth, must determine the *status* of the issue.[2] Hence, if a slave, taken by her master temporarily to a State where slavery does not exist, or a fugitive slave in such a State is delivered of a child, the mother's condition of slavery in either case remaining unchanged, the offspring are slaves.[3]

§ 80. Another conflict of laws arises where the domicile is changed subsequent to the birth, and the law of the new domicile, in which the trial of the question of freedom is heard, is different.  In such a case the *lex fori* yields, not only from comity, but because the *status* of the offspring being determined *eo instanti* upon the birth, a change of resi-

[1] Sidney v. White, 12 Ala. (N. S.) 731; Spotts v. Gillespie, 6 Rand. 566.

[2] Graham v. Strader, 5 B. Monroe, 179 ; S. C. 7 Ibid. 635.

[3] For the discussion of the question as to the effect of the voluntary removal of a slave into a State not tolerating slavery, for a temporary purpose, see post, ch. vii.  I am aware that a decision, at variance with the text, was made by the Supreme Court of Pennsylvania, in The Commonwealth v. Holloway, 2 Serg. & Rawle, 305. That decision, however, was made upon an express provision in their statute, and does not meet the question.  If it was not so made, it would not deserve consideration ; as the real difficulty, viz., the conflict of laws, seems never to have been suggested by either Court or counsel.

dence cannot operate as a change of rights.[1]  This rule as laid down, applies to cases where slavery is recognized and exists in both the original and new domicile. The extent to which the comity of nations requires the tribunals of a State to recognize and enforce the private rights of citizens of another State, will be considered hereafter.

§ 81. A still more complicated case of conflict might arise, where the deed or other instrument, determining the rights of the applicant for freedom, is executed within one jurisdiction, the birth occurs in another, and the trial of the question of freedom is heard in still another. In other words, the *lex loci contractus*, the *lex soli natalis*, and the *lex fori* all differ. In such a case the *lex loci contractus* would generally control the question.[2]  But if it be in conflict with the policy of the law of the forum where the trial is had, the Court will not enforce a rule, contravening the policy of their own government.[3]

§ 81 *a*. If the domicile of the female slave, at the time of the execution of the deed or other instrument of emancipation, be within another jurisdiction, which subsequently becomes the *solum natale* of the child, in that case, the law of the domicile would control the *lex loci contractus*, it being the policy of all the slaveholding States to regulate the condition of all slaves domiciled within their jurisdiction, so long as they remain within that jurisdiction.

[1] Sidney v. White, 12 Ala. (N. S.) 728.

[2] Story's Conf. of Laws, § 242, et seq.; Blackmore v. Phill, 7 Yerger, 452.

[3] Story's Conf. of Laws, § 244, and authorities there cited.

§ 82. We shall hereafter consider, in another connection, the law of domicile, as applied to slaves.[1]
For the present, it is sufficient to state that, as a
general rule, the domicile of the master is that of the
slave, and this not being " of choice" of the slave,
but by operation of law (*necessarium*), by no act of
his can it be changed.[2]

[1] Sections 129–133.
[2] Phillimore on the Law of Domicile, 25, 60.

6

# CHAPTER IV.

§ 83. HAVING ascertained the origin and sources of negro slavery, and having traced that origin to the pure or absolute slavery existing among the tribes of Africa, and having seen that negro slavery is in no wise opposed to the law of nature, except so far as the power to kill or to maim may be claimed therefrom, it follows, that no actual enactment of the legislative power is necessary for its introduction into any country where no municipal law is thereby infringed. Hence, we find it true, that, with the exception of Georgia (where it was at first prohibited),[1] no law is found on our statute books authorizing its introduction.

§ 84. The condition of these slaves in their native country having been one of absolute slavery, including the power over life, such would be their condition in the country to which they were removed, except so far as the same may be modified by the existing laws of their new domicile, and such subsequent legislative enactments as may have been made for their benefit. The law of nature, denying the power over life and limb, being a part of the law of

---

[1] See Stephens's History of Georgia, vol. i.

every civilized state, such power never existed in any of the United States, although it required municipal law to prescribe the punishment for such offences.[1] Many subsequent legislative enactments have been made, regulating the power of the master, and protecting and giving rights to the slave. Having none prior to these enactments, to the municipal law we look for all his rights.

§ 84 a. In the Roman law, a slave was a mere chattel (*res*). He was not recognized as a person. But the negro slave in America, protected as above stated by municipal law, occupies a double character of person and property. Having now ascertained who are and may be slaves in America, a natural division of our subject suggests itself in considering the slave,—first, AS A PERSON, and then, AS PROPERTY.

§ 85. In treating of slaves as persons, we shall inquire of their rights and disabilities, of the authority and rights of the master, and of the relation of slaves to persons other than their masters. To a great extent, these necessarily will be considered together, yet, as far as possible, we shall endeavor to treat them in the order in which they are named.

§ 86. Of the three great absolute rights guaranteed to every citizen by the common law, viz., the right of personal security, the right of personal liberty, and the right of private property, the slave, in a state of pure or absolute slavery, is totally deprived, being, as to life, liberty, and property, under the absolute and uncontrolled dominion of his master,[2]

[1] See The State v. Mann, 2 Dev. Law, 268.

[2] Coke Litt. 116 b; Neal v. Farmer, 9 Geo. Rep. 555; The State v. Mann, 2 Dev. Law, 265; Jackson ex dem. &c. v. Lervey, 5 Cow. 397; Fable v. Brown, 2 Hill Ch. 396.

so that infringements upon these rights, even by third persons, could be remedied and punished only at the suit of the master for the injury done him in the loss of service or the diminution in value of his slave.[1] As before remarked, however, no such state of slavery exists in these States. And so modified is the slavery here, partly by natural law, partly by express enactment, and more effectually by the influence of civilization and Christian enlightenment, that it is difficult frequently to trace to any purely legal sources many of those protecting barriers, the denial of whose existence would shock an enlightened public sense.

§ 87. Statute law has done much to relieve the slave from this absolute dominion, and the master from this perilous power, more especially so far as regards the first great right of personal security. In all of the slaveholding States, the homicide of a slave is held to be murder, and in most of them, has been so expressly declared by law.[2] In Georgia,

---

[1] Authorities cited above. The rule seems to be held different in North Carolina; the battery of a slave by a third person, being held indictable. State v. Hall, 2 Hawks, 582. Upon close examination, however, the decision seems to be based upon a usage sanctioned by the acquiescence of the legislature. In Athens the same rule applied. See Smith's Dict. of Gr. and Rom. Ant. "Servus." But murder of a slave was punished; see same, and authorities cited. In Rome, the master might kill the slave at pleasure, until a constitution of Claudius enacted that it should be murder. Suetonius Claud. 25.

[2] Rev. Code of N. C. 192; Statutes at Large of S. C. vol. vi, 158; New Digest (Cobb) Geo. 785, 982; Laws of Alabama (1823), 639; Hutchinson's Code Miss. 519; Civil Code, Louisiana, Art. 192; Rev. Code of Missouri, ch. xlvii, art. viii, § 39; Laws of Ten-

Alabama, Texas, and Arkansas, the provisions for the protection of the person of the slave are inserted in their respective Constitutions, thus making it a part of the fundamental law, and beyond the reach of ordinary legislation. Nor has the legislation of the States stopped at the protection of their lives, but the security of limbs and the general comfort of the body are, in most of the States, amply provided for, various penalties being inflicted on masters for their cruel treatment; which will be more particularly considered in a subsequent chapter.

§ 88. The question has been much mooted, whether in the absence of statute laws, the homicide of a slave could be punished under the general law prescribing the penalty for murder. By some courts it has been held, that so soon as the progress of civilization and Christian enlightenment elevated the slave from the position of a mere chattel, and recognized him for any purpose as a person, just at that moment, the homicide of him, a human being, in the peace of the State, with malice aforethought, was murder. So long as he remained purely and unqualifiedly property, an injury upon him was a trespass upon the master's rights. When the law, by providing for his proper nourishment and clothing, by enacting penalties against the cruel treatment of his master, by providing for his punishment for crimes, and other similar provisions, recognizes his existence as a person, he is as a child just born, brought for the first time within the pale of the

nessee, Car. & Nich. 676; Laws of Texas (Hartley), 76; Statutes of Arkansas (1848), 48.

law's protecting power; his existence as a person being recognized by the law, that existence is protected by the law.[1]

§ 89. It has been objected to this conclusion, that if the general provision of the law against murder should be held to include slaves, why would not all other penal enactments, by the same course of reasoning, be held to include similar offences when committed on slaves, without their being specifically named? The reply made is twofold. 1st. The law, by recognizing the existence of the slave as a person, thereby confers no rights or privileges except such as are necessary to protect that existence. All other rights must be granted specially. Hence, the penalties for rape would not and should not, by such implication, be made to extend to carnal forcible knowledge of a slave, the offence not affecting the existence of the slave, and that existence being the extent of the right which the implication of the law grants. 2d. Implications of law will always be rebutted by the general policy of the law, and it is clearly against the policy of the law to extend over this class of the community, that character of protection which many of the penal statutes are intended to provide for the citizen.

[1] State v. Reed, 2 Hawks, 454; The State v. Tackett, 1 Hawks, 217; McGren v. Cato's Executors, Minor's (Ala.) Rep. 8; Middleton v. Holmes, 3 Porter, 424; The State v. Jones, Walker's Miss. Rep. 83; Fields v. The State, 1 Yerger, 156; Kelly & Little v. The State, 3 S. & M. 518. See also The Commonwealth v. Booth, 2 Va. Cases, 394; and The Commonwealth v. Turner, 5 Rand. 678; Worley v. The State, 11 Humph. 172.

§ 90. In addition to these reasons, some of the courts have striven to assimilate the condition of the slave to that of the villain in Britain, and thence to apply to slavery here such rules as were applicable to villanage there. That no such identity exists as would justify this conclusion, has been as strenuously demonstrated.[1] Other courts have applied to

[1] Neal v. Farmer, 9 Geo. 555; The Commonwealth v. Turner, 5 Rand. 683; Fable v. Brown's Exr. 2 Hill Ch. 390. That slavery existed among the Saxons prior to the Norman invasion, there can be no doubt; and, as far back as the laws of King Aethelbirht, we find penalties prescribed for the homicide of a slave by a stranger. Ancient Laws and Institutes, 3. So, in the laws of King Alfred, we find, "He who smiteth his own slave, and he die not on the same day, though he live (but) two or three nights, he is not altogether so guilty, because it was his own property; but if he die the same day, then let the guilt rest on him." Ibid. 22; with which compare Exodus, ch. 21 : 20, 21. So also by the laws of King Etheldred, "If an Englishman slay a Danish thrall, let him pay for him with a pound." Ancient Laws, &c., 122. The penalty differed much from that for slaying a freeman. So among the laws of William the Conqueror, "Si quis convictus vel confessus fuerit, in jure alium occidisse, det were suum, et insuper domino occisi, manbote viz. pro homine libero x sol, pro servo, xx sol." Ibid. 203. Among the laws of William, we also find, "Item si servi permanserint sine calumpnia per annum et diem in civitatibus nostris vel in burgis, vel muris vallatis, vel in castris nostris, a die illâ liberi efficiantur; et liberi a jugo servitutis sue sint in perpetuum." Ibid. 213. Strabo informs us that during the Anglo-Saxon times, slaves were one of the principal English exports. Strabo, Lib. IV, p. 199 (Ed. Paris, 1620); Barr. on Stat. 274. (Consult here Studies on Slavery, 304.)

Britton says (fol. 77), that villanage commenced after Noah's flood; the conquerors making villains of the vanquished "to use at their pleasure," "a user al so pleasur." See also Brooks's Abr., title Villenage, pl. 65. The old writers, Bracton, Britton, and Fleta, use Villanus and Servus as synonymous. Bracton, 6 b, 7,

the master and slave, the principles of law applicable to masters and apprentices. This proposition,
however, has not been adhered to with any tenacity.
Another able judge assumes the position, that " the
true state of the slave must be ascertained by reference to the disabilities of an alien enemy, in which
light the heathen were anciently regarded."[1]

§ 91. To all of this reasoning and these conclusions other courts have withheld their assent, and
while they acknowledge that the feelings of humanity, and the dictates of conscience enlightened by
Christianity, would lead them to these conclusions,
yet they have been unable in the law itself to feel
themselves justified in so declaring it. In their
view, the slave remains in a state of pure slavery,
until relieved by legislative enactment, and the provisions of those enactments are the extent of their

24 b, 25, et seq.; Brit. c. xxxi; Fleta, Lib. IV, ch. xi; see 2
Black. Comm. 92; Burrill's Law Dict. Villein.

The Norman Conquest, with its introduction of feudal tenures,
so far modified the condition of the Saxon slaves, as to make the
conditions of villains materially different from that of African
slaves. Yet, it is an undoubted fact, that African slavery not only
existed in fact, in England, but was recognized fully by its courts,
prior to the decision in Somersett's case. "The personal traffic
in slaves resident in England," says Lord Stowell (in the case of
the slave Grace, 2 Hagg. Adm. Rep. 105), "had been as public
and as authorized in London, as in any of our West India Islands.
They were sold on the Exchange, and other places of public resort,
by parties themselves resident in London, and with as little reserve
as they would have been in any of our West India possessions.
Such a state of things continued without impeachment, from a
very early period, up to nearly the end of the last century." See
also pages 108, 109. The decision in Somersett's case was in 1772,
prior to our Revolution.

[1] Fable v. Brown's Exr. 2 Hill Ch. 391, 392.

rights and protection; that by the rules for the construction of statutes, which are adopted to regulate the conduct of citizens, slaves are not included within their provisions unless specifically named ; that though murder is defined to be the killing of a human being, &c., yet rape is defined to be the carnal forcible knowledge of a female, and if the killing of a slave be murder, the carnal forcible knowledge of a female slave is rape; and further, that the fact that every slaveholding State has, by penal enactment, provided punishment for such offences when committed on the persons of slaves, is a legislative declaration that such offences were before that time unprovided for. That the Colonies having adopted the common law, and negro slavery having no existence in Great Britain, there could be necessarily no provision of that law in reference to it, and consequently the power of the master until limited by legislation was absolute.[1] This view of the question seems to have prevailed in the courts of the British West Indies, as appears from the act passed in Jamaica, in 1792, providing punishments for the murder and maiming of slaves.[2]

§ 92. The view we have taken of the law of nature leads us to a different conclusion from either of these, viz., that by that law, and without statutory enactment, the homicide or maiming of a negro slave is prohibited and unlawful, but that it requires statutory enactment to provide punishment for such

[1] Neal v. Farmer, 9 Geo. Rep. 555; Fable v. Brown's Exrs. 2 Hill Ch. 395; State v. Fleming, 2 Strobh. 464.
[2] 1 Brown's Civil Law, 106, note.

offences. Such statutes having been passed long since in all the slaveholding States, the question arises now only collaterally; and generally upon the point whether the master is bound to prosecute criminally, before entering his civil complaint for damages.

§ 93. The same course of reasoning that would make the killing of a slave murder, without statutory enactment, would extend to the offences of manslaughter, mayhem, wounding, and assault with intent to murder, all of these affecting the life of the slave.[1] It would not extend to an ordinary battery, and it would seem clear upon principle, that the battery of a slave, without special enactment, could not be prosecuted criminally.[2] The master's civil remedy would be the only mode of redress against a stranger. Where the battery was committed by the master himself, there would be no redress whatever, for the reason given in Exodus 21 : 21, "for he is his money."[3] The powerful protection of the master's private interest would of itself go far to remedy this evil. Legislators, however, have taken care, as before remarked, in all the States, to protect

---

[1] Fields v. The State, 1 Yerger, 126; see State v. Piver, 2 Hayw. 79; State v. Raines, 3 McCord, 533.

[2] A different rule has been adopted in North Carolina, so far as the battery by a stranger is concerned. The Court seem, however, to base their decision upon usage, acquiesced in by the Legislature. State v. Hall, 2 Hawks, 582; see also Commonwealth v. Booth, 2 Virginia Cases, 394. In accordance with the text, see The State v. Maner, 2 Hill (So. Ca.), 454; Hilton v. Caston, 2 Bailey, 98.

[3] The State v. Mann, 2 Dev. (Law) Rep. 263; The Commonwealth v. Booth, 2 Virginia Cases, 394.

by stringent enactments, the slave from the cruel treatment of his master.

§ 94. The protection of the person of the slave depending so completely upon statute law, it becomes a question of importance, what words in a statute would extend to this class of individuals? Generally, it would seem that an Act of the Legislature would operate upon every person within the limits of the State, both natural and artificial;[1] yet, where the provisions of the statute evidently refer to *natural* persons, the courts will not extend them to *artificial*.[2] Nor will statutes ever be so construed as to lead to absurd and ridiculous conclusions.[3] Experience has proved what theory would have demonstrated, that masters and slaves cannot be governed by the same laws. So different in position, in rights, in duties, they cannot be the subjects of a common system of laws.[4] Hence, the conclusion, that statutory enactments never extend to or include the slave, neither to protect nor to render him responsible, unless specifically named, or included by necessary implication.[5]

[1] Smith's Commentaries on Statute, &c., § 544. If, from a view of the whole statute, the intention of the legislature to include slaves is manifest, they will be considered as included in the word "person." State v. Edmund, 4 Dev. 340.

[2] Blair v. Worley, 1 Scammon, 178.

[3] Smith's Commentaries, &c., §§ 517, 518, et seq.; Domat's Civil Law, Bk. I, tit. i, § 2, pl. 7; United States v. Fisher, 2 Cranch, 400; Reports of Judges, 7 Mass. 523.

[4] Per Nisbet, J., in Neal v. Farmer, 9 Geo. 579.

[5] I am aware that a different rule has been adopted in Virginia. See Dolly Chapple's case, 1 Virginia Cases, 184; Commonwealth v. Carver, 5 Rand. 660. In accordance with the text, see Wash

§ 95. Statutes having declared and affixed penalties to the offences affecting the personal security of slaves, it behooves us to inquire, how far the peculiar relation of the slave may affect the defences of those charged with a violation of these statutes. It would seem that from the very nature of slavery, and the necessarily degraded social position of the slave, many acts would extenuate the homicide of a slave, and reduce the offence to a lower grade, which would not constitute a legal provocation if done by a white person.[1] Thus, in The State v. Tackett, it was held competent for one charged with the murder of a slave to give in evidence that the deceased was turbulent, and insolent, and impudent to white persons.[2] And an assault or striking by a slave would, in many cases, amount to a justification of a homicide, which, in a white person, would only mitigate the offence.[3] If the slave is in a state of insurrection, the homicide is justifiable, in most of the States, by statute. And if a slave is killed, who, being found at an unlawful assembly, combining to rebel, refuses to surrender and resists by force, the homicide is justifiable.[4]

§ 96. But while the law, from the necessity of the case, will thus subject the slave to the partial con-

v. The State, 14 S. & M. 120; Opinion of Nott, J., in The State v. Whyte & Sadler, 2 N. & McC. 175.

[1] Pierce v. Myrick, 1 Dev. 345.

[2] 1 Hawks, 210; see also Ex parte Boylston, 2 Strobh. 41.

[3] Arthur v. Wells, 2 Rep. Con. C. 314; The State v. Cheatwood, 2 Hill (So. Ca.), 461; State v. Crank, 2 Bailey, 75.

[4] Smith v. Hancock, 4 Bibb's Rep. 222. In Maryland, see Dorsey's Laws, &c., 65, 93.

trol of all the freemen of the country, yet it will not sanction any wanton violation of the person of the slave. Thus, it has been held, that a white citizen is not justified in shooting a negro who he orders to stop, and who refuses to do so, even though the negro be a fugitive or runaway.[1] And in the case of Witsell v. Earnest and another, it was held, that even though the negro be suspected of a felony, and be a fugitive, a person not clothed with the authority of law to apprehend him, cannot lawfully kill such slave while flying from him;[2] nor would an overseer be justified in shooting a negro who fled from punishment.[3]

And so, also, the mere fact that the party committing the homicide was a patrolman, and in the exercise of his duties as such, will not justify the killing of a slave flying from him.[4]

§ 97. No settled rule can be laid down as to the extent of the justification which the circumstances of each case may unfold. This we may say, the law looks favorably upon such conduct as tends to the proper subordination of the slave; but at the same time looks with a jealous eye upon all such conduct as tends to unnecessary and cruel treatment.

§ 98. The personal security of the slave being thus protected by express law, becomes *quasi* a right belonging to the slave as a person.[5] How far may

---

[1] Arthur v. Wells, 2 Rep. Con. C. S. C. 314.

[2] 1 Nott & McC. 182.

[3] The State v. Will, 1 Dev. & Bat. 166; Copeland v. Parker, 3 Ired. 513.    [4] Brooks v. Ashburn, 9 Geo. Rep. 298.

[5] I cannot agree with the Court, in South Carolina, that "every

the slave go to protect that right? Subordination
on the part of the slave is absolutely necessary, not
only to the existence of the institution, but to the
peace of the community. The policy of the law,
therefore, requires that the slave should look to his
master and the courts to avenge his wrongs. The
rule, therefore, that justifies the freeman in repelling
force by force, applies not to the slave.

If, however, the life or limb of the slave is en-
dangered, he may use sufficient force to protect and
defend himself, even if in so doing he kills the ag-
gressor.[1]   Such seems to have been the civil law.[2]

§ 99. The law in its mercy goes still farther, and
while it will not justify the slave in resisting force
by force, except in the case stated, yet, in regard for
the frailty of human nature, if the passions of the
slave be excited into unlawful violence by the in-

attempt to extend to the slave positive rights, is an attempt to reconcile inherent contradictions." Kinloch v. Harvey, Harp. 514.
Nor that "in the very nature of things, he is subject to despotism."
Ex parte Boylston, 2 Strobh. 43.   There is no inconsistency in
speaking of the rights of a slave, where those rights are well defined by law, nor is there any inherent difficulty in enforcing those
rights by law, even against his own master.   Every statute passed
to protect the life or limb of the slave, gives to him a right to the
protection provided.   And if the law omitted, the Court should provide a remedy.   The slaves of other countries have positive rights,
and yet are not relieved from slavery.

[1] The State v. Will, a negro, 1 Dev. & Bat. 121–165, a well-con-
sidered cause, decided by Judge Gaston.   Per Thatcher, J., in
Kelly & Little v. The State, 3 S. & M. 526; Dave v. The State,
22 Ala. N. S. 33.   Says Blackstone, "Self-defence, as it is justly
called the primary law of nature, so it is not, neither can it be,
in fact, taken away by the law of society."   Vol. iii, ch. i; see
also Puffendorf, Lib. II, ch. v, § 10, p. 151; Montesquieu, Bk.
XV, ch. xvi.

[2] "Vim vi defendere, omnes leges omniaque jura permittunt."

humanity of his master or others, it will extenuate
the offence, and if a homicide be committed, will
hold these circumstances as a rebuttal of the presumption of malice.[1] This extenuation has been
by some courts confined to cases of homicide by
a slave of one of his own condition, the reason
given being " a stern and unbending necessity."[2] I
cannot yield my assent fully to this proposition as
being well-founded in law. The duty of the slave
to obey, and his habit of subordination, would require a greater provocation to justify an " infirmity
of temper or passion;" but still there are circumstances, where such provocation might be given, especially by others than the master, as to reduce the
offence by the slave from murder to manslaughter.[3]

§ 100. In some of the States the statutes provide
only for the punishment of the murder of a slave,
without specifying or referring to the minor offences
of manslaughter, or an assault with intent to murder, being most probably an oversight on the part
of the draughtsman. In such a case, a verdict of
guilty of manslaughter, it would seem, would leave
the Court to pass judgment as if no statute had been
enacted.[4]

[1] Per Gaston, J., in State v. Will, 1 Dev. & Bat. 171; see also
Dave v. The State, 22 Ala. N. S. 33. This principle was carried very
far in the case of The State v. Cæsar, 9 Ired. 391, where the slave
was declared guilty only of manslaughter, for killing a white man,
who was beating his friend. The Chief Justice dissented, and I
think, properly.

[2] John v. The State, 16 Geo. 203; William v. The State, 18
Geo. 356.

[3] See post, §§ 322, 323; and The State v. Jarrott, 1 Ired. 76;
Dave v. The State, 22 Ala. 33.

[4] The State v. Piver, 2 Hayw. 79.

§ 101. The law is different, however, as to the offence of an assault with intent to murder, for the statute, by making the killing of a slave murder, constituted the offence, at the same time, a felony. And, according to the common law, an attempt to commit a felony, even though the felony be created by statute, is indictable: such attempt being a misdemeanor.[1]

§ 102. Before leaving the subject of the homicide of slaves, it is, perhaps, well to remark, that where a slave is killed, the presumption of law is the same as in other cases of homicide, that it was done maliciously.[2] On account of the frequent and necessarily private relation of master and slave, remote most generally from the presence and view of any white person competent to be a witness, this presumption may and must often operate to the prejudice of the slayer, there being no means of proving the provocation given. Under this view, the Act of South Carolina provides, that where the homicide is committed, and no competent witness is present at the time to testify to the whole transaction, the affidavit of the accused is admitted before the jury, explanatory and exculpatory of his conduct on the occasion.[3] In the other States, upon principle, it would seem, that while the presumption is admitted, the jury should consider the peculiar relations of master and slave, as to some extent rebutting its force and effect.

[1] The State v. Maner, 2 Hill (So. Ca.), 453; 1 Hawkins's Pleas of the Crown, 73, 113.   [2] The State v. Cheatwood, 2 Hill, 464.
[3] The State v. Raines, 3 McC. 533.

# CHAPTER V.

§ 103. WITH reference to the minor offences created by statute, protecting the person of the slave from torture, wounding, maiming, and cruel and inhuman treatment, the great diversity of the statutory provisions and penalties prescribed in the different States, renders it impossible, within the limits of this treatise, to analyze carefully each statute, and consider its practical operation. A few general remarks, upon the general current of legislation, will suffice our purpose.

§ 104. On account of the perfectly unprotect and helpless position of the slave, when his master is placed in opposition to him : not being allowed to accumulate property, with which to provide means for the prosecution of his rights; his mouth being closed as a witness in a court of justice; his hands being tied, even for his own defence, except in the extreme cases before alluded to; his time not being at his service, even for the purpose of procuring testimony; and his person and conduct being entirely under the control of him against whom he stands arrayed, the courts should, and do, feel themselves to be his guardian and protector, and will

7

provide for the defence of his rights, as for a ward of the Court. Hence, in some of the States, by statute, the court is required to assign him counsel learned in the law;[1] and, in others, the very penalty affixed to a conviction for cruel treatment by the master, is the emancipation of the slave.[2] In others, the penalty is, in part, the sale of the slave.[3]

§ 105. This is one of the most vulnerable points in the system of negro slavery, and should be farther guarded by legislation. Large compensation should be provided for informers, upon the conviction of the·master of cruel treatment; and perhaps the best penalty that could be provided upon conviction, would be not only the sale of the particular slave cruelly treated, but of all the slaves owned by the offender, and a disqualification forever of owning or possessing slaves.

§ 106. As to what amounts to cruel treatment, is a question which necessarily, to some extent, must be submitted to the jury.[4] The general principle would be, that the master's right to enforce obedience and subordination on the part of the slave should,

[1] Constitution of Arkansas, Art. IV, § 25; of Missouri, Art. III, § 27; Rev. Stat. of N. Ca. 583; Rev. Code of Va. 787, and others.

[2] Civil Code of Louis. Art. 192. In Tennessee, if a slave is not "comfortably fed and clothed," the master is bound to pay for everything he steals. Caruthers & Nicholson's Digest, 675.

[3] By the Constitutions of Alabama and Texas, in such cases, the slave shall be sold by law. Laws of Ala. 638; Hartley's Digest, 76.

[4] Kelly & Little v. The State, 3 Sm. & M. 518; The State v. Bowen, 3 Strobh. 573.

as far as possible, remain intact. Whatever goes beyond this, and from mere wantonness or revenge inflicts pain and suffering, especially unusual and inhuman punishments, is cruelty, and should be punished as such. And though the statute creating the offence specifies particular acts of cruelty, yet it has been held, that other acts of cruelty, though of a minor grade than those specified, were indictable under the general description of cruel punishment.[1]

§ 107. Another consequence of slavery is, that ✳ the violation of the person of a female slave, carries with it no other punishment than the damages which the master may recover for the trespass upon his property.[2] Among the Romans there was also given the master, an action for the corruption of his slave, in which double damages were given.[3] This, however, was founded also upon the idea of the injury to the property. Among the Lombards, if a master debauched his slave's wife, the slave and his wife were restored to their freedom.[4] The laws of King Alfred provided a pecuniary compensation to the master for the ravishment of his slave.[5] These laws are suggestive of defects in our own legislation.

It is a matter worthy the consideration of legis-

[1] The State v. Wilson, Cheves R. 163.

[2] Dig. Lib. XLVII, tit. x, § 25.

[3] Digest, Lib. XI, tit. 3, § 1; Lib. XLVIII, tit. v, § 6; Lib. XLVII, tit. x, § 25; Heinec. Antiq. Rom. Lib. III, tit. iii, § 9.

[4] Lib. I, tit. 32, § 5.

[5] Ancient Laws, &c. 35. The penalty against a male slave for a rape of a female slave was, "let him make *bot* with his testicles." Ibid.

lators, whether the offence of rape, committed upon a female slave, should not be indictable; and whether, when committed by the master, there should not be superadded the sale of the slave to some other master. The occurrence of such an offence is almost unheard of; and the known lasciviousness of the negro, renders the possibility of its occurrence very remote. Yet, for the honor of the statute-book, if it does occur, there should be an adequate punishment.[1]

§ 108. Having thus inquired into the condition of the slave in reference to personal security under the laws of the United States, it might be profitable to compare this condition with that of slaves in other countries and at other ages. Among the Jews the killing of a slave went unpunished, unless the death was immediate. If the master maimed the slave by putting out an eye or knocking out a tooth, the slave was thereby emancipated.[2] A similar law was enacted by Alfred the Great, as to the murder of a slave by his master, though no civil punishment was prescribed.[3] Among the Anglo-Saxons the murder of a slave by his own master was entirely unpunished by the civil courts.[4] If the homicide was committed by a stranger, the punishment was the payment to the master of *a pound*.[5] So, also, the laws of Henry I, of England. " Qui servum suum occiderit suum peccatum est et dampnum; si

---

[1] See Montesq. Book XV, ch. xi.

[2] Exodus, ch. xxi, v. 20, 21, 26, 27.

[3] Ancient Laws and Institutes, 22.

[4] Ancient Laws and Institutes of England, 272, n. cii.

[5] Ancient Laws, &c. 122; Laws of King Ethelred, § 5; so, also, Laws of William the Conqueror, Ibid. 213.

ipso die, quo vulneratus est, vel alio modo afflictus, tanquam in manibus domini sui moriatur crudelius est et gravius, sicut in lege Moysis scriptum est."[1] When Saxon slavery became modified, and feudal villanage took its place, the murder or maiming of a villain was indictable, but no other cruel treatment was within the interdict of the law.[2] The Roman law gave the master absolute power over the life and limbs of the slave. He might maim or destroy them at pleasure. It is related of a citizen that he caused the head of a slave to be cut off, for the gratification of a guest who had never witnessed such an exhibition.[3]

Subsequently, however, by a constitution of Claudius, the killing of a slave was declared murder; and certain cruel treatment worked an emancipation of the slave.[4] And by a previous constitution of Antoninus, if the master was convicted of cruel treatment to his slave, he was compelled to sell him,

---

[1] Ibid. 253. By the laws of Henry I, the penalty on a stranger for the murder of a slave was increased to a larger fine. Ibid. 251.

[2] Smith's Master and Servant, xxvii. An appeal of murder was given to the villain for the murder of his father. The judgment on conviction was the freedom of the villain. Co. Litt. 123 a.

[3] Juvenal, Sat. V, represents a lady ordering the death of her slave, who was represented to her as being innocent. Her answer was :

"Nil fecerit esto,—
Sic volo, sic jubeo, stet pro ratione mea voluntas."

So, also, he represents another lady, in Sat. VI, 223, exclaiming :
"O, demens ! ita servus homo est ?"

[4] Sueton. Claud. 25, cited in Smith's Dict.

and the slave was empowered to make his complaint to the proper authority.[1]

§ 109. In ancient Athens, the life and person of a slave were protected by law. And in case of cruel treatment by his master, the slave could take shelter in the temple of Theseus, and there claim the privilege of being sold by him.[2]

By the provisions of the Code Noir, a negro slave in the French West Indian Islands, by cruel treatment, was forfeited to the crown,[3] and owners convicted of such offences were obliged to sell all the slaves they had, and incapacitated from afterwards holding such property.[4]

In the Spanish and Portuguese colonies the laws seem still more favorable for the slave. Ill-usage entitled the slave to enfranchisement, or else a sale to another master, or the purchase of his own freedom upon a fair valuation.[5]

Among the German states, the *jurisdictio patrimonialis* gave to the lord or patron the right to chastise in moderation (*modice castigandi*) their serfs or prædial slaves.[6] But among the ancient Germans

---

[1] Seneca, De Benef. iii, 22; Heinec. in Elem. Jur. Pandec. Pt. I, Lib. I, § 134, says, "Verum etiam omnis sævitia dominorum extra ordinem vendicatur."

[2] Xenoph. De Rep. Ath. i, 10; Eurip. Hec. 287, 288; Meier. Att. Proc. p. 403; Smith's Dict. of Gr. and Rom. Ant. "Servus," and many authorities there cited. Becker's Charicles, 276, et seq.     [3] Code Noir, Art. 42.

[4] Les Annales du conseil souverain de la Martinique, tome i, pp. 282–284, cited in Stephens on West Indian Slavery, vol. i, 119.

[5] See Stephens, on West Indian Slavery, vol. i, 119, and authorities there cited.

[6] Heinec. Elem. Jur. Pand. Lib. I, § 137.

and Franks, the master exercised the "jus vitæ necisque," though we are told, "non atrociter, sed tum demum si servi hostilem induissent animum."[1]

After the introduction of Christianity, though the homicide of a slave was unpunished by law, the Church inflicted penalties therefor.[2] Subsequently, about the twelfth century, it was modified by law, as stated by Heineccius, into the *jurisdictio patrimonialis.*[3]

§ 110. The law of slavery in the British East Indies (being the Hindoo and Mohammedan Law, adopted and enforced by the British courts),[4] treated the slave as the absolute property of the master, made no provision for the protection of the slave from the cruelty of his master, not limiting the master's power, even over the life and limb of the slave.[5]

In ancient Spain, Gaul, Poland, Russia, Bohemia, Denmark, Sweden, Belgium, and Helvetia, the power of the master or lord over his slave or serf was absolute, he being the sole judge in all cases, and being allowed to coerce "verberibus flagellis, aliisque pœnis."[6] This differed from the condition of the

---

[1] Potgiesser, De Stat. Serv. Lib. II, cap. i, §§ 4, 6, 7.

[2] Ibid. § 10.  [3] Ibid. §§ 28-33.

[4] Slavery in India, by W. Adams, 26; Harrington's Analysis of Laws, vol. i, pp. 1, 5, 6, 20, 67, 68; McNaghten's Hindoo Law, vol. i, p. 113.

[5] Colebrooke's Official Report, found in Harrington's Analysis, and also in Appendix to Adam, on Slavery in India, pp. 246, 247.

[6] Potgiesser, De Statu Servorum, Lib. II, cap. i, §§ 37, 38, and authorities cited.

slave at Rome in later days in this, that the master's power over the latter, though recognized by law, was subject to the supervision of the civil courts, while among the German nations and those of German extraction, the master or lord had jurisdiction independent of other courts, of all questions touching the vassal or slave.[1]

[1] Potgiesser, De Statu Servorum, Lib. II, cap. i, §§ 39, 40, and 41.

# CHAPTER VI.

## OF PERSONAL LIBERTY.

§ 111. The right of personal liberty in the slave is utterly inconsistent with the idea of slavery, and whenever the slave acquires this right, his condition is *ipso facto* changed. Hence, the enjoyment of it for a number of years has been held to be strong presumptive evidence of former emancipation.[1]

§ 112. Blackstone defines this personal liberty to "consist in the power of locomotion, of changing situation or moving one's person to whatsoever place one's own inclination may direct, without imprisonment or restraint, unless by due course of law."[2] The slave, while possessing the power of locomotion, moves not as his own inclination may direct, but at the bidding of his master, who may, of his own will, imprison or restrain him, unless he thereby infringes some provision of statute law. So utterly opposite is the position of the slave from that of the freeman in respect to this right, that we could not better define his condition, than to say it is the reverse of that of the freeman.

[1] The State v. Hill, 2 Speers, 150; Hunter v. Shaffer, Dudley (Ga.) Rep. 224; Fox v. Lambson, 3 Halsted, 275; Linam v. Johnson, 2 Bailey, 137.

[2] B. I, p. 134.

§ 112 a. But while the slave's power of locomotion is thus within the absolute control of the master, no third person has any right to restrain or imprison him, except by order of the master, or in cases provided by law. Hence, disobedience of a slave to the order of a person who has no right to control him, in the absence of statute law, would be no justification to such person for a battery or other injury committed on the slave.[1]

§ 113. Reasons of policy and necessity, however, require that so long as two races of men live together, the one as masters and the other as dependents and slaves, to a certain extent, *all* of the superior race shall exercise a controlling power over the inferior.[2] If the slave feels that he is solely under the power and control of his immediate master, he will soon become insolent and ungovernable to all others. If the white man had, then, no right by law to control, the result would be, the excitement of angry passions, broils, and bloodshed. Hence have arisen, in the States, the various police and patrol regulations, giving to white persons other than the master, under certain circumstances, the right of controlling, and, in some cases, correcting slaves. But if the white person exceeds the authority given, and chastises a slave who has given no provocation, he is liable for the trespass.[3]

§ 114. Necessarily, much of the time of the slave

---

[1] White v. Chambers, 2 Bay. 70. This case goes still farther, and holds, that insolence from the slave would not justify a battery. See also ante, § 96.

[2] Ex parte Boylston, 2 Strobh. 43; ante, § 96.

[3] Caldwell v. Langford, 1 McMul. 275.

is not employed in his master's service. The long hours of the night, the Sabbath day, and the various holidays, are times when, by the permission of masters, slaves enjoy a *quasi* personal liberty. At such times, it cannot be expected that the watchful eye of the master can follow them. Frequent and large collections of them would necessarily occur, and, having no business to occupy their thoughts and conversation, mischief and evil would be the consequence of their assemblage. It has been found expedient and necessary, therefore, in all the slaveholding States, to organize, in every district, a body of men, who, for a limited time, exercise certain police powers, conferred by statute, for the better government of the slave, and the protection of the master. Upon these policemen or patrol, for the time, greater powers and privileges are necessarily conferred, for the execution of their office, in controlling the liberty and movements of the slave.

§ 115. The power and authority of the patrol, however, are limited by the statutes prescribing them, and they are not at liberty to overleap these bounds.[1] Hence, in South Carolina, it was held, that under the authority to disperse unlawful assemblies of negroes, the patrol had no right to interfere with an open assemblage, for the purpose of religious worship, where white persons were also assembled.[2] Nor with an orderly meeting of slaves, with the consent of their masters, upon the premises of a slaveholder,

---

[1] Per Johnson, J., in Bell v. Graham, 1 N. & McC. 281; Tate v. O'Neal, 1 Hawks, 418.

[2] Bell v. Graham, 1 N. & McC. 281.

with his permission and occasional presence.[1] Nor can the patrol correct a slave giving no provocation, who is without his master's inclosure, with a permit or ticket authorizing it.[2]

If the patrol inflict excessive punishment upon a slave, they will be liable to the master for the trespass. Some degree of discretion, however, is necessarily allowed them.[3]

§ 116. The necessity for patrol regulations being to control slaves when not under the control of their masters, it would seem that the patrol, upon principle, could never interfere with the master's control of his own slave, and upon his own premises.[4] It would require very express enactment to justify such interference.

§ 117. Yet the master's privilege extends only to his own slaves, and he cannot so act towards them as to interfere or injure his neighbors. Hence, the enactments in many States, against persons permitting assemblages of the slaves of others upon their premises, without the consent of their owners.[5] Hence, also, a master, in many States, is prohibited from furnishing spirituous liquors to his own slaves in such quantities as to enable them to furnish others.[6] Hence, also, in almost all the States, the penalties against the master for permitting his slaves

---

[1] State v. Boozer, 5 Strobh. 21; The State v. Boyce, 10 Ired. 536.      [2] Caldwell v. Langford, 1 McMul. 275.

[3] Tate v. O'Neal, 1 Hawks, 418; see ante, § 96.

[4] The State v. Boozer, 5 Strobh. 21.

[5] Commonwealth v. Booth, 6 Rand. 669; Commonwealth v. Foster, 5 Grat. 695; State v. Brown, 8 Humph. 89.

[6] The State v. Weaks, 7 Humph. 522.

to hire their own time, or to go at liberty, to the injury of others.[1]

§ 118. To restrain the slave altogether from leaving his master's premises, during the time that he is not employed in his master's business, would be unnecessarily harsh towards that dependent class. Hence, by the permission of the master, the slave may be allowed to travel the highway, or to visit and remain at other places; in which event, he is not subject to be controlled or corrected by the patrol, unless found violating some provision of law.[2] The evidence of such permission is called a *permit* or *pass*. The particularity with which it should be written, and what it should contain, must necessarily depend upon the requisition of the statutes regulating patrols. A substantial compliance with the statute is sufficient.[3] On the other hand, the master is not permitted to violate the whole policy of the legislation of a State by giving his slave a " permit" or " pass" for an indefinite or unreasonable period of time, especially if it professes to allow the slave privileges forbidden to the slave, and penal in the master.[4]

§ 119. From this *quasi* liberty of the slave, during the Sabbath and other holidays, flow many interesting questions as to the liability of the master or hirer for the acts of the slave at such times, which will be considered hereafter.

[1] Commonwealth v. Gilbert, 6 J. J. Marsh. 184; Parker v. Commonwealth, 8 B. Monr. 30.

[2] The State v. Boozer, 5 Strobh. 21.

[3] Caldwell v. Langford, 1 McMul. 275.

[4] Jarrett v. Higbee, 5 Monroe, 550, 551.

20. The slave being deprived of the right of personal liberty, cannot, by any act of his, obtain it without the consent of his master. Hence, though he escapes from the actual personal control of the master, and while a fugitive enjoys actual liberty, he is at all times subject to be retaken, and placed again under the power of the master. In fact, by placing himself beyond the pale of the master's protecting power, and being, for the time and *pro tanto*, in a state of rebellion to his lawful authority, he deprives himself of the exemption from the interference of strangers, which at home he enjoys, and becomes, to a limited extent, an outlaw in the community. As such, he may be arrested and imprisonec  y any one, even on the Sabbath day, just as a criminal caught *flagrante delicto*.[1]

§ 121. Any person harboring or concealing him, or aiding or abetting him in making his escape, is not only liable to the master civilly,[2] but, in all the States, is made responsible criminally.

Any person hiring or employing a runaway slave, is responsible to the master for his services; and this is true with or without notice to the employer, of the fact of his being a fugitive, the rule in such cases being analogous to that adopted in reference to masters and apprentices.[3] And although the master is

[1] Abrahams v. The Commonwealth, 1 Robinson's Virginia Rep. 675; Commonwealth v. Griffith, 2 Pick. 12; Johnson v. Tompkins et al. 1 Baldw. C. C. 571; Jarrett v. Higbee, 5 Monroe, 552.

[2] Trongott v. Byers, 5 Cowen, 480. Such was also the Roman law, Smith's Dict. "Servus;" see also The Laws of King Ina, §§ 24, 29; Ancient Laws and Institutes, pp. 51, 52.

[3] Trongott v. Byers, 5 Cowen, 480; James v. Le Roy et al. 6

bound to furnish necessary food and clothing to his slave, yet the wrongdoer, in such a case, could not set-off against the master's claim, advances made to the slave, however necessary they were.[1]

§ 122. The master may recapture his slave at any time or place, whether in a slaveholding or non-slaveholding State; and in order to do so, he may enter upon the premises of another without being guilty of a trespass, provided he does so peaceably, and without committing any breach of the peace.[2] Such was the rule in reference to a master and his apprentice at common law; and an advertisement, by the master, in a public newspaper, of his runaway apprentice, has been held sufficient authority to justify a third person in entering upon the premises of another to arrest the apprentice.[3] Such was the rule, also, in reference to the lord and his villain, provided the recapture was within a year and a day; and this privilege extended to any portion of the realm to which the villain may have escaped. Thus Fleta: " Servus fugitivus non solum infra annum et diem capi poterit in feodo domini, sed ubicunque inventus fuerit in regno, dum tamen recenter post

John. 273. So also the law of King Aethelstan, " Et qui alterius hominem suscipiet intra marcam vel extra, quem pro malo suo dimittat et castigare non possit; reddat regi centum viginti solidos, et redeat intus unde exivit, et rectum faciat ei sui servi ut antea." Ancient Law, &c. 92.

[1] Trongott v. Byers, 5 Cowen, 480.

[2] Johnson v. Tompkins et al. Bald. C. C. R. 581; Collomb v. Taylor, 9 Humph. 689; Bogard v. Jones, Ibid. 739; Prigg v. The Commonwealth of Pennsylvania, 16 Peters, 541.

[3] State v. Kerr et al. Addison's Pa. Rep. 325; cited with approbation by Justice Baldwin, in Johnson v. Tompkins et al. Baldw. C. C. R. 581.

fugam sequatur, comprehendi poterit, etiam impune retineri."[1]   Fugitive villains, upon recaption, were branded in the forehead.[2]

§ 123. According to the Roman law, the master's rights over his slaves were in no wise affected by his running away.[3]   A class of persons called *Fugitivarii* made it their business to recover runaway slaves.   The master's right of recaption extended everywhere in the realm, and it was the duty of all authorities to give him aid in recovering the slave. The fugitive slave when captured was branded in the forehead.[4] Such cruel punishment was sometimes added, that Ulpian relates an instance of one who killed himself for fear of returning to his master.[5] No length of time nor acquisition of honors debarred the master's right of recovery.[6]   It was otherwise, however, if another possessed him as a slave.[7]   An action was given to the master against any one who persuaded the slave to fly to a statue for refuge.[8]

§ 124. Fugitive slaves were the subject of recapture in the French Empire during the middle ages. And the Emperor Charlemagne is applauded for providing, that if a lord claimed his villain or slave (*colonus*

---

[1] Fleta, Lib. IV, cap. xi, § 23.

[2] Mahoney, see 4 Harr. & McC. 295.

[3] Digest, II, tit. iv, De Fugitivis.

[4] Smith's Dict. "Servus," p. 1038.

[5] Referred to by Heinec. De Reliq. &c. Exer. xviii, § 32, Op. tom. ii, 688.

[6] The reason is curious, "Qui injuste aufugit, seque alicubi pro libero gerit, sui ipsius fur habetur, nec unquam ideo libertatem adquirit," &c.   Heinec. De Prescrip. &c. Exer. xxvi, § 10; see also Code, Lib. XI, tit. xlvii.                     [7] Ibid.

[8] Heinec. Elem. Jur. Pand. Pt. VII, Lib. XLVII, § 128.

*sive servus*), who had escaped beyond his territory, he was not to be given up until strict inquiry was made as to the truth of the claim.[1]

§ 125. In all the German states fugitive slaves were the subjects of recapture. And no length of prescription could bar the master's claim. Thirty years' possession by another master was subsequently declared a bar. Among the Lombards, thirty years' enjoyment of freedom prescribed the master's claim.[2] The law of the Visigoths enacted severe penalties against those who concealed a slave, refused to deliver him to a judge, released him from his chains, aided him in his flight, or gave him a refuge. It also prescribed the condition of his wife, who married him supposing him to be free, and also of the children born of such a marriage. In some cases, *stripes* were provided as the punishment.[3] Most of the German states made provision by law for the delivery of the fugitives from other states.[4] If the delivery of the fugitive slave was refused, a war frequently ensued.[5] To avoid these controversies, the emperors at different times prescribed a certain length of time to peaceable residence, after which the master's rights were barred.[6] Some of the em-

---

[1] Hallam's Mid. Ages, Vol. I, Pt. II, ch. ii, p. 89, n.

[2] Heinec. De Præscrip. &c. Exer. xxvi, § 11; Opera, tom. ii, p. 895.

[3] Heinec. Elem. Jur. Germ. Lib. II, tit. xxix, § 355.

[4] Ibid.

[5] Heinec. De Præscr. &c. Exer. xxvi, § 12, citing Lehmann, Chron. Spir. Lib. VII, cap. lxxi; Hertius, De Hom. Prop. Sect. iii, § 10. See also Potg. Lib. II, cap. ix, § 20.

[6] Potg. Lib. II, cap. ix, § 20.

perors refused to receive fugitives within their
states to the prejudice of their masters.[1]

§ 126. The right of recapture existed in ancient
Greece, and branding was a common punishment
for a runaway slave.[2]

In the West Indies, the punishment of a fugitive
was very severe. By the "Code Noir" he was
branded and his ears cut off, for the first and second
offences, and for the third, he lost his life. In the
Spanish colonies he was hung, if absent longer than
six months.[3] Up to the year 1819, a fugitive slave
who had been absent for thirty days, was hung in
the English colony of Barbadoes.[4]

§ 127. The Church, since the apostolic day, has
ever followed the example of Paul in restoring to his
master the fugitive Onesimus, and in which Paul
only pursued the teaching of the Spirit of the Lord,
that instructed Hagar in the wilderness to return
and submit herself to the hand of her mistress.
Saint Basil gave full instructions on the subject of
fugitive slaves, requiring all the inferior clergy,
where refuge was sought in the convents or other
sacred places, after having enlightened and made

---

[1] Potgiesser gives the decrees of Frederick II, Henry VI, Rudolphus I, Ludovicus IV, Lib. II, cap. ix, § 21.

[2] Becker's Charicles, 279.

[3] Code Noir. Schœlcher, Colonies Françaises, p. 102. The severity of these provisions accounts for the great number of fugitives, who, under the name of *Maroons*, infested their mountains. Napoleon the Great decreed the sale of any free black, and his family, if he was detected harboring a fugitive slave. Schœlcher, 103.

[4] Substance of the three Reports of Commissioners on the Law of the West Indies, p. 13.

them better, to restore them to their masters.[1] So, by the decrees of several councils, any person advising a slave to abandon the service of his master, or advising him not to serve with good faith and the most profound respect, was subject to the anathema of the Church.[2]

[1] S. Basil. Regul. fus. Tractat. Int. xi; translated in Cassagnac's Voyage aux Antilles, tom. ii, 416.

[2] Cassagnac's Voyage aux Antilles, tom. ii, 440; Bishop England's Letters to Forsyth.

# CHAPTER VII.

SLAVES ESCAPING OR CARRIED INTO OTHER STATES—
PERSONAL STATUTES, AS APPLIED TO SLAVES.

§ 128. THE fugitive slave may escape beyond the
limits of the State of the master's residence. If the
place of his refuge is a slaveholding State, there is
no doubt that his condition of slavery is not thereby
affected, and that by the comity of nations, he would
be delivered up upon the requisition of the master.

A more difficult and vexed question arises when
the place of his refuge is a State where slavery
does not exist. A conflict of laws then exists, the
proper solution of which staggered the judgment of
Lord Mansfield,[1] has placed in such direct anta-
gonism the opinions of the ablest of foreign jurists,
that Judge Story was forced to exclaim, "Non nos-
trum inter vos tantas componere lites,"[2] has engaged
for more than half a century the judicial mind of
America; and even while I write is mooted and
argued as an unsettled question in the courts of
more than one of the non-slaveholding States.

§ 128 a. Such a question I approach with diffidence,
and ask only the judgment of honesty and candor,

[1] Somersett Case, 20 Howell's State Trials, 21.
[2] Story's Conflict of Laws, § 58, et seq.

for the conclusions to which I may arrive. In considering it, I shall not confine the investigation to fugitives, but shall inquire also how far the condition of the slave is changed by the voluntary removal of his master into a non-slaveholding State. If, upon examination, we shall find that in the latter case, under any circumstances, the condition of slavery continues, *a fortiori* it will continue in the former where the removal is *invito domino*.

§ 129. A preliminary question arises as to what constitutes the domicile of a slave. We have seen that, as a general rule, it is that of the master. And this not being of choice of the slave, but by operation of law (*necessarium*), by no act of his can it be changed.[1]

§ 130. That mere residence in a country without the *animus permanendi*, does not effect a change of domicile, so as to subject the resident to the personal laws of the country, is well settled by the jurists of all civilized nations, as we shall see. It is frequently a question of great nicety to determine what facts will amount to a change of domicile, and many criteria are laid down to aid in elucidating this question.[2] It would lead us too far from our main sub-

---

[1] Phillimore, on the law of Domicile, 25, 60. So Menochius, in treating of Domicile, says, "Servus enim pro nihilo habetur cum mortuo comparetur." De Presumptionibus, Presumptio, xxx, § 19, p. 1035, quoted at length in Appendix to Phillimore; Burge Comm. on Col. Law, &c. i, pp. 33, 702, 751; see also 2 Martin, Lin. Rep. N. S. 408; Anderson v. Garrett, 9 Gill. 120.

[2] Phillimore, on the Law of Domicile, pp. 101, 150, to which the inquiring reader is referred. See also Mascardus, De Probationibus, Conclusio, dxxxv; quoted at large in Appendix to Phillimore.

ject to follow the many interesting questions arising
from this source, though each of them may, at some
time, in practice need investigation in connection
with the subject now discussed.  We must content
ourselves, here, with laying down the general rule,
that the length of time of the residence, and the
intention of remaining (to be decided from all the
circumstances, and even against express declarations), are the important criteria in most cases, and
that these must coexist in order to constitute a new
domicile.[1]  For the intention to change a domicile,
without the actual removal, will not effect a change.
And, on the other hand, many jurists hold, that no
length of time of residence, without the *animus remanendi*, will effect a change of domicile.  Thus
Mascardus : Domicilium non contrabitur etiam per
mille annos, si quis habet animum recedendi.[2]  And
adds, " So I was taught by the chief of all interpreters of the law, by Bartolus."[3]  Many of the
civilians, however, held, that residence for ten years
(*decennalis habitatio*) created a legal presumption of
change of domicile; while others again supposed it
to be a matter within the discretion of the judge,
according to the circumstances of the particular case.[4]
Lord Stowell entered his protest against the doctrine,
that the mere fact that the original residence was
for a *special* purpose, and with the *animus revertendi*,
should perpetually bar the presumption of a change

[1] Phillimore, 146, and American authorities there cited.

[2] De Probationibus, Conclusio, dxxxv, Summarium, 12, vol. i,
248.                              [3] § xiii, 249.

[4] Phillimore, 141; Pothier, Coutumes des Duché, Bailliage et
Prévôté d'Orléans, ch. i.

of domicile, and insisted, that "a general residence might grow on a special purpose."[1]

§ 131. There can be no doubt that such a presumption would arise, if the residence were continued after the "special purpose" ceased to exist.[2] And we might add, that a vague definite intention to return to one's country at some future time, is not sufficient to rebut the presumption of a change of domicile. Thus Lord Thurlow: "A person's being at a place, is *prima facie* evidence that he is domiciled at that place, and it lies on those who say otherwise to rebut that evidence."[3] It may be rebutted, no doubt. A person travelling, on a visit, he may be there for some time on account of his health or business; the case of soldiers, ambassadors, &c. But what will make a man's domicile or home, in contradistinction to these cases, must occur to every one. A British man settles as a merchant abroad; he enjoys the privileges of the place; he may mean to return when he has made his fortune, but if he die in the meantime, will it be maintained that he had his domicile at home?[4] If the residence be not voluntary, but by virtue of authority, such as a military officer's, at a post to which he has been

[1] 2 Robinson's Adm. Reports, pp. 224, 225; see also Stanley v. Bemis, 3 Hagg. Ec. Rep. 373.

[2] Pothier, Coutumes des Duché, Bailliage et Prévôté d'Orléans, ch. i, § 1; Phillimore, on the Law of Domicile, 148.

[3] This is true, yet "animus mutandi domicilium nunquam presumitur, nisi probetur." Mascardus, De Probationibus, vol. i, p. 248. (Turin. 1591.)

[4] Bruce v. Bruce, reported in a note to Marsh v. Hutchinson, 2 Bos. & Pul. 219; see also Elbers & Kraffts v. The United Insurance Co. Johnson's Cases; Guvier v. O'Daniel, 1 Binney, 349.

ordered by his superior, then the change of residence does not evidence an intention to change the
domicile.[1]

§ 132. Another rule, perhaps, deserves to be
noticed, and that is the domicile of origin (which is
"that arising from a man's birth and connections")[2]
must prevail, unless it be proved that the party has
acquired another by residence, and abandoning his
domicile of origin.[3]

Hence it would follow, that a citizen of a non-
slaveholding State cannot evade the law by claiming
a domicile in a slaveholding State, and thus seek the
protection afforded by the comity of nations. Nor
will the mere removal, temporarily, to a slaveholding State, effect this; there must be a *bonâ fide*
change of domicile; an abandonment of the domicile
of origin.

§ 133. As the *animus* or intention is a very material question in determining the place of domicile, it
is perhaps well to remark, that the *oral declaration*
of the party, as well as his letters, are admissible in
evidence, to be weighed according to the circumstances under which they were spoken or written.[4]

---

[1] Opinion of Judge Campbell, in the Dred Scott case, p. 101.

[2] Sommerville v. Sommerville, 5 Vesey, 570. "Est autem ori-
ginis locus in quo quis natus est, aut nasci debet, sicut forte reipsa
alibi natus esset, matre in peregrinatione parturiente." I. Lv. t. i,
§ 91.

[3] See Decisions of Lord Chancellor Cottenham, in Munro v.
Munro, 7 Clarke & Finnelly; Report of Cases, in the House of
Lords, 842. See Phillimore, p. 101, where the opinions and deci-
sions of foreign jurists and courts are collected.

[4] Phillimore, on the Law of Domicile, 112; Munro v. Munro,
7 Clarke & Finnelly, 842; Sommerville v. Sommerville, 5 Vesey,

In general questions of this kind, the intention is ascertained from motives, pursuits; on conditions of the family and fortune of the party. And no change will be inferred, unless evidence shows that one domicile was abandoned, and there was an intention to acquire another.[1]

§ 134. Having disposed of this preliminary inquiry, we resume our investigation. As a general rule, the capacity or incapacity of persons is to be governed by the law of the place of their domicile.[2] Huber lays it down, as a universal doctrine, that *personal qualities,* impressed upon any person by the law of any place, surround and accompany him everywhere, with this effect: that wherever he goes he enjoys, and is subject to, the same law that such persons elsewhere enjoy and are subject to.[3] All foreign jurists agree upon this as a general principle, though expressed differently; varying, however, widely among themselves as to what are personal and what real statutes.[4] Thus Boullenois: "Ces

570. Such also is the French law, Code Civil, t. iii, Du Domicile, § 105; and the Spanish law, Codice Civile, t. iii, Del Domicilis, § 68.

[1] Justice Campbell, in the Dred Scott case, p. 101, and authorities cited by him.

[2] Œuvres D'Aguesseau, tom. v, p. 256, 257, 8vo. edition; Pothier, Int. Coutumes D'Orleans, Int. ch. i, § 7; D'Argentré, Coutume de Bretagne, Art. 218, Glos. vi, n. 5, et suiv.

[3] "Qualitates personales, certo loco, alicui jure impressas, ubique circumferri et personam comitari, cum hoc effectu, ut ubique locorum eo jure, quo tales personæ, alibi gaudent vel subjecti sunt, fruantur et subjiciantur." Huberus, De Conf. Leg. Lib I, tit. iii, § 12.

[4] Story's Conflict of Laws, ch. iv, on Capacity of Persons. Œuvres D'Aguesseau, tom. v, 256.

lois personelles affectent la personne d'une qualité
qui lui est inhérente, et la personne est telle par-
tout."[1] So Rodenburg: "Cum de statu ac conditione hominum queritur, uni solummodo judici et
quidem domicilii, universum in illâ jus sit attribu-
tum." "Whenever it becomes necessary to inquire
into the state or condition of persons, there is but
one judge, viz., that of his domicile, to whom the
whole question is to be referred."[2] "Hinc," says
Hertius, "status et qualitas personæ regitur (regun-
tur) a legibus loci, cui ipsa sese per domicilium sub-
jecit."[3] "Hence, the state and quality of a person are
governed by the laws of that place to which, by his
domicile, he subjects himself." Froland, Bouhier,
Pothier, Fœlix, Stockmannus, and others, lay down
the same rule.[4]

§ 135. Vinnius goes farther, and applies the rule
directly to the question of slavery, thus: "Status
est personæ conditio aut qualitas quæ efficit ut hoc
vel illo jure utatur, ut esse *liberum*, esse *servum*, esse
ingenuum, esse libertinum, esse alieni, esse sui juris."[5]
"The *status* is that condition or quality of a person,
which makes him free or slave, noble or ignoble,
capable or incapable, by whatever law he may be
judged."

---

[1] 1 Prin. Gen. p. 4.　　[2] De Div. Stat. tit. i, ch. iii, §§ 4–10.

[3] Hertius, De Collis. Leg. § 4, n. 5, p. 122.

[4] Story's Conf. of Laws, 3d edit. § 51 a. I cannot forbear quoting
the language of Stockmannus, for the sensible reason he gives for
the rule: "Unde, recte, cum qui inhabilis est in uno loco, etiam in
alio inhabilem censeri; et si aliter statuamus, incertus et varius erit
personarum status; cum tamen uti personam ubique eandem, ita
qualitatem personæ inherentem, velut ejus accidens, ubique unifor-
mem esse conveniat." Decis. 125, § 6.

[5] Vinnius, Lib. I, De Jure Personali, tit. iii, Introd.

In fact, so general is this principle, that we find it announced as maxims : " Habilis vel inhabilis in loco domicilii est habilis vel inhabilis in omni loco."[1] " Capable or incapable in the place of domicile, is to be capable or incapable everywhere." And also, " Quando lex in personam dirigitur, respiciendum est ad leges illius civitatis, quæ personam habet sub-jectam."[2] " When the law is directed to the person, we must look to the laws of that state of which the person is a subject." The figure used by Potgiesser, in defining the meaning of *status*, is still stronger : " Omnis autem homo, quicunque fuerit, vivit in statu quodam, qui eum, *velut umbra corpus ubique comitatur*, et sine quo ut agens considerari nequit."[3] " Every man, whoever he may be, lives in a certain *status*, which accompanies him everywhere, as the shadow does the body, and without which he cannot be considered as an actor."

§ 136. Among American writers, we find the same broad principle distinctly acknowledged and laid down. Wheaton says, " In general, the laws of the state applicable to the civil condition and per-sonal capacity of its citizens, operate upon them even when resident in a foreign country. Such are those universal personal qualities, which take effect from birth, &c. . . . . . The laws of the state affecting all these personal qualities of its subjects, travel with them wherever they go, and attach to them in whatever country they are resident."[4]

---

[1] Boullenois, Dis. sur les conflits des lois, Ed. 1732, Disc. Prel. p. 20 ; Règle, 10.

[2] Hertius, De Collis. Leg. § 4, Art. 8, p. 123, ed. 1737.

[3] De Statu Servorum, Proleg. § 11.

[4] Wheaton's Elements of International Law, Part II, ch. ii, § 6,

Burge, the only English writer upon the conflict of laws, agrees that this is the general rule.[1]

§ 137. If. there is an actual change of domicile, *animo remanendi,* a different principle applies, and the better opinion undoubtedly is, that the law of the new domicile governs as to capacity.[2] This is a case very materially different from that of a sojourner for pleasure, or on business; and a disregard to this difference we conceive, as we shall hereafter show, has misled many of the courts in their decisions in reference to the question under consideration.

§ 138. The general principle that the capacity or incapacity of a person is governed by the law of his domicile, has been frequently recognized in the English courts. It more frequently arises in reference to questions connected with marriage and divorce, infancy, or legitimacy. Thus, in Beasley v. Beasley,[3] the Court say, " There is a preliminary consideration, the capability of the parties to contract marriage; and the true question is, whether that capability is to be determined by the law of Scotland or the law of England. The former would say, the parties are capable; the latter would say, they are incapable. The parties in this case being domiciled in England, though the marriage was consummated in Scotland, they were held incapable, and the mar-

p. 132. He refers, as an authority, to Pardessus, Droit Commerciale, Pt. VI, tit. 7, ch. ii, § 1, and to Fœlix, Droit International Privé, Lib. I, tit. i, § 31.

[1] Treatise on Col. and For. Law, vol. i, § 7.

[2] Story's Conf. of Laws, §§ 55, 69, et seq., and authorities cited.

[3] 3 Hagg. 639.

riage void." So, in the case of Sheddon v. Patrick,
the law of the State of New York was enforced by
the English courts in reference to the legitimacy of
a child born before the marriage of the parents.
The same decision was made in the Strathmore
Peerage case.[1]  In accordance with these cases is
the declaration of Lord Stowell, in Dalrymple v.
Dalrymple.[2]  " Being entertained in an English
court, it must be adjudicated according to the principles of English law, applicable to such a case. But
the only principle applicable by the law of England
is, that the validity of Miss G.'s marriage rights
must be tried by reference to the law of the country
where, if they exist at all, they had their origin.
Having furnished this principle, the law of England
withdraws altogether, and leaves the legal question to
the exclusive judgment of the law of Scotland."[3] With
equal clearness does Lord Ellenborough state the rule
in Potter v. Brown, when he says, " We always import
together with their persons the existing relations of
foreigners as between themselves, according to the
laws of their respective countries ; except, indeed,
where those laws clash with the rights of our own
subjects here, and one or other of the laws must

---

[1] These two last cases I take from the argument of counsel, in
Doe v. Vardill, 5 Barn. & Cr. 438; see also that case.

[2] 2 Hagg. Consist. Rep. 59.

[3] See also Birdwhistle v. Vardill, 9 Bligh. 45.  In this case the
Court refused to extend the principle to the inheritance of realty
situate in England.  It is unnecessary for our purposes to examine
the correctness of this exception from the general rule; suffice it
to say, it is at war with the opinions of all foreign jurists on this
subject.  See Story's Conf. of Laws, § 93, r.

necessarily give way, in which case our own is entitled to the preference."[1]

§ 139. The same principle, that the personal *status*
is to be governed by the law of the domicile, has
been frequently recognized by the courts of the
United States.

§ 140. Having established the general principle
that the *status* of a person is to be determined by
the law of his domicile, it becomes us next to inquire whether the condition of slavery is one of the
exceptions to the rule, or is embraced within its
general operation.

To determine these questions, we must seek for
the reasons upon which exceptions to the rule are
based.    Huber gives us that reason as follows:
"Rectores imperiorum id comiter agunt, ut jura
cujusque populi, intra terminos ejus exercita, teneant
ubique vim suam, quatenus nihil potestati aut juri
alterius imperantis ejusque civium præjudicetur."[3]
"The rulers of nations observe this principle through
comity, that the laws of each state, enforced within
its own limits, shall retain the same force everywhere, so long as no injury is done to the power
or laws of the state where they are sought to be
enforced."

§ 141. The rule and the exceptions are here
given together. The laws of a nation have no extra
territorial effect *per se*. But the recognition and
enforcement of these laws in a vast variety of cases,

---

[1] 5 East, 131.

[2] Saul v. His Creditors, 17 Martin, R. 590.  See a masterly
exposition, by Lockwood, J., in Willard v. The People, 4 Scam.
472.                        [3] De Conf. Leg. Bk. I, tit. iii.

have been found to contribute so largely to promote justice between individuals and to produce a friendly intercourse between the sovereignties to which they belong, that courts of justice have continually acted upon it as a part of the voluntary law of nations.[1]

Thus far the comity of nations requires the courts to go. Whenever the enforcement of the foreign law is contrary to the policy or prejudicial to the interests of the state where its recognition is invoked, the courts will " prefer the laws of their own country to that of the stranger."[2]   For example, if two parties contract a marriage within one jurisdiction, and subsequently remove to another domicile, the question as to the validity of the marriage, as a general rule, will be determined by the law of the domicile at the time of the marriage.   But if the marriage, according to the law of their new domicile, were incestuous, or if the husband sought to retain more than one wife, because polygamy was allowed by the law of his former domicile, incest and polygamy being contrary to the policy of the law of his new domicile, that law would be enforced by the courts.[3]

§ 142. Having arrived at the reason of the exception, the question recurs, how far would the recognition of slavery interfere with the policy or be prejudicial to the interest of a non-slaveholding nation? This question we will first examine upon principle, and then upon authority.

[1] See remarks of Taney, C. J., in Bank of Augusta v. Earle, 13 Peters, 589.

[2] Per Porter, J., in Saul v. His Creditors, 17 Mart. 596; Story's Conf. of Laws, § 32.

[3] Story's Conf. of Laws, §§ 113, 113 a (3d Ed.).

If the residence of the slave in the new domicile was *animo remanendi*, there can be no doubt that to continue his *status* as a slave, would be to introduce a new system of servitude, violative of the policy of the laws of his domicile, where such a system is not recognized, but may possibly have been abolished by law. No nation could require of another, through comity, to change its social system, or to establish within its bounds an institution contrary to the policy of its laws. The conclusion is manifest, that a master removing to a non-slaveholding State, with a view to a change of domicile, and carrying with him his slaves, would thereby emancipate them.

§ 143. On the other hand, if a citizen of a slave-holding State, removing to another where slavery was established, should be compelled by necessity or misfortune to pass through the territory of a non-slaveholding State with his slaves, it is equally clear, upon the principles before stated, that the *status* of the slave is not changed; and the declaration, by the courts of such a State, that this transit contravened the policy of their laws, or was prejudicial to the interests of their government, would be viewed by all candid minds as a mere pretence and evasion. I shall, hereafter, consider how far the government of such State might go in prohibiting such transit, without violating the law of nations. I am considering the question now in the absence of such express prohibition.

§ 144. I am aware that to this position it may be replied, in the words of Lord Mansfield, that "Slavery is so odious, that it can exist only by positive law;"[1]

---

[1] See Commentary of Lord Stowell on this remark of Lord Mansfield, in 2 Hagg. Adm. Rep.

and that, so soon as the slave is removed beyond the limits of the slaveholding State, he is beyond the influence of the positive law. But mark! admitting that it exists by positive law, the conclusion is in direct violation of the principle we have established, that the courts of every nation will enforce " the positive law" of every other nation,[1] except where it contravenes its own policy. Does it contravene that policy?

§ 145. " Slavery," it is said, " is a state of despotism, and it is contrary to the policy of a free government to recognize despotism in any shape." Is this a true proposition? The government of Great Britain is a free government; that of Russia is despotic. The Czar of Russia visits Westminster with his court. Is their allegiance *instanter* dissolved? Stripped of his power, would the Czar stand before a British court with no other power over his suite but that of a British citizen? I am aware that it may be replied, that the intercourse of courts and the comity of nations have established certain principles governing the rights and privileges of sovereigns, and even of their ambassadors. Yet that comity which will recognize the rights of the sovereign is too weak to enforce the rights of the citizen.

§ 146. But let us sift the proposition. " Slavery is despotism." For the sake of the argument, granted. " It is contrary to the policy of a free

---

[1] Equally unfounded is the remark in Forbes v. Cochran, 2 Barn. & Cress. 448, that " the reason why a foreign slave is free in England, is because there is no law to restrain him." There is a law to restrain him,—the law of his domicile, enforced by the English courts, *ex comitate.*

government to recognize despotism in any shape." By the policy of a government, we are to understand that uniform and fundamental principle which is evidenced by the general tenor of its acts. The policy of a free government then, would be to secure liberty and the blessings of liberty to all who owe it allegiance. A Quixotic crusade against the institutions of other governments has never been acknowledged as being embraced within that policy. The transit of the master with his slave, in the case supposed, interferes not with the liberty of any citizen, nor the fruition of that liberty. It does not bring the labor of the slave in competition with free labor. In no possible light can it be seen, that the rights, or interests, or liberties, of the citizen, are thereby impaired. And hence the inevitable conclusion, that the policy of the government is not contravened.

§ 147. We must be careful to distinguish between the phrases, "contrary to the law of a government," and "contrary to the policy of a government," as many things may be contrary or different from the law of a government, which at the same time may not be contrary to its policy. Thus, a marriage by the civil law legitimates antenuptial children. *Aliter* by the common law. Yet the courts of all countries where the common law is adopted, recognize the legitimacy of such children, when such is the law of the domicile of the parents at the time of the marriage.

Hence, the fact that slavery is not recognized, or is actually abolished by the laws of a State, does not of itself make it "contrary to the policy of the State," under any circumstances, to recognize sla-

very.   Another step is necessary.   Some detriment
to the rights, interests, liberties, or morals, of the
people, or to the laws of the State, must be shown,
to constitute the right sought to be enforced "contrary to the policy of the State."

§ 148. We must be careful, also, to distinguish
between the recognition of a right which is sought
to be permanently enjoyed within the limits of a
nation, and of a right, the temporary enforcement
of which is sought, *ex comitate*, to secure its ulterior
enjoyment elsewhere.   The former may be against
the policy of a nation, while the latter is not.   Thus
polygamy being, in Christian nations, deemed *contra
bonos mores*, is prohibited by the civil and criminal
codes of all such nations.   Were a Turk with his
harem, therefore, to seek, in a Christian nation, permanently to reside, he would be forced to abandon
his plurality of wives.   The right he seeks would
be detrimental to the morals of the people, and contrary to the law of his new domicile.   But if, in
passing from his own to some other nation where
polygamy is allowed, by stress of weather or other
cause, he should be forced to enter within a Christian port, or to pass over the territory of a Christian
nation, could it be supposed that he thereby subjected himself to a criminal prosecution for bigamy;
or that his wives were relieved from the obligations
of the marriage tie the instant their feet trod the
soil of a Christian nation?

§ 149. In thus noticing the objections that might
be raised to the truth of the proposition, that the
mere transit of the slave through the territory of a
non-slaveholding State, does not emancipate him, I
have not pretended to reply to the declaration (it

does not deserve the name of argument where principles are discussed), that " the air of a free state is too pure for a slave to breathe."[1] I am aware that this fashionable piece of eloquence originated in France as early as 1738, when one of the counsel, in his zeal, announced among other things, " La France, mère de la liberté, ne permet aucuns esclaves," and " Il n'y a en France aucuns esclaves, et la coutume y est telle que, non seulement les Français, mais aussi les étrangers, prenant port en France, et criant *France et Liberté*, sont hors de la puissance de celui qui les possédait."[2] I am aware that English lawyers of high fame have been willing to reiterate the declaration in the presence of excited multitudes, and perhaps in the hearing of an intimidated court; that even judges have been found who were willing gravely to announce, as a principle, the outburst of Parisian enthusiasm.

§ 150. I am also aware that, at the time the sentiment was announced in France, and until the time of the great Revolution, there were in that nation serfs or " mainmortes, whose condition, if it were not strictly speaking slavery, undoubtedly bore a very strong resemblance to that *status*."[3] That at

---

[1] It is a little curious, that so much influence should be given to the air. Heineccius informs us, that the air of some countries, *ipso facto*, makes some persons slaves. Speaking of the various sources of slavery, he says, " Per commorationem in illis locis, ubi aer dicitur servos facere." Elem. Jur. de Pand. Lib. I, § 138.

[2] 13 Causes célèbres. Argument of M. Le Clerc, p. 549.

[3] 20 Howell's State Trials, .1369; see also Encyclopædia, tit. Mainmorte. M. Favre, Cod. Lib. VII, tit. iii, def. 3, says of the *mainmortes* of France, " Negari non potest, quin servis proxime accedant, illamque naturalem libertatem, quæ hominibus omnibus

the time it was caught up in England, and proclaimed as a principle, " the laws of England had
not rejected servitude." Villanage was worn out,
but the law of villanage was unrepealed upon the
statute-book.[1] That at that moment thousands of
West Indian slaves were owned by residents in
England. That at the very time that pæans of
triumph were being sung over the abolition of
slavery in the West Indies, a larger body of slaves
were under British rule and governed by British
law in the East Indies.[2] That the slave-trade was
carried on to furnish her with slaves, and that such

communis est, valde immunitam habeant." President Boubier
quotes this opinion with approbation. Observ. sur la Cout. du
Duché de Bourgogne, ch. lxiv, § 3. He says, " On nous donne
en effet pour axiome de notre Droit Français que toutes personnes
sont franches en ce Royaume ; et que sitôt qu'un esclave a atteint
les marches d'icelui, se faisant baptiser, il est affranchi. Mais il
est certain que cela doit seulement être entendu du droit dont nous
usons depuis quelques siècles. Car tout le monde convient, que
non seulement sous les deux premières races de nos Rois, mais
même sous les premiers de la troisième, on ne connoissoit point cette
espèce d'affranchisements dont je viens de parler ; en sorte qu'il
etoit permis d'avoir des esclaves autant qu'on en vouloit, ou qu'on
pouvoit avoir." Obser. ch. lxiv, p. 420. Again, speaking of *mainmortes personnels*, he says, " Ce qui fait voir l'erreur de ceux qui ont
prétendu qu'il n'y avoit point de servitude personelle en notre province." Ibid. The children of *mainmortes* followed the condition of
the father. Ibid. Because the wife, according to the custom of Burgundy, follows the condition of the husband. Ibid. ch. lxvi, § 56.
Even if she is a noble. Ibid. § 74.

[1] 20 Howell's State Trials, 74. Argument of Mr. Dummig.
Lord Mansfield himself, thirteen years later, declared that "villains
in gross, may, in point of law, subsist at this day" (1785). 4
Douglas, 302. (26 E. C. L. R. 369.)

[2] Slavery in India, by W. Adam, 626.

slavery continues and is authorized by British law to this day.[1] That long after Grœnewegen had written, that in Holland, "ejusque nomen (servitus) apud nos exolevit," there was in that country involuntary servitude for life, and death the penalty for non-performance;[2] and that when the same sentiment was applauded in the courts of Scotland, an hereditary servitude for life, and with few if any privileges above slavery, existed, and continued long after to exist, in the salt-works and collieries of that country.[3] The sentiment was pleasant to speak and gratifying doubtless to hear, and would be very appropriate in a popular harangue, on the festival of the anniversary of some day sacred to liberty. But it weighs nothing in a court where questions of law are decided according to the principles of law.

§ 151. In support of the proposition we have advanced, that the bare transit of a slave through the territory of a non-slaveholding State, does not change his *status* of slavery, another principle of the law of nations might be invoked, viz., that strangers have a right to pass with their property through the territories of a friendly nation.[4] And the question of what is " property," is to be decided by the laws of the domicile of the owner.[5]

§ 152. Two positions upon principle we consider as established. First. Upon a change of domicile

---

[1] Slavery in India, by W. Adam, 31, 129, 218.     [2] Ibid. p. 75.

[3] 20 State Trials, 7, note; see also Barrington's Observations on Anct. Stat. 1 Rich. 2, note. ·

[4] Vattel, Law of Nations, Bk. II, ch. ix, §§ 123–136; Puffendorf, Bk. III, ch. iii, §§ 5–10.

[5] Vattel, Bk. II, ch. viii, § 81.

from a slaveholding to a non-slaveholding State, *animo remanendi*, the *status* of the slave is changed, and he becomes free. Second. The mere transit of a slave, either from necessity or convenience, through the territory of a non-slaveholding State, does not change his *status* or condition of slavery. Between these extremes there are many intermediate points. The temporary residence for business or pleasure of a master with his slave, the sojourning for a season for health, or the constant travelling in search of novelty and pleasure, in short, the many varied circumstances, differing, and distinguishing each case as it arises. On the one hand, the mere announcement by the master of an intention to return to his domicile, at some future and uncertain period, should not operate so as to introduce, by such an evasion of the law, into a State an institution repugnant to its laws. On the other, a mere detention for a limited season of a master, by business or pleasure, could not operate so as to change the *status* of his slave, when he thereby in no way contravenes the policy of the local law.

§ 153. Where then is the line to be drawn? So long as the residence of the master and his slave is *bonâ fide* for a *temporary* purpose, it would seem the comity of nations would protect the master's right. Whenever this privilege of temporary residence is used to evade the law (as at the time of the trial of Somersett's case, when there were in the British Isles 15,000 slaves), it would be the duty of the courts to refuse to extend the principle of comity. In fact, upon all questions of this character, much necessarily has to be left to the discretion of the courts. In his Conflict of Laws, Judge Story says, "Upon the continent of Europe some of the principal states have silently suffered their courts to draw this portion of their jurisprudence (viz., questions arising under the comity of nations), from the analogies furnished by the civil law, or by their own customary or positive code. France, for instance, composed as it formerly was of a great numbe of provinces, governed by different laws and customs, was early obliged to sanction such exertion of authority by its courts, in order to provide for the constantly occurring claims of its own subjects, living and owning property in different provinces, in a conflict between the different provincial laws. In England and America, the courts of justice have hitherto exercised the same authority in the most ample manner; and the legislatures have in no instance (it is believed) interfered to provide any positive regulations. The common law of both countries has been expanded to meet the exigencies of the times, as they have arisen, and so far as the practice of nations or the *jus gentium privatum* has been supposed to furnish any general principle, it has been followed out with a wise and manly liberality."[1]

§ 154. Upon this examination of the principles upon which the comity of nations enforces, in every state, the laws of other and foreign governments, we arrive at three conclusions :

1. That where there is a change of domicile, from a slaveholding to a non-slaveholding nation, the *animus remanendi* works of itself and *instanter*

[1] Conflict of Laws, § 24.

(simul ac imperii fines intrarunt) the emancipation of the slave.

2. That the mere transit of the master with his slave, either from necessity or convenience, through the territory of a non-slaveholding state, does not change the *status* of the slave.

3. That, as a general rule, where there is a *bonâ fide* temporary residence of a master, *with his slave*, in a non-slaveholding nation, the *animus revertendi* will protect the master's rights in his slave to the extent of his personal service, and the right to return with him to his domicile. At the same time, if this privilege is used to evade the local laws of the nation with reference to slavery; or the exercise of it becomes so general as to interfere with the policy, or be prejudicial to the interest of the government or its people, the courts will not violate the principles of comity in refusing their aid to enforce these rights.

§ 155. It will be remarked, that in this investigation we have been considering the principles governing the courts of distinct and totally independent nations. How far these principles will be modified, and with how much greater force the requisitions of comity should apply to the States of this Union, bound together by a common constitution, and forming all together, in one view, a single sovereignty, we shall consider fully hereafter.

# CHAPTER VIII.

§ 156. HAVING examined, upon principle, the question, whether the condition of slavery is an exception to the general rule, that the *status* of an individual is to be determined by the law of his domicile, and having arrived at certain conclusions, our next duty is to consider how far these conclusions are supported by the authority of adjudged cases or the opinions of distinguished jurists.

§ 157. Judge Story, in his Conflict of Laws,[1] says, " There is a uniformity of opinion among foreign jurists and foreign tribunals, in giving no effect to the state of slavery of a party, whatever it might have been in the country of his birth, or of that in which he had been previously domiciled, unless it is also recognized by the laws of the country of his

---

[1] Section 96. Burge, in his Treatise on Colonial and Foreign Law, vol. i, p. 738, makes the same assertion, almost verbatim; evidently with Judge Story's work before him; and refers to the same authorities with Judge Story, viz., Christinæus and Grœnewegen. Burge also refers to the Conflict of Laws, as an authority, and the later editions of that work refer to Burge as an authority. It is easy to multiply authorities in this way.

actual domicile, and where he is found, and it is sought to be enforced."

Let us examine into the correctness of this broad statement;[1] and we will first inquire as to the opinions of foreign jurists, and next the decisions of foreign tribunals.

§ 158. In support of his statement, as to the opinions of foreign jurists, Judge Story quotes as follows: "Christinæus states this as a clear rule, affirmed by judicial decisions, 'Propter libertatis personarum usum, hîc per aliquot sæcula continue observatum.' Grœnewegen, speaking of slavery, says, 'Ejusque nomen, hodie apud nos, exolevit. Adeo quidem ut servi qui aliunde huc adducuntur, simul ac imperii nostri fines intrarunt, invitis ipsis dominis, ad libertatem proclamare possint. Id quod et aliarum Christianarum gentium moribus receptum est.'"[2] These are the only foreign jurists that the research of the learned and indefatigable commentator has been able to array in favor of an opinion of great practical moment. Let us inquire who these writers are; the weight to which their opinions

---

[1] As a precedent for disputing the opinions of a jurist so learned in the law, I extract the following from the Life and Letters of Joseph Story, by his son. In the case of Rust v. Low, a note of Lord Hale's to Fitzherbert's Natura Brevium was quoted by the opposing counsel. Mr. Story, in opening, said, " I think I shall satisfy the Court that Lord Hale is mistaken." " What! Brother Story," said Chief Justice Parsons, " you undertake a difficult task." " Nevertheless," was my father's reply, "I hope to satisfy your Honors that he has really misapprehended the authorities on this point." He satisfied the Court of Lord Hale's error. Vol. i, pp. 116–118.          [2] Conf. of Laws, § 96.

are entitled; and the extent to which these opinions
go.

§ 159. Christinæus was a Belgian lawyer of the six-
teenth century, and the work from which this extract
was made was entitled, " Practicarum Quæstionum,
Rerumque, in Supremis Belgarum Curiis, actarum et
observatarum, Decisiones." Grœnewegen was also a
Dutch lawyer, and the work from which the extract
was made was entitled, "De Legibus abrogat, in Hol-
landiâ," &c. It will be seen, from the very subject of
these works, that neither of these authors pretended to
enter upon the great field of International Law, but
their investigations were confined to the local laws of
their own nation. In proof of which, I am inclined,
from a cursory examination, to believe that this is
the only place in the treatise of Judge Story, on the
Conflict of Laws, in which Grœnewegen is cited as
an authority. In fact, were it not for a note, in
which the commentator states that " Grœnewegen
cites many authorities in support of his opinion," I
should shrewdly suspect that the extract above
quoted came secondhand, as I find the same *verbatim* in a note to Mr. Hargraves's argument, in the
celebrated Somersett case.[1] These then, indeed, are
*foreign jurists;* but their opinion should weigh little
upon a branch of jurisprudence which was foreign
to the subject of their studies; and more especially
should it conflict with the opinions of those who
have made the conflict of laws and the comity of
nations the subject of earnest and lifelong investigation.

[1] 20 Howell's State Trials, 62.

§ 160. But let us see what is the extent to which these opinions go. The quotation from Christinæus is, " Propter libertatis personarum usum, hîc per aliquot sæcula continue, observatum." Which literally means : " This has been observed, here, uninterruptedly for some ages, with a view to the security of personal liberty."[1] Upon examining the context, it appears that Christinæus was referring to the question now under consideration, and makes this statement upon the authority of Molanus, Lib. III, Canonic. ch. 34. Not having access to this book, I cannot test his accuracy. He certainly does not pretend to argue the question, but merely states an historical fact.[2]

§ 161. The quotation from Grœnewegen is, "Ejusque nomen hodie apud nos exolevit. Adeo quidem ut servi, qui aliunde huc adducuntur, simul ac imperii nostri fines intrarunt, invitis ipsis dominis, ad libertatem proclamare possint. Id, quod et aliarum Christianarum gentium moribus receptum est." Rendered thus, " And its name at this time hath grown out of use among us. So much so indeed that slaves who are brought hither from elsewhere, so soon as they shall have entered the limits of our government, even against the will of their masters, can appeal to the Judiciary (*proclamare*), in behalf of

[1] Burge, in his Treatise on Colonial and Foreign Law, vol. i, p. 749, states, that Christinæus and Gudelin, in this case, both agreed that if the slave returned to the slaveholding State, the original *status* revived.

[2] It would appear, from Van Leuwen's Roman Dutch Law, Lib. I, ch. v, and the authorities there cited, that the decision referred to by Christinæus, was founded on some local statute or edict.

their freedom. Which hath also been adopted among the usages of other Christian nations." Upon this authority I remark, that the author is giving only the law of Holland, and we know not but that it was so ordained by statute.[1] But even were he speaking of the law of nations, under a particular set of circumstances, the quotation would be correct law; were the slaves brought within the realm, *animo remanendi*, we have seen that the effect described by Grœnewegen would follow. But under a different state of facts we have seen that this effect would not follow. The objection then that I make to the quotation as law is, that it does not specify under what circumstances such is the law.[2] As a *universal* principle we have seen that it is incorrect. The context here too might place the author right; unfortunately I have not access to it.[3] Certain it is,

[1] Since writing the above, I find my suggestion partially confirmed. The following is Mr. Henry's translation of the first and second articles of the Customs of Amsterdam, as collected by Rozeboom. "Within the city of Amsterdam, and its freedom, all men are free, and none are slaves. Also, all slaves who shall come or be brought within this city and its freedom, are free, and out of the power of their masters, and their wives," &c. Henry's Points in Manumission, 160.

[2] By-the-by, the same objection applies to all that Judge Story says on the subject of slavery, in his work on the Conflict of Laws. Usually accurate and minute, he seems nowhere to consider that the circumstances under which the slave comes within the jurisdiction of another State, affects in any manner the question as to his *status*. See §§ 25, 27, 96, et seq.

[3] Since writing the above, by the kindness of Professor Greenleaf, a short time before his decease, I have a copy of the entire title, and find that my criticism is correct. The words quoted are all the author says upon the subject, and he is not pretending to discuss the question under our consideration.

this quotation does not justify the declaration of the " uniformity of foreign jurists on this subject."

§ 162. But even if this authority fully supported Mr. Story, that author should have been aware that in 1736, the Supreme Court of Holland, with the celebrated Bynkershœk as its President, in a case of a fugitive slave, declared the law to be precisely the reverse of the quotation from Grœnewegen, and just as we are now contending to be correct.[1] To put an end to all further doubt upon this question, a statute was passed 23d May, 1776, confirming the law as pronounced by the Supreme Court.[2]

§ 163. But to show there is no such "uniformity,"

[1] This case is reported in the Observations of the Society of Advocates on Grotius's Introduction to the Laws of Holland. I have availed myself of Mr. Henry's translation, and, as it is accessible to but few, I give here the case in full. " A slave named Claas, who had run away from his mistress, at Curaçoa, and got to Holland, was reclaimed there on the part of his owner; and on proceedings being instituted before the magistrates of Amsterdam, the slave obtained a sentence in his favor. On appeal to the Provincial Court, on the 23d of March, 1736, the following sentence was given. 'The Court having heard the report of the Commissaries, before whom the parties have appeared, and seen the *procès-verbal*, with the other vouchers and documents, annul the sentence of the magistrates of the city of Amsterdam, . . . and declare the appellant entitled and permitted, by means of a substitute schout of Amsterdam, or a marshal of this Court, to take the respondent out of the place wherein he is now confined, and ship him on board the first vessel bound to Curaçoa,' &c. The slave appealed from this judgment to the Supreme Court, who 'having maturely deliberated on and weighed and considered everything pertaining to this matter,' affirmed the decision of the Provincial Court, 3d July, 1736." Henry's Points in Manumission, 156, et seq.; see also Van der Linden's Laws of Holland, Bk. I, ch. ii, § 3.                                        [2] Ibid. 159.

Vinnius, with whose works no jurist in America was better acquainted than Judge Story, and who was writing upon the very subject we are now considering, the *jus personale*, as we have before seen, applies the general rule as to capacity directly to the slave. "Item, jus personæ hîc esse, quod statum et conditionem personæ sequitur. Nam status ipse est personæ conditio aut qualitas, quæ efficit ut hoc vel illo jure utatur, ut esse *liberum* esse *servum*, esse ingenuum, esse libertinum, esse alieni, esse sui juris."[1] "A personal statute is that which follows the *status* and condition of the person. For *status* itself is that condition or personal quality which makes one free or slave, noble or ignoble, capable or incapable, by whatever law considered." With this opinion of Vinnius, Huber agrees,[2] whose treatise, "De Conflictu Legum," was the model, after which Judge Story wrote his work, "On the Conflict of Laws."

§ 164. So Heineccius, speaking of fugitives: "This indeed is no hindrance to the master, who may claim his slave wherever found. So far is this restriction from taking the slave from his master, that there may be no safe refuge for him while a fugitive, not even in the prefects and estates of kings themselves. This appears from the Capitularies of the Kings of the Franks, in which we read thus : 'If any slaves belonging to the Church, or any freeman, take refuge in our jurisdiction, and are

---

[1] Lib. I, De Jure Personali, tit. iii. This opinion of Vinnius did not escape Judge Story's notice; as we find this very sentence quoted by him in the same treatise on the Conflict of Laws, § 93, c.

[2] Lib. I, tit. i, c. iii.

demanded by their masters or their agents, if the
governor or steward shall perceive that he cannot
justly hold them within our dominion, let him eject
them, and let their masters take possession of them."[1]
John Voet, after declaring the effect of personal
statutes, following the person everywhere, and applying it to questions of infancy, nobility, legitimacy,
&c., adds, " Nec ullâ mutatione loci, aut illam quam
habet exuere, aut aliam induere posse qualitatem."
"And by no change of place can one put off the
*status* which he has, or put on another which he has
not."[2]

§ 165. The modern civilians uniformly extend
the rule, that personal statutes follow the person into
any jurisdiction, to the question of freedom and
slavery. Thus, Rodenberg, after stating the general rule, gives a reason for it : " Cum enim, ab uno
certoque loco statum hominis legem accipere ne-
cesse esset, quod absurdum earumque rerum natu-
raliter inter se pugna foret, ut in quo loco quis iter
facierit, aut navigans delatus fuerit, totidem ille
statum mutaret aut conditionem ; ut uno, eodem-
que tempore hîc sui juris, illîc alieni futurus sit," &c.
"Because it must be necessary for the law to determine a man's *status* from a single and certain place,
to avoid the conflict and absurdity which would
arise, that whenever one made a journey, or was
driven by sea, so often he would change his *status*
and condition, so that at one and the same time,
*here* he would be free, and *there* he would be subject

---

[1] Opera, vol. ii, 896; De Præsc. § 12.
[2] John. Voet, Lib. I, tit. iv, Parts II, § 7.

to another."[1]  He extends this expressly to feudal
vassals, stating that such is the concurrent testimony
of the jurists, with two exceptions.[2]

§ 166. Boullenois, in his extended work on Personal Statutes, comments upon this statement of
Rodenberg at some length, and concurs with his
opinion.  He cites and rebuts the contrary view
taken by M. Guizot.[3]  Bouhier, speaking of Personal
Statutes, says, " Telles sont les loix qui fixent l'age
de la puberté, et de la majorité ; celles qui règlent
*la qualité de la personne libre ou non libre.*"  " Such are
the laws which fix the age of puberty and majority ;
those which regulate the *status* of a person, whether
free or slave."[4]  Merlin on the same point says, " Tels
sont les statuts qui regardent la naissance, la légitimé,
la liberté," &c.,—" Such are those which look to birth,
legitimacy, freedom," &c.,—and adds, " Le statut de
domicile règle l'état de la personne, et sa capacité ou
incapacité personnelle."  " The law of the domicile re-
gulates the age of the person and his personal capacity or incapacity."[5]  Froland agrees fully with these,
and gives the rule broadly without exception.[6]

 § 167. Of English jurists we have no works from
which to deduce opinions upon this question.  In
truth, the English lawyers seem to have been

---

[1] Cap. iii, § 4.                    [2] Cap. v, § 17.

[3] Traité de la Personalité, Observation xxxi, tom. i, pp. 876, 878 ;
see also tit. i, ch. ii, Obs. iv, where he quotes, as authority,
Queen Elizabeth, "I do not wish my sheep marked with any other
mark than my own."

[4] Observations, &c., ch. xxiii, § 16, p. 452.

[5] Répertoire de Jurisprudence, mot Statut.

[6] Mém., de Stat.

strangers to the discussions among the jurists on the continent.[1] Outside of their reports, we have the opinion of only two of their learned jurists. In 1740, some difficulties having been suggested upon this question, the English colonists applied to the then attorney and solicitor general of England (afterwards Lord Hardwicke and Lord Talbot), for their opinion; which, after due consideration, was given, to the effect that the carrying of a negro slave from the colonies to England, did in no manner interfere with the master's control over him.

[1] 20 Howell's State Trials, 81.

# CHAPTER IX.

§ 168. WE come now to consider how far adjudged cases in the courts of foreign tribunals sustain the declaration quoted from the "Conflict of Laws," and contravene the conclusions to which we have arrived.

We have already alluded to the decision of the Supreme Court of Holland, in the case of the slave Claas.[1]

In France, the first and only case which comes to us in such a form as to be reliable,[2] is found in the thirteenth volume of the "Causes Célèbres," p. 492, and is entitled, "La liberté réclamée par un nègre contre son maître." This cause occurred in 1738, and the slave was liberated by the Court. In the argument of counsel in this case, there is a great deal of declamation about France, "Mère de la Liberté," "the

[1] Note to § 162.

[2] The cases mentioned by Bodin, De Republicâ, Lib. I, cap. v, and referred to by Mr. Hargrave, in his argument in the Somersett case, are too indefinitely reported to be commented on. The latter is admitted, by Mr. Hargrave, to be wrong, being violative of the rights of an ambassador, whose slave, it seems, could breathe, even the pure air of France. See ante, note to § 150.

free air of France being too pure for a slave to breathe," &c.; which was as foreign to the case as it was unbecoming a court professing to decide upon principles of law. The facts of the case, and the questions at issue, were simply as follows. In 1716, Louis XVI, hearing that many of the colonists in the French West Indies were desirous of bringing or sending their slaves to France for the purpose of being instructed in the doctrines and practices of the Church, and of being taught in some art or trade, and that such colonists were fearful that thereby they would recover their liberty, issued an edict, "concernant les esclaves nègres des colonies," in which, after reciting these fears, it is decreed that such colonists may bring or send any of their slaves to France, for these purposes, there to remain, upon complying with certain prescribed regulations; and the edict further provided that, on failure to comply with these regulations, the negroes shall become free, and the owners shall lose all property in them.[1]

[1] This edict, after reciting, *inter alia*, "Comme nous avous été informés, que plusieurs habitans de nos îles de l'Amérique désirent envoyer en France quelques—uns de leurs esclaves pour les confirmer dans les instructions et dans les exercices de notre religion, et pour leur faire apprendre quelque art et métier, dont les colonies recevroient beaucoup d'utilité par le retour de ces esclaves; mais que ces habitans craignent que les esclaves ne prétendent être libres en arrivant en France, ce qui pourroit causer aux dits habitans une perte considérable, et les détourer d'un objet aussi pieux et aussi utile—

"Le Roi ordonne que si quelques uns des habitans des colonies, ou des officiers employés dans l'état veulent amener avec eux des esclaves nègres, de l'un ou de l'autre sexe, en qualité de domestiques ou autrement, pour les fortifier dans la religion, &c., les propriétaires seront tenus, d'en obtenir la permission des gouverneurs

A master of St. Domingo carried with him, in 1738,
to France, a negro slave, and *failed* to comply with
the requisitions of the edict.   The only questions
submitted in that case and decided by the Court
were, 1st. Whether the party claiming the negro
was such a person, as by the French King's edict
of October, 1716, was permitted, under certain formally prescribed conditions, to bring slaves from the
French West Indian Colonies into France, and to
retain them there? 2d. Whether he had performed
those conditions?[1]

§ 169.  It is evident that in this case the question
now under consideration could not arise.   That the
Government of France had the right to prescribe
such regulations in reference to slaves coming from
their own colonies is unquestionable, and all that
the court decided was, the regulations had not been
complied with.   Such was the view taken of this
case (when cited in the argument of the Somersett
case) by Lord Mansfield.   "As to France," said he,
"the case stated decides no farther than that king-

généraux ou commandans, dans chaque isle; laquelle permission
contiendra le nom  du propriétaire, celui des esclaves, leur age et
leur signalement.

"Les propriétaires des dits esclaves seront pareillement obligés
de faire enregistrer la dite permission au greffe de la jurisdiction
du lieu de leur résidence, avant leur départ, et en celui de l'ami-
rauté du lieu de débarquement, dans huitaine après leur arrivée
en France."

After other things, it provides, "faute par les maîtres des esclaves
d'observer les formalités prescrites par les précédens articles, les
dits esclaves seront libres, et ne pourront être réclamés."   See 20
Howell's State Trials, pp. 12, 15, notes.

[1] 20 Howell's State Trials, 12, note.

dom, and there freedom was claimed, because the slave had not been registered in the port where he entered conformably to the edict of 1716."[1]   It may be said, however, that the very existence of such an edict, would show the opinion of the jurists of the day, that under the law as it previously existed, such a permission from the government was necessary to authorize the introduction of slaves.   This is doubtless true, for we have seen that the object of the edict was to allow the slaves to remain in France an indefinite time, and that such a residence would, upon the principles heretofore discussed, work an emancipation of the slave.

§ 170.  In Scotland,[2] two cases are reported in the Dictionary of Decisions.   The first, of Sheddan v. A Negro, occurring in 1757, the latter, of Knight v. Wedderburn, in 1778.   In the first case, during the investigation the negro died, and the point was not determined.   The case of Knight v. Wedderburn

[1] 20 Howell's State Trials, 70.

[2] It may be well to remark, that in the Scotch Elementary Treatises or Institutes, the subject of the Comity of Nations obtains no place, and consequently, their authority is arrayed directly on neither side.   Forbes, whose Institutes of the Law of Scotland, were published in 1722, says, "Slaves are those who are at the arbitrary will of their masters, and may be sold by him as his goods.   We have no vestiges of slavery remaining in Scotland, except in coal-heavers and salt-makers;" vol. i, 73.   These, he states, "without any express paction, are inthralled or astricted during their life;" "and may be recovered by him from any unlawful possessor, to whom they unwarrantably revolt from their master's service."   Ibid.   See also Erskine's Institutes of the Law of Scotland, Bk. I, tit. vii, § 61.   He adds, § 62, that "there appears nothing repugnant, either to reason or the peculiar doctrines of Christianity, in a contract, by which one binds himself

(1778), we will examine more fully. The facts were, " The commander of a vessel in the African trade, having imported a cargo of negroes into Jamaica, sold Joseph Knight, one of them, to Mr. Wedderburn. Knight was then a boy, seemingly about twelve or thirteen years of age. Some time after Mr. Wedderburn came over to Scotland, and brought this negro along with him, as a personal servant. The negro continued to serve him for several years without murmuring, and married in the country. But afterwards, prompted to assert his freedom, he took the resolution of leaving Mr. Wedderburn's service, who being informed of it, got

to perpetual service under a master, who, on his part, is obliged to maintain the other in all the necessaries of life ;" and cites for his authority, Grotius de Jure Bel. Lib. II, ch. v, § 27. He adds, as a peculiar fact, that " by the practice of Holland, negro slaves, as soon as they set their foot in the Dutch territory, may assert their freedom from servitude, in spite of their masters;" but does not pretend that such was the law of Scotland. We have, therefore, negatively his authority that such was not the law of Scotland.

McDouall, in his Institutes of the Law of Scotland, Bk. I, tit. ii, says, that "slavery, in a proper sense, does not take place with us, though it was anciently our law." He admits "the state of coaliers and salters resembles, in some respects, that of slaves," meets the idea that " slavery is inconsistent with Christian liberty," and declares that "this opinion has no support from the apostolical doctrine," and adds, "if it had prevailed in primitive times, it is probable the Roman Empire would never have embraced Christianity; for it had, in a great measure, been a forfeiture of men of substance of those days, by withdrawing from them their property in their slaves."

There certainly is nothing in these principles, announced by these writers on Scotch law, inconsistent with the position we maintain, that slavery is lawful where not abolished, and forms no exception to the general rule, that the personal *status* is decided by the law of the domicile.

him apprehended on a warrant of the justices of the peace." The case being brought before the Sheriff of the County (Perthshire), after some procedure, he decided : " That the state of slavery is not re- cognized by the laws of this kingdom, and is incon- sistent with the principles thereof ; that the regula- tions in Jamaica concerning slaves, do not extend to this kingdom, and repelled the claim to perpetual service of the defender, Mr. Wedderburn." This cause was argued at length before the Court of Ad- vocates, counsel for the master contending that *he had a right to his perpetual service in Scotland*, or to send him back to the plantations. Counsel for the negro do not seem to deny, that if the negro had been enslaved in Jamaica according to any prin- ciple recognized by the law of nations, " on the grounds of equity, the court would give effect to the laws of other countries ;" but they insist that this negro being a child at the time he was carried to Jamaica, could be enslaved "on force and usurpation alone, which no writer on the law of nations has vindicated as a justifiable origin of slavery." That the law of Jamaica was consequently unjust, and could not be supported. This view of counsel was sustained by the Court, whose decision is given in these words : " The Court were of opinion that the dominion assumed over this negro under the law of Jamaica, *being unjust*, could not be supported in this country to any extent ; that therefore the defender has no right to the negro's service for any space of time, nor to send him out of the country against his consent."[1]

[1] 20 Howell's State Trials, note, pp. 1–7. It is a fact worthy

§ 171. This is the case in which Judge Story says that it was solemnly adjudged, that "no effect whatever" would be given to the state of slavery, "whatever it might have been in the country of his birth," unless it was also recognized by the laws of the country where it is sought to be enforced. On the contrary, I remark, upon this case, 1st. That directly the opposite principle is adjudicated, the counsel admitting, and the decision of the Court sustaining the counsel, that if the slavery of the negro, in Jamaica, was justifiable, under the law of nations, the Court would give it effect in Scotland. The decision is based upon the want of title in the master under the "law of nations."[1]

2d. The facts show a case in which, upon the

of note, that such was the public feeling at the time of the decision of this case in Scotland, and Somersett's case in England, that even the men of literature prepared arguments to be read in the courts. That "faithful chronicler," Boswell, has retained Dr. Johnson's argument in this case, and it is worthy of examination, as being "the seed argument in the propagation of abolition doctrines." Fletcher's Studies on Slavery, 68. The course of reasoning followed, is confirmatory of the view taken in the text, as to the ground on which this decision is based. 2 Boswell's Life of Johnson, 132.

[1] Were it necessary, in this connection, to show that there are circumstances under which slavery is justifiable, and recognized by the law of nations, I would refer to Judge Story's own decision, in the case of La Jeune—Eugénie (2 Mason R. 90), where, in spite of the strong anti-slavery feeling, which biassed and warped his judgment whenever the question of slavery came before him, he says, "Sitting in an American Court of Judicature, I am not permitted to deny that, under some circumstances, slavery may have a lawful existence; and that the practice may be justified by the condition or wants of society, or may form a part of the domestic policy of a nation."

principles we have heretofore investigated, the
comity of nations would not have required the
courts of Scotland to have enforced the laws of Jamaica. For it seems that the negro had been actually domiciled in Scotland for "several years," and
had been permitted there to marry; and the *animus
remanendi* appears from all the facts of the case.

So far then from opposing the views I have advanced, this case goes farther than principle would
require, in giving effect to the *status* of a slave, in
a new domicile.

§ 172. I come now to examine the decisions of
the English courts.

Before doing so, it will be well enough to consider,
historically, the position not only of England, but
of the English law, at the time when the leading
decisions were made; not for the purpose so much
of avoiding the effect of the decisions, but with a
view to ascertain the amount and sources of information of the courts and counsel, in order to determine the weight to which their *dicta* are entitled.[1]

---

[1] We are too frequently prone to give weight to a name, without
going back to weigh the value of an opinion from the circumstances, &c., under which it was made. Because a Judge has
exhibited great learning on one branch of the law, we err in attributing to him the same position on every branch. The opinion of
Sir Isaac Newton on a branch of science, *e. g.*, Geology, to which
his attention was never devotedly turned, would not weigh a feather
with scientific men of this generation, in opposition to the researches
or opinions of others, much less distinguished, but much better acquainted with the subject. So, in law, Coke, Holt, and Mansfield,
should weigh no more on a branch of jurisprudence foreign to their
studies. Of course, the *onus* is upon the *declarant*, to show that
any branch of the law escaped their attention.

It is a fact too notorious to require proofs, that the commerce of England had never extended itself sufficiently to feel the trammels of the strict and almost rude rules of the common law, until the days of Lord Mansfield, to whom was due the honor, and in whom was the capacity of, developing that system of mercantile law which the necessity of the times required.

It is but a fair inference from this fact, combined with many others, suggesting themselves to any student of history, that her international communication, prior to that period, was very limited with the nations of Europe. The consequence was (what the reports demonstrate), that questions of international law were very rare in the courts of England. To the bench and to the bar, therefore, no inducements were held out for a close investigation and study of this (at this day) important branch of jurisprudence. Confirmatory of these views is the fact, that Judge Story's work on the Conflict of Laws, was the first treatise in the English language on this important subject; and the only treatise within the library of the English jurists, until the work of Mr. Burge, on "Foreign and Colonial Law."[1]

§ 173. Chancellor Kent says, "The doctrine of the *lex loci* is replete with subtle distinctions and embarrassing questions, which have exercised the skill and learning of the earlier and more distinguished civilians of the Italian, French, Dutch, and German schools, in their discussions on highly im-

[1] Story's Conf. of Laws, § 10 ; Burge's Comm. on For. and Col. Law, Ded. p. 10.

portant topics of international law.  These topics were almost unknown in the English courts prior to the time of Lord Hardwicke and Lord Mansfield, and the English lawyers seem generally to have been strangers to the discussions on foreign law by the celebrated jurists in continental Europe."[1]  In this opinion Mr. Burge agrees; for, in the Dedication of his work, he says, " This branch of jurisprudence (Conflict of Laws) does not appear to have excited the interest of English lawyers."[2]

§ 174.  The first case in the English Reports, touching the question, is that of Butts v. Penny.[3] It was an action of trover for ten negroes and a *half*. The special verdict found, that the negroes were infidels, subjects to an infidel prince, and usually bought and sold as merchandise.  That the plaintiff had bought them, and was in possession of them, and that the defendant had taken them out of his possession.  The Court held, that negroes are, " by

---

[1] 2 Kent's Comm. Lect. xxxix, p. 455; see also Life and Letters of Story, vol. i, 224.

[2] Burge, on For. and Col. Law, Ded. p. x.

[3] 2 Lev. 201; 3 Keb. 785; 15 Viner's Abr. 549, title Negro. I have not alluded to the case of the Russian slave, relied on by Mr. Hargrave, in his argument in the Somersett case, because we have no report, nor record of any sort, of that case.  Nor has there been produced any evidence from the court-roll, of the existence of such a case.  Mr. Hargrave relies on a single observation in Rushworth's Historical Collections, vol. ii, p. 468.  It is worthy of notice, simply because we there find, for the first time, the announcement of the false and ridiculous proposition that " the air of England was too pure for a slave to breathe in."  I think I am justified in saying it is false, when Mr. Sumner, in his labored attack upon the Fugitive Slave Law, in the Senate of the United States, was forced to acknowledge that the claim was unfounded.  ·

usage, *tanquam bona*, and go to administrator until
they become Christians, and thereby they are enfranchised." This decision seems to be speaking of
their *status* under the law of England.

§ 175. The next case is that of Gelly and Cleve,
determined in the Common Pleas (at Hil. Term, 5
W. & M.); and of which we have it stated, in 1 Ld.
Raym. 147, that it was "adjudged that trover will
lie for a negro boy, for they are heathens, and therefore a man may have property in them, and that the
Court, without averment made, will take notice that
they are heathens."

§ 176. The next case is that of Smith v. Gould,[1]
where trover was brought for a negro, and other
articles of merchandise. Verdict for plaintiff, and
damages for the negro, £30. In arrest of judgment
it was contended, that trover did not lie, because
the owner's property was *not absolute;* "he could
not kill him as he could an ox." The Court held
that *trover* did not lie, " but seemed to think that
in *trespass quare captivum suum cepit* the plaintiff
might give in evidence that the party was his negro,
and he bought him."

§ 177. The next case is that of Chamberlain v.
Harvey,[2] which was an action of trespass for taking
a negro. The special verdict found, " that the father
of the plaintiff was possessed of this negro and of
such a manor in Barbadoes, and that there is a law
in that country which makes the negro a part of the
real estate. That the father died seized, whereby

---

[1] 2 Salkeld, 666 ; 2 Lord Raym. 1274.
[2] 1 Lord Raym. 146 ; 3 Ibid. 129; Carth. 396; 5 Mod. 186;
15 Viner's Abr. 549, title Negro.

the manor descended to the plaintiff as son and heir, and that he endowed his mother of this negro and a third part of the manor. That the mother married Watkins, who brought the negro into England, where he was baptized without the knowledge of the mother. That Watkins and his wife are dead, and that the negro continued several years in England, and that the defendant seized him," &c. After argument at the bar several times, it was adjudged that the action would not lie, there being no averment of a " per quod servitium amisit." The reasons for this decision are not given in Lord Raymond's Reports: whether the form of action was defective, or the baptism of the negro released him from slavery, or his residence in England had given him a new domicile there, is not stated. The substance of the report is given above. In 5 Mod. it is said, " The Court were of opinion that no action of trespass would lie for the taking away a man generally, but that there might be a special action of trespass for taking his servant *per quod*," &c. The same reason is given for the decision in 15 Viner. There the Court says, a negro " is no other than a slavish servant," and the master can maintain no other action than trespass *per quod*, &c.

§ 178. There is one other case reported in Salkeld,[1]

---

[1] Vol. ii, 666. Barrington, in his Treatise on Statutes, 1 Ric. II, says: " It is laid down that trover will lie for a negro, in 2 Lev. 201; and it seems to be agreed by the two cases in Salkeld (vol. ii, 666), that some kind of action will lie for a negro, though not an action of trover. I cannot say, indeed, that these cases are well reported. The term slave is certainly not unknown to our law; as by 1 Edw. VI, ch. iii, a vagabond, an idle servant, is to become

Smith v. Brown and Cooper, the accuracy of which is exceedingly doubtful. The report states that it is an action of indeb. assumpsit for £20, for a negro sold "in parochiâ beatæ Mariæ de Arcubus in Warda de Cheape," and verdict for plaintiff, and on motion in arrest of judgment, Holt, C. J., held, " that as soon as a negro comes into England he becomes free ; one may be a villain in England, but not a slave." Et per Powell, J., " The law took no notice of a negro." Holt, C. J., " You should have averred in the declaration that the sale was in Virginia, and that by the laws of that country negroes are saleable." " Therefore ·he directed the plaintiff should amend." "Then the Attorney-General coming in, said, they were inheritances, and transferable by deed, and not without; and nothing was done." Such is the substance of the report. Its accuracy is doubtful, 1st. Because it gives neither date nor location to the cause, but leaves it to be inferred that it was in B. R. from the names of the Judges presiding. 2d. Because it states that the same case is found in Lord Raymond, in which it does not appear. 3d. From internal evidence of inaccuracy, viz., the allowance of an amendment, after judgment and upon the hearing of a motion in arrest, a proceeding unheard of in the King's Bench. And, also, the statement that negroes were inheritances in Virginia at that date, and transferable only by deed. 4th. Lord

a slave to his master, and the expression is frequently repeated in that statute." (p. 240, notes.) The same view of these cases seems to be taken by the Reporter, in note to Noel v. Robinson, 1 Vernon, 453.

Mansfield gave another reason for its inaccuracy, "that it was upon a petition to Lincoln's Inn Hall after dinner; probably, therefore, might not, as he believes the contrary is not unusual at that hour, be taken with much accuracy."[1] Perhaps the reporter at that hour was more accurate than the Judges. 5th. Because the reason given by the Court for its judgment, viz., that the contract was laid in London, and should have been laid in Virginia, was directly opposed to all the usage and practice of the courts, which required such an allegation in all such contracts, and which allegation was not traversable.

§ 179. In Noel v. Robinson, Mr. Sergeant Maynard's case was cited, wherein it is stated that "by his advice an action of trover was brought, and judgment obtained for the *fourth* part of a negro."[2] This is the only reference I find to this case.

§ 180. These are the reported cases to be found in the English reports, prior to the great case of the negro Somersett. Upon them, we may remark, that in them all, excepting Chamberlin v. Harvey, there is a distinct recognition of the property of the master in the slave under the laws of England. It must be admitted that the views of the courts seem indistinct, and the reports are very meagre. The idea of the lawfulness of the enslavement being dependent on the infidelity of the negro, was, at that day, a very common one. The author of the Mirror seems to recognize such a distinction (c. 2, § 23), and the

---

[1] 20 Howell's State Trials, 70; Justice Best, in Forbes v. Cochrane & Cockburn, 2 B. & C. 448, agrees that this case is inaccurately reported.    [2] 1 Vernon, 453.

particularity with which the fact is found in each of the special verdicts in the cases referred to, would strengthen the supposition that such was the opinion of the courts. It is an undoubted historical fact, that such an opinion prevailed among the planters in both the English and French colonies, and induced many to deny to their slaves Christian instruction and baptism. Hence, the application and inquiries of the English planters to Lord Talbot and Lord Hardwicke, and their celebrated answers, to which we have had occasion to refer. And hence, also, a provision in the "Code Noir," with reference to the baptism of negroes in the French colonies. Lord Mansfield states, that the question was considered on a petition in Lincoln's Inn Hall, "on the earnest solicitation of many merchants, to know whether a slave was freed by being made a Christian. And it was resolved,'not."[1] In Sir Thomas Grantham's case, it appeared that "A. brought a man-monster from the Indies, having the perfect shape of a child growing out of his breast, except the head (as an excrescency), and showed him for profit. This man turned Christian and was baptized, and detained from A." On a *homine replegiando* the Court bailed him.[2]

§ 181. None of these cases certainly contravene the positions we occupy with reference to the duty of the courts in enforcing the comity of nations. Whether they are sufficient to show that negro slavery once existed in England (against which idea

[1] 20 Howell's State Trials, 70.
[2] 15 Viner, 306, title Hom. Repl. 3 Mod. 120.

all the ingenuity of Mr. Hargrave is brought to bear), it is unnecessary for us to inquire, nor is it necessary for us to show.[1]  The case of Chamberlin v. Harvey, even if decided upon the ground that the negro's residence in England had released him from the master's control, would not be opposed to the views we have advanced, for the length of residence and the circumstances attending it, placed the master's rights beyond the pale of comity.

§ 182.  We come now to consider the leading case of the negro Somersett.[2]  The questions arose upon a return to a writ of habeas corpus, served upon Captain Knowles, of the ship Ann and Mary.  He produced the body of Somersett, the negro, and returned for cause of detainer, that Somersett was a negro and native of Africa, in the regular course of the slave-trade, bought, carried to Virginia, and sold to the claimant, Charles Stewart.  That, on the first day of October, 1769, said Stewart left America on a voyage to England, "having occasion to, and for the purpose of, transacting certain affairs and business in this kingdom, and with an intention to return to America as soon as the said affairs and business should be transacted."  That Stewart brought the negro along with him, to attend and serve him during his stay, and with an intent to carry him back when his business should be finished; "which affairs and business are not yet transacted, and the intention of the said Stewart to return to America hath hitherto continued and still continues."

[1] See the remarks of the Court of Appeals of Maryland, in Mahony v. Ashton, 4 Har. & McH. 323, 324, upon these cases.
[2] 20 Howell's State Trials, i, 82, S. C. Lofft.

That the negro served Stewart from the time of his arrival until the 1st October, 1771, when he abandoned the service without the consent of his master. That Stewart then delivered the negro to˙ the respondent, Knowles, for the purpose of being carried back to America to be sold.

Upon this return, argument was had at great length. On the adjournment over of the Court, Lord Mansfield said : " The distinction was difficult as to slavery which could not be resumed after emancipation, and yet the condition of slavery in its full force could not be tolerated here. Much consideration was necessary to define how far the point should be carried. The Court must consider the great detriment to proprietors, there being so great a number in the ports of this kingdom, that many thousands of pounds would be lost to the owners by setting them free. (A gentleman observed no great danger, for in a whole fleet usually there would not be six slaves.) As to France, the case stated de-. cides no farther than that kingdom ; and there freedom was claimed, because the slave had not been registered in the port where he entered, conformably to the edict of 1706. Might not a slave as well be freed by going out of Virginia to the adjacent country, where there are no slaves, if change to a place of contrary custom was sufficient? A statute, by the Legislature, to subject the West India property to payment of debts, I hope will⋅ be thought some proof ; another act divests the African Company of their slaves, and vests them in the West India Company ; I say, I hope these are proofs the law has interfered for the maintenance of the trade in slaves and the transferring of slavery. As for want of application properly to a court of justice, a common servant may be corrected here by his master's private authority. Habeas corpus acknowledges a right to seize persons by force, employed to serve abroad. A right of compulsion there must be, or the master will be under the ridiculous necessity of neglecting his proper business by staying here to have their service, or must be quite deprived of those slaves he has been forced to bring over. The case as to service for life, was not allowed, merely for want of a deed to pass it."

§ 183. After farther argument, the decision was delivered as follows:

LORD MANSFIELD.—The question is, if the owner had a right to detain the slave for the sending of him over to be sold in Jamaica. In five or six cases of this nature, I have known it to be accommodated by agreement between the parties; on its first coming before me, I strongly recommended it here. But if the parties will have it decided, we must give our opinion. Compassion will not, on the one hand, nor inconvenience on the other, be to decide, but the law; in which, the difficulty will be principally from the inconvenience on both sides. Contract for sale of a slave is good here; the sale is a matter to which the law properly and readily attaches, and will maintain the price according to the agreement. But here, the person of the slave himself is immediately the object of inquiry; which makes a material difference. The next question is, whether any dominion, authority, or coercion, can be exercised in this country, on a slave according to the American laws? The difficulty of adopting the relation without adopting it in all its consequences, is indeed extreme; and yet many of those consequences are absolutely contrary to the municipal law of England. We have no authority to regulate the condition in which law shall operate. On the other hand, we think the coercive power cannot be exercised.

'Tis now about fifty years since the opinion given by two of the greatest men of their own or any times (since which no contract has been brought to trial, between the masters and slaves). The service performed by the slaves, without wages, is a sheer indication they did not think themselves free by coming hither. The setting 14,000 or 15,000 men at once free, loose, by a solemn opinion, is much disagreeable in the effects it threatens. There is a case in Hobart (Coventry and Woodfall), where a man had contracted to go as a mariner; but the now case will not come within that decision. Mr. Stewart advances no claims on contract; he rests his whole demand on a right to the negro as slave, and mentions the purpose of detainure to be the sending of him over to be sold in Jamaica. If the parties will have judgment, *fiat justitia ruat cœlum*, let justice be done, whatever be the consequence. 50*l.* a head may not be a high price; then a loss follows to the proprietors of above 700,000*l.* sterling. How would the law stand with respect to their settlement; their wages? How many actions for any slight coercion by the masters? We cannot, in any of these points, direct the law, the law must rule us. In these particulars, it may be matter of weighty consideration what provisions are made or set by law. Mr. Stewart may end the question by discharging or giving freedom to the negro. I did think, at first, to put the matter to a more solemn argument. But if my brother agree, there seems no occasion. I do not imagine, after the point has been discussed on both sides so extremely well, any new light could be thrown on the subject. If the parties choose to refer it to the Common Pleas, they can give them that satisfaction whenever they think fit.

An application to Parliament, if the merchant think the question of great commercial concern, is the best, and perhaps the only method of settling the point for the future. The Court is greatly obliged to the gentlemen of the bar who have spoke on the subject; and by whose care and abilities so much has been effected, that the rule of decision will be reduced to a very easy compass. I cannot omit to express particular happiness in seeing young men, just called to the bar, have been able so much to profit by their reading. I think it right the matter should stand over; and if we are called on for a decision, proper notice shall be given.

TRINITY TERM, JUNE 22, 1772.

LORD MANSFIELD.—On the part of Somersett, the case which we gave notice should be decided this day, the Court now proceeds to give its opinion. I shall recite the return to the writ of habeas corpus as the ground of our determination; omitting only words of form. The Captain of the ship, on board of which the negro was taken, makes his return to the writ in terms signifying that there have been, and still are, slaves to a great number in Africa; and that the trade in them is autho- rized by the laws and opinions of Virginia and Jamaica; that they are goods and chattels; and, as such, saleable and sold. That James Somersett is a negro of Africa, and long before the return of the King's writ, was brought to be sold, and was sold to Charles Stewart, Esq., then in Jamaica, and has not been manumitted since; that Mr. Stewart, having occasion to transact business, came over hither, with an intention to return, and brought Somersett to attend and abide with him, and to carry him back as soon as the business should be trans- acted. That such intention has been, and still continues; and that the negro did remain, till the time of his depar- ture, in the service of his master, Mr. Stewart, and quitted it without his consent; and thereupon, before the return of the King's writ, the said Charles Stewart did commit the slave on board the Ann and Mary to safe custody, to be kept till he should set sail, and then to be taken with him to Jamaica, and there sold as a slave. And this is the cause why he, Captain Knowles, who was then, and now is, commander of the above vessel, then and now lying in the river of Thames, did the said negro, committed to his custody, detain; and on which he renders him to the orders of the Court.

We pay all due attention to the opinion of Sir Philip Yorke and Lord Chief Justice Talbot, whereby they pledged themselves to the British planters, for all the legal consequences of slaves coming over to this kingdom or being baptized, recognized by Lord Hard- wicke, sitting as Chancellor, on the 19th of October, 1749, that trover would lie. That a notion had pre- vailed, if a negro came over or became a Christian, he was emancipated, but no ground in law; that he and

Lord Talbot, when Attorney and Solicitor General, were of opinion that no such claim for freedom was valid; that though the Statute of Tenures had abolished villains regardant to a manor, yet he did conceive but that a man might still become a villain in gross by confessing himself such in open court. We are so well agreed that we think there is no occasion of having it argued, as I intimated an intention at first, before all the Judges, as is usual, for obvious reasons, on a return to a habeas corpus; the only question before us is, whether the cause on the return is sufficient? If it is, the negro must be remanded; if it is not, he must be discharged. Accordingly, the return states that the slave departed and refused to serve, whereupon he was kept to be sold abroad. So high an act of dominion must be recognized by the law of the country where it is used. The power of a master over his slave has been extremely different in different countries. The state of slavery is of such a nature that it is incapable of being introduced on any reasons, moral or political, but only positive law, which preserves its force long after the reasons occasion, and time itself from whence it was created, is erased from memory. It is so odious that nothing can be suffered to support it but positive law. Whatever inconveniences, therefore, may follow from a decision, I cannot say this case is allowed or approved by the law of England, and therefore the black must be discharged.

§ 184. This decision has been given at length for several reasons, besides the fact of its being the leading case upon which many subsequent rulings have been made. One of those reasons is, that many expressions and opinions have been attributed to Lord Mansfield, which are nowhere included in or inferable from his opinion, but which have been taken from the arguments of counsel, especially that of Mr. Hargrave, written out long after the decision, and which it is not pretended were ever delivered upon the hearing.[1]  Thus, even Lord Camp-

[1] See note to page 23; 20 Howell's State Trials.

bell has reported Lord Mansfield as having said that " the air of England has long been too pure for a slave to breathe," and that " villanage had ceased in England and could not be revived,"[1] none of which appears in this report, and which we have the authority of Lord Mansfield for asserting that he never said. For, in a case arising thirteen years thereafter, he stated that the decision " went no farther than that the master cannot by force compel the slave to go out of the kingdom,"—and in the same case decided, that " villains in gross may, in point of law, exist at that day" (1785).[2]

§ 185. Before examining minutely the decision itself it is worthy of remark, that the report, as well as cotemporaneous history show, that there was a great deal of public feeling and excitement created by the investigation of the case. This is evidenced

[1] Lives of Chief Justices, vol. ii, 320 (Amer. Ed.). Lord Campbell gives a decision at length of Lord Mansfield's, and refers, as his authority, to 20 Howell's State Trials ; not one word of which will be found in the report referred to. The report of Lord Campbell, moreover, is entirely inconsistent with the whole bearing and manner of Lord Mansfield in this case. His is a polished, firm, bold, literary production, closing with the Latin quotation, "Quamvis ille niger, quamvis tu candidus esses." Lord Mansfield's is a vacillating, doubting, irregular, disjointed effusion, unworthy of his greatness. For fear that I did Lord Campbell injustice, I addressed him a letter requesting his authority for this decision. In reply to this, he says, in a courteous note, dated Aug. 27th, 1855, " I am not able to refer you to any printed authority for the words of the judgment of Lord Mansfield, in Somersett's case, as I have given it. It agrees, in substance, with the printed reports, and I have every reason to believe that it is quite correct."

[2] Rex v. Inhabitants of Thames Ditton, 3 Douglas, 300 (26 E. C. L. R. 367).

by the report in many instances.  The indecorous
interruption of the Court by a bystander, while delivering its judgment on the first argument.  The
fact that the counsel for the respondent acknowledged it to be his " misfortune to address an audience, the greater part of which he feared were
prejudiced the other way.  That he found it necessary to disclaim intimating a wish in favor of slavery
by any means," and to defend his appearance by referring to his " duty to maintain those arguments
which are most useful to Captain Knowles ;" and
that in concluding his argument he was weak enough
to forget the Court and address the audience, and
after making his apologies, to express the " hope, that
he should not suffer in the opinion of those whose
honest passions are fired by the name of slavery ;"
and the farther hope, " that he had not transgressed
his duty to humanity."[1]  The fact of the inflammatory character of the arguments for the negro, and
the still more pregnant fact, the vacillating, doubting, unusual, and it might be truly added, discreditable manner in which the opinion of the Court was
delivered.[2]  All of these facts, apparent upon the
face of the report, show that the public feeling was
oppressive to the counsel, and had its influence upon
the Court.  Contemporaneous history confirms this
inference, the exciting questions of abolition of the

---

[1] Argument of Mr. Dunning, 20 Howell's State Trials, 71–75.

[2] This fact did not escape attention at the time.  The decision was
declared to be a " delphic ambiguity," and the question left in
" grand uncertainty."  Pamphlets were written, *pro* and *con*, to
explain and to attack.  See Just Limitation of Slavery, by Granville Sharp, and Appendix, Nos. 8 and 9.

slave-trade, and West India emancipation being just then taking hold of the public mind and conscience, and " Wilkes and Liberty" being the popular tocsin. The fact that Dr. Samuel Johnson, the despot over the literary world of that day, prepared an argument upon this question, to be used in the case of Knight and Wedderburn, in the Scotch Courts, almost cotemporaneously with this case, is confirmatory of this opinion.[1]

Without desiring in any manner to disparage the deservedly great reputation of the great jurists that delivered this opinion, it is nevertheless unquestionably true, and so admitted by his biographers and eulogists, that a prominent defect in his character was a want of that moral courage (that my Lord Coke possessed in such an eminent degree) that could withstand every influence when the law demanded his obeisance.[2]

§ 186. The arguments of the counsel in this case (written out and reported at length in 20 Howell's State Trials), go far to sustain the opinion expressed by Chancellor Kent, of their ignorance at that time upon these vexed questions of International Law. The subject of the Comity of Nations is never mentioned, *eo nomine*, by either of them; and the principles of that comity (the only ground on which the master's rights could be supported), are never even obscurely alluded to by the counsel representing his interests. On the contrary, Mr. Dunning, the leading counsel for the master, yielded the whole

[1] 2 Boswell's Life of Johnson, 132.

[2] Campbell's Lives of the Chief Justices, vol. ii, p. 437 (Amer. Ed.).

question, when he admitted, in his argument, the broad proposition, that "the municipal regulations of one country are not binding on another" (p. 73). In fact, the only allusion to the doctrine of comity, deserving the name, made on either side, seems to be an afterthought of Mr. Hargrave, in writing out his argument for publication, where he speaks of the *lex loci* (p. 60); and then his application of the doctrine shows either strange ignorance, or a wanton perversion. And this was evidently not mentioned on the hearing, as his view is neither met by the opposing counsel, nor alluded to by the Court. It is true that it is said (p. 71), that "the Court approved Mr. Alleyne's opinion of the distinction how far municipal laws were to be regarded;" but Mr. Alleyne's argument shows no distinction to have been drawn by him. He says (p. 68), "Slavery is not a natural, it is a municipal relation; an institution, therefore, confined to certain places, and necessarily dropped by passage into a country where such municipal regulations do not exist." If this be the distinction to which the Court alludes, they place themselves very much in the category of the counsel.

§ 187. The truth is, the arguments show—what the decision of the Court clearly demonstrates—that the case was placed upon an entirely false issue, viz., whether or not African slavery could be introduced into England. The justly celebrated argument of Mr. Hargrave is all directed to show that "the law of England will not admit of a new slavery" (p. 35). The argument of the counsel for the master strove to demonstrate that the law of England recognized slavery in villanage; and that, at most, it would modify the state of absolute slavery to that of servitude for life. The true ground, that the law of the domicile determined the *status* of the slave, and that the English Courts, through comity, were bound to enforce the municipal law of that domicile, when it did not interfere with the policy or become prejudicial to the interests of England, was never suggested to the consideration of the court.[1]

§ 188. When we come to examine the decision of the Court, we find it equally wide of the mark. Lord Mansfield seems to have arrived almost in view of the point, when he said, "The now question is, whether any dominion, authority, or coercion, can be exercised, in this country, on a slave, according to the American laws? The difficulty of adopting the relation, without adopting it in all its consequences, is indeed extreme; yet many of those consequences are absolutely contrary to the municipal law of England. We have no authority to regulate the conditions in which law shall operate." His great mind, unaided, seems to have almost borne him to the true solution; one step farther, and there would have been no difficulty; the step subsequently taken by Lord Stowell, when he declared that in cases coming under the Comity of Nations, the business of the English law was simply to bring the parties to a hearing; and that

[1] Lord Stowell says, "The arguments of counsel, in that decisive case of Somersett, do not go farther than to the extinction of slavery in England, as unsuitable to the genius of the country, and the modes of enforcement." Case of Slave Grace, 2 Hagg. Admr. 109.

effected, she stepped back, and left the decision to
the municipal law of the foreign state.  But Lord
Mansfield seems to have sunk under the oppression
of the difficulties, and, instead of taking the other
step, goes rambling off in a dislocated jargon, about
"*fiat justitia, ruat cœlum;*" "50*l.* a head not a high
price;" suggestions to Mr. Stewart to emancipate his
negro, in order to relieve the Court, &c. &c., which,
taken altogether, is by no means calculated to advance his fame.[1]

§ 189.  The final judgment of the Court, delivered
some five months thereafter, shows clearly what has
been formerly stated, that the case was decided upon
a false issue, viz., whether African slavery would be
lawful under the municipal law of England.  Say
the Court, "The state of slavery is of such a nature
that it is incapable of being introduced on any
reasons, moral or political, but only by positive law."
"Whatever inconveniences, therefore, may follow
from the decision, I cannot say this case is allowed
or approved by the law of England; and, therefore,
the black must be discharged."  It would seem unquestionable, that this decision denied the right of
introducing a slave *animo remanendi.*  Yet Lord
Mansfield, in a subsequent case, where a slave was
introduced and retained in England, declared that
this "determination went no farther than that the
master cannot, by force, compel the slave to go out

---

[1] Since penning this paragraph, I have been pleased to see that
this decision made a similar impression upon the minds of the profession soon after its delivery.  See Argument of Luther Martin,
Attorney-General of Maryland, in 1799, in case of Mahoney v.
Ashton, 4 Har. & McH. 320, 321.

of the kingdom."[1]   Barrington, in his Observations on Statutes, published shortly after the decision, refers to this case, and corroborates the remarks just quoted of Lord Mansfield.   He says, "There hath lately, indeed, been a celebrated judgment in the Court of King's Bench, with regard to a black servant; but I conceive that the only point determined in that case was, *that a master hath not a right to send such a slave out of the kingdom, in order that he may be sold.*"[2]

§ 190. Lord Stowell, in the case of the slave Grace, decided in 1827 (2 Hagg. Adm. Rep. 94), has reviewed, at some length, the decision in Somersett's case; and while he disclaims the "presumption of questioning any *obiter dictum* that fell from that great man" (Lord Mansfield), he combats, and successfully, the only foundation upon which the decision is based, viz., that "slavery cannot be established without positive law."   He says (p. 107), "I trust, I do not depart from the modesty that belongs to my situation, and I hope to my character, when I observe that *ancient custom* is generally recognized as a just foundation of all law.   That *villanage*, which is said to be the prototype of slavery, had no other origin than ancient custom; that a great part of the common law itself, in all its relations, has little other foundation than the same custom."   Of the judgment in the case, he says (p. 109), "There is hardly anything else that is ex-

[1] Rex v. Inhabitants of Thames Ditton, 4 Douglas, 300 (26 E. C. L. R. 367).

[2] The italics are his own.   Observ. on Statutes 1 Ric. II, p. 312 (5th Edition, 1796).

pressed, save several well-merited civilities to the
gentlemen of the bar; and some expressions of contempt for the danger and jealousy that might be
encountered, but of which none ever appear to have
occasioned any reasonable alarm." Of the very
favorite expression of later days, "that the air of
England was too pure for a slave to breathe," Lord
Stowell says, with well-deserved sarcasm (p. 109),
"How far *this air* was useful for the common purposes of respiration, during the many centuries in
which the two systems of villanage maintained their
sway in this country, history has not recorded."

§ 191. And as conclusive proof that this case
went no farther than Lord Mansfield declared in
the case in Douglas, is the fact, that for fifty years
after the decision in Somersett's case, slaves were
continually brought from the West Indies to England, the masters relying upon their voluntary
return. Says Lord Stowell, in the case cited, p. 112,
"Black seamen have, ever since, navigated West
India ships to this island, but we have not heard of
other Somersetts, nor has the public been much
gratified with complaints of their desertion." "And
what excuse is to be offered for Lord Mansfield, who
long survived the change of the law which he had
made, and yet never interposed in the slightest
manner to correct the total misapprehension, if it
is so to be considered, of the law which he himself
had introduced." (p. 114.)

§ 192. Having examined the decision of the Court
as made, let us view the case made by the return, in
the light of those rules which we have deduced from
the principles of international law governing these

questions.    It appears that the master had been residing two years in England with this slave, "for
the purpose of transacting certain business," and
" with the intention of returning to America at the
close of that business."   The nature of that business, and the probable duration of the master's stay,
are not stated.   The farther fact appears, upon the
hearing, that near 15,000 slaves were at that time,
under various pretexts, introduced into England.   It
is a doubtful question whether, under such circumstances and with so vague a return, the Court would
not have been justified in the exercise of its discretion, in "refusing to extend the principle of
comity."[1]

§ 193.  The judgment of the Court, upon the case
made, therefore, does not necessarily contravene the
principles we have laid down.   The reasons given
by the Court for that judgment, we dissent from.
Those reasons, not the case, have been the fruitful
source of erroneous decisions, as our farther review
of the cases will abundantly show.

§ 194.  In the case of Williams v. Brown,[2] decided
in 1802, the question incidentally arose as to the condition of a fugitive slave, who, having enjoyed freedom
in England, voluntarily returned to the West Indies,
whence he had fled.   The Court of Common Pleas
were unanimous in the opinion, that his state of slavery existed upon his return.   Which decision was

---

[1] This appears to be the view of this case taken by Lord Stowell,
in a letter to Judge Story, and which view was fully approved by
the latter.   Life and Letters of Story, vol. i, 555, 558.

[2] 3 Bos. & Pul. 69.

affirmed, as we shall see, upon elaborate argument, in
the subsequent case of the slave Grace.

§ 195. The next case in England, worthy of attention, is that of Forbes v. Cochrane & Cockburn
(decided in 1824).¹ The question made there, and
decided by the Court, does not, in any manner, affect
the point under review; and Bayley, J., who de-
livers the judgment of the Court, expressly waives
"giving any opinion" upon the question, whether
" a slave, the instant he leaves his master's plantation, and gets upon other land where slavery is not
tolerated, becomes, *ex necessitate,* to all intents and
purposes, a freeman." Nor would it be necessary to
refer to the case, except that some of the Judges, in
concurring in the judgment, had taken occasion to
throw out *dicta* that have been since referred to as
law. Let us examine these *dicta.*

Holroyd, J., asserts broadly, that " the moment a
slave puts his foot upon the shores of this country,
his slavery is at an end." The reason is given thus :
" He ceases to be a slave in England, only because
there is no law which sanctions his detention in slavery." The reason given is not true. There *is a
law* in England which sanctions his detention. That
law is the municipal law of the domicile of the master, and which, by comity, the English Court is
bound to enforce, under certain circumstances. The
difficulty with Justice Holroyd is, that he does not
discriminate between the cases of the introduction
of slavery as a permanent institution, and the intro-

¹ 2 Barnewall & Cresswell, 448 (9 E. C. L. R. 138–150).

duction of a slave for a temporary purpose. Best, J., seems to have worked himself into a passion before he had an opportunity of delivering his opinion, and in the outset, gives notice that his "feelings are excited," and may "betray him into some warmth of expression."

This warning would be a sufficient justification to the cool inquirer after truth for passing by his opinion, but proper respect suggests a moment's examination. He speaks of slavery as "a crime;" denies that "in any case an action has been held to be maintainable in the municipal Courts of England, founded upon a right arising out of slavery;"[1] declares the law of Florida to be "anti-christian" and "contrary to the law of God," and consequently should not be recognized, and concludes by declaring that it was a maxim, that the comity of nations "cannot prevail in any case where it violates the law of our own country, *the law of nature, or the law of God.*" If it were necessary, *oyer* might be claimed of this maxim, as to its latter branch, and Justice Best would be probably puzzled to produce it. However, the necessity does not exist, for African slavery violates neither the one nor the other.

§ 196. In the case of the slave Grace, which subsequently arose before Lord Stowell in the Admiralty Court, the question was, whether upon the return of a slave to the slaveholding state, the master could

---

[1] In addition to the cases referred to by us, there was before the Court, at this time, the then recent case of Madrazzo v. Willes, 3 B. & A. 353, where Justice Best himself gave judgment for the plaintiff for 18,180*l.*, the value of a cargo of slaves.

assert his authority over her, or whether she was free? The decision of Lord Stowell maintained the authority of the master, holding that the Somersett case did not decide that the removal to a non-slave-holding state worked an emancipation, but simply that the courts of England would not lend their aid to enforce his rights.[1]

In this case, Lord Stowell enters upon the examination of the question with great candor. He unhesitatingly affirms that African slavery not only existed *in fact*, but was recognized by the courts prior to the case of Somersett. He refers particularly to the judgment of Lord Chancellor Hardwicke, in 1749, sustaining the counsel he had previously given the colonists as Sir Philip Yorke, and says that this judgment was reversed by Lord Mansfield. He speaks of Lord Mansfield's decision as " a change of the law," and as law which Lord Mansfield " himself had introduced."[2]

§ 197. Such are the English authorities. Those prior to Somersett's case, would seem to recognize slavery as existing under the municipal law of England. The *dicta* of some of the Judges in the later cases go to the opposite extreme, while that of Lord Stowell sustains it in full. At the date of the former there seems to have been but little information on the peculiar questions of international law. At the date of the latter, there seems to have been much excitement and zeal on the subject of slavery and the slave-trade, which the judicial ermine could

---

[1] 2 Hagg. Adm. Rep. 94.        [2] Pages 109, 114.

not exclude from the courts of justice.[1] About them all we may remark, that in no single case was the question made and decided as to the extent to which the comity of nations required the enforcement of the foreign law in the courts of England.

[1] Lord Stowell, even in a letter to Judge Story, glories in the appellation of "an abolitionist." Life and Letters of Story, vol. i, 555.

# CHAPTER X.

§ 198. WE have thus examined the opinions of foreign jurists and the adjudged cases in foreign courts, to see whether their decisions controvert the correctness of those conclusions to which upon principle we arrived.[1] We must think that to the honest

---

[1] Ante, § 174. Through communications in the public journals, I see the decision of a cause very lately (1856), in the highest judicial tribunal of Prussia, where the question was distinctly made and ruled as I lay down the law. Not having an authoritative report, I cannot insert it in the text. " The case was that of Dr. Ritter, a citizen of Brazil, against one Marcinello, his slave, whom he had brought to Berlin, where he told him he would simply treat him as a servant, but on his return home he should expect him to re-enter on his former condition. The slave, however, left his master, and instituted a suit against him, praying that he be called upon to prove his property within a given period, or be forever debarred, &c. The local tribunal of Berlin gave judgment in favor of the slave, but the Court of Appeals reversed this judgment, and the Supreme Court of Justice confirmed the judgment of the Court of Appeals. Mr. Grund also adds that, in the written reasons for this decision, which are always furnished by the Judges in Germany, the Court held that Dr. Ritter had good cause to claim Marcinello as his slave; it being proved that the relation of master and slave subsisted, and still

candid mind those conclusions remain, if not supported, at least uncontradicted, by the authorities.

§ 199. If these are the principles upon which the
slaveholder's rights would be adjudicated in the
courts of foreign independent nations, should the
same principles determine the relative rights of
master and slave within the States of the Union?
And is the obligation to observe this comity greater
or less among the States of this Union, than among
totally independent States? These questions demand now our consideration.

§ 200. The very name "Comitas inter communitates" exhibits the foundation of these principles. It
is comity, courtesy, founded upon mutual respect, and
promotive of mutual interest, the offspring of commerce and enlightenment, the handmaid of justice
and peace. Surely it does not require an argument
to prove that there is nothing in the nature of the
union of these States, which weakens those bonds
that bind together even independent States.

§ 201. On the contrary, the obligation to re-

subsists lawfully in Brazil, the domicile of both the plaintiff and
defendant; that by the plaintiff's own confession, defendant had
bought him for a certain sum of money; that it was proved by a
competent witness, a merchant by the name of Ree, that Marcinello, while at Rio Janeiro, lived in the defendant's house as a slave,
using the language and wearing the badge of servitude (going
barefooted), by which slaves in Brazil are recognized; and, finally,
because Marcinello's name occurs in the passport as a slave, belonging to the defendant. The relations between master and servant
are regulated by the laws of the country where both are domici-
liated, and a promise on the part of the master, within a certain
limited time and space not to use his rights over his slave to the
fullest extent, is not tantamount to their relinquishment."

spect and observe this comity, is greater upon the
Courts of the States of this Union, than upon the
Courts of independent States. The very Union
itself was framed to establish justice, insure domestic tranquillity, and promote the general welfare of
the people of these United States. If, then, we
mete out to each other no farther privileges, no
greater courtesy than if no bond of union existed,
"what thanks have we? Do not the publicans the
same?" Wherein is this Union made "more perfect," if it leaves the courts of the several States
regulating the rights of the sister States, by the
scanty courtesy of foreign tribunals? So long as
this Union exists, there is but one body, though
many members. The States are not foreign to each
other, for every purpose; and more especially in the
application of those principles of comity, which are
calculated so much to "insure domestic tranquillity."
The language of Judge Lockwood[1] is as praiseworthy
for its patriotism, as it is remarkable for its clear
legal conclusions. "The relations we sustain to our
sister States, also, furnish strong reasons why the
law of comity should be expanded, so as to meet
the exigencies arising out of that relation. What,
then, are the relations we sustain to other States,
which ought to affect our public policy towards
them? They are not foreign States. We are
bound up with them by the Constitution of the
United States into a Union, upon the preservation
of which no one can doubt that our own peace and
welfare greatly depend. Other nations may cherish

[1] Willard v. The People, 4 Scammon, 475.

friendly relations with each other, and endeavor to promote alliances and frequent intercourse, from fear of foreign war, or a desire of commercial prosperity. But to us, these relations and this intercourse, have a value and importance which are inestimable. They are the grounds of safety for our domestic peace, and for our hopes of the continuation of the happy government under which we live. Whatever injures one State, injures the others. It is, consequently, our duty to consult the good of all the States, and so to frame and administer our laws, that we give our sister States no real cause of offence. We ought to do them all the kind offices in our power, consistently with our duty to ourselves. Thus will be produced that concord, that union of affection and interest among the States, which may prove an enduring cement to that happy and glorious Union, upon the continuation of which our hopes of domestic peace and rational freedom so eminently depend. By the law of nations, it would be considered just cause of complaint, if we should arbitrarily refuse to the citizens of foreign nations at peace with us, permission to pass through our territories with their property. If this be so, as regards the citizens of foreign nations, how much greater propriety does there exist that we should extend this boon, if boon it be, to our fellow-citizens, who are also our friends, our neighbors, our relations. That our denial to the people of our sister States to have the right of passage for themselves and their slaves, would inflict on them a most serious injury, cannot be doubted. The bitterness which usually characterizes border animosities admonishes us of

the propriety of cultivating, by every just means in
our power, that social intercourse with our neighbors
which will be productive of mutual esteem and good
will.   Should we refuse them the privilege of taking
their slaves through our State, would there not be
danger that such refusal would engender feelings, on
their part, not favorable to a continuance of our
happy union?   Are there reasons of sufficient magnitude to induce us to risk such consequences?   I
think not.   Our interest, our duty, our love to our
whole country, conspire to prove the propriety of
allowing our fellow-citizens of our sister States, the
right to travel through this State, either as emigrants
or travellers, with their slaves, unless serious injury
will result to ourselves by giving such permission.
How injury can result to the people of this State,
by such a permission, I am entirely at a loss to conceive.   On the contrary, it might be shown that in
many instances it was to their decided advantage."

§ 202. This general view is confirmed by a closer
examination of our frame of government.   A refusal
on the part of an independent nation to extend to
another the benefit of this comity, would leave to the
nation thus treated the alternatives, either to reta-
liate, through her own courts, or to cease all commercial intercourse with the offending nation; or, if the
magnitude of the case justified it, to declare war for
this denial of her rights, under the Law of Nations.[1]
How is it with the States of this Union?   If Mas-

___

[1] Such wars have been waged, for the refusal to deliver up fugitive slaves.   Heineccius, De Præscr. &c. Exr. xxvi, § 12, citing
Lehmann, Chron. Spir. Lib. VII, cap. lxxi; Hertius, De Hom:
propr. Sect. iii, § 10.

sachusetts denies to Georgia the benefit of this comity, what alternatives has Georgia? She cannot cease commercial intercourse, because, under the Constitution, Congress has exclusive control over that subject. She cannot declare war, for of that power, also, is she divested by the terms of Union. She cannot even stipulate by treaty for the allowance of this comity to her citizens, for, by the same clause (Sect. X, Art. I), is she prohibited from entering into any agreement or compact with another State. The poor, miserable alternative of retaliating through her own courts, is all that is left to her—one little calculated to "secure domestic tranquillity." It cannot be believed that the wise framers of our Constitution, whose foresight and providence amounted almost to "prophetic ken," have left so fruitful a source of disturbance,—so dangerous a rock of offence, without some principles to govern us and some power to enforce. For every other conceivable cause of difficulty between the States provision is made, and the tribunals pointed out by which the conflicting rights are to be decided; and every power is taken away from the States, which, it was supposed, could be used for the purpose of annoying or vexing each other. Thus, the laying of tariffs on articles brought from other States, the regulation of commerce generally between the States, the keeping a standing army, or ships of war, &c., are all prohibited to the States. And, in other cases, where prohibition was impossible, but difficulties might arise, the duties of the several States are clearly defined;—such as the cases of fugitives from justice, and from service, the privileges of citizens, the credit given to judicial proceedings, &c.  Under this view of the Constitution (without stopping to inquire how far the several States have yielded any portion of their sovereignty), the conclusion is inevitable, that the spirit of this compact of Union imposes a weighty obligation upon every State composing it, with scrupulous nicety to extend to the citizens of every other State, the full measure of their rights under the Comity of Nations.[1]

§ 203.  It may at some day become a question of great practical importance, what remedy is provided, if any, to the other States, for the enforcement of this comity upon a State disposed to disregard this obligation.  For instance, if one State should enact that while, by the comity of nations, her courts are bound to enforce the municipal law of the other States in certain enumerated cases; yet, by virtue of her sovereign right to regulate all her internal affairs, she enacts that her courts shall thenceforward cease to respect this comity, and to enforce this law.  Are the other States remediless?  Can it be possible that the rights of the citizens of all the other States, are thus placed at the mercy of a refractory State?

§ 204.  In the supposed case, the issue stands thus: The remaining States demand of the offending State, through her courts, to enforce their municipal laws, in those cases where, by the comity of nations, those laws should decide the rights of the parties.  She

---

[1] See 3 Story Comm. on Const. § 1303; Green v. Sarmiento, 1 Peters C. C. R. 78, 79; Opinion of Livingston, J., in Mills v. Duryee, 7 Cranch, 486.

refuses to do so.   The other States cannot declare
war.   They cannot lay a tariff on her productions.
They cannot even purchase from her their peace.
They can look only to the Constitution, and the
powers granted thereby, for redress.   Do they provide for the case?

§ 205.  The fourth Article of the Constitution of
the United States seems to have for its principal
object the regulation of the intercourse of the several
States with each other.   The first and second sections of this Article are exclusively devoted to this
object.   An anxious solicitude is evidenced in these
sections to provide for every possible cause of difficulty between the several States.   Prominent and
first in these provisions stands this section:

" Full  faith  and  credit  shall  be  given  in  each
State  to  the  public  *acts*,  records,  and  judicial  proceedings  of  every  other  State.   And  the  Congress
may, by general laws, prescribe the manner in which
such *acts*, records, and proceedings, shall be proved,
and *the effect thereof.*"

§ 206.  That the words " public acts" refer to the
laws of the several States, is admitted by all commentators upon this clause.[1]   And this opinion was
acted on by the Congress of 1790 (composed partly
of the men who framed this instrument), when, in
the act passed to carry out this section, they provided for the authentication of the acts of the legislatures.[2]   If there could be any doubt on this point,

---

[1] Story, on the Constitution, vol. iii, § 1298; Bayard's Exposition of the Constitution, 120; Sergeant's Constitutional Law, 386.

[2] Statutes at Large, vol. i, p. 122; see U. S. v. Amedy, 11
Wheat. 407.

the history of the clause would remove it. In the original draft of a Constitution reported by the Committee, the words were inserted in full, "acts of the legislature,"[1] and was so agreed to. The present verbiage was adopted subsequently, when another more important alteration was made in the clause. In the first draft it read, " Full faith and credit shall be given, in each State, to the acts of the legislatures, and to the records and judicial proceedings of the courts and magistrates of every other State." No power, it will be perceived, was given to Congress to enforce this obligation on the States. The clause, as thus reported, was almost a transcript of a similar provision in the Articles of Confederation. The resolutions of instructions, passed by the Convention, and referred by them to the Committee of Detail, solemnly declared that Congress ought to possess the right " to legislate in all cases in which the harmony of the United States may be interrupted by the exercise of individual legislation."[2] In accordance with, and in the spirit of this instruction, originated the second clause of this section, reported thus by the Committee : "And the Legislature shall, by general laws, prescribe the manner in which such acts, records, and proceedings, shall be proved, and the effect which judgments obtained in one State shall have in another." " Congress may" was substituted, by amendment, for " Legislature shall ;" and then a motion was made to amend by substituting the words " and the effect thereof," for the words

[1] Proceedings and Debates of Convention, 267.
[2] Secret Proceedings and Debates, &c. 250.

"and the effect which judgments obtained in one State shall have in another." In other words, to make the power general, instead of confining it to the effect of judgments only. The amendment was carried by the vote of six States against three, and thus came the present verbiage of this clause.[1] Moreover, Mr. Madison's report of the debates on this section, shows conclusively that the framers of the instrument understood, by "public acts," the "statute laws." Thus, "Mr. Wilson and Dr. Johnson supposed that the acts of the legislatures should be included for the sake of acts of insolvency," &c.; and Mr. Randolph proposed a substitute, reading: "the act of any State, whether legislative, executive, or judicial."[2]

§ 207. What is the full force and meaning of the words "and the effect thereof?" A diversity of opinion has arisen among learned courts as to the proper construction of these words; some referring them to the authentication, and limiting the power of Congress to prescribing the effect of such authentication as evidence.[3] Others referring them to the "acts, records, and judicial proceedings," and thereby conferring on Congress the power of prescribing the effect of such acts, records, and judicial proceedings.[4]

[1] Journal of Convention, pp. 228, 305, 320, 321; 3 Story, on Constitution, § 1298.        [2] 5 Elliott's Debates, 488.

[3] Opinion of Livingston, J., in Hitchcock v. Aicken, 1 Caine's Rep. 471; Bissell v. Briggs, 9 Mass. 443 (Sewall, J., dissenting).

[4] Opinions of Radcliff, J., Kent, J., and Lewis, C. J., in Hitchcock v. Aicken, 1 Caine's Rep. 471; Armstrong v. Carsons, 2 Dall. 302; Bartlett v. Knight, 1 Mass. 401; Green v. Sarmiento, 1 Peters C. C. Rep. 78; see Federalist, No. xlii.

The history of this clause, given in the foregoing section, favors the latter construction.

In addition to the facts stated, it appears that when the clause was under discussion, Mr. Madison advocated it upon the express ground, that " he wished the Legislature (Congress) might be authorized to provide for the execution of judgments in other States, under such regulations as might be expedient.  He thought this might be safely done, and was justified by the nature of the union." Mr. Governeur Morris moved to commit, with the clause, the following proposition, which was done *nem. con* " The Legislature shall, by general laws, determine the proof and effect of such acts, records, and proceedings."[1]  This last proposition, agreed to without a dissenting voice, seems to place beyond question the construction put upon this section by the framers of it.  In the Virginia Convention, the Constitution underwent a most critical examination, section by section.  The stern State Right views of Mr. George Mason were alarmed at this clause, and he said, " How far it may be proper that Congress shall declare the effects of acts, I cannot clearly see into."  Mr. Madison replied, that " this was a clause which was absolutely necessary," and it was adopted without a dissenting voice.[2]  So that it appears that the conventions ratifying, as well as the framers of this clause, so construed it.  And such seems to be the interpretation of it by the Supreme Court of the United States, in the leading case of Mills v. Duryee,[3]

---

[1] 5 Elliott's Debates, 488.         [2] 3 Elliott's Debates, 584.
[3] 7 Cranch, 481; Hampden v. McConnell, 3 Wheaton, 234.

which has been adopted and approved ever since. In that case Mr. Justice Johnson dissented from the opinion of the Court, insisting that "*faith and credit* were terms strictly applicable to evidence," and that the record of a judgment authenticated under the Act of 1790, was only *primâ facie* evidence of indebtedness.   And considerable difference of opinion exists in the courts, as to the effect of the Act of 1790, declaring that the records, " authenticated as aforesaid, shall have such faith and credit given to them in every court within the United States, as they have, by law or usage, in the courts of the State from whence the said records are taken;" the one side holding that Congress, though authorized to declare the effect of the judgment in this act, has declared only the effect of the record as evidence; the others contending, that under this act Congress has declared the judgment as conclusive as in the State where it is rendered.   This controversy is foreign to our purpose, and reference is made to it only to show that neither side necessarily deny the construction of the clause in the Constitution to which we lean, though some of the advocates of the latter opinion have done so, as we have seen above.

§ 208.  We cannot forbear here to quote a portion of the very satisfactory reasoning of Mr. Justice Washington, in construing this clause of the Constitution.   In the case of Green v. Sarmiento,[1] he says, " That the intention of the Constitution to invest Congress with the power to declare the judgments of the courts of one State conclusive in every

---

[1] 1 Peters C. C. Rep. 78, 79.

other, and even to clothe them with a still more extended force and effect, corresponded with the strong and unambiguous expressions used in this article, will appear from the following considerations. First. It is presumable that the enlightened framers of that instrument knew that by the general comity of nations, and by the long-established rules of that country, whose decisions were once of binding authority in the United States, and to a certain period were still observed and adopted, a foreign judgment might be made the foundation of an action here, and was *primâ facie* evidence of its own correctness. It is highly probable, therefore, that the Constitution intended something more than merely to recognize an established rule of law. . . . If nothing more was meant, the provision was certainly unnecessary. It would on the contrary seem more natural that the Constitution, which was intended to 'form a more perfect union,' and a more close and intimate connection of the States than had existed under the Confederation, would consider the judgments of the several States in relation to each other as domestic rather than foreign judgments. Secondly. The change of the language of this section of the Constitution from the parallel section of the Articles of Confederation, affords a strong reason for the opinion, that the former was intended to give to the judgments of each State, within the other States, a more extensive force and effect than the rule of law, founded on mere comity, had allowed to foreign judgments."

§ 209. Mr. Story, in his Commentaries on the Constitution, when considering this section, indulges

in a similar train of thought. "It is hardly conceivable," he says,[1] " that so much solicitude should
have been exhibited to introduce, as between con-
federate States, much less between States united
under the same national government, a clause
merely affirmative of an established rule of law,
and not denied to the humblest or most distant
foreign nation. It was hardly supposable that the
States would deal less favorably with each other on
such a subject, where they could not but have
a common interest, than with foreigners. A motive of a higher kind must naturally have directed
them to the provision. It must have been to 'form
a more perfect union,' and to give to each State a
higher security and confidence in the others by attributing a superior sanctity and conclusiveness to
the public acts and judicial proceedings of all. There
could be no reasonable objection to such a course ;
on the other hand, there were many reasons in its
favor. The States were united in an indissoluble
bond with each other. The commercial and other
intercourse with each other would be constant and
infinitely diversified; credit would be everywhere
given and received, and right and property would
belong to citizens of every State in many other
States than that in which they resided."

§ 210. The attention of these learned jurists was
turned only to the evils which would flow from a
denial by the States to each other, of those principles of enlightened comity, which applied more
directly to the judgments and records of the courts;

[1] Vol. iii, § 1303.

and the possibility of such evils, in their judgment, justified the enlightened framers of the Constitution in inserting the section now under consideration. When we look to the still greater and momentous evils which would flow from a denial by the States to each other, of those principles of comity by which, under certain circumstances, the citizen carries with him into another State the protection of the municipal law of his domicile, the necessity for such a provision in the Constitution in reference to the laws of the several States is much more obvious, and every consideration suggested in favor of the exercise of such a power in reference to judgments, applies with tenfold power to the exercise of it in reference to the laws.

§ 211. Yet it is an undeniable fact, that the nature and extent of this power given to Congress, while it has undergone scrupulous investigations so far as records and judgments are concerned, has never attracted attention in the courts in that more important light, viz., the declaring the effect of the laws of one State, over the citizens of that State and their property, when within the territorial jurisdiction of another. In this light, this clause of the Constitution is not deserving the comment of the Federalist, that it "can be of little importance under any interpretation which it will bear."[1]— Nor does it afford an argument against this construction, that hitherto so important a power has remained dormant and unnoticed. The occasion for its exercise, so long as good faith and comity exist

---

[1] Federalist, No. xlii.

between the States, can never arise.   " The Constitution," says the Supreme Court, "was not intended
to provide merely for the exigencies of a few years,
but was to endure through a long lapse of ages, the
events of which were locked up in the inscrutable
purposes of Providence.   It could not be foreseen
what new changes and modifications of power might
be indispensable to effectuate the general objects of
the charter; and restrictions and specifications which,
at the present, might seem salutary, might in the
end prove the overthrow of the system itself.
Hence, its powers are expressed in general terms ;
leaving to the legislature from time to time to adopt
its own means, to effectuate legitimate objects, and
to mould and model the exercise of its powers as
its own wisdom and the public interests should require."[1]

§ 212. It may be replied, that this is a construction dangerous to the rights and sovereignty of the
States, by which, carried to its utmost limits, Congress might declare the legislative acts of one State
binding upon the citizens and property of every
other State.   But, *non sequitur*, it could be as well
and more plausibly argued, that because Congress
can declare the effect of a judgment, and render that
conclusive which before was only *primâ facie* evidence, a power never denied, that Congress might
go farther, and give to the judgments of one favored
State a priority of lien throughout the United States.
This clearly cannot be done, and the same reason
defeats both conclusions.   Congress can give no

---

[1] *Martin, heir of* Fairfax v. Hunter's Lessee, 1 Wheat. 304.

effect to a judgment in another State, which it did not have under the laws of the State where rendered. It may authorize it to follow into another State property upon which its lien had attached in its own State, but it cannot give it a lien on property upon which the laws of the State where it is rendered are powerless to create a lien. Congress may declare it to be record evidence, and hence conclusive, for such it is in the State where it is rendered; but it cannot provide a process to issue thereon against the body of the defendant in another State, when no such process is authorized in the State of its rendition.

§ 213. So, likewise, of the legislative acts of a State. It is not within the power of Congress to extend their effect over persons or property to which they did not apply *proprio vigore,* but it is within the competency of Congress to declare their effect and extend their protection over such persons and property wherever found within the limits of the United States. If, in the exercise of this power, Congress should infringe upon any of those rights reserved to the States, for example, the control *bonâ fide* of their internal police regulations, the act would be unconstitutional and inoperative.[1] It may be a difficult question to decide, where the State's power to regulate police ends, and when this power is exercised *bonâ fide.* This must be left necessarily to the wisdom of the respective governments, and the purity and independence of the judiciary.

[1] See Prigg v. Commonwealth of Pa. 16 Peters, 471, 625; Willard v. The People, 4 Scammon, 470.

§ 214. Our conclusion then is, that should any one of the States prove so recreant to the great obligation resting upon her under the bond of union, as by legislative enactment to deny to the citizens of the other States, who may be within her borders, the protection of their municipal laws, to which they are entitled under the comity of nations, a corrective power is lodged by the Constitution in the Congress of the United States. Hence, should any State, by its local enactments, deny to the slaveholder, those privileges and protection which we have seen are awarded to him, through comity, by the courts of independent nations, it would be the solemn, though delicate duty of the national legislature, to exercise this power in his behalf.

§ 215. From this view of the nature and powers of the Union, under the Constitution, our conclusions, upon mere abstract reasoning, would be, that the rules heretofore deduced from the principles of the comity of nations, as recognized by independent States, with increased sanction apply to the courts of the several States.   Those rules were,

1st. That where there is a change of domicile from a slaveholding to a non-slaveholding State, the *animus remanendi* works of itself, and *instanter*, a change of the *status* of the slave so long as he remains within that territory.

2d. That the mere transit of the master with his slave, either from necessity or convenience, through the territory of a non-slaveholding State, does not change the *status* of the slave.

3d. That as a general rule, where there is a *bonâ fide* temporary residence of a master with his slave in a non-slaveholding State, the *animus revertendi* will protect the master's right in his slave, to the extent of his personal service, and the right to return with him to his domicile. At the same time, if this privilege is used to evade the local laws of the State in reference to slavery, or the exercise of it becomes so general as to interfere with the policy or be prejudicial to the interest of the government or its people, the courts will not violate the principles of comity in refusing their aid in enforcing these rights.

# CHAPTER XI.

§ 216. HAVING arrived at those rules which ought
to govern the decision of this delicate question, let
us examine the adjudged cases, to see how far they
have been recognized by the Federal and State courts.
It would be proper to premise, that with us, as in
England, these peculiar questions of international
law have not, until lately, received that attention to
which they were entitled. Having adopted, almost
universally, the common law of England, and with
it many of its unfounded prejudices against the civil
law, the profession have confined their researches
very generally to those fountains whence the common law flowed. Upon these questions, we have
seen that they were indeed " broken cisterns." Mr.
Story, it is true, broke through the barriers, and has
enriched his many valuable treatises with the wisdom of the continental jurists. Unfortunately for
us, however, upon the question we are now considering, he permitted his anti-slavery prejudices to bias
his judgment and blind his vision; and his work on
the " Conflict of Laws" has rather tended to make
the " darkness visible," than to place upon a sound

basis the determination of the question at issue.[1] The same prejudices have necessarily, to a great extent, entered into the adjudication of the several courts; the cases generally arising in a non-slave-holding State, and the decisions being pronounced generally by anti-slavery men. Hence, we find in almost every decision, the announcement of the erroneous principle, that African slavery is contrary to the law of nature, and is supported solely by municipal law; a position which, we think, is successfully shown to be incorrect.

§ 217. This question has never been directly decided by the Supreme Court of the United States. It was alluded to in the argument and decision of the case of Prigg v. The Commonwealth of Pennsylvania,[2] but only incidentally, it not being at all necessary to the decision of that case. The opinion was written out by Mr. Justice Story, and his *dicta* upon this question deserve our notice. He says: "By the general law of nations, no nation is bound to recognize the state of slavery, as to foreign slaves within its territorial dominions, when it is in opposition to its own policy and institutions, in favor of the subjects of other nations where slavery is recognized. If it does it, it is as a matter of comity, and not as a matter of international right. The state of

---

[1] To such an extent did this prejudice carry him, that in the case of La Jeune Eugenie, he held the "slave-trade to be a violation of the law of nations," against the decision of every court in England and America. Upon which decision Mr. Wildman, an English writer, remarks, that it is "elaborately incorrect." Wildman's International Law, 11.

[2] 16 Peters, 610.

slavery is deemed to be a mere municipal regulation, founded upon and limited to the range of territorial laws. This was fully recognized in Somersett's case. It is manifest, from this consideration, that if the Constitution had not contained this clause (in reference to fugitive slaves), every non-slaveholding State in the Union would have been at liberty to have declared free all runaway slaves coming within its limits, and to have given them entire immunity and protection against the claims of their masters; a course which would have created the most bitter animosities, and engendered perpetual strife between the different States."

§ 218. In this extract, truth and error are strangely blended; a characteristic of all that fell from this distinguished jurist on the subject of slavery. The proposition announced in the outset, is true, being the exception, viz., "when it is in opposition to its own policy and institutions." The second clause is ridiculous, viz., "if it does it, it is a matter of comity," &c., for when did a nation, through comity, ever recognize the municipal law of another, "in opposition to its own policy?" That these principles were settled in Somersett's case, we have shown to be untrue, as they were never alluded to, and could not be settled. And then his conclusion, that "from this consideration," &c., the clause in the Constitution is the only protection of the slaveholding States, is a perfect *non sequitur*. Or rather, in more logical phrase, it is a *petitio principii;* for he assumes the fact to exist, that the recognition of foreign slavery would be violative of the interests and policy of the non-slaveholding States. The closing remark is eminently true, that the denial of this comity, on the part of the non-slaveholding States, would be "a course creating the most bitter animosities, and engendering perpetual strife between the different States." That such would have been the law, in the absence of the clause in the Constitution referred to, we cannot admit. We adopt rather, the more satisfactory and enlightened opinion of Mr. Justice Baldwin, that "the Constitution does not *confer* but *secures* the right to reclaim fugitive slaves against State legislation."[1] To which latter opinion the Supreme Court of the United States, in the late case of Jones v. Van Zandt, have given their unqualified approval.[2]

§ 219. The case of Butler v. Hopper,[3] decided by Mr. Justice Washington, on the Circuit, proceeds entirely and correctly upon the local law of Pennsylvania, which protected the sojourner in the use of his slave. This act, in this particular, was affirmatory of the principles for which we are contending; and the decision in Butler v. Hopper was correct, in the absence of the local law.

§ 220. Vaughn v. Williams,[4] decided by Mr. Justice McLean, on the Circuit, affirms the principle, that an owner of slaves who takes them into a non-slaveholding State, keeps them at labor for six months, announces his determination to become a resident of such State, and in pursuance thereof casts his vote at elections, thereby forfeits his right to them as slaves.

[1] Johnson v. Tompkins et al. 1 Baldwin's Rep. 571.
[2] 5 Howard, 229.
[3] 1 Wash. C. C. R. 499.     [4] 3 McLean's Reports, 530.

§ 221. In Jones v. Van Zandt,[1] the same Judge presiding, this *dictum* appears : "If a person held in slavery go beyond the jurisdiction where he is so held, and into another sovereignty where slavery is not tolerated, he becomes free.  And this would be the law of these States, had the Constitution of the United States adopted no regulation upon the subject."  No argument or authority is offered to support this *dictum*, and the only remark necessary for our purpose is, that in the decision on appeal of this case by the Supreme Court, the very opposite doctrine is asserted, and acquiesced in by the whole Court, Justice McLean being one of them.[2]

§ 222. In Strader et al. v. Graham,[3] where slaves who had been temporarily taken to Ohio, returned to Kentucky, and subsequently sought to base a claim for freedom thereon, the Supreme Court held that it had no jurisdiction; the question being one which belonged exclusively to the State of Kentucky. "The condition of the negroes, therefore, as to freedom or slavery, after their return, depended altogether upon the laws of that State, and could not be influenced by the laws of Ohio."  I am not prepared to sanction, fully, this statement; for, if the residence in Ohio has effected the emancipation of the slave, that *status* would not be changed by a return to the slaveholding State.

§ 223. We come now to consider the case of Dred Scott v. Sanford, decided by the Supreme Court, December Term, 1856.[4]  The question we are con-

---

[1] 2 McLean's Rep. 601.

[2] Jones v. Van Zandt, 5 Howard (U. S.), 229.

[3] 10 Howard, 2.              [4] 19 Howard, 1.

sidering was only incidental to the point decided, which was identical with that decided by Lord Stowell, in reference to the slave Grace, and was adjudicated by the Court in accordance with that decision. The Chief Justice (Taney), who delivered the opinion of the Court, did not pretend to consider the point we are arguing; Mr. Justice Nelson expressly declined to enter upon the investigation. Others of the Court did, and we will examine briefly their views. Mr. Justice Daniel comments upon the Somersett case, and restricts the decision to the mere question of the detention of the slave in bondage, within the realm of England, and shows how the decision of Lord Stowell so restricts it.

§ 224. But Mr. Justice Campbell enters more at large upon the question, and shows a familiarity with it, exhibited in few judicial opinions reported in our books. In the absence of any prohibitory law he shows, that the slave would not be liberated by the accident of his introgression into a State, and adds: "The relation of domestic slavery is recognized by the law of nations, and the interference of the authorities of one State with the rights of a master belonging to another, without a valid cause, is a violation of that law."[1] He shows that the reclaiming of slaves was universally allowed by the public law of Europe for many years, and that it was first curtailed by the enactment of laws of prescription in favor of privileged communes. Bremen, Spire, Worms, Vienna, and Ratisbon, in Germany; and Carcassonne, Béziers, Toulouse, and Paris, in France,

[1] 19 Howard, 101.

acquired these privileges at an early period. This fact explains the cases, referred to by Bodin, and cited in the discussion of the case in "Causes Célè-bres," already referred to. He then examines the Somersett case, and shows the extent of that decision, especially as explained by Lord Stowell in the case of the slave Grace, and affirms this latter decision. He ridicules justly the excited and inflammatory declamation of the French advocates, in the case of Verdelin, and shows how unfounded was the pretence, that negro slavery, and other bondage equally as severe, never existed in England.

§ 225. Mr. Justice McLean, in his dissenting opinion, maintains the opposite doctrine; basing his whole argument upon the principle asserted by Judge Story in Prigg v. The State of Pennsylvania, that "the state of slavery is deemed to be a mere municipal regulation, founded upon and limited to the range of the territorial laws." Having shown that this is not correct, in a former chapter, it is unnecessary to consider the corollaries drawn therefrom.[1] We may remark, that Judge McLean refers to several cases decided by the Supreme Courts of Missouri and other States, in almost all of which, upon examination, it will be found that the slave acquired a domicile in the free State; and hence, on returning to a slaveholding State, carried the *status* acquired in the new domicile. A principle we have seen to be perfectly correct, unless it be against the policy of the old domicile to allow the increase of free negroes within it. We admit, however, that there

[1] 19 Howard, 135-170.

are cases where the Judges in slaveholding States have carelessly recognized the deduction drawn from the Somersett case.

§ 226. Mr. Justice Curtis also dissented. He lays down clearly and correctly the rule as to personal statutes following the person, and says, "that the laws of a country do not rightfully operate upon and fix the *status* of persons within its limits *in itinere*, or who are abiding there for definite temporary purposes, as for health, curiosity, or occasional business." That it is true that a State may, by law, declare its determination not to recognize this comity, and such a law the courts must obey. But until such a law is passed, "it is not within the province of any judicial tribunal to refuse such recognition from any political considerations, or any view it may take of the exterior political relations between the State and one or more foreign States, or any impressions it may have, that a change of foreign opinion and action, on the subject of slavery, may afford a reason why the State should change its own action." Applying these principles to the case before him, Judge Curtis finds that *law* in the *ordinance* which prohibited involuntary servitude or slavery within the territory of Wisconsin, where the negro had been taken. He argues the question at length upon the several provisions of the statute, and adds, "I must conclude, therefore, that it was the will of Congress that the state of involuntary servitude of a slave, coming into the territory with his master, should cease to exist." (p. 200.) If this was a correct inference, the law is correctly expounded by him. We must dissent from this inference. The

principle, however, as we have laid it down, is fully
recognized and clearly stated.[1]

§ 227. We come now to consider the decisions of
the courts of the several States. From their great
number, we are not allowed to examine them with
that minuteness that would otherwise be desirable.
We shall look briefly at the adjudications of each
State.

Prominent and chiefly relied on by those who hold
the opposite opinion stands the case of The Commonwealth v. Aves, decided in Massachusetts.[2] The
case was elaborately and well argued by counsel on
both sides. The points were distinctly made before
the Court. The claim of the master was placed
upon its proper basis by his counsel, Mr. Curtis; and
no better answer could be made to the decision of
the Court, than is furnished in the published brief
of the counsel. The Court admit the doctrine, that
the personal *status* of the slave is not changed by
the removal into a non-slaveholding State; and the
general principle, that by the comity of States, the
courts of one will recognize and enforce, in certain
cases, the municipal laws of the other. But the
Court decides that this doctrine does not apply, "because if it did, it would follow as a necessary consequence that all those persons, who, by force of local
laws, and in all foreign places where slavery is permitted, have acquired slaves as property, might
bring their slaves here and exercise over them the
rights and power which an owner of property might
exercise, and for any length of time short of acquir-

[1] 19 Howard, 197 et seq.          [2] 18 Pick. 193–225.

14

ing a domicile; that such an application of the law
would be wholly repugnant to our laws, entirely inconsistent with our policy and our fundamental
principles, and is therefore inadmissible." In a subsequent portion of the decision, the Court disclaims
giving any opinion " upon the case where an owner
of a slave in one State is *bonâ fide* removing to another State where slavery is allowed, and in so doing,
necessarily passes though a free State; or where, by
accident or necessity, he is compelled to touch or
land therein, remaining no longer than necessary."

§ 228. The difficulty into which the Court has
fallen, is almost self-evident. If the master can control the slave for an hour, while passing *in tran-
situ*, why will not the same law protect him for a
day, a week, a month? The only sensible distinction is, that the courts will protect him so long as
that protection contravenes not their own public
policy, and no longer. The Court errs, in saying,
that "a necessary consequence" of applying the doctrine of comity to the case then at bar, was, that it
would protect all masters in any residence "short of
acquiring a domicile." There might be such a case
truly "repugnant to their laws," and hence without
the pale of comity; while the case then at bar was
in no wise repugnant to their laws, as was clearly
shown by the argument of Mr. Curtis. Moreover,
as Mr. Justice Curtis shows in his decision in the
Dred Scott case, just examined, this is a question
for legislative and not judicial discretion. Until the
legislature speak, either directly or by necessary inference, the courts are bound to respect the comity

of States. This case has been since followed by the Courts of Massachusetts.[1]

§ 229. In Connecticut, this question was directly made and decided, in the case of Jackson v. Bullock,[2] the year succeeding the decision in Commonwealth v. Aves (1837). It was not necessary to the case, on account of a statute of Connecticut, upon which a majority of the Court rested their decision. The Court divided in their opinion, three Judges affirming the case Commonwealth v. Aves, and two maintaining the principles for which we contend. The majority of the Court declined to enter upon the examination of the authorities upon this question, adopting simply the decision in the case referred to. Our remarks in reference to that case, consequently apply to their decision. It is a curious fact, however, that the majority state that "it had been conceded that the master could claim nothing by comity," when that was the very question before them for decision. The dissenting opinion of Mr. Justice Bissell, concurred in by Church, J., is able, liberal, and convincing. Grasping the whole subject, while he admits his sympathies to be with the slave, he drives away every prejudice, and boldly follows to those conclusions to which principle and law guided him. So far from considering it to be conceded that the master claimed nothing from comity, he understood his rights to rest solely upon it. Clearly laying down the general rule as to *status*, and the principles of comity, he necessarily is brought

---

[1] Commonwealth v. Taylor, 3 Metc. 72.
[2] 12 Connecticut Rep. 38.

to consider the question,—the only question in such cases,—does the enforcement of such comity contravene the public policy of the State, or the rights of its citizens? His argument upon this question is worthy of great consideration. "Do the claims set forth in this return, so far clash with the rights of our citizens, and are they so opposed to the institutions and the essential interests of this community, as that the law of the domicile must yield? This, as it seems to me, is the whole inquiry, and it lies within very narrow limits."

§ 230. "The discussion, however, has taken a wide range, and many considerations have been urged upon us, which, in my judgment, have very little to do with the case to be decided. Much has been said of the injustice and immorality of slavery; and both moral and political writers have been summoned to our bar to bear testimony to the enormities of the system. Those considerations might very properly be urged, and have their influence elsewhere. They might with propriety and should have been addressed to our pilgrim fathers, when they were about to introduce the system, and to bring this foul stain upon our otherwise free institutions. They may properly enough be urged upon the legislative department of the government. And I am not about to deny the propriety of urging them upon the moral sense and feelings of the community. With these topics, and with the excitement that is abroad on this subject, whether favorable or adverse to the present claim, I can have nothing to do. Sitting here to administer the law, I cannot undertake to be wiser than the laws and constitution of my country, nor purer than those great and good men by whom they were ordained. As a citizen and as a man I may admit the injustice and immorality of slavery; that its tendencies are all bad; that it is productive of evil, and of evil only. But as a jurist, I must look at that standard of morality which the law prescribes. 'Whatever,' says Chief Justice Marshall, 'might be the answer of a moralist to the question, a jurist must search for its solution in those principles of action, which are sanctioned by the usages, the national acts, and the general assent of that portion of the world of which he considers himself a part, and to whose bar the appeal is made.'

"Again, it has been urged, that slavery is opposed to the laws of nature and of God; that its existence among us is forbidden by our obligation to these laws; and that they are paramount to the law of the domicile.

"I may be permitted to inquire here, what is the precise meaning of this argument; and how far it is intended to be carried? Is it meant that the whole law of slavery is absolutely void? And that no obligation whatever can grow out of it? Is it to be seriously urged, that no obligation, no contract, bottomed on slavery, as a system, can be enforced in our courts of justice? Unless the argument is to be carried this length, it is difficult to see its application to the case; and before we can be called upon to take this ground, we must be asked to denounce a system, which has prevailed among us for more than a century, to blot out from our statute-book the various enactments by which it has been recognized and regulated, and to reverse the repeated decisions of this Court.

"Again, it is insisted with much apparent reliance on the objection, that if we hold this return to be sufficient, we sanction and adopt the whole law of slavery, as it exists in Georgia, and that we establish their system among us, with all its odious and revolting features. I cannot so understand the law. The simple inquiry upon this demurrer is, whether the claim of the respondent, as stated on the return, conflicts with our laws? It might as well be urged, were a native of Hindostan to come here to reside for a season, that by allowing him to retain the custody of his infant child, we adopted the laws and the customs of Hindostan in regard to that relation, and of course must allow the parent either to sacrifice his child to his idols or expose him to perish.

"And again: it has been urged, that if we suffer this respondent to take his slave with him to Georgia, she will there be subjected to all the rigors and injustice of their system. This may be true; and we may regret that it is so; but are we, therefore, to say that she is emancipated? The State of Georgia, in the exercise of her

undoubted rights as a sovereign State, has enacted laws
upon this subject, which she deems essential to the security of her citizens, and the protection of their interests;
and so long as she enforces these laws within her own
jurisdiction, we surely are not to sit in judgment upon
them. If, indeed, she seeks to enforce them here, and
calls upon our tribunals to assist in so doing, we may
then, as we are now called upon to do, determine
whether their execution here will conflict with our own
laws and institutions."

§ 231. In Pennsylvania, as early as 1780, an act
was passed providing for the abolition of slavery,
but excepting from its operation " slaves attending
upon delegates in Congress, foreign ministers and
consuls, and persons passing through or sojourning
in" the State. In case of sojourners, it was " provided, that such slaves be not retained in the State
longer than six months." Many decisions have been
made, construing this statute, in none of which have
the views of the Court denied the principles for
which we contend.[1]

In New York, Rhode Island, and New Jersey,
similar statutes were passed soon after the adoption
of the Federal Constitution.[2]

§ 232. In Illinois this question underwent a most
searching and thorough examination in the case of
Willard v. The People.[3] It was well argued by the
counsel, and fully considered by the Court. The
case made was that of the transit of a master with

---

[1] See Butler et al. v. Delaplaine, 7 Serg. & Rawle, 378; Commonwealth v. Halloway, 6 Binney, 213; 1 Browne, 113; 1 Watts,
155; 4 Yeates, 204; Addis, 284; 2 S. & R. 305.

[2] 1 Revised Laws of New York, 657; Laws of Rhode Island
(Ed. of 1798), 607; Laws of New Jersey, 679.

[3] 4 Scammon Rep. 461–477.

his slave through the territory of Illinois. The whole Court concurred in the opinion, that the master's rights were in no wise affected by this transit; and Justice Scates, who delivered the opinion of the Court, says, "It would be productive of great and irremediable evils of discord, of heartburnings, and alienation of that kind and fraternal feeling which should characterize the American brotherhood, and tend greatly to weaken the common bond of union among us, and our nationality of character, interest, and feeling. It would be startling, indeed, if we should deny to our neighbors and kindred that common right of free and safe passage which foreign nations would hardly dare deny. The recognition of this right is no violation of our Constitution. It is not an introduction of slavery into this State, as was contended in argument, and the slave does not become free by the Constitution of Illinois, by coming into the State for the mere purpose of passage through it."

Lockwood, J., and Wilson, C. J., while concurring in the judgment of the Court, were not satisfied with the narrow grounds on which it was based. The former delivered a separate opinion, in which the latter concurred, placing the decision upon the broad ground of "comitas inter communitates;" denying that it contravened the policy of the State, or introduced slavery therein.

§ 233. In Indiana, a similar view has been taken of the law. On a return to a habeas corpus, before Justice Morris, the question was distinctly made. He says: "By the law of nature and of nations, and the necessary and legal consequences resulting from the civil and political relations subsisting between the citizens as well as the States of this federative republic, I have no doubt but the citizen of a slave State has a right to pass, upon business or pleasure, through any of the States, attended by his slaves or servants; and while he retains the character and rights of a citizen of a slave State, his right to reclaim his slave would be unquestioned."[1]

§ 234. In Kentucky, in an early and leading case, this doctrine underwent investigation, and the distinction contended for, drawn clearly by the Court, viz.: that a "fixed residence," or being domiciled in a non-slaveholding State, would operate to release the slave from the power of the master; but that the transient passing or sojourning therein, had no such effect. The Court argues the question at great length, and upon the law of nations, and adds: " If nations, amidst all their jealousies and thirst for power, could adopt such rules to govern themselves, with regard to their neighbors, how much stronger is the reason and propriety of the rule when applied between the different branches of the American family? Can it be for a moment supposed that any one of them would reject a principle so strongly based in reason, propriety, and the nature of things?"[2] The subsequent decisions in Kentucky, maintain clearly the distinction laid down in this leading case.[3] In the last case, before the Court of Appeals of

[1] 3 Amer. Jurist, 407.
[2] Rankin v. Lydia, 2 A. K. Marsh. 467.
[3] Bush's Rep. v. White and wife, 3 Monroe, 104; 1 Bibb, 423; Graham v. Strader, 5 B. Monr. 173; 7 B. Monr. 635; Davis v. Tingle et al. 8 B. Monr. 545; 9 B. Monr. 565. In 8 B.

Kentucky,[1] all the previous cases are ably reviewed by Chief Justice Marshall, and the decisions defended both upon principle and authority.

§ 235. In Missouri there have been numerous adjudications. In the early and leading case of Winny v. Whiteside,[2] the Court maintained that a traveller through a non-slaveholding territory, does not thereby lose his property in his slave, " nor do we believe that any advocate for this portion of the species ever seriously calculated on such a decision." The true criterion was, whether the master, " by his length of residence, indicated an intention of making that place his residence, and that of his slave." In many of the later cases this true criterion is preserved.[3] In the case of Julia v. McKinney,[4] though the decision of the Court is right upon the facts, yet the majority of the Court, in giving their reasons, lost sight of the true distinction. Wash, Judge, however, in his dissenting opinion, tenaciously held to the question of *intention*, as the criterion; and in the subsequent case of Nat v. Ruddle,[5] the Court again returned to their old mooring. In two subsequent cases, the Court seem to adopt a new test, viz., whether the master made any unnecessary delay in the non-slaveholding territory, thereby placing an incident and fact as the criterion,

Monr. 546, the query is suggested, whether the owner of a life interest in a slave can, by domiciling him in another State, defeat the rights of the remaindermen.

[1] 9 B. Monr. 565.

[2] 1 Missouri Rep. 472.

[3] La Grange v. Chouteau, 2 Missouri, 19; Milly v. Smith, Ibid. 37; Ralph v. Duncan, 3 Missouri, 194; Nat v. Ruddle, Ibid. 400.

[4] 3 Missouri, 270.          [5] Ibid. 400.

instead of the intention of becoming resident.[1] In a still later case, Robert v. Melugen, however, the Court base their decision upon the question of intention.[2]

§ 236. In Louisiana, the true distinction was early taken in the case of Lunsford v. Coquillon.[3] The Court state that great stress was laid upon the removal to Ohio, *"with the intention of settling, and it is this circumstance which governs the case."* There has been no variation in the subsequent decisions.[4]

§ 237. In Virginia, the opinions of the courts have been equally clear. Lewis v. Fullerton,[5] an early case, established that the removal of a slave into a non-slaveholding State, "for a mere transitory purpose, and with the *animus revertendi*," did not effect the emancipation of the slave. And this decision has been not only followed, but distinctly approved in the subsequent cases.[6]

§ 238. In Maryland, this question underwent the earliest and perhaps most thorough investigation which, at that time, it had ever received on this side of the Atlantic. The case arose in 1799, upon a negro, brought by Lord Baltimore from England; and Somersett's case was invoked to show that the mere fact of the foot of a slave touching British soil, worked an emancipation. The case was most tho-

---

[1] Rachel v. Walker, 4 Missouri, 350; Wilson v. Melvin, Ibid. 592.　　　　　　[2] 9 Miss. 170.

[3] 14 Martin's Rep. 401.

[4] Josephine v. Poultney, 1 La. Ann. R. 329; Louis v. Cabarrus et al. 7 Louis. Rep. 170.　　　　[5] 1 Rand. 15.

[6] Hunter v. Fulcher, 1 Leigh, 172; Gilmer, 143.

roughly and learnedly argued upon the law of England, the argument following, to a great extent, the course pursued by the counsel in Somersett's case. The Court of Appeals denied the authority of that case, and held that the negro was still a slave.[1] In this case, the principle of the comity of nations was not invoked nor considered. The subsequent cases, however, seem to be in accordance with this principle.[2]

§ 239. This review of the decisions of the courts of the Union, shows that the weight, both of numbers and authority, preponderate in sustaining those conclusions to which we arrived upon principle, and we may safely say that neither of those Courts whose decisions are opposed to these conclusions, have either met or attempted to answer the arguments from which they must inevitably follow. We may add, that in all of the States, it has been held, wherever the question arose, that upon the slave being subsequently found within a slaveholding State, the master's rights and authority were not impaired by the temporary sojourn of the slave within the limits of a non-slaveholding State.[3]

[1] Mahony v. Ashton, 4 Harr. & McH. 322.

[2] David v. Porter, 4 Harr. & McH. 418; Porter v. Butler, 3 Harr. & McH. 168.

[3] Story's Conf. of Laws, § 96 a (3d Ed.); Collins v. America, 9 B. Monr. 575; Batty et al. v. Horton, 5 Leigh, 622; Hunter v. Fulcher, 1 Leigh, 179; Lewis v. Fullerton, 1 Randolph, 15; Louis v. Cabarrus et al. 7 Louisiana, 170; Graham v. Strader, 7 B. Monr. 635. Judge Tucker, in his opinion, in 5 Leigh, 622, seems to lay stress upon the fact that there was no judgment of the Courts of the free State, declaring the slave free. In that event, he seems

to think the judgment would be conclusive everywhere. In this opinion, he is opposed to Judge Roane and the whole Court of Appeals, in the case of Lewis v. Fullerton, 1 Rand. 15, where it was held that a judgment on a *habeas corpus,* in Ohio, in favor of the slave, does not establish his right to freedom in Virginia. It seems clear that the judgment could not be conclusive, unless the master was a party to the case; nor, indeed, until Congress should by law prescribe the effect of such judgments in other States. See also 5 B. Monr. 173.

# CHAPTER XII.

SAME SUBJECT CONTINUED.—FUGITIVE SLAVES, AND OF
THE RIGHT OF THE MASTER TO REMOVE THE SLAVE.

§ 240. HAVING thus shown, upon principle and
authority, that the voluntary removal of a slave, by
the master, into a non-slaveholding State, does not
necessarily, but only in specified cases, emancipate
the slave, it follows, *a fortiori*, that the escape of the
slave into a non-slaveholding State would not impair the master's rights.[1] For even in Holland, where,
according to Christinæus and Grœnewegen, the
comity of nations is disregarded, when invoked in
behalf of a master, the decisions have never been
extended to fugitives; on the contrary, they are expressly withdrawn from the operation of the decision.[2]

§ 241. In the United States, this latter question
is provided for in the fundamental law. The Constitution of the United States, in the fourth Article and

[1] Louis v. Cabarrus et al. 7 Louisiana, 170.

[2] Van der Linden, on the Laws of Holland, Bk. I, ch. ii, sect.
iii, translated by J. Henry, and authorities there cited. In the
West Indies, prior to the abolition of slavery by Great Britain, the
extradition of fugitives was universal. After that time, the British
Islands became the house of refuge for them; the Governors refusing to deliver them up. Schœlcher, Colonies Françaises, 115.

2d Section, providing, that "no person held to service or labor in one State, under the laws thereof, escaping into another, shall, in consequence of any law or regulation therein, be discharged from such service or labor, but shall be delivered up on claim of the party to whom such service or labor may be due."[1]

§ 242. In 1793, Congress passed an act for the purpose of carrying this provision into execution.[2] This act was found to be ineffectual, on account of submitting the owner to the State Courts and Judges for the adjudication of his rights. In 1850, a more stringent and effectual statute was passed, constituting Federal officers for the execution of its provisions. When we come to examine the master's right to the slaves as property, we may consider more minutely the provisions of these acts, and the decisions of the Courts upon them.[3]

§ 243. For nearly fifty years the Act of 1793 was executed and enforced without its validity or constitutionality being seriously questioned.[4] In Massachusetts, in 1823, the question was directly made as to its constitutionality, and the Supreme Judicial'

---

[1] Statutes at Large of U. S. vol. i, p. 302.

[2] Ibid.

[3] For the present, we refer only to some of the cases. See Hill v. Low, 4 Wash. C. C. Rep. 327; Ex parte, Simmons, Ibid. 396; Ibid. 461; Baldwin's C. C. R. 577, 579; Prigg v. Commonwealth of Pa. 16 Peters, 539; Stuart v. Laird, 1 Cranch, 299; 1 Wheat. 304; 6 Ibid. 264; Jones v. Van Zandt, 2 McLean's C. C. R. 596.

[4] Opinion of Judge Story, Prigg v. Comm. of Pa. 16 Peters, 621; Wright v. Deacon, 5 Serg. & Rawle, 63; Glen v. Hodges, 9 John. R. 67; In the matter of Clark, 9 Wend. 219; Jack v. Martin, 12 Wend. 311.

Court were unanimous in affirming the validity of the statute, although there was a dissenting opinion upon a collateral point.[1] In New York, in 1834, the same question came before the Supreme Court, and the constitutionality of the act unanimously affirmed.[2] Nor indeed has any court in any of the States ever declared these acts to be void, yet their validity has been distinctly denied before the courts, and though there fully and unqualifiedly sustained, is still denied even in the highest legislative department of the government.[3] In Prigg v. The Commonwealth of Pennsylvania (1836), the question was most elaborately discussed before the Supreme Court of the United States; and though the Court differed in their reasons for the judgment rendered, yet they were unanimous in the opinion of the constitutionality and validity of the Act of 1793. Judge Story, who delivered the opinion of the majority in that case, argues the question with convincing ability.[4] In Jones v. Van Zandt (1847), the Supreme Court of the United States again unanimously affirm the validity of the act.

[1] Commonwealth v. Griffith, 2 Pick. 11–19.
[2] Jack v. Martin, 12 Wend. 323.
[3] Appendix to Cong. Globe, vol. xxv, p. 1100.
[4] 16 Peters, 539–674. Mr. J. Wayne says (p. 637), " All of the Judges concur in the declaration that the provision of the Constitution was a compromise between the slaveholding and the non-slaveholding States, to secure to the former fugitive slaves as property. All of the members of the Court, too, except my Brother Baldwin, concur in the opinion, that legislation by Congress, to carry the provision into execution, is constitutional; and he contends that the provision gives to the owners of fugitive slaves all the rights of seizure and removal which legislation could give; but he concurs

§ 244. With such an unbroken chain of authority
upon the side of this legislation, it would be an act
of supererogation in a work of this character to discuss at length the arguments of the objectors. These
arguments are diligently collected, and most elaborately, ingeniously, and eloquently presented, by Mr.
Sumner, in a speech delivered before the Senate of
the United States, on the 26th of August, 1852. No
better reply need be given to that speech than that
contained in the speeches of Senators on that occasion; and more especially that of Mr. Badger,
whose effort is as distinguished for its logical reasoning as its withering sarcasm.[1] I cannot refrain from
quoting, in this connection, from the opinion of Mr.
Justice McLean, in Prigg v. The Commonwealth,
&c.,[2] one portion of his reply to the favorite argument, that this clause in the Constitution is a compact between the States, and must be executed by the
States and not by the General Government. "The
necessity for this provision was found in the views
and feelings of the people of the States opposed to
slavery; and who, under such an influence, could
not be expected favorably to regard the rights of the
master. Now, by whom is this paramount law to
be executed? It is contended that the power to
execute it rests with the States. The law was designed to protect the rights of the slaveholder against
the States opposed to those rights; and yet by this
argument, the effective power is in the hands of

in the opinion, if legislation by Congress be necessary, that the
right to legislate is exclusively in Congress."
    [1] Appendix to Congressional Globe, vol. xxv, p. 1102, et seq.
    [2] 16 Peters, 661.

those on whom it is to operate. This would produce a strange anomaly in the history of legislation.
It would show an inexperience and folly in the
venerable framers of the Constitution, from which,
of all public bodies that ever assembled, they were,
perhaps, most exempt."

§ 246. Among the Saxons, although the master
had a perfect dominion over the slave within the
kingdom, yet, in many cases, and especially upon
the conversion of the slave to Christianity, the master was prohibited from transporting and selling him
without the realm, "et maxime infidelibus, ne anime
in dampnacionem vendantur, pro quibus Christus
vitam impendit."[1] And thus the Saxon slave enjoyed one of the fruits of liberty, the right of remaining within the kingdom. So, also, the villains
*regardant*, in England; the colliers, in Scotland; the
*coloni* or *adscriptitii glebae*, of Rome; the helots of
Sparta, and the penestæ, of Thessaly,[2] while under
the dominion of the master, could not be removed
from the land to which they were attached. The
Roman slaves generally, however, might be removed
by the master at will, without the realm. Such is
the condition of the African slave in America.

[1] Ancient Laws, &c. 145, 162, 208; Laws of Ethelred, viii, §
5; Laws of King Cnut, Sect. iii; Laws of William the Conqueror,
§ 41.

[2] Smith's Dict. of Greek and Roman Antiq. "Servus."

# CHAPTER XIII.

## OF THE PRIVILEGE OF A SLAVE TO BE A WITNESS.

§ 247. ONE of the consequences of the want of liberty in the slave is his disqualification to be a witness in cases affecting the rights of freemen. This disqualification has been the prolific theme for much complaint and abuse of the system. Mr. Stephen, and his imitator and copyist, Mr. Stroud, have declared the rule unparalleled, and without "the authority of any country, either ancient or modern."[1] They deny positively its origin in the common law, and refer it to the civil law, declaring, at the same time, that we have increased its rigors. Yet, we find it to exist wherever we find negro slavery, and even where slavery has ceased, the disqualification is continued in some of the United States,[2] showing that it is founded not only upon the servile condition of the negro, but also upon his known disposition to disregard the truth. We shall examine the correctness of the charge made by Mr. Stephen and Mr. Stroud.

[1] Stephen, on West Indian Slavery, 166, et seq.; Stroud's Sketch, &c. 70, et seq.

[2] Ohio, Illinois, Iowa, &c.

§ 248. How stands the common law ?   The term
" law," according to the common law, is defined to
be " a freeman's privilege of being sworn in Court
as a juror or witness."   A freeman only was deemed
to be "*othesworth*," and this privilege of being sworn
was one of the distinctive traits and characteristics
of a "liber et legalis homo."   It was otherwise called
" frank law," and sometimes " the law of the land."[1]
So Bracton, speaking of a freeman's loss of this privilege, says: "Perpetuam infamiam incurrant et legem
terræ amittant, et ita quod nunquam postea ad sacramentum admittantur, quia de cetero non erunt *othesworth* nec ad testimonium recipientur."[2]   " They
incur perpetual infamy and lose their privilege of
the law, so that never afterwards are they admitted
to the sacrament, and, among things, shall not be
'*othesworth*,' or received as witnesses."   This was a
part of the punishment of jurors who had been convicted of a false verdict.[3]   So Blackstone says that
in the " wager of law" or " trial by battle," if either
party pronounced the horrible word " craven," he
was condemned "amittere liberam legem," and therefore never to be put upon a jury, or admitted as a
witness in any cause.[4]   And this is probably the

[1] Burrill's Law Dictionary, Frank Law; Jacob's Law Dict.
Frank Law; see also Cromp. Jur. 156.   The laws of King Withraed expressly forbade the "theow," or slave, his oath, § 23; Ancient Laws and Institutes, 18.

[2] Bracton, folio, 292 b.

[3] Glanville, Lib. II, c. iii; Co. Litt. 294 b.

[4] 3 Black. Comm. 340; see to same effect, Co. Litt. 6 b; Fortesc.
ch. xxvi.

true origin of the rule that excludes from testifying persons convicted of infamous offences.   Fleta gives this as the reason : " Repellitur autem sacramento infamis, qui alias convictus fuerit de perjurio, quia jam legem liberam amisit, nec ulterius dignus est legis libertate gaudere quia publice in legem commisit."[1]   "The infamous person convicted of perjury is denied the sacrament, because he has lost his privilege of the law, nor is he ever worthy to enjoy this liberty, because of this public disregard of it."

§ 249. Subsequently, when feudal tenures were substituted for the former servitude, and the villain gradually became to be considered as a freeman, as against every one, save his lord, it seems that the privileges of a freeman (and among others, that of being sworn as a witness), were extended to him. This, however, is itself a matter of doubt, and it is very possible that it was not until tenure by villanage fell into entire disuse, that the villain was admitted as a witness.[2]

§ 250. The civil law in excluding the testimony of slaves, gave precisely the same reason for the exclusion as the common law : "Etenim testis, homo *liber* esse debet."[3]   The civil law extends the dis-

---

[1] Fleta, Lib. IV, cap. viii, § 2.   This is a much more sensible reason for, and origin of the rule, than the one given by Baron Gilbert, in his Treatise on Evidence, 142, 143, and which has been adopted by subsequent writers.   See McNally, Ev. 207 ; 1 Phillips, on Ev. 14, 15 ; 1 Starkie, on Ev. 83 ; 1 Greenl. on Ev. § 372.

[2] Hallam's Mid. Ages, Pt. II, ch. ii, p. 91, n.; Smith, on Master and Servant, Introd. p. 28.

[3] Huber, Prælec. Lib. XXV, tit. v, § 2.

credit arising from the menial occupation, even to the hireling,—domestici testimonii fides improbatur.[1]

§ 251. Whether founded upon the same reason or not, certain it is that this rule of exclusion has been universal, wherever slavery or villanage has existed.[2] By the Code Noir, the evidence of slaves was excluded in all cases in the French Colonies, whether for or against freemen or slaves. The Judges were allowed to hear their evidence, as suggestions to illustrate other testimony, but they were prohibited from drawing thence, " aucune présomption, ni conjecture, ni adminicule de preuve."[3] The same rule obtained in the British West Indies, and it is a little remarkable that the commissioners appointed to inquire into their condition, with a view to meliorating the *status* of the slave, hesitated to recommend a different rule, except in criminal cases.[4] Among the Jews, Josephus informs us that the testimony of servants was rejected " on account of the ignobility of their soul."[5]

§ 252. So universal was this rule of exclusion in

---

[1] Leg. 3, Cod. 4, 20.

[2] In Greece. See Becker's Charicles, 278; Recueil des Historiens, tom. xiv, Pref. p. 65; Hallam's Mid. Ages, Pt. II, ch. ii; Taylor's Law Glossary, 425; Du Cange, Glossary, Voce "Servus," vol. vi, p. 451; Potgiesser, De Statu Serv. Lib. I, cap. iii.

[3] Code Noir, Art. 30. By the French Civil Code, the *domestique* or menial servant is disqualified as a witness; the Court, in its discretion, being allowed to hear his evidence. Touillier, Droit Civil Français, vol. ix, p. 496.

[4] Substance of the Three Reports, p. 450 (London, 1827).

[5] Antiquities of the Jews, Bk. IV, ch. viii, § 15. Mr. Stroud doubts the truth of this, because Deuteronomy is silent on this subject. Sketch, &c. p. 69, note.

the middle ages, that the Church specified as an element of its early persecution the admission against them of the testimony of slaves.[1]    And afterwards, by their decrees, the Pope rejected slaves as accusers and witnesses.[2]

§ 253. In the United States the rule is enforced, without exception, in all cases where the evidence is offered for or against free white persons.[3]    In most of the States this exclusion is by express statutes.[4] In others, by custom and the decision of the Courts.[5] In all the slaveholding States, and in Ohio, Indiana, Illinois, and Iowa, by express statute, the rule has been extended to include free persons of color, or emancipated slaves.[6]    This is right upon principle, as we shall see hereafter, when we come to consider the effect of manumission upon the *status* of the slave.    In all the slaveholding States the negro is a competent witness in cases where slaves or free negroes are the only parties.[7]    And this testimony

[1] Neander's Hist. of the Church, Translation, vol. i.

[2] See Bishop England's Letters to Forsyth, 42, quoting decree of Stephen I, and others.

[3] Winn. Adm. &c. v. Jones, 6 Leigh, 74.

[4] Civil Code, Louisiana, Art. 177; N. C. Rev. Stat. 583; Rev. Code of Virginia, 663; Dorsey's Laws of Maryland, 56, 564; Stat at Large of S. C. vi, 489; vii, 427; Hutchinson's Mississippi Code, 515.

[5] In Georgia.    Berry v. The State, 10 Geo. 519.    See provision in Alabama Code, § 3318.

[6] Jordan v. Smith, 14 Ohio Rep. 199; Rusk v. Sowerwine, 3 Har. & J. 97.

[7] The State v. Samuel, a slave, 2 Dev. & Bat. 177.    In Delaware, the testimony of free negroes is admitted on criminal prosecutions, in some cases.    Rev. Code of 1852, p. 381.    In some States, the testimony of a single negro must be corroborated.    N.

PRIVILEGE OF SLAVE TO BE A WITNESS.     231

has been allowed even where a white person has been vouched upon his warranty by one of the parties.[1] In suits where negroes are the only parties, the same rules of evidence govern, as to competency and admissibility and relevancy, as in ordinary cases, except perhaps that marriage not being recognized among them, that *quasi* relation does not exclude the evidence of either.[2]

§ 254. The negro being excluded as a witness, his declarations to others, as a general rule, are of course inadmissible.[3] There are exceptions, however, founded partly in the necessity of the case; in other cases the declarations are admissible upon other rules of evidence. Thus, the declarations of a negro to a physician or others as to the symptoms of his disease, or the seat of his sufferings, are admissible in evidence;[4] but his declarations as to the cause of his injury or disease, or as to the length of time of its existence or duration, are inadmissible.[5]

§ 255. And again, if a white person refers to a negro for information, the declarations of the negro, under such circumstances, are admissible against the person so referring, he having thereby given credit to and adopted as his own the statement of the

C. Rev. Stat. 581; Stat. at Large of S. C. vii, 356; Dorsey's Laws of Maryland, 92.

[1] Meechum v. Judy, 4 Miss. 361.

[2] The State v. Samuel, 2 Dev. & Bat. 177; The State v. Ben, 1 Hawks, 434.     [3] Tumey v. Knox, 7 Monroe, 91.

[4] Opinion of Owsley, J., in Tumey v. Knox, 7 Monr. 92; Brown v. Lester, Ga. Dec. Pt. I, p. 77; McClintock v. Hunter, Dudley, S. C. 327; Marr v. Hill, 10 Mo. 320.

[5] Tumey v. Knox, 7 Monroe, 90; McClintock v. Hunter, Dudley, S. C. 327.

negro. So if a person accused of a crime, agrees that a negro shall tell all he knows, the declarations of the negro in his presence, and uncontradicted by him, are admissible in evidence against him.[1] The silence of a party, as a general rule, however, would not make the declarations of a negro in his presence admissible against him, for the law would not require of a free white person to deny the misstatements of every negro in his presence. The circumstances must be such as to require the party, as a reasonable man, to pay attention, and give a denial to the statements of the negro, in order to render them admissible in evidence against him. Where a conversation is heard between a negro and a white person, the remarks of the negro may be given in evidence against the white person, in all cases, by way of inducement, and as illustrating the remarks of the white person.[2] So, also, it is admissible for a witness to state that he was induced to waylay a party, suspected of a design to commit a felony, from information derived from a negro, this being only in explanation of the witness's own conduct.[3] And, it has been held that on the trial of an accessory to a murder committed by slaves, the confessions of guilt by the slaves were admissible to prove that fact.[4]

§ 256. That this universal exclusion of a negro from testifying may, in many supposable cases, operate harshly and to the defeat of justice, especially in reference to the cruel treatment of slaves, is an undeniable fact; and yet it is equally true, that the

Berry v. The State, 10 Ga. 520, 521.          [2] Ibid.
[3] Whaley v. The State, 11 Ga. 123.
[4] State v. Simes, 2 Bailey, 29.

indiscriminate admission and giving credit to negro testimony would not only, in many cases, defeat justice, but would be productive of innumerable evils in the relation of master and slave. Even Mr. Stephen admits that " it might be right even wholly to exclude the testimony of slaves, when the master has any interest in the cause. They ought never, perhaps, to be heard, but when he himself is no party, and would, if called as a witness, be free from every exception."[1] He admits further, that the testimony should always be wanting in credit, because of the " general presumption against his moral character, more especially in the article of veracity."[1] That the negro, as a general rule, is mendacious, is a fact too well established to require the production of proof, either from history, travels, or craniology.[1]

§ 257. Perhaps it might be well to permit the negro to testify as to the cruel treatment of himself or his fellows by persons other than his master, when no competent white witness is present to testify as to the transaction. In such case, the credibility of his testimony should be specially submitted to the jury, and the accused should be allowed to state, under oath, his own version of the transaction, the credibility of which testimony should also be submitted to the jury. Under such a rule, in most cases, the jury would arrive at a very correct verdict, notwithstanding the objectionable character of all the evidence. In some such extreme cases, it appears that the civil law admitted the testimony

[1] Stephen, on West Ind. Slav. vol. i, p. 177.          [2] Ibid.
[3] See Jones, on the Religious Instruction of Negroes.

of slaves. " Causa sit ardua, ad reipublicæ spectans utilitatem, aut aliæ desint probationes."[1]   But this did not extend to civil cases.[2]   And, in ancient Athens also, in cases of murder, the testimony of slaves was received with credit.[3]

---

[1] Voet, Comm. ad Pandect, Lib. XXII, tit. v, § 2.
[2] Heinec. De Lubric. Jur. Sup. Exer. xvii, § 17.
[3] Plato, Leg. xi, 937; see Becker's Charicles, 270.

# CHAPTER XIV.

## OF THE RIGHT OF PRIVATE PROPERTY.

§ 258. OF the other great absolute right of a free-man, viz., the right of private property, the slave is entirely deprived. His person and his time being entirely the property of his master, whatever he may accumulate by his own labor, or is otherwise acquired by him, becomes immediately the property of his master.[1] If he has several masters, his gains belong to them all *pro rata*.[2] Though our law allows of no *peculium* to the slave, yet, as a matter of fact, such *peculium* is permitted, *ex gratiâ*, by the master.[3] And such was the Roman law, for the *peculium* of the slave was there a matter not of right but of favor; of which the master might at any time deprive him.[4]

§ 259. Such was the condition also of the English

---

[1] Jackson v. Loovey, 5 Cow. 397; 1 Bailey, 633; 2 Hill's Ch. 397; 2 Rich. 424; 6 Humph. 299; 1 Stewart, 320; 5 B. Monr. 186.

[2] Heinec. Elem. Jur. Pars VII, Lib. XLV, § 26.

[3] Mr. Stephen admits the fact to exist in the West Indies, vol. i, 61. Louisiana allows the *peculium* by statute.

[4] Institutes, Lib. II, tit. ix, § 3; Gaius, i, 52; Domat. Prel. Bk. tit. ii, sect. ii, § 97; Huberi Præl. Lib. II, tit. ix, 162 e; Heinec. Elem. Jur. Lib. III, tit. xviii; Smith's Dict. of Antiq. "Servus."

villain, for, "quicquid acquiritur servo, acquiritur domino," saith my Lord Coke.[1] Fleta gives the rule in almost the same words: "Quicquid per ipsum juste acquiritur, id domino acquiritur; et cum ipse a domino suo possideatur, nihil possidere potest, nec aliquid proprium habere."[2] So also Glanville: "Notandum est quod non potest aliquis, in villenagio positus, libertatem suam propriis denariis suis quærere," &c. "It is to be remembered that a villain cannot even seek to purchase his own liberty with his own money."[3] The villain might acquire and convey, however, provided he did so before the lord took possession of his acquisitions.[4] The earnings of an apprentice, and everything purchased therewith, in the same way, belong to his master.[5]

§ 260. The same rule prevails in every country where negro slavery exists. In the Spanish, Danish, and French West Indian colonies, by express statute, the slave was permitted to accumulate enough to purchase his freedom.[6] Among the Germans, the *homines proprii* originally could hold no property.[7] At a later day they were allowed to accumulate and hold all exceeding the stipulated wages, "*operas et censum.*"[8] The same rule exists in the East Indies.[9]

[1] Co. Litt. Lib. II, § 172.      [2] Lib. IV, ch. xi, § 4.
[3] Lib. V, ch. v.      [4] Co. Litt. Lib. II, § 173.
[5] Smith, on Master and Servant, 80, 81; Salk. 68; Reaves, Dom. Rel. 343.
[6] Schœlcher, Colonies Françaises, and Colonies Etrangères, vol. ii; Stephen, on West Indian Slavery, i, pp. 60, 119, and authorities there cited; Gurney's West Indies.
[7] Potg. De Statu Serv. Lib. II, cap. x.
[8] Heinec. Elem. Jur. Lib. I, § 85.
[9] Adam, on Slavery in India, 246, 247.

§ 261. If a slave obtains valuable property, by finding, his possession is considered that of his master; and the master may maintain an action against any one who receives or forcibly takes such property away from the slave.[1] If the slave be in the possession of one not his master, e. g., a hirer, according to the Roman law, the possessor could claim no gains of the slave, except it arose from his own labor or by means of the property of the possessor.[2]

§ 262. The slave in Rome could not assent to take a legacy, except by his master's order; and in such case, the legacy vested immediately in the master.[3] Certain slaves who had no master, could not, therefore, give assent, and the legacy was simply void.[4] If a legacy were given to an African slave, there seems to be no reason why the legacy should be void, and if delivered by the executor to the slave, the title would vest immediately in the master.[5] The master, however, cannot bring suit for such a legacy, as he cannot bring suit upon an executory contract with his slave.[6] So if a chattel

[1] Brandon v. The Huntsville Bank, 1 Stewart, 320; Fable v. Brown Exr. 2 Hill's Ch. 396.

[2] Ulpian, Frag. tit. xix; Inst. Lib. II, tit. ix, § 4.

[3] Gaius, ii, 87, et seq.; Inst. Lib. II, tit. ix, § 3; Heinec. Elem. Jur. Lib. II, tit. xiv, § 536.

[4] Smith's Dict. of Antiq. "Servus," and authorities there cited.

[5] Williams v. Ash, 1 How. U S. 1. By the Civil Code of Louisiana, a legacy to one occupying the position of a *statuliber* was good, and was preserved for him till he became free. If he died before this time, it reverted to the donor and his heirs. Arts. 193, 195.

[6] Fable v. Brown Exr. 2 Hill's Ch. R. 378, 396; Hall v. Mul-

were given and delivered to a slave, the title thereto would vest in the master; and it seems if land were conveyed to a slave, and possession given, by parity of reasoning, the master would be seized of the land.[1]

§ 263. A slave cannot take by descent, there being in him no inheritable blood.[2] This was true of the Roman slave: they were not objects of cognation or affinity.[3] The same provision is inserted in the Civil Code of Louisiana. By it, however, the succession to the estate of free persons, related to the slave and which the slave would have inherited had he been free, may pass through him to a manumitted descendant.[4]

§ 264. The slave not being capable of acquiring property, it follows, that he cannot convey or give it away. Thus, Fleta, in enumerating those who cannot make donations, expressly includes slaves.[5]

---

lin, 5 Har. & J. 190; Leech v. Cooley, 6 S. & M. 93; aliter, Alston v. Coleman et al. 7 Ala. N. S. 795; 5 How. (Missis.), 305; Trotter, Admr. v. Blocker and wife, 6 Porter, 269.

[1] Per Harper, C. in Fable v. Brown Exr. 2 Hill, Ch. R. 396. See also remarks of Colcock, J., in Gregg v. Thompson, 2 Rep. Cons. Ct. 332.

[2] Jackson v. Lervey, 5 Cowen, 397; Opinion of Dulany, 1 Har. & McH. 560, 561.

[3] Taylor's Elements of Civil Law, 429; Heinec. Antiq. Rom. Lib. II, tit. vii, § 1; Opera, tom. iv, p. 402; and also of the German, Potgies. De Stat. Serv. Lib. II, cap. xi. This was only partially true of the agrestic slaves. Their children remained on the land, and inherited all agricultural tools and household goods. Ibid. § 23.

[4] Civil Code, Art. 176. From this right of the master arose the feudal doctrine of *mortuaries*. Ibid.

[5] Lib. III, cap. iii, § 10.

As a consequence, a slave cannot make a testament, and this was true even in those nations where the slave was allowed his *peculium;* on his death, it belonged to his master.[1]

[1] Taylor's Law Glossary, note to Servitus est, &c.; Potg. De Statu Serv. Lib. II, cap. xi.

# CHAPTER XV.

OF CONTRACTS BY SLAVES, AND HEREIN OF MARRIAGE.

§ 265. IN this connection we may properly notice another disability of the slave, and that is, his inability to contract, or to be contracted with.[1]  In this respect the Roman law differed from ours to this extent, that the *peculium* of the slave might be reached by his creditors, and in the event of subsequent manumission, the creditors might prosecute their debts, previously contracted.[2]  Sometimes, also, it was agreed between the Roman master and his slave, that the slave should purchase his freedom with his *peculium*, when it amounted to a certain sum, and it would seem as if such contracts were enforced.[3]  These privileges, however, were *ex gratiâ*. Strictly the slave could acquire nothing by contract, " Servus nec persona est, nec sibi quidquam adquirit, sed domino.   Ergo et stipulatione sibi nihil."[4]

[1] Hall v. Mullin, 5 Har. & J. 190; Gregg v. Thompson, 2 Rep. Con. Ct. S. C. 331; Jenkins v. Brown, 6 Humph. 299 ; 5 Cowen, 397 ; Emerson v. Howland et al. 1 Mason, 51; Bland and another v. Dowling, 9 Gill & J. 27.

[2] Smith's Dict. of Gr. and Rom. Ant. "Servus," and authorities cited.   Inst. Lib. IV, tit. vi, de Actionibus, § 10.

[3] Tacit. Ann. xiv, 42.

[4] Heinec. Elem. Jur. Lib. III, tit. xviii.

§ 266. In this respect, also, our slave differs from the ancient villain, who might contract, and enforce his contracts, even as against his lord.[1]  The same seems to be true of the Russian serf,[2] the German, and the Polish slave.[3]  But this principle is true of the African slave, wherever he exists.[4]

§ 267. Hence, it follows, that an agreement by the master with his slave, to give to the slave all of his earnings, beyond stipulated wages, is not binding on the master; and, however it may be opposed to good morals, the master can sue for and recover such earnings from a third person, with whom they have been deposited by the slave.[5]  If, however, these earnings were accumulated by the slave, prior to the purchase by his master, they belong to his former owner, and do not pass with the title to the slave.[6] If the depositary of the slave, at his request, invest the fund in real or personal property, taking the title in his own name, the master cannot recover the property, nor make the purchaser a trustee for him.  He can only recover the sum deposited by his slave.[7]

[1] Co. Litt. Sect. 177; Bro. Abr. tit. Villenage, pl. 14, 50, etc.

[2] The Knout and The Russians.

[3] Heinec. Elem. Jur. Lib. I, § 85; Potgies. De Statu Servorum, Lib. II, cap. ii, § 13; Wraxall's Memoirs of Court of Berlin, vol. ii, let. 21.

[4] Stephens, on West Indian Slavery, 58.

[5] Jenkins v. Brown, 6 Humph. 299; Gist v. Toohey, 2 Rich. 425.

[6] Shanklin v. Johnson, 9 Ala. N. S. 275.  This authority sustains only the latter proposition.  The former is equally true.

[7] Shanklin v. Johnson, 9 Ala. N. S. 271.  The case of Sally v. Beatty, 1 Bay, 260, extended this principle very far; "farther," says Judge O'Neal, 2 McMul. 471, "than I desire to go."  Both

§ 268. If the contract with the slave be fully executed, the property conveyed to the slave becomes
*instanter* the property of the master; and the property conveyed by him, upon his master's implied
assent, vests in the contracting party.[1]   An executory contract, however, such as a promissory note, payable to a slave, vests no right of action in the master.[2]

Hence, also, an executory contract with the master to emancipate the slave, cannot be enforced by
the slave, not even though made with a third person,
the slave being no party thereto.[3]   Though it may
be enforced by the parties themselves.[4]

§ 269. In some of the States, the contract by the
master with the slave for his emancipation, has been
excepted *in favorem libertatis* from the general rule
as to the contracts of slaves, and such contracts
have been enforced.[5]   Indeed, it may be worthy of
inquiry, how far contracting with his slave by implication emancipates him?[6]   In several of the
States, contracts with slaves (mechanics, &c.) made
by third persons, with the implied consent of the
master, are expressly prohibited.

§ 270. The inability of the slave to contract ex-

Judge and jury seemed carried away with enthusiasm, at the " extraordinary benevolence of the wench."

   [1] Gist v. Toohey, 2 Rich. 425; Carmille v. Admr. of Carmille, 2
McM. 470; Hobson v. Perry, 1 Hill, 277.

   [2] Gregg v. Thompson, 2 Rep. Con. Ch. 331; Fable v. Brown,
2 Hill Ch. 378; 2 Rich. 425; Gist v. Toohey, 2 Rich. 425.

   [3] Gatliff's Admr. v. Rose et al. 8 B. Monr. 633; Beall v.
Josephs, Hardin's Rep. 51.

   [4] Thompson v. Wilmot, 1 Bibb, 422.

   [5] Victoire v. Dusseau, 4 Martin (La.), 212.

   [6] Keane v. Boycott, 2 H. Black. 573; see post, § 369.

tends to the marriage contract, and hence there is no recognized marriage relation in law between slaves.[1] This was true of the Roman slaves. There was among them a recognized relation, termed " contubernium," from which certain consequences flowed, especially after manumission. For instance, it was incest for a manumitted slave to contract marriage with his manumitted sister.[2] The same effects have been held to flow from a marriage during slavery, after manumission, in Louisiana. In fact, the courts there seem to hold, that after manumission, the marriage contract becomes valid for all purposes.[3]

§ 271. The marriage relation existed among the villains of England. If the villain neife married a freeman, she became thereby enfranchised, and her husband compensated her lord for her loss.[4] And, e converso, it would seem, that if a villain married a free woman, the woman became a neife.[5] If the father

[1] Jackson v. Lervey, 5 Cowen, 397; The State v. Samuel, 2 Dev. & Bat. 177; see Opinion of Mr. Dulaney, in App. to 1 Har. & McH. R. 560, 561.

[2] Dig. Lib. XXIII, tit. ii, § 14; Cooper's Notes to Institutes, 420; Taylor's Elements, Civil Law, 429; Smith's Dict. Gr. and Rom. Antiq. "Servus."

[3] Girod v. Lewis, 6 Martin R. 559.

[4] Bro. Abr. Villenage, pl. 10; Lit. Lib. II, cap. xi, § 187. Upon the death of her husband, however, she returned to her former state of slavery. Mirror, ch. ii, § 18. This seems approved by Lord Coke. Co. Litt. 123.

[5] Co. Litt. 123, says, "And when a bondman marrieth a free-woman, they are all one person in law; and *duæ animæ in carne unâ; and uxor subjecta est viro et sub potestate viri.*" See also Bro. Abr. tit. Villenage, Pl. 23, 39. Such, certainly, was the law of France. Marculfi Formulæ, L. II, 29. And of Burgundy and Lombardy.

and mother were both villains, and belonged to different lords, the issue were equally divided between the respective masters.[1]

§ 272. The marriage relation existed at a later day among the *homines proprii* of the German nations.[2] But until the ninth century, the contubernial relation alone was recognized.[3] Potgiesser boasts that the Germans were the first who united their servants together in the name of Christ.[4] Without the consent of the master, however, the marriage was void, and the parties punished severely.[5]

§ 273. It seems that the Hebrew law did not recognize marriage among slaves of other than Hebrew origin, but a relation existed similar to the *contubernium* of Rome. Certain it is, that the separation of the man from his wife and children, was in certain cases expressly commanded.[6]

§ 274. The marriage of free men and women with slaves was very much discouraged by the laws, civil and ecclesiastical, of the middle ages. Heavy penalties were annexed, and the right was even conceded to parents to kill a daughter who persisted in such

Potgies. Lib. II, cap. ii, § 30. In Flanders, a man that married a villain became one himself, after living with her for a twelvemonth. Recueil des Historiens, tom. xiii, p. 350. So, also, among the Franks. Potgies. Lib. II, cap. ii, § 31.

[1] Qui vero procreantur ex nativâ unius et nativo alterius proportionabiliter inter dominos sunt dividendi. Coke Litt. 123.

[2] Heinec. Elem. Jur. Lib. I, § 85.

[3] Potgies. Lib. I, cap. iii; Lib. II, cap. ii.

[4] Lib. II, cap. ii, § 10.          [5] Ibid. §§ 12, 13, et seq.

[6] See Potgies. Lib. II, cap. ii, § 2, and authorities cited by him, from the opinions of Jewish Rabbins.

an alliance. The question was submitted to the See of Rome, whether a freeman might put away a wife, taken from the servile class, and take a freewoman to his bed. Leo responded in the affirmative.[1] Among the Germans three years were given to a free woman to repent of her course and dissolve the relation. In such case, however, the issue pending the coverture were slaves.[2]

§ 275. The contract of marriage not being recognized among slaves, of course none of its consequences follow from the contubernial state existing between them. Their issue, though emancipated, have no inheritable blood.[3] In trials of slaves, they may be witnesses for and against each other.[4] Yet as the fact of cohabiting, and living together as man and wife, is universal among slaves, and the privileges of parents over children, in correcting and controlling them, are universally acceded to them, in all trials of slaves for offences committed by them, these relations are recognized by the Courts, and the merciful extenuations of the law, to the conduct of the husband and father, are extended to the slave standing in the same situation.

§ 276. How far this contubernial relation between slaves may be recognized and protected by law, is a question of exceeding nicety and difficulty. The unnecessary and wanton separation of persons stand-

[1] Potgies. Lib. II, cap. ii, § 37; see note to § 271.
[2] Ibid. Lib. II, cap. ii, § 34.
[3] Jackson v. Lervey, 5 Cow. 397.
[4] The State v. Samuel, 2 Dev. & Bat. 177. In this case it is held, that the recognition of this state of concubinage, in many of the statutes of North Carolina, does not legalize the marriage, so as to give any of the effects of the marriage relation thereto.

ing in the relation of husband and wife, though it
may rarely, if ever, occur in actual practice, is an
event which, if possible, should be guarded against
by the law.   And yet, on the other hand, to fasten
upon a master of a female slave, a vicious, corrupt-
ing negro, sowing discord, and dissatisfaction among
all his slaves ; or else a thief, or a cut-throat, and to
provide no relief against such a nuisance, would be
to make the holding of slaves a curse to the master.
It would be well for the law, at least, to provide
against such separations of families by the officers
of the law, in cases of sales made by authority of
the Courts, such as sheriffs' and administrators' sales.
How much farther the lawgiver may go, requires
for its solution all the deliberation and wisdom of
the Senator, guided and enlightened by Christian
philanthropy.[1]

§ 277. The incapacity of a slave to contract,
being a part and consequence of his personal *status*,
extends to every place he may go, so long as he remains a slave.   D'Aguesseau gives the incapacity
to contract as an illustration of the meaning and
effect of a personal statute.[2]  Hence, a fugitive slave,
though he may be in a State where slavery does not
exist, is still incapable of contracting, his *status* remaining unchanged.[3]   And, even though the slave
be afterwards manumitted, he cannot be made responsible upon a contract entered into while in a
state of slavery.[4]

[1] See the Act in Georgia, on this subject.
[2] Œuvres, tom. v, 256, 8vo. ed.
[3] Giles v. Hodges, 9 Johns. R. 67 ; Trongott v. Byers, 5 Cow.
480 ; Per Lord Alvanley, Williams v. Brown, 3 Bos. & Pul. 71
[4] Free Lucy and Frank v. Denham's Admr. 4 Monr. 169.

# CHAPTER XVI.

## OF SUITS FOR FREEDOM.

§ 278. ANOTHER disability of the slave, which may be properly considered in this connection, is his inability to be a suitor in any of the Courts of justice, either as plaintiff or defendant, except in suits for freedom, which, in most of the States, is provided for and regulated by statute.[1] This was the rule of the civil law,[2] of the ancient Britons,[3] Germans, and Franks, and other European nations.[4] This disability extends to *statuliberi*, or those whose manumission takes effect *in futuro*.[5] It accompanies the slave to every jurisdiction, so long as his *status* is unchanged. It has been held, however, that for a trespass upon his

[1] Bland & Woolfolk v. Negro Beverly Dowling, 9 Gill & J. 19; Amy v. Smith, 1 Litt. 326; Cateche et al. v. The Circuit Court, &c. 1 Miss. 608; Matilda v. Crenshaw, 4 Yerg. 303; Susan v. Wells, 3 Brev. 11; 4 Gill, 249; Berard v. Berard, 9 Louis. 156; Free Lucy, &c. v. Denham's Admr. 4 Monr. 169.

[2] Taylor's Elem. of Civil Law, 429; Heineccius gives the reason, "ut nec servus, qui persona plane non est, agere possit." Elem. Jur. de Pand. Pars II, Lib. V, § 14. The suit for freedom was termed "Actio de liberali causâ." Dig. Lib. IV, 8, 32.

[3] Fleta, Lib. IV, cap. xi, §§ 1, 4.

[4] Potgiesser, Lib. II, cap. i, §§ 17, 37.

[5] Dorothée v. Coquillon, 19 Mart. L. R. 350.

person, while within the jurisdiction of a non-slave-holding State, he might maintain an action.[1]

§ 279. As before remarked, in all the States the negro may institute proceedings to recover his freedom, when unlawfully detained in bondage. Many of the States prescribe by statute the nature and form of the proceedings,[2] and in such case it must be strictly pursued.[3] In others, these are mere creatures of the Court. Trespass for an assault and false imprisonment is frequently adopted as the form of action.[4] In many of the States, a guardian or *prochein ami* appears in behalf of the slave, and is responsible for the costs.[5] To avoid vexatious and unfounded suits, the slave not being liable to be mulcted in costs, other States require a previous application to the presiding Judge, and, on a *primâ facie* case being made, liberty is granted to the slave to appear *in formâ pauperis*, and counsel are assigned for him.

[1] Polydore v. Prince, 1 Ware, Dist. Ct. Rep. 410.

[2] Georgia, New Dig. 999, 1011; Mississippi, Hutchinson's Code, 523; Maryland, Dorsey's Laws, &c. 341; Virginia, Rev. Code (1849), 464; Alabama, Code of 1852, §§ 2049–2055; Arkansas, Dig. of 1848, ch. 74, p. 543; Missouri, Rev. Stat. (1845), ch. 69, p. 531; Delaware, Rev. Code (1852), ch. 80, Sect. 20.

[3] Richard v. Demors, 5 S. & M. 609; Peters v. Van Lear, 4 Gill, 249. But see Union Bank of Tenn. v. Benham, 23 Ala. 143. Whereas, against creditors of the nominal master, another proceeding was allowed.

[4] Matilda v. Crenshaw, 4 Yerg. 303; Pleasants v. Pleasants, 2 Call. 293; Evans v. Kennedy, 1 Haywood, N. C. 422.

[5] The civil law, to the time of Justinian, required the slave to appear by next friend, called *adsertor*. The difficulty of finding persons to occupy this position, induced him to allow them to appear directly. Cod. Lib. VII, 17, 1.

[6] Missouri, Rev. Stat. 1845, ch. 69; Arkansas, Dig. of 1848,

§ 280. In other States, to prevent slaves from harassing their masters with unfounded suits, the Courts were allowed, in their discretion, to cause corporal punishment to be inflicted upon the claimant, if the jury should return a verdict adverse to his claim of freedom.[1] Mr. Stroud has compared this legislation to the "feast of Damocles," considering the "conduct of Dionysius supreme beneficence compared with the terms of mercy contained in this act."[2] It is the only judgment that can be entered against a slave, and when we remember that it is entered at the suit of the master, who can by law, at his own pleasure, inflict the same punishment, and that it is regulated by the discretion of a disinterested and impartial and humane Judge, sworn to administer the law in mercy, the provision seems indeed to be very unnecessary and ineffectual (having for its object more the deterring of the slave from an unfounded suit, than his actual punishment), yet it certainly does not deserve the denunciation with which Mr. Stroud has treated it. In other States, penalties have been affixed upon the attorney prosecuting the case, or others aiding and abetting in the cause, where the claim of freedom proves to be unfounded.[3]

ch. 74; Bodine's Will, 4 Dana, 476; Dempsey v. Lawrence, Gil. 333.

[1] In South Carolina. Georgia, New Digest, 971. Query, Does not the Act of 1837 repeal this provision? Ibid. 1011.

[2] Sketch, &c. 79.

[3] Maryland, Dorsey's Laws, 341; Virginia, Rev. Code (1849), 465. By the civil law, the slave could appear only by his next friend (*adsertor*), of whom security was required for the person of the slave, and also for costs. Justinian abolished this law, and

§ 281. These various restrictions, while founded upon a regard for the peace and protection of the master, are unnecessary, public opinion being a sufficient guarantee against such an evil. They are in fact dead letters on the statute-book, as the reports of the several States will make manifest. They serve only as food for the appetite and texts for the pens of Abolition fanatics, and had better be expunged.

§ 282. The freedom of the claimant frequently depends upon the will of his previous master. Until admitted to probate, it is inchoate, and the question has arisen, whether the slave thus emancipated may propound the will for probate? It is not strictly a suit for freedom. It is merely to establish a part of the title, and being slaves until their title to freedom is established, the disability as slaves to sue attaches to them. In some of the States it has been held, that they might propound,[1] even where the will emancipates upon a future or uncertain contingency.[2]

§ 283. The course most consonant with principle, would seem to be for the slave to institute his suit for freedom, and upon the trial to prove the execu-

allowed the slave to appear by attorney. Cod. VII, 17, 1. See Livy, Bk. III, ch. xlvi; Henry's Points in Manumission, 43, et seq.

[1] Ben Mercer et als. v. Kelso's Admr. (so says the Reporter), 4 Grattan, 106; Bodine's Will, 4 Dana, 476.

[2] Bodine's Will, 4 Dana, 476. The civil law gave an equitable action to compel the performance of a trust under a will, in favor of freedom. Dig. 40, 5, 17. In Tennessee, by special Act (1829), if the executor refused to apply to the County Court for its assent, the slaves might file a bill by their next friend. Fisher's Negroes v. Dabbs, 6 Yerger, 119.

tion of the will, his inability to propound being a sufficient reason why the will has not been passed upon by the Probate Court; or else, pending the suit for freedom, to allow the slave to file a bill in equity, compelling the executor to propound, or at least to produce the will for probate.[1] Such a bill has been allowed at the instance of slaves manumitted by will, to compel the executor to make application to the County Court for the assent necessary to make valid the manumission.[2] And a similar proceeding has been allowed against the executor of a will of another than the master, by which will the slaves were required to be purchased and manumitted.[3]

§ 284. To prevent the removal of the applicants for freedom, pending the suit, many of the States require the person having them in possession to give bond and security for their forthcoming.[4] In others, where no such provision is made, a bill in the nature of a *quia timet*, lies at the instance of the slave.[5] And even the statutory provision has been held no bar to a bill for the purpose.[6]

[1] Isaac et al. v. McGill, 9 Humph. 616; Wade et al. v. Amer. Col. Soc. 7 S. & M. 663; Peters et al. v. Van Lear, 4 Gill. 249.

[2] Isaac et al. v. McGill, 9 Humph. 616; see also Peters et al. v. Van Lear, 4 Gill. 249.

[3] Marie v. Avart, 6 Mart. Louis. R. 731.

[4] Georgia, New Digest, 1011; South Carolina, Carpenter v. Coleman, 2 Bay. 436; Tennessee, Act of 1817, c. 103; Alabama, Code of 1852, § 2052. A similar provision in civil law. See Henry's Points, &c. 47, n.

[5] Sylvia & Phillis v. Covey, 4 Yerg. 297; Fenwick v. Chapman, 9 Pet. 475.

[6] Sylvia & Phillis v. Covey, 4 Yerger, 297; see Harriet v. Ridgely, 9 Gill. & J. 174.

§ 285. The suit for freedom is allowed only to those who are actually free, and are wrongfully detained in bondage. Hence, it does not lie to·enforce an executory contract, by which freedom is promised to the slave. Here the plaintiff is still a slave, and the disability of the slave to sue attaches to him.[1] We shall see hereafter how far such contracts are binding on the master. We may remark here, that if a slave is bequeathed to a legatee for the purpose of manumission, this is good reason for a specific performance, if the executor, or other person having him in possession, refuses to deliver him up.[2]

§ 286. The suit for freedom is viewed favorably by the courts, on account of the imbecile condition of the claimants,[3] and may be instituted wherever the slaves may be held in custody, although the right to freedom accrued under the laws of another jurisdiction.[4] Nor will the courts require any nicety or technicality in pleading.[5] It must be commenced, however, against the person actually claiming and holding them, and not against a previous owner who has parted with the possession.[6] It may be brought against the executor of a deceased owner, although creditors may be interested in the issue.[7] Where

---

[1] Henry v. Nunn, 11 B. Monr. 239.     [2] Code, 7, 5, 17.

[3] Hudgins v. Wright, 1 Hen. & M. 143; Lee v. Lee, 8 Pet. 44. Such was the civil law. See Henry's Points in Manumission.

[4] Rankin v. Lydia, 2 A. K. Mar. 467.

[5] Pleasants v. Pleasants, 2 Call. 350; Hudgins v. Wright, 1 Hen. & Munf. 134; McMichen v. Amos et al. 4 Rand. 134.

[6] John et al. v. Walker, 8 B. Monr. 605.

[7] Fenwick v. Chapman, 9 Pet. 461. The judgment is not conclusive against the creditors. Allen v. Negro Jim Sharp, 7 Gill. & J. 96.

the claim to freedom of several slaves depends upon the same title and proof, a joint action, by them, has been allowed.[1] The propriety of this, however, where the action sounded in *tort*, has been questioned and denied.[2] The common law allowed two or more to join in the writ *de homine replegiando*.[3] The right to bring the suit for freedom is personal; and hence, so long as the negro is content, no one else can sue for him. Nor can his freedom be set up as a defence against a suit by his nominal master, for trespass to him, or other action founded on his possession.[4]

§ 287. The issue made in all suits for freedom, is the right of the claimant to liberty. It is not competent, therefore, to seek a recovery by showing a want of title in the defendant.[5] Like all other plaintiffs, the claimant must remove the *onus probandi* which is upon him.[6] If the alleged freeman had been in the enjoyment of freedom, the civil law cast the *onus* upon the master, he being defendant.[7] A personal inspection is not only allowable but

[1] Harris v. Clarissa et al. 6 Yerg. 227; Coleman v. Dick & Pat, 1 Wash. 233; Peters v. Van Lear, 4 Gill, 249.

[2] Violet and another v. Stephens, Lit. Sel. Cas. 147; Beaty v. Judy, 1 Dana, 103.

[3] Thomas's Coke, vol. iii, p. 340, n. 2.

[4] Calvert v. Steamboat Trinoleon, 15 Miss. 595.

[5] Harriet v. Ridgely, 9 Gill. & J. 174; Berard v. Berard, 9 Louis. R. 157; Johnson v. Tompkins et al. Bald. C. C. R. 577.

[6] Vaughn v. Phebe, Mart. & Yerg. 20; Berard v. Berard, 9 Louisiana R. 157; Mary v. Morris et al. 7 Louis. R. 135; Hudgins v. Wright, 1 Munf. 134, 138. Such was the civil law also. Dig. 40, 12, 7, 41.

[7] De Except. Dig. 44, 1, 12.

proper for the jury; and the color of the applicant, whether white or black, affords a corresponding presumption for or against his freedom.[1] The rules of evidence, in such cases, are the same as in ordinary cases.[2] Hearsay or reputation is admissible to prove pedigree,[3] but is inadmissible to prove any specific fact which is in its nature susceptible of being proved by witnesses who speak from their own knowledge.[4] Hence, it is not allowable to prove by hearsay or general reputation, that the ancestor of the applicant was free.[5] So the declarations of a previous owner are admissible or not, according as they were made before or after parting with possession.[6] So, also, the manner of attacking the credibility of witnesses, is the same; and evidence that the applicant's witness associated with negroes, is inadmissible.[7] On account of the condition of subjection of the slave, and the control of the master, admissions made by him against his right to freedom,

[1] Hook v. Nancy Pagee and her children, 2 Munf. 379; Hudgins v. Wright, 1 Hen. & M. 133; Gentry v. Polly McMinnis, 3 Dana, 385. See ante.

[2] Mima Queen and child v. Hepburn, 7 Cranch, 295; Field v. Walker, 23 Ala. 155.

[3] John Davis et al. v. Wood, 1 Wheat. 6; Vaughn v. Phebe, Mart. & Yerg. 5; Pegram v. Isabel, 2 Hen. & M. 193.

[4] Mima Queen and child v. Hepburn, 7 Cranch, 290.

[5] Davis et al. v. Wood, 1 Wheat 6; Walls v. Hemsley et al. 4 Har. & J. 243; Gregory v. Baugh, 4 Rand. 611; aliter, 4 Harr. & McH. 63; see also 2 Leigh, 665; 1 Hen. & M. 142.

[6] Gentry v. Polly McMinnis, 3 Dana, 382; Garnett v. Sam & Phillis, 5 Munf. 542; Free Jack v. Woodruff, 3 Hawks, 106; Caroline v. Burgwin, 3 Dev. & Bat. 28.

[7] Thomas v. Pile, 3 Har. & Mc. H. 241.

should be received with great caution, and allowed but little weight.[1]

§ 288. Though the slave is allowed thus to sue and become a party in court, yet until judgment affirms his right to freedom, he is a slave.[2] Hence, he is not entitled in the progress of the cause to make affidavit for the purpose of changing venue, or otherwise to be heard as a freeman.[3] His guardian, or *prochein ami*, may be heard in his behalf, or, where he sues directly in his own name, his attorney.

§ 289. The question has been much discussed, whether, upon a verdict establishing the freedom of the applicant, damages, or hire, should be given to the plaintiffs. In some of the States, such damages are given by special statute.[4] In the absence of statutory enactment, in analogy to other actions, many of the courts have allowed damages by way of *mesne* profits, some from the time of the commencement of the suit,[5] and others for the whole period of their illegal detention, together with the expenses of litigation.[6] In others still, the question of da-

---

[1] Vincent v. Duncan, 1 Missouri R. 214. The civil law excluded it altogether. Cod. 7, 16, 6.

[2] The civil law was otherwise. He was entitled to his liberty, *pendente lite*, by giving security for his appearance. Henry's Points in Man. 51.

[3] Queen v. Neale, 3 Har. & J. 158; Peter et al. v. Hargrave et al. 5 Grat. 14.

[4] In Georgia, New Digest, 971; Virginia, Rev. Code (1849), 465.

[5] Gordon v. Duncan, 3 Miss. 385; Matilda v. Crenshaw, 4 Yerg. 299.

[6] Pepoon v. Clarke, 1 Rep. Const. Ct. S. C. 157.

mages is made to depend upon the *bona fides* of the defendant's claim.[1] Other courts insist, and with great force, that the peculiar condition of the slave, and relation that he bears to the white race, the difficulties surrounding the master, and the interest of the freedman himself, render it inexpedient to make his freedom relate back farther than the judgment pronouncing him free. In these courts all damages are refused.[2] Unless allowed by statute it is usually recovered in a subsequent suit.[3]

§ 290. The effect of the judgment in favor of or against the freedom of the applicant is governed generally by the same rules with other judgments. Hence, the record of such judgment establishing the freedom of the ancestor is not evidence, unless between parties or privies. Between them it is not admissible to sustain the application of a descendant born prior to the judgment,[4] but is admissible and conclusive evidence in favor of or against issue born subsequent to the judgment.[5] A judgment against

[1] Scott v. Williams, 1 Dev. Law, 376; Woolfolk v. Sweeper, 2 Humph. 88, 96; Phillis v. Gentin, 9 Louis. 208; Thompson v. Wilmot, 1 Bibb, 422.

[2] Peter et al. v. Hargrave et al. 5 Grat. 12; Paul's Admr. v. Mingo et al. 4 Leigh, 163; Henry et al. v. Bollar et al. 7 Leigh, 19; Pleasants v. Pleasants, 2 Call. 250.

[3] Woolfolk v. Sweeper, 2 Humph. 88. Under the civil law, a freedman, wrongfully claimed as a slave, might sue for the calumny. Cod. 7, 16, 30.

[4] Davis v. Wood, 1 Wheat. 6; Pegram v. Isabel, 1 Hen. & M. 388; aliter, Vaughn v. Phebe, Martin & Yerg. 5; see also Pegram v. Isabel, 2 Hen. & Munf. 199, Judge Tucker's Opinion. See James v. Jones, 10 Humph. 334.

[5] Chancellor v. Milton, 1 B. Monr. 25; Alexander v. Stokely, 7 Sergt. & R. 299; Shelton v. Barbour, 2 Wash. 64; Pegram v.

the claim for freedom would be a bar to another suit
in the name of a different next friend.[1]  The record
of the judgment in favor of freedom is also admissible as *primâ facie* evidence of an eviction, against
the warrantor of the title who was vouched by the
party.[2]

§ 292.  The same rule was early adopted as to villains in England.  In trespass, for taking a villain,
it appeared that the ancestor in a former suit, in
which it was alleged that he was a villain regardant,
had answered that he was free, and verdict accordingly.  The son relied upon this finding as an es-
toppel, and it was so held.[3]

§ 293.  There suit for freedom, not being for the
recovery of property, is not within the ordinary
statutes of "limitation of actions," and on account
of the poverty, general ignorance, and enslaved condition of the applicants, no length of time will be
held by the Courts to bar the right to sue.[4]  Nor
will the applicant be estopped by the fact of allowing himself to be sold as a slave without giving
notice of his claim to freedom.[5]  On the other hand,

Isabel, 2 Hen. & Munf. 193 ; Roberts v. Smiley, 5 Monr. 271.  But
see Wood v. Stephen, 1 S. & R. 175.

[1] The rule was formerly different by the civil law, but Justinian
adopted the rule laid down in the text.  Cod. 7, 17, 1.

[2] Roberts & Co. v. Smiley, 6 Monr. 270; Brown v. Shields, 6
Leigh. 440.             [3] Year Books, 13 Ed. IV, 2, 3, 4.

[4] Gentry v. McMannis, 3 Dana, 382; Gatliff's Admr. v. Rose,
8 B. Monr. 631.  Per Roane, J., in Hudgins v. Wright, 1 Hen.
& Munf. 141.  Such was the civil law.  Cod. 7, 22, 2, 3.

[5] Guillemette v. Harper, 4 Rich. 186.  Such was the civil law,
but an action lay against him in favor of the deceived purchaser.
Dig. Lib. XL, 12, 14.

it appears, no length of time of the enjoyment of freedom will bar the master's rights. Such was the Roman law, and the same principle was generally adopted among the Franks and Germans.[1] The lord of the villain, on the contrary, it seems, had to reclaim him within a year and a day.[2]

§ 294. Frequently strong prejudices exist in the minds of jurors either in favor or against the claim of freedom. Such jurors are not "indifferent between the parties," and though no bias may exist in the particular case, yet such general prejudice should be allowed as a challenge to the favor.[3]

§ 295. In trial of questions of freedom among the Franks and Germans, where the right was doubtful, it was decided by "wager of battle." And then the alleged slave was allowed to enter the lists in his own behalf. In other cases, he who detained him from the master "waged the battle" for him.[4] It is probable, that in this species of causes was the "wager of battle" first introduced as an appeal to Deity to favor the right. It seems to have arisen as a sequence to the "wager of law :" where neither party could bring the requisite *compurgatores*, one of them would propose to produce his own unsupported

[1] Heinec. De Præscr. &c. Exr. xxvi, §§ 10, 11; Opera, vol. ii, 894, 895; Potgies. De Stat. Serv. Lib. II, cap. ix, § 16, et seq. The civil law allowed a prescription of thirty years to avail, in some cases. Henry's Points in Man. 71.

[2] Fleta, Lib. IV, cap. xi, § 23.

[3] Mima Queen v. Hepburn, 7 Cranch, 290; Chouteau v. Pierre, 9 Miss. 3.

[4] Potgies. De Stat. Serv. Lib. II, cap. ix, §§ 14, 15.

oath, and challenge the other party to deny by his oath, in which event the appeal was to arms.[1]

[1] Thus the law of the Frisians, " Si aut calumniator, aut ille cui calumnia irrogata est, se solum ad sacramenti mysterium perficiendum obtulerit, et dixerit : ego solus jurare volo si tu audes negare sacramentum meum, et armis mecum contende ! Faciant etiam illud si hoc eis placuerit; juret unus, et alius neget, et in campum exeant." Potgies. Lib. II, cap. ix, § 14.

# CHAPTER XVII.

OF OTHER DISABILITIES OF SLAVES.

§ 296. THE marriage relation not being recognized among slaves, none of the relative rights and duties arising therefrom, belong strictly to the slave. We have before noticed the fact that, in the Criminal Courts, the contubernial relation is so far recognized that the motives and acts of slaves, charged with crimes, are adjudged accordingly. We may make the same assertion in reference to the relation of parent and child. In some of the States, both of these relations are so far recognized by the legislature, as to provide by statute against their disruption in public sales.

§ 297. From the very nature of slavery, it is impossible for the slave to hold any office of public or private trust. He consequently cannot be executor to a will, nor guardian to a ward.[1] In this respect villanage in later days differed widely from African slavery, the villain being capable of acting as executor, and in such capacity being allowed to bring suit even against his lord.[2]

§ 298. Possessing none of the privileges of citizenship, the slave is not bound to any of its duties. He

---

[1] Civil Code Louis. Art. 177.    [2] Lit. Inst. Lib. II, § 191.

may, however, rightfully bear arms in a war under the orders of his master.

§ 299. A slave cannot be constituted an agent for a third person other than the master.[2] He may, however, act as agent for his master or employer, and, where the master's or employer's affirmation of the agency is proved, he will be bound by the acts of his agent.[3] This affirmation may arise from acts as well as express authority. Thus, where a slave has been in the habit of purchasing goods of a tradesman, upon the credit of the master, and the bills are paid without complaint, or notice not to continue the credit, the master's assent to the agency will be presumed. The presumption, however, is against the agency, and the *onus* lies upon the tradesman to prove its existence.

§ 300. The Roman master employed his slave as his agent in a great many capacities. They were their factors in the management of business, mechanics and artisans, and some were employed as readers, amanuenses, and copyists.[4] They were sometimes employed as electioneerers for their masters, and were then called *monitors*, and sometimes *fartores* (stuffers), "because they stuffed their master's name in the ears of the citizens."[5]

---

[1] Grotius, De Bel. et Pace, Lib. V, ch. v, § 3. He cites Aristotle, in support of this principle. See also Puffendorf, Lib. VIII, ch. ii, note.

[2] The State v. Hart, 4 Ired. 246.

[3] The State v. Hart, 4 Ired. 250; Chastain v. Bowman, 1 Hill S. C. 270.

[4] Smith's Dict. of Gr. and Rom. Antiq. verb. "Servus."

[5] Heinec. Antiq. Rom. Lib. IV, tit. xviii, § 77 (Op. vol. iv, 631).

§ 301.  For the protection of the community, many of the States have, by special enactment, prohibited masters from employing slaves in certain capacities, where the opportunity and temptation to injure others were placed before them, such as employing them in drug stores, or to administer medicine, even to other slaves not belonging to. the master.[1]

[1] Macon v. The State, 4 Humph. 421.

# CHAPTER XVIII.

## OF OFFENCES COMMITTED BY SLAVES.

§ 302. WE have already seen that statutory enactments never extend to or include the slave, neither to protect nor to render him responsible, unless specifically named or included by necessary implication.[1] The result is, that the ordinary penal code of a slaveholding State does not cover offences committed by slaves, and the penalties thereby prescribed cannot be inflicted upon them. A moment's reflection would show the propriety of this principle. To deprive a freeman of his liberty, is one of the severest punishments the law can inflict; and one of the most ordinary, especially when the penitentiary system is adopted. But to the slave this is no punishment, because he has no liberty of which to be deprived. Every slaveholding State has, hence, found it necessary to adopt a slave code, defining the offences of which a slave may be guilty, and affixing the appropriate penalties therefor.[2] We

[1] Ante, § 94.

[2] In South Carolina, it has been held, that the expression, "if the crime by law deserve death," applied by implication to the slave all capital crimes defined in the code. The State v. Posey, 4 Strobh. 125. The Alabama Code specifies how far slaves and free persons of color are within its provisions, § 3305.

shall, hereafter, consider how far free negroes have been included therein, and the reasons for this course.

§ 303. If the general penal code does not include slaves, it must follow, that where the presence of two or more persons is necessary, under that code, to constitute an offence, slaves cannot be enumerated so as to make out the offence against the white persons present. Thus, if by statute the presence of three persons is necessary to the commission of a riot, two white persons cannot be found guilty on proof of the presence of a slave aiding and abetting.[1]

So, also, a person gaming with a slave cannot be convicted under the general provisions against gaming; and if there be no statutory penalty, must go unpunished.[2]

§ 304. Another and interesting question arises, as to how far a white person may become an accessory before the fact, to a slave. There seems to be no difficulty in saying that a white person and a slave may jointly commit an offence, and each be tried and punished under their respective codes, although the punishments may vary. A difficulty, however, arises (in the absence of statutes) with reference to accessories. For instance, the ordinary penal code prescribes that the punishment for accessories before the fact shall be the same with that of the principal. The punishment, by the slave code, prescribed for an assault with intent to murder a white person, is

---

[1] I am aware that it was decided otherwise in The State v. Thackam & Magson, 1 Bay. 358, but, as I conceive, against principle.        [2] State v. Pemberton & Smith, 2 Dev. 281.

death; while for the same offence by a white man, it is merely imprisonment. If, then, a white man was convicted as an accessory to a negro, in this offence, what punishment would be inflicted on him? The principal's punishment is death. Can the accessory's be the same? The difficulty is easily relieved, by a provision, by statute, making the punishment the same as if the principal had been a white person. There being no legal difficulty in the way of a white person being accessory to a person capable by law of committing a crime, even if that person is his own slave, the Courts, without legislation, might construe the punishment to be as indicated above.[1]

§ 305. If the criminal act is committed by a slave under the compulsion of the master, who has the right to enforce obedience, the law considers the slave as the mere passive instrument in the hands of the master, and inflicts punishment on him. And if the person, commanding the slave to commit the offence, be not the master, still, if the act is done under such influence, the person commanding is treated as a principal offender. In some of the States, this principle has been extended to persons persuading slaves to commit offences.[2]

§ 306. In minor offences, the command of the master would be a perfect defence to the slave, obeying, in good faith, such command.[3] In graver offences,

[1] The State v. Posey, 4 Strobh. 103.

[2] See Statutes in Georgia on this subject, New Digest (1851), 780, 781.

[3] By express statute, in South Carolina, Statutes at Large, vii, 343; see also New Digest of Statutes of Georgia, 780, 781.

and especially capital crimes, public policy would
forbid such a defence as a justification, while it
would be always admitted in extenuation or as explanatory of the motives of the offender.

§ 307. The condition of the slave renders it impossible to inflict upon him the ordinary punishments, by
pecuniary fine, by imprisonment, or by banishment.[1]
He can be reached only through his body, and hence,
in cases not capital, whipping is the only punishment which can be inflicted. In the case of manslaughter, some of the States prescribe branding on
the cheek as an additional punishment, more particularly with a view to protect distant and innocent
purchasers from negroes who have been guilty of a
homicide.[2] The extremes, death and whipping, being
the only available punishments, it becomes necessary, in forming a slave code, to throw all offences
under the one or the other. Hence, many offences
are, from public policy, necessarily made capital,
which, when committed by a white person, are not.
Such are, rape upon a white female; arson in a town
or city; attempts to poison; insurrection, &c. This
necessity has been felt in every country where there
has been slavery, and this consequent difference in

[1] In Maryland, banishment is prescribed in some cases.  Dorsey's
Laws, 702; also in Virginia, Rev. Code (1849), 106, 753, 754.

[2] The earlier slave codes provided other punishments, mutilating
the bodies of the slaves, such as slitting the nose, cutting off the
ears, castrating, &c.  These have been gradually abolished and
superseded.  See Dorsey's Laws of Maryland, 777.  Mr. Stroud
comments at length on the former law; but does not allude to the
repealing act, which had been in existence six years before his
sketch was published.

punishments for the same offence, when committed by a freeman or a slave, has always existed.

§ 308. Another consequence of being restricted to these two modes of punishment is, that in all offences not capital, very great discretion necessarily must be given to the tribunal trying the offence, in regulating the amount of punishment for each individual case. The varying circumstances of the case, the previous character of the offender, the condition of his health, &c., render it impossible for a scale of punishments to be adopted, leaving nothing to judicial discretion. Protected as the slave always is by the presence and interest of his master, no ill consequence to him ever follows this discretion.

§ 309. These peculiarities as to the punishment inflicted for the offences, thus shown to be necessary, are the fruitful theme for vituperation and abuse against the slaveholding States, by Mr. Stroud, in his "Sketch of the Laws of Slavery," in which he has only copied from Mr. Stephen similar strictures on the Penal Laws of the British West Indies. Theoretically it may be considered an evil, that the list of capital offences should be enlarged. Practically the punishment is never inflicted undeservedly. The slave's situation is such that the temptation to commit the higher offences is very slight, and only the most vicious are ever guilty of them. Executions of slaves for any of these offences are very rare.

§ 310. Every State, by its code, has constituted the tribunals before whom slaves charged with offences shall be tried. The minor offences are usually disposed of by courts called together for the purpose, so as to avoid delay and costs. Capital offences are, in most of the States, tried before the highest County Courts; and every guard, thrown around the citizen to protect his innocence, is allowed to the slave.[1] Counsel is not only allowed, but if the master fails to afford it, by the laws of all and the Constitutions of some, the. Courts are bound to appoint counsel.[2] It being the duty of the master to protect the slave, and furnish him everything necessary to that protection, he cannot abandon him when charged with an offence. It is his duty to furnish him with counsel; if he fails to do so, he will be liable for reasonable fees to such counsel as afford that protection which he was bound to give.[3] It would seem, however, that when counsel is appointed by the Court, the master is not liable, as the attorney is then discharging a duty incumbent on him, by virtue of his relation to the Court.[4]

§ 311. A fair trial by jury, in all graver cases, is

[1] Maryland, Dorsey's Laws, &c. 92; Virginia, Rev. Code (1849), 753, 754; North Carolina, Rev. Statutes (1837), 581, 582, &c.; South Carolina, Statutes at Large, vii, 354 et seq.; Georgia, Cobb's New-Digest (1851), 851, 982, 986, 1019; Alabama, Code of 1852, 595; Mississippi, Hutchinson's Code, 521, 949; Arkansas, Dig. of 1848, Part XII, ch. li; Missouri, Rev. Statutes (1845), 413; Tennessee, Caruthers & Nich. Dig. 675, 683; Texas, Hartley's Digest, § 2539 et seq.; Delaware, Rev. Code (1852), ch. lxxx, § 25.

[2] See Rev. Statutes of North Carolina (1837), 583; Rev. Code of Virginia (1849), 787; Constitution of Arkansas, § 25; Constitution of Missouri, Art. iii, § 27.

[3] See Macon v. Davis, 13 Ga. 68; Rev. Stat. of North Carolina, 583; Rev. Code of Virginia, 787; Code of Alabama (1852), § 3329; Hutchinson's Miss. Code, 522.

[4] Manning .v. Cordell, 6 Miss. 471.

granted by the statutes of every State; and the same safeguards, to secure impartiality, are thrown around their selection, as is afforded to a citizen charged with a like offence.[1]

So, also, that principle of law which protects a citizen from being twice charged criminally with the same offence, throws its shield over the slave. So that, if an inferior Court take cognizance of an act committed by a slave, and inflicts punishment therefor, this sentence may be pleaded in bar in a higher tribunal, where the slave is charged capitally for the same offence.[2]

§ 312. The same rules which govern the Courts, as to the frame of the indictment and the order of pleading in ordinary cases, apply to cases against slaves, except where they are necessarily inapplicable from the nature and condition of the slave.[3] Descriptive allegations in the indictment should therefore be made with reasonable certainty;[4] and if the Court be of limited jurisdiction, the facts necessary to give jurisdiction should be stated.[5] If, however, the Court is of general jurisdiction, these allegations are unnecessary.[6]

§ 313. The right of the master to control his

---

[1] In the following States, by their Constitutions, Alabama, Missouri, Arkansas, Texas. By statutes, Maryland, Virginia, North Carolina, South Carolina, Georgia, Kentucky, Tennessee, Louisiana, Mississippi. In North Carolina, by Act of 1793, the jury must be of slave-owners. See State v. Ivin, 1 Dev. 142.

[2] Ex parte, Jesse Brown, 2 Bailey, 323. In Georgia by statute, Cobb's New Dig. 984.

[3] The State v. Posey, 4 Strobh. 103.

[4] Wash v. The State, 14 S. & M. 120.

[5] State v. Peter, Geo. Dec. Pt. I, 46.

[6] Anthony v. The State, 9 Geo. 264.

slave is subordinate to the right of the State to hold the slave amenable to its laws; but it continues even during the trial of the slave, so far as it does not interfere with the latter and superior right. Hence, the master, during the progress of the cause, may make consents and waivers which will be binding on the slave, such as agreements to a mistrial, or the withdrawal of a juror.[1]

All motions or responses to motions, must be made by the master or the counsel of the slave.

§ 314. A consequence of the subordination of the master's rights to the superior rights of the State is, that the master cannot legally obstruct his arrest or assist his escape. For the latter case, many of the States have provided penalties.[2] Independent of these, the master would not only be an accessory after the fact, but any sale of the slave, even to an innocent purchaser, would be void, as against public policy.[3]

§ 315. The rules of evidence are the same as those which are administered in other criminal cases,[4] except that slaves and free persons of color are competent witnesses for or against the prisoner.[5] Hence, it is illegal to admit in evidence the opinion of the committing magistrate, that the slave was guilty of

---

[1] Elijah v. The State, 1 Humph. 102.

[2] Georgia, New Dig. (1851), 975.

[3] Doughty v. Owen, 24 Miss. 404.

[4] The State v. Ben, 1 Hawks, 434. In Georgia, by express statute, Cobb's New Dig. (1851), 986.

[5] In Maryland and South Carolina, their testimony must be corroborated by pregnant circumstances. Dorsey's Laws, &c. 92; Stat. at Large, vii, 356.

a capital offence.[1]   So, also, the good character of the slave: is admissible to repel the presumption of guilt.[2]   And, on the other hand, his bad character cannot be placed in issue, except in the same manner as that of other persons charged with a crime. So, as a general rule, confessions made by slaves are admissible in evidence on the same terms as in other cases, but they should be received with great caution, and allowed but little weight, especially when made to the jailor or arresting officers, for the habit of obedience in the slave compels him to answer all questions of the idlest curiosity, while his mendacious disposition will always involve even the most innocent in the most contradictory inconsistencies.

§ 316. Is the master a competent witness for or against the slave ?   In the former case he has large pecuniary interests in securing an acquittal.   In the latter, in many of the States, he is liable for costs on conviction, and, *quoad hoc*, is a party to the case. The better opinion is, that he is a competent witness in either case.   In the words of Chief Justice Henderson, " the interest at stake being so entirely different from that which is brought forward to protect the witness from giving evidence, or to exclude him if willing, is not to be weighed in the same balances with mere pecuniary interest.   It is so transcendent in its nature, that its weight is not to be ascertained by mere money balances."[3]

[1] Allen v. The State, 9 Geo. 492.

[2] Pierce v. Myrick, 1 Dev. 345 ; Dave v. The State, 22 Ala. N. S. 33.

[3] The State v. Charity, 2 Dev. 547.   The judgment of the Court was the other way; but I adopt, as the better law, the dissenting.

§ 317. A more difficult question is presented in the admissibility of confessions made by the slave to the master. The former is bound, and habituated to obey every command and wish of the latter. He has no will to refuse obedience, even when it involves his life. The master is his protector, his counsel, his confidant. He cannot, if he will, seek the advice and direction of legal counsel. Every consideration which induces the law to protect from disclosures confidential communications made to legal advisers, applies with increased force to communications made by a slave to his master. Moreover, experience shows, that the slave is always ready to mould his answers so as to please the master, and that no confidence can be placed in the truth of his statements. Such communications should be excluded from the jury; nor should they be admitted even if the master was willing to testify; for, unfortunately, there are many masters who would not have the moral courage to plead their privilege, under such circumstances.[1]

§ 318. Slaves, not being included in the ordinary criminal laws, cannot be bailed by the master after commitment, and before trial, unless by express statutory provision. Should bail be allowed, the master and his sureties might be responsible on their bond as a voluntary obligation, but the officer taking it would be liable for an escape.

§ 319. We shall see hereafter how far the master

opinion of the Chief Justice. In Georgia, he is made, by statute, a competent witness. New Dig. 974.

[1] The State v. Charity, 2 Dev. 543; especially the able Opinion of C. J. Henderson.

is liable for the acts of his slave. Criminal acts not done by his order, do not create a responsibility upon the master. Hence, in the absence of express statute, he would not be liable for the costs upon a conviction. In nearly all the States, this question has been regulated by statute. On the other hand, he would have no claim upon the State for his loss, arising from the execution of the slave. In some of the States, to induce masters not to screen their slaves from prosecution for offences, a part or all of the value of a slave executed is paid by the State.

§ 320. It will not be within our plan to analyze the several slave codes of each State, and specify the acts which, when committed by slaves, are declared thereby to be crimes; nor to point out the tribunals established in each State, for the trial and punishment of these crimes. These laws vary somewhat in the several States, being more or less rigid, according to the situation and feelings of the citizens of each. Thus, in some States, insolence of a slave towards a white person, is an offence for which he may be tried and punished.[1] While, in most of the States, such conduct is left to be punished by the master on complaint, or redressed by the person so offended by chastisement, he being liable for any excess.[2] It follows, from what we have previously said, that no Court has jurisdiction of offences by slaves, except those to which such jurisdiction is granted by statute.[3]

[1] Per O'Neal, J., in Ex parte Boylston, 2 Strobh. 41; Hutchinson's Mississippi Code, 517.
[2] State v. Jarrott, 1 Ired. 76.
[3] See State v. Mary Hage, 1 Bailey, 275.

§ 321. If the statute defining the crimes of which slaves may be guilty, does not enumerate them, but after specifying capital crimes, declares that " all other offences," when committed by slaves, shall be punished, &c.,[1] the Court must look to the general penal code for the " other offences," in their nature applicable to slaves, and cannot punish for any act not thereby declared penal.[2]

§ 322. We have heretofore considered how far the slave is justified in repelling force by force.[3] "Vim vi defendere, omnes leges omniaque jura permittunt." "To repel force by force, all systems of law permit." But as a certain amount of force is legally exercised over the slave, to justify his resistance by force it must appear that such resistance was necessary to protect his right of self-preservation, either as to life or limb. But even this must be received with some qualification, for if the slave was originally the wrongdoer, and resisting lawful authority, he cannot afterwards justify a homicide, by showing a reasonable sense of imminent danger to his own life.[4]

§ 323. We have also seen that, while the homicide of a white person by a slave may be the offence of manslaughter,[5] yet the same provocation which will so reduce the offence in a citizen, will not in a slave. A legal provocation for a slave, is such as, having due regard to the relative condition of the

---

[1] As in Georgia, New Dig. 987.

[2] See Grady v. The State, 11 Geo. 253.

[3] Ante, §§ 98, 99.

[4] Dave v. The State, 22 Ala. N. S. 35; The State v. Will, 1 Dev. & Bat. 121.        [5] Ante, § 99.

white man and the slave, and the obligation of the latter to conform his instinct and his passions to his condition of inferiority, would provoke a well-disposed slave into a violent passion.[1] Hence, the mere fact of an engagement, on a sudden heat of passion, would not of itself form such a provocation.[2]

§ 324. Subordination and obedience being not only the duty of the slave, but absolutely necessary to the preservation of social order, insubordination, and insurrection or rebellion, are offences recognized and punished severely in all the States. The slave becomes an outlaw so soon as he places himself in a state of insurrection, and by many of the codes his homicide is justified. It becomes, then, a question of importance to define accurately what constitutes the offence of insurrection or rebellion. Mere insubordination does not, else every fugitive slave would be in a state of insurrection; and yet, to a certain extent, every runaway is rebelling against the authority of the master. On the other hand, it is not necessary that there should be a concerted plot or conspiracy, on the part of several slaves, to constitute an insurrection, else a single slave might defy all peaceable attempts to recapture him. The ingredients, therefore, necessary to place a slave in a state of insurrection or rebellion are, that he

---

[1] The State v. Jarrott, 1 Ired. 76. An able Opinion by Judge Gaston.

[2] Ibid. In The State v. Cæsar, 9 Ired. 391, the beating of prisoner's friend by drunken rowdies, was held a sufficient provocation by a majority of the Court. But *quære* of the correctness of this decision? Had it been his wife, or his child, there would have been more excuse for the sudden heat of passion.

should be openly resisting *lawful* authority, and that this resistance should be by such force as indicates an intention to maintain it to the shedding of blood.[1]

§ 325. It follows from this, that a master, overseer, or employer, cannot be justified in killing or maiming a slave merely for the purpose of subduing him.[2]  Nor would either of these, or a patroller, be authorized to maim or kill a slave who is seeking, without such force, to escape from their control.[3] Much less would one, who had no lawful right to control the slave, be protected in perpetrating such acts.[4]

§ 326. A question suggests itself here which, perhaps, would more properly be considered hereafter, in connection with the master's rights for illegal interference with and trespasses upon his slave; and that is, how far a third person, who persuades or compels, or otherwise induces a slave to commit a crime by which his life is forfeited, is liable to the master in damages for the injury to his property.  It has been held, properly, that if a person furnishes spirituous liquors to a slave, sufficient to intoxicate him, and this drunkenness causes the slave to expose himself so as to produce death, the person furnishing the liquors is liable to the master for the value of his slave.[5]  On principle, it would seem, that if the

---

[1] See Dave v. The State, 22 Ala. N. S. 33.

[2] Wooley v. The State, 11 Humph. 172.

[3] Ante, § 96; Brooks v. Ashburn, 9 Ga. 298; The State v. Will, 1 Dev. & Bat. 166; Copeland v. Parker, 3 Ired. 513.

[4] Arthur v. Wells, 2 Rep. Con. C. S. C. 314; 1 Nott & McC. 182.

[5] Harrison v. Berkeley, 1 Strobh. 125.

crime by the slave is the immediate and proximate effect of the conduct of the person commanding or persuading, he would be liable to the master in damages. But if the crime cannot be traced as the natural and proximate consequence of such person's misconduct, and uncontrolled by the agency of the slave himself, he is not liable.[1]

[1] Kelly v. The City Council, 4 Rich. 426.

# CHAPTER XIX.

## OF MANUMISSION, AND HEREIN OF DIRECT MANUMISSION BY DEED.

§ 327. WE come next to consider in what manner the slave may be relieved from his bondage, and the effect of such release. Manumission is as universal as slavery; wherever the latter existed, the privilege of being relieved therefrom has concurrently been acknowledged, more or less trammelled by formalities or conditions, according to the policy of the State.[1]

The act, manumission, derives its name from the Roman law. The English writers adopted with the name, the definition and explanation. Thus Glanville: "Est libertatis datio, nam quamdiu quis in servitute est, manui et potestati sui domini suppositus est; et cum manumissus fuerit, ipse est a manu et potestate domini sui liberatus."[3] "It is the gift of liberty; for one in slavery is supposed to be in the hand or power of his master, and when he is manumitted, he is liberated from the hand and power

[1] Colchester v. Lyme, 13 Conn. 277.

[2] Institutes, Lib. I, tit. v.

[3] Lib. V, ch. v; Lib. II, ch. xiv; see also Bracton, Lib. I, ch. v, § 8; Brit. fol. 78.

of his master." So Littleton : " Manumittere quod
idem est quod extra manum, vel extra potestatem
alterius ponere."[1] " To manumit, which is to place
one beyond or without the hand (*manum*) or power
of another."

§ 328. The right to manumit a slave, arising from
the power of the owner of property to renounce his
right to him, requires no permission or sanction of
law to give it validity and effect. On the contrary,
it requires the most explicit prohibition of law to
restrain this right.[2] Considerations of public policy
have imposed restraints upon, and in some cases prohibited entirely, the exercise of this right.[3] We will
consider these as we progress in this investigation.
Unrestrained by statute, then, every owner may
manumit his slave, provided he or she labors not
under some disability, such as nonage, or coverture,
or lunacy, or duress.[4]

§ 329. Manumission being the disclaimer of
ownership, of course no one can manumit who is not
the owner.[5] Hence, one of several joint owners

[1] Sect. 204; see Coke's Comments.
[2] McCuthen et al. v. Marshall et al. 8 Peters, 238.
[3] Ibid. Montesquieu, in vindication of the necessity and policy
of such restraints, mentions the fact of the freedmen among the
Volsinienses, becoming masters of the suffrages, making an abominable law, giving themselves the right of lying first with the girls
married to the free born. Esprit des Lois, Liv. XV, ch. xvii.
[4] In some States, infants above a certain age, though still minors,
may manumit. Minney v. Cartwright, 3 Marsh. 493. Like all
other contracts by infants, the manumission is only defeasible by
him. 10 John. 132. The civil law allowed minors to manumit
under certain circumstances. Henry's Points in Manumission.
[5] Ferguson et al. v. Sarah, 4 J. J. Marsh. 103; Wallingsford v.
Allen, 10 Peters, 583. So a deed by the true owner will not effect

cannot, and the result would be the renunciation of his right to the benefit of his co-tenants; the exercise of it, by the slave, being inconsistent with their rights.[1]  Such was the German law : "Servus communis ab uno sociorum, e manu dimissus illico, liber non fieret, quin potius altera pars servi accresceret alteri socio, qui in manumissionem non consensisset."[2] "A slave held in common, and manumitted by one of the co-tenants, will not be made free, but rather the interest of the other tenant, who did not consent to the manumission, will be increased to that extent."

The manumission is effectual so far as to deprive the person manumitting of his interest, which he cannot recall.[3]

§ 330. So the persons entitled only to the use and profits of slaves cannot manumit them, they having no title.  Thus the ecclesiastics could not manumit the slaves attached to the Church.  In favor of liberty, one of the councils decreed, that such manu-

emancipation against one who has held by adverse possession for the period limited by the statute.  Givens and another v. Mann, 6 Munf. 191.  Such was also the civil law.  Voet, ad Pandectas, tit. De Rei Vindicatione, N. 17.

[1] Thompson v. Thompson, 4 B. Monr. 505.  This was in accordance with the civil law right, "jus accrescendi."  Justinian, however, decreed that the joint owner should accept a fair compensation for his interest from the slave.  Dig. xl, 12, 30; 2 Inst. tit. 7; contra Oatfield v. Waring, 14 John. R. 188.  The rule of this case is correct, perhaps, when the co-tenant manumitting has exclusive possession.  His co-tenant may treat the manumission as a conversion.  Even this, however, would be at his election.

[2] Potgies. De Stat. Serv. Lib. IV, cap. ii, § 3.

[3] Thompson v. Thompson, 4 B. Monr. 505; 8 Id. 544.  In the latter case, it is held, that if a majority of the co-tenants join in the manumission, the gift of liberty is perfect.  But *quære?*

mission should be valid if the ecclesiastics would replace *two* slaves for every *one* thus manumitted.[1]

So, a tenant for life cannot enfranchise the slave, to the destruction of the interests in remainder; and as the law cannot recognize a temporary freedom, the gift would operate as a renunciation of the life-estate in favor of the remaindermen.[2] On the contrary, the remaindermen may manumit, to take effect at the death of the tenant for life.

So, also, in those States where the widow is entitled to one-third of her husband's personal estate, a clause of manumission in his will cannot affect her rights.[3] In fact, even the State cannot manumit a slave so long as slavery exists, without the master's consent.[4]

§ 331. So, again, a person may not manumit his slave, so as to relieve himself from any forfeiture or liability which he may have incurred by reason of such ownership, either for the support of the aged and infirm, or for damages for injuries done to another. Nor can an insolvent manumit his slaves to the damage of his creditors.[5] The Roman law re-

---

[1] Potgies. Lib. IV, cap. ii, § 4.

[2] See Tom Davis v. Tingle, 8 B. Monr. 542.

[3] See Virginia Rev. Code, 525; Miss. Rev. Code, 386; 2 Litt. & Swift's Dig. 1246.

[4] Allen v. Peden, 2 Law Rep. 638.

[5] Allen v. Jim Sharp, 7 Gill & J. 96. The *onus* of impeaching the deed lies on the creditor. 7 Gill & J. 96. If the slave has actually enjoyed freedom under the deed of manumission, and the deed is set aside, not for fraud, but simply as avoiding the rights of creditors, it has been held, that it was effectual till set aside, and issue born pending the time are free. Parks v. Hewlett, &c. 9 Leigh, 511; Union Bank v. Benham, 23 Ala. 143.

quired that it should be done with intent to defraud, else it should be valid. The same distinction is recognized in some of the States.[1]

So, also, the Roman law forbade persons condemned to die, or those condemned to slavery as a punishment to manumit their slaves.[2]

§ 332. Almost every State has placed some restraint as to the slaves capable of being manumitted. Thus, the old and sick, who would become burdens on the community, and the young and feeble, incapable of supplying their own wants, are by many laws forbidden the right of emancipation; certain ages being specified between which the right of accepting freedom is allowed.[3]

So, also, the disposition to manumit has in some countries so depopulated the farms and multiplied the number of idle drones, that restrictions have been found necessary as to the number emancipated.[4]

Restraints on manumission were common in all the English West Indies prior to the Emancipation Act. Manumission by implication was not recognized. In St. Vincents, one hundred pounds sterling

[1] Ayliffe's Pandect of Civil Law, Bk. II, tit. viii, p. 90. Ferguson et al. v. Sarah, 4 J. J. Marsh. 103. See Revised Code of Virginia, 434; Mississippi Rev. Code, 386; Civil Code of Louisiana, Art. 190; 2 Litt. & Swift's Digest, 1155.

[2] Ayliffe, as above. The Lex Aelia Sentia, and Lex Junia Norbana, were the principal laws restraining manumission. The Lex Fusia Caninia was made to prevent imprudent manumissions by will.

[3] Trudeau's Exr. v. Robinette, 4 Martin (La.), 577.

[4] Potgies. Lib. IV, cap. ii, § 6. Thomas, Dissertat. de Imped. Manumis. cap. iv.

was required to be paid into the treasury, for each slave sought to be manumitted.[1]

§ 333. Manumission may be either *in presenti* or *in futuro*, unless restricted by statute. In the latter case the condition of slavery remains until the time when the manumission takes effect.[2] Such persons are called by the Roman law *statuliberi*. In the meantime, their issue are slaves. In the former case, the manumission takes effect immediately, and their future issue are free. A reservation in the deed that the issue shall be slaves, would be void.[3] We have, under a former chapter, considered the several questions arising from these general principles as to the *status* of the issue, and shall not repeat them here.[4]

§ 334. There is no middle ground between slavery and freedom; no such thing as qualified freedom, or qualified slavery. If the negro is a slave, he cannot enjoy any of the rights of a freeman, denied to other slaves. If he is free, he cannot be forced to submit to any bonds, not imposed on other free persons of color.[5]

§ 335. At the same time the law does not prohibit a master, either in a sale, or gift, or bequest, from inserting a provision looking to the comfort of a slave, such as the payment of a small annuity, the en-

---

[1] 2 H. Black. 514, note.
[2] Mayho v. Sears, 3 Iredell, 227.
[3] Fulton v. Shaw, 4 Rand. 597.
[4] Ante, chap. iii, §§ 70 to 82.
[5] Henry v. Nunn, 11 B. Monr. 239; Wynn et al. v. Carroll et al. 2 Grat. 227.

forcement of humane treatment, &c.[1]  And, though
the slave has no legal remedy by which to enforce
such provisions, a condition for the forfeiture of the
title upon a failure to perform, would be enforced in
favor of the person entitled in such an event.

§ 336. Manumission may be either direct and in-
tentional, or indirect and by implication; of the former
class are manumission by deed, by will, or by contract; of the latter, are manumission by effect of
law, either foreign or domestic, and by implication.
We will consider of these as far as possible in the
order in which they are named.

§ 337. Manumission by deed has been as ancient
as the art of writing;[2] but in this class we include
not only written deeds, but every express act, *inter
vivos*, granting liberty to the slave.  These were very
various in different nations.

No particular formality was prescribed by the
Grecian laws, nor were such required at Rome
during the earlier days of the kingdom and republic.  Subsequently, by various decrees, certain prescribed forms were to be complied with ; and, at a

---

[1] Spalding v. Grigg. 4 Geo. 75; Drane v. Beall, 21 Ga. 23.  But
see Cunningham v. Cunningham, Conf. Rep. 353.

[2] The following is the form of an ancient deed of manumission :
"Te illum aut illum ex familiâ nostrâ a presente die, ab omni vinculo servitutis absolvimus, ita ut deinceps, tanquam si ab ingenuis
parentibus fuisses procreatus, vitam ducas ingenuam, et nulli
hæredum aut prohæredum nostrorum vel cuicunque servitium nec
libertinitatis obsequium debeas, nisi soli Deo, cui omnia subjecta
sunt; peculiari concesso, quod habes, aut deinceps elaborare poteris."
Marculfus, Lib. II, forms 32, 33, 34.  For various forms, see Du
Cange's Glossary, "Manumissio;" also Appendix to Potgiesser,
p. 920 et seq.

still later day, the consent of a tribunal, established
for that purpose, was necessary to make valid the
manumission. The usual forms were the *census lus-*
*tralis*, the *vindicta*, and the *testamentum*.[1] The first
was effected by the master's entering the name of
the slave upon the list of citizens. The second was
the stroke from the *vindicta*, or freedom-rod, of the
prætor.[2] The last was by will, thus: *Cicero, si neque*
*censu, neque vindicta, nec testamento liber factus est,*
*non est liber.*[3] The former mode went into disuse
about the time of Vespasian. Constantine substituted in its place the manumission *in sacrosanctis*
*ecclesiis*, whereby, in the presence of the congregation, on a feast day, either orally or in writing, declared the slave to be free. In the time of Justinian
other modes were allowed, as by letter, in the presence of friends, &c.[4] Among the Germans and
Lombards, the manumission in the church, *circa*
*altare*, gave the name of *tabularii* to the freedmen.
A mode peculiar to the Franks was, for the master
to strike a small piece of money (*denarius*) from
the hands of the slave in the presence of the king.
These freedmen were called *denariales*.[5] Another

[1] Brown's Civil Law, Bk. I, ch. iii.

[2] After the slave was tapped with the *vindicta* or prætor's rod,
his head was shaved, and the cap of liberty put upon it. Hence,
doubtless, the origin of the liberty cap elevated on a wand, in the
hands of the Goddess of Liberty.

[3] Heinec. Elem. Juris. Lib. I, tit. v, § 94 et seq.

[4] Heinec. as above. Justin. Inst. Lib. I, tit. v, §§ 1, 2; Ayliffe's
Pand. 90. Potgiesser throws some doubt upon Constantine's being
entitled to the credit of originating this mode of manumission.
Lib. IV, ch. iv, § v.

[5] These occupied a more honorable position than the ordinary
freedmen. Potgies. Lib. IV, cap. iii, § 7.

mode among the Lombards was to carry a slave to a point where two roads crossed, and then to utter, in the presence of witnesses, these words: " De quatuor viis, ubi volueris ambulare, liberam habeas potestatem."[1] There were other modes, *per Hantradam, per impans, per sagittam, per arma,* in *mallo publico,* &c., practised among these nations, but not worthy a specific description.[2]

§ 338. In England, similar modes of manumission were adopted from the earliest time. Manumission at the altar is provided for as early as the laws of King Withraed.[3] Full directions to be followed at the County Court are given in the laws of William the Conqueror, even to the " libera arma, scilicet lancea et gladium," which were to be given to the freedmen. The laws of Henry I prescribed four different places where manumission might be effected: *in ecclesiâ, vel mercato, vel comitatu, vel hundreto,* and a record thereof is required to be kept. The reason given is rather curious: " Quia multi potentes volunt, si possunt, defendere homines suos, modo pro servo, modo pro libero, sicut interim facilius sit."[4] It would seem from this, that the difference between the actual condition of the slave and the bondman was not very distinctly marked.

§ 339. In America, unless restricted by statutory regulations, it has been held, in accordance with the principles of the common law, that no formal mode

---

[1] Heinec. Elem. Jur. Germ. Lib. I, tit. ii, §§ 49 to 53 ; Potgies. De Stat. &c. Lib. IV, cap. iii.

[2] Potgies. De Stat. Serv. Lib. IV, cap. i, § v.

[3] Ancient Laws and Institutes of England, 17.

[4] Ibid. 213, 254.

or prescribed words were necessary to effectuate the manumission of slaves ;[1] that it might be effected by parol, and any words were sufficient which evidenced a renunciation of dominion on the part of the master, either *in presenti* or at a specified future period.[2] On the contrary, declarations of an intention, however specific, will be insufficient, unless subsequently carried into effect.[3]

§ 340. In every slaveholding State, however, restrictions, more or less stringent, have been placed upon the manumission of negro slaves, and conditions prescribed to regulate the exercise of this privilege by the master. According as the policy of the legislation of each State inclined for or against the increase of a free colored population, so the tendency of the Courts has been either to adopt the maxim of the civil law, " In obscurâ voluntate manumittentis favendum est libertati,"[4] or, on the other hand, to hold the exercise of this privilege by the master within the strict letter of the law. The result is, a contrariety of decisions, varying more according to the " latitude" of the Courts than the ability of the Judges. Our course shall be " the middle way, in which is safety."[5]

---

[1] Lewis v. Simonton, 8 Humph. 189 ; Fox v. Lanbron, 3 Halst. 275.

[2] The State v. Admrs. of Prall, Coxe, 4 ; Geer v. Huntington, 2 Root, 364.

[3] The State v. Frees, Coxe, 259 ; Bazzi v. Rose, &c. 8 Mart. 149 ; In the matter of Nan Mickel, 14 John. 324 ; 19 John. 53.

[4] Dig. Lib. L, tit. xvii, § 179.

[5] For the laws as to manumission :
In Maryland, Dorsey's Laws, &c. 337, 342, 597.
" Virginia, Revised Code, 458-9, and note to 459.

§ 341. Where the law requires the manumission to be by "instrument in writing," no formal words are necessary. A certificate or letter of manumission will be a compliance with the statute.[1] If there be a condition precedent to its taking effect, such as that the slave shall serve faithfully a certain period of time, then the deed takes effect only when that condition is performed.[2] If, however, the manumission be immediate, and there is a subsequent reservation of services, the slave is emancipated, notwithstanding a failure to perform those services.[3] A sale, subsequent to the deed in the former case, and prior to the performance of the condition, would convey a perfect title to the purchaser. In the latter, the sale would pass no title, the master having parted with his dominion.[4]

§ 342. To effect manumission by a written instrument, it must show a renunciation, by the master,

In North Carolina, Revised Statutes (1837), 585 et seq.
" South Carolina, Stat. at Large, viii, 442, 443, 459; Abstract of Slave Laws by Judge O'Neal.
" Georgia, Cobb's New Dig. (1851), 983, 991, 1125.
" Alabama, Code of 1852, §§ 2044, 5 to 8.
" Mississippi, Hutchinson's Code, 523, 539.
" Louisiana, Civil Code, Art. 184 et seq.
" Arkansas, Dig. of 1848, 65, 476.
" Missouri, Digest of Statutes (1845), ch. 167, Art. 2.
" Tennessee, Caruthers & Nicholson's Dig. 277 et seq.
" Texas, Hartley's Digest, Constitution, 37.
" Delaware, Rev. Code (1852), ch. 80, sec. 5.
[1] Minney v. Cartwright, 3 Marsh. 493.
[2] Julien v. Langlish, 9 Mart. (La.) 205; Dunlap v. Archer, 7 Dana, 30; Kettletas v. Fleet, 7 John. 324.
[3] Isaac v. West, 6 Rand. 561.
[4] Thrift v. Hannah, 2 Leigh, 300; Case of Tom, 5 John. 365.

of his dominion over the slave. Hence, a mere
permit to the slave " to go about his lawful business," with the addition, " this is not to operate as
a pass if he should ever return to the State of Maryland, but he shall be liable to be taken up and treated
as a slave," was held not to be a manumission, the
negro having returned to Maryland.[1] But, if there
be an actual manumission, such a condition subsequent, would be inconsistent with the gift, inoperative and void.[2]

§ 343. Wherever the State has prescribed certain
formalities which must be complied with, or placed
any restrictions upon the exercise of the power of
manumission, it is necessary to show a compliance
with these formalities or restrictions, before the deed
can take effect.[3] Thus, if the statute requires the
registry of the deed, the slave is not free until the
record is complete.[4] So, where the assent of the
State, through its Legislature, or County Court or
other officer, is necessary to manumission, the act is
not complete until such assent is given.[5] It seems,

[1] Maverick v. Stokes, 2 Bay. 511; 1 Brev. 273.

[2] Spencer v. Dennis, 8 Gill. 314; Forward v. Thamer, 9 Grattan, 537.

[3] Clara v. Meagher, 5 Har. & J. 111; 14 John. 324; 19 Ib. 53;
The State v. Emmons, 1 Penn. 10; Roberts v. Mellugen, 9 Miss.
170.   But see State v. Pitney, Coxe, 165; Reuben v. Parrish, 6
Humph. 122.

[4] Givens v. Mann, 6 Munf. 191; Donaldson v. Jude, 1 Bibb,
57 (see 2 J. J. Marsh. 230); Sawney v. Carter, 6 Rand. 173;
Thrift v. Hannah, 2 Leigh, 300; Miller v. Herbert, 5 Howard,
U. S. 72.

[5] Bryan v. Dennis, 4 Florida, 445.   Held otherwise in Tennessee.   8 Humph. 185; 10 Ibid. 332.

however, that this assent may be given even before the deed is executed; and in that event the deed takes effect immediately.[1]   It is not necessary, in those States where the assent of a Court is required to be given on certain conditions, that the order of the Court should show that these conditions were complied with.   The judgment of the Court will be conclusive until set aside, and cannot be collaterally attacked.[2]   It is not conclusive, however, as to facts recited outside of the action of the Court. Thus an order, that a slave be manumitted "agreeably to a deed which said G. had filed," is not conclusive evidence that such a deed was duly executed.[3]

§ 344.   In several of the States domestic manumission, that is, manumission to take effect within the State, is prohibited, the increase of free negroes being declared against their policy.   Of course all deeds or wills attempting to manumit in opposition to such policy, are *pro tanto* void.[4]   But even in these States it is allowed, by deed or will, to provide for the immediate transfer of the slaves to some other State or country where manumission is allowed,

---

[1] 6 Yerg. 119; or afterwards see Donaldson v. Jude, 2 Bibb, 57.

[2] Samson v. Burgwin, 3 Dev. & Bat. 28; Hartsell v. George, 3 Humph. 255; Greenlow v. Rawlings, 3 Humph. 90; Stringer v. Burcham, 12 Ired. 41; Lewis v. Simonton, 8 Humph. 185.   Even in another State.   Maria v. Alterbery, 9 Miss. 369; see Cully v. Jones, 9 Ired. 168, as to the effect of a failure to give bond, when required by the Court.

[3] Talbot v. David, 2 A. K. Marsh. 603.

[4] Moses v. Deniger, 6 Rand. 561; Finley v. Hunter, 2 Strobh. Eq. 208.

for the purpose of being there emancipated.[1] If, however, the provision is made for a *future* emigration for that purpose, it would be void; it being in contravention of that public policy to increase the number of *statuliberi* within the limits of the State. Hence, in a gift of slaves to A. for life or years, and at the expiration of that estate, a provision for their emigration to a foreign State, for the purpose of manumission, the latter provision would be void.[2] But a bequest of slaves to an executor, requiring him to apply to the Legislature for a special act, allowing their manumission within the State, and on failure to obtain that, directing their transmission to another country for this purpose, would be valid.[3] And a direction to the executor to pay a legacy to such slaves, in their new home, would be valid, notwithstanding their incapacity to take while slaves.[4]

§ 345. Any attempt to avoid the operation of these acts, forbidding manumission by a trust, either open or secret, for the benefit of the slave, will be

[1] Cox v. Williams, 4 Ired. Eq. 15; Thompson v. Newlin, 8 Ired. Eq. 32; Wooten v. Becton, Ibid. 66; Vance v. Crawford, 4 Geo. 445; Sibley v. Maria, 2 Florida, 553; Wade v. Am. Col. Soc. 7 S. & M. 663. But this is prohibited in South Carolina; and it was held that the act applied to a will, admitted to probate before the passage, of which *quære?* 2 Rich. Eq. 43; see 7 Humph. 388.

[2] Pinckard v. McCoy, 22 Ga. 28; Drane v. Beall, 21 Ga. 23; Thornton v. Chisolm, 20 Ga. 338.

[3] Cleland et al. v. Waters, 19 Ga. 35.

[4] Vance v. Crawford, 4 Ga. 445; Wade v. Amer. Col. Soc. 7 S. & M. 663; Cooper v. Blakely, 10 Ga. 263; Cameron v. Com. of Raleigh, 1 Ired. Eq. 436; Cooper v. Blakely, 10 Ga. 263.

illegal and void.[1]   And such trust may be proven by parol, outside of the deed.[2]

§ 346. The trust being void, does the deed or will convey any title to the trustee? If he had no agency in creating the illegal trust, was not a party to the attempt to evade the law by assenting thereto, or agreeing to carry out the same, then the trust only is void, and the trustee takes the title freed from the illegal trust.[3]  But the whole conveyance or bequest is void if the trustee was a *particeps criminis* in the attempt to violate or evade the law. The grantor himself might not be heard, however, to set up his own wrong; and the principle, *in pari delicto*, &c., has been held to apply where the statute does not declare the deed to be absolutely void.[4]

So, also, an illegal bequest of freedom in remainder to slaves, after a life-estate, does not destroy or render the latter ineffectual.[5]

§ 347. A question of some nicety arises, where a deed of manumission is made in a State allowing thereof, and to take effect at a future time, but before that period arrives the slave is carried into another State, where such manumission is prohibited. When

---

[1] White v. White, 1 Dev. & Bat. 260; Wright v. Lowe, 2 Murph. 354; The State v. Singlebury, Dudley, S. C. 220; Cunningham v. Cunningham, Conf. Rep. 353.

[2] Robinson v. King, 6 Geo. 539.

[3] The State v. Singlebury, Dudley, S. C. 220; Weathersby v. Weathersby, 13 S. & M. 685; Broughton v. Telfer, 3 Rich. 431; Cline v. Caldwell, Hill, S. C. 423; Smith v. Dumoody, 19 Ga. 666; Drane v. Beall, 21 Ga. 23.

[4] Cline v. Caldwell, 1 Hill, S. C. 423.

[5] Dougherty v. Dougherty, 2 Strobh. Eq. 63.

the period arrives, what is the *status* of the slave? Although the legislature had prohibited manumission within the State, and the increase of a free colored population is not desired, until the legislature either refuse ingress into the State to negroes occupying the position of *statuliberi*, or otherwise declares its will, the *lex loci* must, upon principle, control and give freedom to the slave.[1] In such case, it has been held, that the applicants for freedom must prove, as a fact, the existence of the *lex loci*.[2] The propriety of this ruling we must doubt. We have seen that, in the absence of statutory inhibition, the right to manumit was undoubted. The presumption of law therefore is, that the owner has such a right by the *lex loci*, and the party suggesting statutory restrictions should prove them.[3]

§ 348. If, however, the deed or will is made with reference to slaves within another jurisdiction, or is made with a view to evade the laws prohibiting manumission in another State, the Courts of that State will not regard the *lex loci*, but will enforce their own statutes.[4] So, also, if slaves are sent out of the State and emancipated, with a view to return

[1] Sidney v. White, 12 Ala. N. S. 728; Nancy v. Snell, 6 Dana, 148, 151; Reuben v. Parrish, 6 Humph. 122; Sam v. Fore, 12 S. & M. 413; Sidney v. White, 12 Ala. 728.

[2] Sam v. Fore, 12 S. & M. 413; Sidney v. White, 12 Ala. 728; Remick v. Chloe, 7 Miss. 197.

[3] These remarks do not apply to the case in 12 Ala. There the applicant set up that the law of Tennessee, in construing certain deeds differing from the general current of decisions, he was rightly required to prove it.

[4] Lewis v. Fullerton, 1 Rand. 15; Mahomer v. Hooe, 9 S. & M. 247.

after emancipation, being a fraud on the law, the manumission is void.[1]

§ 349. Although a deed of manumission is not good against the claim of creditors, if the grantor is insolvent, yet it is good until set aside in the proper court. Hence, the executor of the grantor cannot treat such manumitted slave as assets, but must resort to his legal remedy to vacate the deed.[2] A court of equity has jurisdiction for this purpose, and may frame a decree so as to sell the negro only for a term of years, if thereby the creditors will be paid.[3] Issue born after the deed, and before its vacation, are free.[4] If the deed is made by the insolvent, with a view to defeat creditors, it is still good against him.[5]

§ 350. If a deed of manumission be of doubtful construction, the usual rules of interpretation should be applied; and, among others, that it is to be taken most strongly against the grantor.[6] If it be lost, secondary evidence of its contents may be admitted. But if lost before registry, parol evidence of its contents will not authorize a record.[7]

[1] Green v. Lane, 8 Ired. Eq. 70. Held otherwise in Blackmore v. Phill, 7 Yerg. 452.

[2] Allen v. Sharp, 7 Gill. & J. 96; Snead v. David, 9 Dana, 350; Thomas v. Wood, 1 Md. Ch. Dec. 296.          [3] Ibid.

[4] Parks v. Hewlett, 9 Leigh, 511; 23 Ala. 143.

[5] So was the civil law.  Cod. vii, 8, 5.

[6] Isaac v. West, 6 Rand. 652. The civil law rule was, that in case of doubt the construction should be in favor of liberty. "In obscurâ voluntate manumittentis favendum est libertati." See Dig. xxxv, 2, 32. Pothier lays down the same rule, in notes to tit. De Regulis Juris.

[7] Mimey v. Cartricht, 3 A. K. Marsh. 493.

§ 351. Sometimes the courts presume a deed of manumission when the owner permits the slave, for a number of years, to do acts inconsistent with a state of slavery. It is a question generally submitted to the jury, but upon which the courts, in different States, vary in their rulings.[1] This presumption may, of course, be rebutted by proof of acts inconsistent with freedom.[2]

§ 352. If the record shows that the Court has acted on a case not authorized by the statute, the judgment is of no effect. As in North Carolina, the petition was to emancipate the slave "when the owner thinks proper;" and the decree granted permission "on the owner's complying with the statutes;" it was held, that the proceeding was invalid.[3]

---

[1] Burke v. Joe, 6 Gill & John. 136; Wells v. Lane, 9 John. 144; Miller v. Reigne, 2 Hill S. C. 592; State v. McDonald, Coxe, 332; Wilson v. Barnett, 8 Gill. & J. 159; State v. Hill, 2 Speers, 150; Stringer v. Burcham, 12 Ired. 41; Anderson v. Garrett, 9 Gill. 120; Henderson v. Jason, 9 Gill. 483.

[2] Sampson v. Burguin, 3 Dev. & Bat. 28.

[3] Bryan v. Wadsworth, 1 Dev. & Bat. 384.

# CHAPTER XX.

§ 353. WHAT has been said in reference to manumission by deed, applies with equal force to manumission by will, except in those States where such manumission is prohibited. The number of slaves thus set free has caused, in some of the States, a prohibition of manumission by will.[1] In the absence of that, a testator may order his executor to do that which he himself could have done while in life. There are other questions, however, which arise peculiarly on manumission by will, to which we will now attend.

§ 354. The will must be executed with the same formalities as is necessary to pass title to slaves to other legatees;[2] and if not executed in that manner, it cannot be aided or made effectual by a mere reference to it in some other conveyance.[3] So, also, a nuncupative will cannot effect emancipation where

---

[1] Mississippi, 9 S. & M. 247; Alabama, 14 Ala. 76. In Maryland, deeds of manumission made during the last illness, are void. 2 Har. & McH. 198.

[2] Mullins v. Wall, 8 B. Monr. 445. This was a case of the fraudulent destruction of the will by the heirs.

[3] Henry v. Nunn, 11 B. Monr. 239.

it is insufficient to pass a bequest of slaves.[1] The assent of the executor is as necessary to a manumitting clause as to any other legacy, but this assent may be presumed from his acts.[2]

§ 355. A will having no effect until the death of testator, a sale or gift of the negro, to whom freedom was bequeathed by the testator in his lifetime, is *pro tanto* a revocation of the will.[3] But it takes effect immediately after death, and hence, a child born after the death of testator and before probate of the will, of a slave manumitted by the will, is free.[4] And this is true, even if the manumission is conditional upon the slave's electing to go to Liberia.[5]

The mere expression of a desire, in a will, that a slave shall be free, does not amount to a manumission, if, from other provisions, it appears that the intention of testator was not to part with the dominion over such slave.[6] Nor would a bequest of freedom, if the executor or heir shall be willing, according to the civil law, amount to manumission.[7]

§ 356. In construing a bequest of freedom, some of the courts have announced that the law favors liberty, and hence, the courts will incline in favor

[1] Cooke v. Cooke, 3 Litt. 238; aliter, where it would pass a bequest of slaves, even though the statute requires manumission to be done by writing. Phœbe v. Boggers, 1 Grat. 129.

[2] Nicholas v. Burruss, 4 Leigh, 289; Nancy v. Snell, 6 Dana, 148.

[3] Matter of Nan Mitchell, 14 John. 324; Stewart v. Williams, 3 Md. 425.          [4] Black v. Meaux, 4 Dana, 188.

[5] Graham v. Sam, 7 B. Monr. 403.

[6] Rucker v. Gilbert, 3 Leigh, 8; Taylor v. The American Bible Soc. 7 Ired. Eq. 201.          [7] Dig. Lib. xxx, 1, 75.

of manumission,[1] while others have announced that
the increase of a free colored population is against
the policy of a slaveholding State, and hence the
courts will incline against manumission.[2]  The true
principle of hermeneutics is, that the Court should
incline neither the one way or the other, but should
inquire, first, what is the intention of testator? and,
second, has he used sufficient words to carry out his
intention?[3]  If, in either of these particulars, the
bequest is insufficient, it must fail, unless in the
latter case the facts make out such a case as, under
the general rules of law, will authorize the Court to
supply words, in which event, such words will be
supplied.[4]

§ 357. We have seen heretofore that manumission cannot be effected to the prejudice of creditors.  If the estate, therefore, is insolvent, the bequest fails,[5] nor can the executor, by assenting to
the legacy before the solvency of the estate is ascertained, deprive the creditors of their right to look
to the slaves as assets.[6]  If there be a sufficiency of
assets, and the executor still refuses to assent, the
slaves cannot commence their petition for freedom,

[1] Nancy v. Snell, 6 Dana, 149; 7 Serg. & R. 378; Cuffy v. Cas-
tillon, 5 Mart. 494.  Such was the rule of the civil law.  "Quoties
dubia libertatis interpretatio est."  Dig. Lib. 1, 17, 20.

[2] Charlotte v. Chouteau, 11 Miss. 193.

[3] See Monica v. Mitchell, 1 Md. Ch. Dec. 355; Robinson v.
King, 6 Ga. 539; Lanham v. Meacham, 4 Strobh. Eq. 203; Cleland v. Waters, 16 Ga. 491.

[4] Cleland v. Waters, 16 Ga. Rep. 496.

[5] Cornish v. Wilson, 6 Gill. 299.

[6] 6 Gill. 299; Fenwick v. Chapman, 9 Peters, 461.  It is good
against him.  Nancy v. Snell, 6 Dana, 155; 9 Peters, 461.

and rely upon these facts to show their right to their liberty, but must institute another proceeding, usually in Chancery, to compel the executor to assent,[1] in which case, the Court does not decree the liberty of the slaves, nor that the executor make deeds of manumission, but that he assent to the legacy.[2] If the executor is an improper person to administer the assets, so as to secure the solvency of the estate, some of the courts have placed the assets in the hands of a commissioner for this purpose.[3] If the executor should wrongfully sell a slave thus manumitted, where there is a sufficiency of assets to pay the debts, the sale would not be good, even to an innocent purchaser, against the claim of the negro to freedom. In fact, the will being of record, is notice to the purchaser.[4]

§ 358. Is real estate assets for the payment of debts, so as to secure the bequest of manumission? In those States where real estate is made assets on the same footing with personalty, for the payment of debts, it should be exhausted before the manumitting clause should fail entirely.[5] If, however, slaves are held as personalty, and the law of the State requires that species of property to be exhausted before the realty should be looked to as assets, upon principle, the right of the heir is

---

[1] Cornish v. Wilson, 6 Gill. 299; Peters v. Van Lear, 4 Gill. 249.

[2] 6 Gill. 299; see also Anderson v. Garrett, 9 Gill. 120.

[3] Graham v. Sam, 7 B. Monr. 403.

[4] Nancy v. Snell, 6 Dana, 149, 151; Patty v. Colin et al. 1 Hen. & Munf. 525; Boyce v. Nancy, 4 Dana, 238.

[5] Thomas v. Wood, 1 Md. Ch. Dec. 296.

superior to that of the manumitted slave. The testator may, by his will, charge his debts upon the realty in order to secure freedom to his slave, in which event, of course, his will should be executed.[1] By the civil law, if a testator bequeathed freedom to a slave, supposing himself to be the owner, when in reality he was not, the heir was bound to purchase him at a reasonable price, to effectuate this purpose.[2]

§ 359. There may be a sufficiency of assets at the death of testator, and subsequent thereto these may, without fault of the executor, prove insufficient, in which event the bequest of freedom must fail.[3] And, *e converso*, if the assets were originally insufficient, and subsequently became sufficient, the bequest is good.[4] If the insufficiency does not amount to the value of the manumitted slaves, a Court of Chancery may order their sale only for a term of years, until the proceeds shall satisfy the debts.[5] If there is a sufficiency of assets, and the executor assents to the manumission, a sale of the manumitted slave under a *fi. fa.* against the executor would be void and convey no title.[6]

§ 360. Before the bequest is declared invalid on

[1] When the intention to manumit, at all events, is manifest, slight words will amount to a charge. The words " after my debts and funeral charges are paid, I devise and bequeath as follows," held sufficient to charge the debts on real estate, in order to give effect to a manumitting clause. Fenwick v. Chapman, 9 Peters, 461.

[2] Dig. xl, 5, 39.

[3] Wilson v. Ann Barnett, 9 Gill. & John. 158.

[4] 9 Gill. & J. 158.

[5] Cornish v. Wilson, 6 Gill. 299; Nancy v. Snell, 6 Dana, 151.

[6] Rice v. Spear, Harper's Law Rep. 20.

account of the insufficiency of assets to pay debts, there should be an accurate account of all the assets subject to this purpose ; and where the realty is so subject, the heir at law should be called in to account therefor.[1] An order passed by the Orphans Court, directing the administrator to sell the slaves, would not be conclusive evidence of the insufficiency of the assets.[2]

§ 361. If the residuum be insufficient to pay the debts, and specific legacies must abate to furnish a fund for this purpose, the question may arise, whether the bequest of freedom to a slave (being estimated as of the value of the slave) should abate *pro rata* with other legacies ? Some of the courts seem to incline against such abatement, on the ground of the favored character of the bequests. Upon principle, it should be treated as other specific legacies, and abate *pro rata* .

§ 362. In those States where manumission by will or domestic manumission is prohibited, the question arises, whether the heirs or distributees at law, or the residuary legatee, is entitled to slaves to whom a void bequest of freedom is given. It has been held that they fall into the residuum.[4]

§ 363. It has been suggested by the courts of one of the States, that a slave is incapable of making a choice ; and hence, a bequest providing for an elec-

[1] Allein v. Sharp, 7 Gill. & J. 96; Thomas v. Wood, 1 Md. Ch. Dec. 296; George v. Corse's Admr. 2 Har. & Gill. 1.

[2] Wilson v. Barnett, 8 Gill. & J. 160.

[3] Nancy v. Snell, 6 Dana, 152, 153.

[4] Roberson v. Roberson, 21 Ala. 273; 7 Ib. 795; Lanham v. Meacham, 4 Strobh. Eq. 203.

tion by the slave, to remain in bondage or be removed
to a non-slaveholding State, would fail by reason of
this incapacity.[1]  This suggestion has not been approved by other courts,[2] and we cannot see the force
of it.  The theory of a complete annihilation of
will in the slave, is utterly inconsistent with all recognition of him as a person, especially as responsible
criminally for his acts.

§ 364. It sometimes occurs, that a testator directs
his slaves to be removed to another State for the
purpose of manumission, and the execution of this
provision becomes impossible, from the refusal of
such State to admit free negroes within its limits.
It has been held, that in such cases the bequest
fails.[3] It may be a question whether, in such a case,
the primary intention of the testator to emancipate
his slaves may not, on the principle of approximation or *cy-près*, be carried out, regardless of the
secondary intention as to the particular manner of
effecting it.

§ 365. Wherever the legislature directs the removal of the slave after emancipation, or imposes
any other condition upon the execution of bequests
of manumission, they must be strictly complied
with.[4] If, however, there is unavoidable delay in
removal, beyond the time specified; or if there is a
fraudulent collusion to violate the law, in order to

[1] Carroll v. Bromby, 13 Ala. 102.
[2] Leech v. Cooley, 6 S. & M. 93; John v. Moreman, 8 B. Monr.
100; 10 Ib. 69; Isaac v. McGill, 9 Humph. 616; Washington v.
Blunt, 8 Ired. Eq. 253.
[3] Nancy v. Wright, 9 Humph. 597; Cleland et al. v. Waters,
18 Ga. Rep. 563.        [4] Spencer v. Dennis, 8 Gill. 314.

deprive the slave of the benefit of the bequest, such failure to comply will not avoid the manumission.[1]

§ 366. We have seen heretofore how slaves, inte- rested under a will, could be heard in a motion to have the will proven, without a violation of the principle which denies, to them, while slaves, the right to sue.[2] We may add here, that if a slave is bequeathed to a legatee for the purpose of manu- mission, this is good reason for a court of equity to decree a specific performance, if the executor, or other person having him in possession, refuses to deliver him up.[3] In those States where domestic manumission is forbidden and foreign emancipation is allowed, a question may arise, how a direction to executors to remove slaves to a foreign State for this purpose, can be enforced ? In the absence of statutory enactment, both public policy and the principles of justice require, that the courts should devise some means by which a faithless executor should be compelled to execute the trust. In similar cases, the civil law gave the slave an equitable action to enforce the trust.[4]

§ 367. A slave being incapable of making a con- tract, and all of his earnings belonging to his master, it would follow necessarily that no executory con- tract between the master and the slave, looking to future manumission, could be enforced, even where the slave could show a complete compliance on his

[1] Wade v. Am. Col. Soc. 7 S. & M. 663.
[2] §§ 283, 284. See also Redford v. Peggy, 6 Rand. 316; and Manus v. Givens, 7 Leigh, 689.
[3] Code, Lib. vii, 5, 17.
[4] Dig. xl, 5, 17; Cod. vii, 16, 25, and 26.

part.[1] Such was the civil law.[2] Yet, under certain circumstances, such contracts have been enforced both under that law and in some of the States.[3] If the contract is for immediate manumission, and made in conformity with law, the master may subsequently enforce from the manumitted slave a compliance with its terms.[4] Such was also the civil law.[5]

§ 368. A very different result follows a contract made by the master, with a third person, for the manumission of the slave. Such a contract, if not forbidden by the law, stands on the same footing with all other contracts, and can be enforced by the parties thereto.[6] The slave, however, is not a party to the contract; nor can he, like another *cestui que trust*, apply for its execution in his favor.[7] Accord-

[1] Beall v. Joseph, Hardin, 51; Cooke v. Cooke, 3 Litt. 238; Bland v. Dowling, 9 Gill. & J. 19; Willis v. Bruce, 8 B. Monr. 548. In Louisiana, these contracts are excepted from the general incapacity of the slave to contract, and if in writing, may be enforced by the slave, after a full compliance with the terms. Victoire v. Dussuau, 4 Mart. 212; 5 Mart. 494.

[2] Dig. xv, 1, 11; Dig. xl, 1, 4; Ibid. 1, 19.

[3] Dig. as above. Stiles v. Richardson, 4 Yeates, 82; Kettletas v. Fleet, 7 John. 324; State v. Prall, Coxe, 4; Sally v. Beaty, 1 Bay. 260.

[4] Keane v. Boycott, 2 H. Black. 511; Williams v. Brown, 3 Bos & Pul. 69; Opinions of Heath, Rooke, and Chambre, JJ.; Commonwealth v. Clements, 6 Binney, 206; Stiles v. Richardson, 4 Yeates, 82; Kettletas v. Fleet, 7 John. 324. Held otherwise in Commonwealth v. Cook, 1 Watts, 155; and Commonwealth v. Robinson, Ib. 158; but placed on a statute of Pennsylvania.

[5] Dig. iv, 3, 8.

[6] Gatliffe's Admr. v. Rose et al. 8 B. Monr. 633; Thomson v. Wilmot, 1 Bibb, 422; Cato v. Howard, 2 Har. & J. 323.

[7] Gatliffe's Admr. v. Rose et al. 8 B. Monr. 633; Dunlap v. Archer, 7 Dana, 30.

ing to the civil law, a slave sold with a covenant that the purchaser should manumit him, became free without farther act.[1] If a future time was specified, he became free at that time.[2]

§ 369. Where manumission is not required to be effected by written instrument, nor otherwise restricted by statute, a contract by a master with his slave, for his manumission, might effect an immediate emancipation by implication; as the master thereby recognizes in the slave the power to contract,—a power belonging only to freemen.[3]

[1] Dig. xl, 8, 9.　　　　　　　　[2] Cod. iv, 57, 4.
[3] Keane v. Boycott, 2 H. Black. 514, and note.

# CHAPTER XXI.

## OF INDIRECT MANUMISSION.

§ 370. WE come now to consider of *indirect* manumission; which may be effected either by the operation of law, or by implication, from the acts of the master.

§ 371. Manumission by operation of law, may be either of foreign laws acting on the slave when properly subject to their influence; or of domestic laws, the violation of which works the emancipation of the slave. We have heretofore considered, at length, the effect of foreign laws upon a slave voluntarily or by flight coming within their jurisdiction; and have laid down the rules which we considered govern such cases.[1] We will not repeat them here. We may add, that as the *animus morandi*, the change of domicile, is essential in order to work emancipation, such animus cannot be imputed to one who is not *sui juris*, and capable of choosing a domicile, such as an infant or one under duress.[2]

§ 372. So, also, one who has only a temporary interest in a slave, as a hirer or even a tenant for

[1] §§ 134–239.

[2] Porter v. Butler, 3 Har. & McHen. 168; David v. Porter, 4 Har. & McHen. 418.

life, cannot destroy the interest of the owner, in fee or in remainder, by changing the domicile of the slave to a foreign State.[1] One of several joint owners could destroy the entire interest; for, having a right to the possession of the slave equally with the others, he can choose a domicile for the slave, and his cotenants must look to him for damages in thus destroying the joint property. But a mortgagor cannot thus destroy the interest of the mortgagee. The slave can recover freedom only by satisfying the mortgage debt.[2]

§ 373. If manumission be once effected by the operation of foreign laws, it is as complete and effectual to secure liberty to the slave, as manumission by deed; and the subsequent return of the negro to the original domicile would not restore to the master the dominion over him.[3] Of course it is otherwise where the residence in the foreign State is temporary, and the *status* of slavery has never been changed, even though the courts of such foreign State refused to aid the master in asserting his dominion within their jurisdiction.[4]

§ 374. Many of the slaveholding States, conceiving it to be their policy not to admit a farther immigration of slaves, except with their masters, *bonâ fide* intending to become citizens, have passed laws

---

[1] Butler v. Delaplaine, 7 Serg. & R. 378; Davis v. Tingle, 8 B. Monr. 545–6.      [2] Milly v. Smith, 2 Miss. 171.

[3] Marie Louise v. Mariot et al. 8 Louis. Rep. 475; Mimey v. Whitesides, 1 Miss. 472; Bland v. Dowling, 9 Gill. & J. 19; Josephine v. Poulteney, 1 La. An. Rep. 329.

[4] Case of slave Grace, 2 Hagg. Ad. Rep. 94; Dred Scott case, 19 How. 1.

prohibiting such immigration, and have annexed various penalties to their violation. In some, one of the penalties is the manumission of the slave.[1] In such States, slaves imported in violation of the law, or whose masters have failed to comply with those requisites as to registry, oath, &c., prescribed by the statutes to avoid evasions, are free.[2] If, however, this is not a penalty prescribed, the slave is not free, though imported in violation of the law.[3]

§ 375. If an infant or *feme covert* should fail to comply with the requisites of the statute, as to registry, &c., the Courts will not permit their failure to work a forfeiture of their title so long as the disability continues.[4] It has been held, also, that an agent intrusted with the importation of the slaves, might comply with the formalities of the statute, even to the taking of the oath prescribed.[5] Nor does the statute apply to any but voluntary importations; and hence, one forced to fly from St. Domingo with her slaves, and temporarily residing in Maryland, was held not to be within the operation

[1] Laws of Maryland, on this subject, Dorsey's Laws, &c. pp. 334, 1108, 1112, 2325; Laws of Virginia, Revised Code, 749; Laws of South Carolina, Stat. at Large, vii, 447.

[2] Henderson v. Tom, 4 Har. & John. 282; Scott v. Ben, 6 Cranch, 1; Boisneuf v. Lewis, 4 Har. & McH. 414; Fulton v. Lewis, 3 Har. & J. 564.

[3] Gomez v. Bonneval, 6 Mart. 626.

[4] Haney v. Waddle, 3 Har. & John. 557; Sprigg v. Mary, 3 Har. & J. 491.

[5] Montgomery v. Fletcher, 6 Rand. 612. A wife may not. McMichen v. Amos, 4 Rand. 134.

of the law.¹ So, if a slave is brought into the State without the consent of the true owner, he does not become free.²

§ 376. If a slave be removed to another State, and acquire a domicile there, the subsequent return of such slave into the State is an importation within the statute.³ If, however, the master's residence in such other State was temporary, on his return with his slaves he need not comply with the formalities prescribed by the statute.⁴

§ 377. Slaves introduced into the State for a mere temporary purpose, as by a hirer for a year, are not imported in violation of the law.⁵ After long possession in the State, the Court may presume a compliance with the statutory regulations.⁶ Under certain circumstances, also, parol evidence has been admitted to supply an omission in the certificate given by the collector of the tax imposed on slaves imported.⁷

§ 378. It is almost unnecessary to say, that where the statute requires the registry of slaves for the

¹ Baptist et al. v. De Volunbrun, 5 Har. & J. 86; Ib. 99, n. *Aliter* if the residence be permanent. Fulton v. Lewis, 3 Har. & John. 564.

² Scott v. London, 3 Cranch, 324; Pocock v. Hendricks, 8 Gill. & J. 421; see also 6 Munf. 12; 4 Rand. 67.

³ Wilson v. Isbell, 5 Call. 425; Sprigg v. Pressly, 3 Har. & J. 493; Betty v. Horton, 5 Leigh, 615.

⁴ Murray v. McClarty, 2 Munf. 393; Barnett v. Sam, 1 Gilmer, 232; Adams v. Leverton, 2 Har. & McH. 382.

⁵ Henry v. Ball, 1 Wheat. 1.

⁶ Mason v. Matilda, 12 Wheat. 590; Abraham v. Matthews, 6 Munf. 159.

⁷ Harry v. Lyles, 4 Har. & McHen. 215.

purpose of gradual abolition, or for any other purpose, and prescribes freedom as a penalty for a non-
compliance, the master failing to comply, forfeits his
interest in the slave.[1]  If he registers by a wrong
name, it has been held that parol evidence was inadmissible to show the mistake.[2]  And the registry
by one not the owner or his agent, has been held
insufficient.[3]

§ 379. In some of the States the exportation of
slaves, under certain circumstances, is illegal, and
emancipation is the penalty.  A violation of such
a statute gives immediate liberty to the slave.[4]  The
carrying of a slave out of the State on a temporary
travel or sojourning, does not come within the inhibition of the law.[5]

§ 380. It remains for us to consider of manumission by implication, from the acts of the master.
Where manumission may be effected by parol, and
no formalities are prescribed by the law, acts of the
master recognizing the slave as a freeman, were held
by the Courts sufficient evidence to presume a previous manumission.  When freedom was declared
upon such evidence, the manumission was implied,
and hence the title, " by implication."  From this
view of its origin, it is evident that manumission
can never be implied in any State where public formalities are required to make it effectual.

§ 381. In the civil law, and especially before any

[1] Giles v. Meeks, Addis. 384.
[2] Lucy v. Pumfrey, Addis. 380.
[3] Elson v. McCullough, 4 Yeates, 115.
[4] Allen v. Sarah, 2 Harring. 434 ; 3 Ibid. 560.
[5] Cross v. Black, 9 Gill. & J. 198.

restraints were placed on manumission, various acts by the master were considered sufficient to justify the Courts to imply freedom; such as appointing the slave guardian or tutor by will;[1] giving him a legacy;[2] living in a state of concubinage with a female slave, and not mentioning her in his will;[3] abandoning him in sickness,[4] and all similar acts showing a withdrawal of the dominion of the master.

§ 382. So it has been held in America, that the bringing of an action by the master against the slave,[5] or a devise of property, real or personal, to the slave by the master,[6] implied manumission.

[1] Inst. i, 14.　　　　　　　[2] Ibid. ii, 14.
[3] Code, vii, 15, 3.　　　　　[4] Dig. xl, 8, 2.
[5] Oatfield v. Waring, 14 John. 188.
[6] Hall v. Mullin, 5 Har. & John. 190; Guillemette v. Harper, 4 Rich. 186. Such implied manumission is expressly forbidden by the Civil Code of Louisiana, Art. 184.

# CHAPTER XXII.

OF THE EFFECT OF MANUMISSION, AND HEREIN OF
THE STATUS OF FREE PERSONS OF COLOR.

§ 383. MANUMISSION once effected, removes forever the dominion of the master, and by no act of his can it be restored;[1] nor can even the legislative power of the State deprive the freedman of his liberty, except for some violation of the law.[2] By the Roman law, the freedman became the client of the master, who, as patron, continued to exercise considerable power over him. This, however, was the result of municipal law.

§ 384. To withdraw his dominion, is the privilege of the master. To incorporate a new citizen into the body politic, is only within the power of the State. The freed negro does not become a citizen by virtue of his manumission. It requires the act of another party, the State, to clothe him with civil and political rights.[3] Before such act he stands

---

[1] The civil law carried this principle so far as to protect freedom acquired by fraud. Dig. iv, 3, 24. See Article 189, of Louisiana Civil Code.

[2] I am aware of the decision in Blackman v. Gordon, 2 Rich. Eq. 43; but I conceive the text to be in accordance with principle.

[3] Crandall v. The State, 10 Conn. 340; Bryan v. Walton, 14 Ga.

in the position of an alien friend, and in the absence
of legislation he would be entitled to all such privileges as are allowed to such residents.[1]  He occupies in such a case the position of the freedmen of
Rome (*liberti* or *libertini*), before the right of citizenship was conferred upon them.[2]  They were capable
of all those rights founded on the *jus naturale* and
*jus gentium*, but not political rights or those apper-
taining to citizenship.  They were as to these in the
same condition with alien friends (*peregrini*).[3]

§ 385.  I regret, in this opinion, to differ from the
conclusions of the Supreme Court of Georgia, in
Bryan .v. Walton, 14 Ga. 185.  I agree with them
as to the *status* of the freed negro in Georgia, but
that *status*, in my opinion, is derived from the legislation of the State, by which he " can act only by
and through his guardian," and by which " he is in
a state of perpetual pupilage or wardship."

§ 386.  Free persons of color, unless restricted by
statute, may contract marriage with those of their
own condition, or any free person capable of contracting.  Intermarriage with the whites is prohibited in a large majority of the States of the Union.
They may make contracts, and dispose of their

185; 1 Meiggs's Rep. 331; N. Bacon's Discourse on the Laws of
England, 35; Decision of J. Daniel, in Scott v. Sandford, 19 How.
83.  The case of the State v. Edmund, 4 Dev. 340, seems to be
otherwise.  A close examination of it, however, shows that it is
merely a construction of a penal statute.  The case of The State
v. Manuel, 4 Dev. & Bat. 20, is placed on the statutes of the State.

[1] See Fable v. Brown's Exr. 2 Hill's Ch. 391.

[2] Inst. Lib. I, tit. v, Art. 3; tit. xvi, § 4.

[3] Kaufman's Mackeldey, Div. II, ch. i, § 119.

estates by will. In the absence of a will, administration will be granted on their estates, and unless otherwise directed by statute, they will be subject to the ordinary and general law of distribution.[1]

§ 387. Public policy has made it necessary for the slaveholding States, by statute, to impose other restrictions upon free persons of color. They have been forced to extend over them their patrol and police regulations, to deny to them the privilege of bearing arms, to require of them the selection of a guardian, who shall stand as patron, and contract for them; to restrain their acquisition of negro slaves as property; to place them on the same footing with slaves as to their intercourse with white citizens; such as purchasing spirituous liquors, &c.[2] These various restrictions, differing in the different States, place the free negro but little above the slave as to civil privileges. Hence, the penal slave

[1] In Georgia, their estates go to their "descendants," which has been held not to include collaterals. Bryan v. Walton, 20 Ga. 512; Akin v. Anderson, 19 Ga. 229.

[2] Maryland, see Dorsey's Laws, 335, 340, 510, 543, 858, 1071, 1072.
Virginia, Rev. Code (1849), 458, 465, 468, 748, 753, 754.
North Carolina, Rev. Statutes (1837), 588, 590, 591.
South Carolina, Stat. at Large, vii, 462 et seq. 474.
Georgia, Cobb's New Dig. (1851) 991–997, 1008, 1010, 1017.
Alabama, Code of 1852, §§ 1033, 1034 et seq.
Mississippi, Hutchinson's Code, 524, 525, 540.
Arkansas, Dig. of 1848, p. 546 et seq.
Missouri, Dig. of Statutes (1845), ch. 123.
Tennessee, Caruthers & Nich. Dig. 330, 354, 355.
Texas, Hartley's Dig. § 2539 et seq.
Delaware, Rev. Code (1852), pp. 144, 145, 146.

code usually embraces the free negro. They occupy, therefore, a position very similar to that of the class of freedmen in Rome known as *dedititii*, whose condition was but slightly removed from that of the slave.[1]

§ 388. The free negro, in the non-slaveholding States, occupies the position we have assigned him, without the restrictions just named, viz., that of alien friends, until the State grants him the rights of citizenship. We have seen, heretofore, his *status* in the several States of the Union.[2] But when a State, by virtue of its sovereignty, grants to the free negro the rights of citizenship, an interesting question arises, under the peculiar form of our government, whether he is thereby incorporated as a citizen of the United States, and entitled to those privileges belonging exclusively to citizens.

§ 389. The universal principle is, that it is the privilege of every government to confer citizenship, and that none have it except those upon whom the privilege has been conferred. Previous to the adoption of the Constitution, every State had the power to adopt persons, within its community, as citizens; and all the whites who had been so adopted prior to that, were recognized as citizens under the General Government. The Constitution evidently intended to give that power, in future, to the General Government, for to it is given the express power to enact

---

[1] Inst. Lib. I, tit. v, § 3; Kaufman's Mackeldey, vol. i, p. 130; Bryan v. Walton, 14 Ga. 204.

[2] Preliminary Historical Sketch, ch. xv.

naturalization laws. That the laws enacted in pursuance of that power, necessarily exclude the introduction of negroes into the body politic, is evident, from the fact that they expressly confine their operation to white persons. Can a State, since the organization of the Federal Government, confer citizenship in that government? The very question answers itself, unless power is expressly given by the Constitution for that purpose. The State can confer citizenship within itself; and all privileges given by the Constitution to citizens of a State, as such, can be claimed by the negro citizen. But those privileges given to citizens of the United States, as such, can be exercised and enjoyed only by those who have been regularly admitted into this body politic. Under these views, it has been decided that a negro citizen cannot sue in the Federal Courts, that privilege being confined to citizens of the United States, and foreign States under certain circumstances.[1]

§ 390. Negroes in the condition of *statuliberi*, to be free at a future day, are protected by the statutes of several of the States, and should be by all, from being removed or fraudulently sold, so as to defeat the future freedom.[2] The introduction of such negroes is prohibited in other States, under severe penalties.[3]

§ 391. In all the slaveholding States, and in many

[1] Scott v. Sandford, 19 Howard, S. C. 1.
[2] Maryland, Dorsey's Laws, 658, 660, 661; Civil Code of Louisiana, Art. 194.
[3] North Carolina, Rev. Stat. (1837), 575.

of the non-slaveholding States, the admixture of negro blood is a disqualification for citizenship. The *quantum* varies in the different States. In many of them, the mode of trial of the question of citizenship is prescribed by statute.

Having concluded our view of the negro slave *as a person*, we shall hereafter consider of those rules of law to which *as property* he is subject. In that investigation we shall find that his nature as a man, and his consequent power of volition and locomotion, introduce important variations in those rules which regulate property in general.

NOTE.—This branch of the subject will be considered in another volume.

# INDEX.

## HISTORICAL SKETCH OF SLAVERY.

---

# LAW OF NEGRO SLAVERY.

(The references are to sections.)

POLICE.
    regulations consequent on slavery, 113, 114.
    power of patrol, 115.
    homicide of slave by, 96.
    assemblies of slaves, 115.
    interference on premises of master, 116.

POLICY.
    of Free State, not violated by temporary holding of slaves, 145.
    how far this extends, 146.
    when rule applies, 147.
    distinction between what is contrary to law and to policy, 147.
    between temporary and permanent rights, 148.
    prohibitions of, extend not to sojourner from necessity, 148.

PRESCRIPTION. (See LIMITATIONS.)

PROMISSORY NOTES.
    to slave, void, 268.

PROPERTY.
    acquisition of, by slave, 258.
    villein, 259.
    law of other countries, 260.
    when found by slave, 261.
    peculium the property of master on death of slave, 264.
    extra earnings belong to master, 267.
    deposits of, 267.
    but not property purchased with, by third person, 267.

RAPE.
    of female slave, not punishable, 107.

REBELLION.
    what is, 323.

REGISTRY.
    omission of, under statutes, 378.

SALE OF.
    when void, 314, and see TITLE.

SET-OFF.
    not allowed for necessaries furnished runaway, 121.

SLAVE.
    defined, 1, 112.
    condition under pure slavery, 86.
    under ordinary, 86.
    partus sequitur ventrem, 70.
    domicile of, 82.

23

WILL, *Continued.*

    operating on slaves in another jurisdiction, 348.

    emancipation by, where prohibited, 353.

    formalities of, required, 354.

    not aided by reference in another instrument, 354.

    assent of executor to manumission by, 354.

    revocation by sale or gift, 355.

    construction of, 355, 356.

    manumission by an insolvent, 357.

    by one supposing himself owner, 358.

    slaves illegally manumitted by, fall into residue, 362.

    where condition of emancipation prohibited by foreign law, of place of performance, 364.

    collusion or delay of executor will not avoid, 365.

    remedy where executor refuses to deliver to legatee for manumission, 366.

www.ingramcontent.com/pod-product-compliance
Lightning Source LLC
Chambersburg PA
CBHW041254040426
42334CB00028BA/3007